CW01072613

CONTRIBUTIONS
TO
MEDICAL PSYCHOLOGY

VOLUME 2

Other Pergamon Titles of Interest

M. HERSEN & A. BELLACK
Behavioural Assessment

L. HERSOV, M. BERGER & A. NICOL
Language and Language Disorders in Childhood

R. GATCHEL & K. PRICE
Clinical Applications of Biofeedback

M. MEACHER
New Methods of Mental Health Care

B. POPE
The Mental Health Interview

S. RACHMAN & G. WILSON
The Effects of Psychological Therapy 2nd Edition

A Journal of Related Interest

BEHAVIOUR RESEARCH AND THERAPY
Editor: S. Rachman, Institute of Psychiatry, London

This journal focuses on the applications of experimental psychology, and especially learning theory, to the modification of maladaptive behaviour, and to the improvement of learning efficacy.

Free specimen copies available upon request.

CONTRIBUTIONS TO MEDICAL PSYCHOLOGY

VOLUME 2

Edited by

S. RACHMAN

Institute of Psychiatry, London

PERGAMON PRESS

Oxford · New York · Toronto · Sydney · Paris · Frankfurt

U.K.	Pergamon Press Ltd., Headington Hill Hall, Oxford OX3 0BW, England
U.S.A.	Pergamon Press Inc., Maxwell House, Fairview Park, Elmsford, New York 10523, U.S.A.
CANADA	Pergamon Press Canada Ltd., Suite 104, 150 Consumers Road, Willowdale, Ontario M2J 1P9, Canada
AUSTRALIA	Pergamon Press (Aust.) Pty. Ltd., P.O. Box 544, Potts Point, N.S.W. 2011, Australia
FRANCE	Pergamon Press SARL, 24 rue des Ecoles, 75240 Paris, Cedex 05, France
FEDERAL REPUBLIC OF GERMANY	Pergamon Press GmbH, Hammerweg 6, D-6242 Kronberg-Taunus, Federal Republic of Germany

Copyright © 1980 Pergamon Press Ltd.

All Rights Reserved. No part of this publication may be reproduced, stored in a retrieval system or transmitted in any form or by any means: electronic, electrostatic, magnetic tape, mechanical, photocopying, recording or otherwise, without permission in writing from the publishers

First edition 1980
Reprinted 1984

British Library Cataloguing in Publication Data

Contributions to medical psychology.
Vol. 2
1. Medicine and psychology
2. Clinical psychology
I. Rachman, Stanley
610'.1'9   R726.5   80-40416

ISBN 0-08-024684-2

Printed in Great Britain by A. Wheaton & Co. Ltd., Exeter

CONTENTS

LIST OF CONTRIBUTORS

BLANCHARD, E. Department of Psychology, New York University at Albany, 1400 Washington Avenue, Albany, New York 12222, USA

HUMPHREY, M. Department of Psychology, St. George's Hospital Medical School, Jenner Wing, Cranmer Terrace, Tooting, London SW17

LEVENTHAL, H. Department of Psychology, University of Wisconsin, Madison, Wisconsin 53706, USA

LEY, P. School of Behavioural and Social Science, Plymouth Polytechnic, Drake Circus, Plymouth, Devon PL4 8AA

MELAMED, B. G. Department of Psychology, University of Florida, Box J-165, JHMHC, Gainesville, Florida 32610, USA

MEYER, D. Department of Psychology, University of Wisconsin, Madison, Wisconsin 53706, USA

NERENZ, D. Department of Psychology, University of Wisconsin, Madison, Wisconsin 53706, USA

PHILIPS, C. Department of Psychology, Institute of Psychiatry, De Crespigny Park, London SE5 8AF

POOLE, A. D. Department of Psychiatry, The University of Western Australia, Nedlands, Western Australia 6009

RACHMAN, S. Department of Psychology, Institute of Psychiatry, De Crespigny Park, London SE5 8AF

RAY, C. Department of Psychology, School of Social Sciences, Brunel University, Uxbridge, Middlesex UB8 3PH

RIPPERE, V. Department of Psychology, Institute of Psychiatry, De Crespigny Park, London SE5 8AF

SANSON-FISHER, R. Department of Psychiatry, The University of Western Australia, Nedlands, Western Australia 6009

STEPTOE, A. Department of Psychology, St. George's Hospital Medical School, Jenner Wing, Cranmer Terrace, Tooting, London SW17

WEISENBERG, M. Department of the Sociology of Health, University Center for Health Sciences, Beer Sheva 84 120, P.O.B. 653, Israel

YOUNG, L. D. Department of Psychology, New York University at Albany, 1400 Washington Avenue, Albany, New York 12222, USA

INTRODUCTION

S. RACHMAN

Institute of Psychiatry, University of London

1. MEDICAL PSYCHOLOGY OR BEHAVIOURAL MEDICINE?

Do these two terms describe the same subject, and does it matter anyway? The answer to the first question appears to be No, and the answer to the second question is Yes. The terms do differ and the differences are significant, but by no means vital. Before considering the merits of the competing terms, it is advisable to take notice of certain activities that are unmistakable signs of scientific movement. New journals are announced, regional and national conferences are arranged, professional societies are formed, and disputes arise about the correct titles and terms which one should use in describing the new activities. All of this activity signifies the emergence of a new subject, medical psychology.

The first journal devoted specifically to the new subject, the *Journal of Behavioral Medicine*, appeared in 1978 and is certain to be followed by competitors, as is the present series of *Contributions to Medical Psychology*. The formation in the U.S. in 1979 of a new professional division dealing with medical psychology is bound to be followed by the establishment of regional, national, and international societies. All of these events are welcome signs of growing interest in the subject and of healthy academic, clinical, and scientific activity.

Given the enormous scope of the subject and the potential for scientific growth, one might question whether it is necessary to quibble about the choice of a title for the emerging subject. Strictly speaking, such debates are not essential, but insofar as they help to clarify one's aims, methods, and range, they can be useful. The most obvious advantage to be had from using the term *medical psychology* is its breadth, encompassing as it does an integration of the common contents and interests of two of the largest of contemporary scientific disciplines. The term is broad, liberal, and inviting. But it has one serious drawback: *medical psychology* has for some years been used loosely to refer to psychiatry, or at least to some aspects of psychiatry. For example, the material published in the *British Journal of Medical Psychology* is predominantly psychiatric. In addition, numbers of psychiatric departments are still described as departments of psychological medicine. As one of the main aims set out by advocates of medical psychology is to expand the application of psychology beyond the traditional and nearly exclusive concern with psychiatry (e.g. Rachman and Philips, 1978, 1980), the confusion between psychiatric psychology and medical psychology is troublesome.

1

The advantages of the term *behavioural medicine* are that it emphasizes the significance of behaviour, it is a new term and hence carries few unwanted associations, and thirdly, it has gained a measure of early acceptance. (The association of
the term with behaviour therapy is historically apt, but may soon be overtaken by
developments within behaviour therapy itself—will we soon be asked to change the
term to *cognitive* behavioural medicine?) The main disadvantage of the term *behavioural medicine* is that it implies an unnecessary restriction to purely behavioural
aspects of medical practice and problems, and may even encourage the neglect of
other aspects of psychological functioning. It may be too narrow. Ideally, one
would like to promote the widest and fullest application of psychological ideas and
methods to medical matters, and those applications are bound to include psychophysiological studies, affective influences, cognitions, and so on. For these reasons,
my preference is for the broader term, *medical psychology*. And now on to matters
of substance.

2. THE THIRD STEP

The first two steps in developing a medical psychology have been taken: the
initial step was a recognition that psychological influences pervade all branches of
medicine, and the second step was the acknowledgement that clinical psychologists'
exclusive concern with psychiatric medicine was no longer justified. The third step
is the construction of properly psychological conceptions of health problems that
àre intended to avoid an uncritical immersion in prevailing medical theories and
practices. An original and constructive step in this direction has been taken by
Leventhal and his colleagues. In their leading chapter, they discuss the advantages
of applying psychological concepts and findings to medical and health problems in
a fresh manner, emphasizing the need for the deliberate introduction of psychological theorizing. So, for example, they examine the concept of self-regulating coping
behaviour in relation to the patient's definition of his illness. This examination
leads to novel conclusions about compliance behaviour, the role of fear in executing
healthy behaviour, the relation between fear and knowledge of health hazards, the
connections between danger and coping behaviour, and so on. They postulate that
effective coping depends largely on two essential components of regulatory behaviour, the presence of a valid and believable danger and an idea of how to cope
effectively with that danger. Their argument is illustrated by case examples and
supported by research findings, including some unusually interesting information
on patients' conceptions of the relations between their symptoms and illness. In all,
the growing knowledge about patients' theories of their illnesses and how these
theories may disagree—even seriously disagree—with their doctors' theories is particularly enlightening, and promises some valuable rewards.

When the first two steps towards a medical psychology were being taken, the
hope was expressed that psychologists would use their conceptions, training, and
knowledge to enrich the theory of medicine (Rachman and Philips, 1975); and
Leventhal's work is an encouraging model. Earlier conceptions of health and illness, antedating the growth of modern medicine, are a fascinating reminder of the
continuing process of re-discovering ourselves. Rippere's chapter on the history of

human melancholy is an entertaining and illuminating account of the history of central ideas about dysphoria and how to cope with it.

3. SCOPE

The contents of this second volume cannot aspire to provide a comprehensive account of the subject, but the chapters do cover some of the major themes that have emerged. At this stage, we have an encouragingly large number of promising possibilities, a few clear successes, and one or two disappointments. The most obvious disappointment is the relative failure of research into biofeedback procedures to produce clinically practical applications. In their critical and comprehensive review of the subject, Young and Blanchard give a sobering account of present knowledge. One other application of medical psychology that has not yet fulfilled our early hopes is the introduction of self-control procedures for modifying behaviour that is harmful to one's health. In the first volume of this series, the small, but significant, progress in helping people to cease smoking was described, and the present volume contains a comprehensive analysis of progress in reducing obesity. Ley's balanced account provides a sound basis for planning the next stage in the surprisingly slow process of shaping effective psychological procedures for helping people to control the weight of their own bodies. Barbara Melamed has established a position of considerable authority by her prescient contributions to the early growth of medical psychology. In this volume, she gives a wide-ranging account of the status of psychological pediatrics that is bound to become a valued stimulus for clinical applications and further research.

On the practical side, one of the earliest and clearest successes has been the development of simple and practical methods for psychologically preparing people who are about to undergo stressful medical or surgical procedures—a subject to which Melamed made valuable contributions. The obstacles to introducing these methods on a wide scale are now being studied, and there is every reason to be optimistic about the prospects for providing assistance to a large number of patients without undue delay. Psychological analyses of the mechanisms involved in successful preparation for unpleasant procedures will require a great deal more effort, but it is a problem of considerable scientific interest and of wide potential significance. It should engage the attention of many psychologists for some time to come.

On the academic side, we have seen a rapid and understandable growth of interest in the intriguing subject of pain. The importance attached to this major problem is reflected by the inclusion of three chapters on the subject—a general review and analysis by Weisenberg, a progress report on head-pain research by Philips, and an introduction to a new subject, the psychological aspects of low back-pain, by Michael Humphrey. Ray's review of research on cancer is also relevant here. In addition to the intrinsic interest of these chapters, each in its own way reflects the growth of new procedures for studying what is for psychologists, a relatively new phenomenon. The complexities of pain phenomena are skilfully elucidated by Weisenberg, and it is just these sorts of complexity that prompted Philips to apply a three-systems analysis to the problem of head pain. Her firmest conclusion is that headache is best construed as a problem of pain, and that view inevitably leads one to consider the critical role of psychological factors. The psychology of pain is the most challenging contemporary problem for medical psychologists. One can safely predict a considerable accumulation of new knowledge and skills during the next five to ten years, and the exciting possibility of developing connections between psychological aspects of pain and endorphins is one that has already sparked some interest.

The successful development of new methods of study is clearly illustrated in the research on psychological aspects of hypertension described by Steptoe. Most of this work involves the use of psychophysiological recordings, whereas the research described by Sanson-Fisher and Poole is an application of naturalistic observation to psychiatric practice in a hospital setting. Given their remarkable results, the authors are justified in recommending the power of direct observation, and I have no doubt that when psychologists apply these methods to the analysis of other branches of medical practice, we will quickly gather some astonishing and useful information. The introduction of new methods is accompanied by a widening scope of the subject, and this is reflected by the inclusion of two chapters on novel subjects—breast cancer (by Ray) and low back-pain (by Humphrey).

4. CONCEPTS

The psychology of medical practice, especially the relationship between the doctor and his patient, remains a subject of central interest in the whole enterprise. It is not too fanciful to hope that the accumulation of scientifically based evidence on the psychological nature of medical practice will lead to widespread improvements and reforms. It is to be hoped that psychologists will not confine themselves to practical aspects of medical practice, notwithstanding their importance. There is a strong case for arguing that the introduction of psychological concepts and methods will, in the long run, have most to contribute to the theory of illness and illness behaviour—it being recognized that at present there is no satisfactory or agreed conception of what constitutes an illness. The weaknesses of present conceptions of illness are nowhere clearer than in psychiatric medicine, but the inadequacies are not confined to that speciality. Leventhal's important chapter encourages the adoption of a fresh *psychological* approach to our conceptions of illness. The anticipated broadening of our concepts of illness and of medical practice is bound to highlight the need for a better understanding of the concept of stress and the connections between stressful events and experiences. A lucid use of the concept can be found in Steptoe's chapter.

On the subject of prevention, it is a truism that effective methods of prevention depend upon a degree of understanding of the disorder concerned. Like most truisms, however, it is not entirely satisfactory, for, as in the case of preparing children for stressful medical or surgical procedures, considerable progress has been made in advance of a satisfactory understanding of the psychological processes involved. In certain respects, current understanding of excessive eating and unnecessary smoking exceeds our knowledge of how and why prevention is defective. Nevertheless, we are already in possession of relatively effective procedures for preparing people for stressful procedures, but have made only small progress towards the development of satisfactory preventive measures for people whose eating and smoking behaviour gives rise to health hazards.

All this evidence of stimulating academic and scientific activity should not however lead psychologists to expect easy and early victories. Even in those aspects of medical psychology where rapid progress is made, one has to allow for the inevitable delays in translating the new knowledge into practice. I have already heard it said that most, or all, of the research into medical psychology is of scant practical value because medical practitioners remain unaware of the new knowledge, or worse, are reluctant to use the knowledge. It would, of course, be idle to ignore the occurrence of resistance to new ideas and new practices, but the medical profession has a record which is in many ways superior to that of other professions. Innovations that are practical and likely to produce manifest improvements in the health of their patients can be adopted quickly. The widening of perspective to include a fuller appreciation of the role of psychological factors in health and illness can be expected to follow the introduction of demonstrably beneficial practices. It is largely up to psychologists to make such demonstrations.

The present series is designed to facilitate such demonstrations and to ensure the transmission of new knowledge—and in so doing, help to stimulate and promote the widening enterprise. It has been said that if psychologists insist on working their own ground—the psychology of health and illness—the coming decade could be the most rewarding in the history of their emerging profession.

REFERENCES

Rachman, S. and C. Philips (1975) *Psychology and Medicine*, Temple Smith, London, and (1978) Pelican Revised Edition, Harmondsworth.
Rachman, S. and C. Philips (1980) *Psychology and Behavioral Medicine*, Cambridge University Press, New York.

THE COMMON SENSE REPRESENTATION OF ILLNESS DANGER

HOWARD LEVENTHAL, DANIEL MEYER and DAVID NERENZ

University of Wisconsin, Madison

CONTENTS

1. INTRODUCTION

Volume 1 of Professor Rachman's *Contributions to Medical Psychology* (1977) is a testament to the rapid growth of the field of medical psychology. With the exception of research on drug abuse and neuropsychology, the field was virtually empty in the early 1960s. The new outcropping of research focuses on a variety of behavioral problems relevant to the determinants of illness and its treatment. These problems include compliance with preventive health behavior and medical regimens, non-chemical alternatives for the treatment of heart disease (biofeedback, relaxation training, weight loss, etc.), psychological preparation for stress reduction, treatment of headache and menstrual distress, motivation for preventive health behavior and health promotion, and studies of life stress and illness. Like medical sociologists before them (see Mechanic, 1978), psychologists have dicovered health and illness, and are rapidly entering the area to solve medicine's behavioral problems; in doing so, they appear to be using extant techniques and theories to answer questions and solve problems posed by medical practice. This is most clearly seen in areas such as compliance with medical regimens and prevention. In compliance, the question seems to be "How do you get patients to take their hypertension (or other) medication?" One possible outcome of such interdisciplinary collaboration is a problem matrix where specific issues in health practice comprise the abscissa and specific behavioral techniques comprise the ordinate. Behavioral researchers fill in the matrix by identifying which intervention procedure best resolves each practice problem (Leventhal and Cleary, 1979; Zifferblatt and Wilbur, 1977).

The degree to which the above picture is an accurate reflection of behavioral medicine might bring joy to those who believe science should solve real-world problems. In our judgment, such a view is misguided. The degree to which psychologists are testing extant technologies to fill in the matrix is a measure of the degree to which the medical tail is wagging the behavioral dog; this forecasts a grim future. If behavioral medicine develops as a collection of technologies which are to be applied to specific practice problems and ignores underlying, explanatory mechanisms, it will fail both as a science and as a problem-solving technology (Leventhal and Cleary, 1979). Theory is essential for the development of science. Theory is a key analytic tool for intelligent practice.

Unfortunately, the area of research on compliance with preventive health behavior and compliance with recommended health regimens—the topical focus of the present paper—typifies this technological approach (see Sackett and Haynes, 1976). With few exceptions (e.g. Ley, 1977), compliance researchers have done little to develop a theoretical base for their discipline (Baranowski, 1979; Meyer, Leventhal and Gutmann, in preparation). Instead, they have accepted the medical practitioner's questions: "Who follows medical orders?" and "How can you get people to follow orders?" They have then proceeded to identify personal factors that distinguish compliant from non-compliant patients; situational factors such as individualized appointments, reduced waiting times, and reduced costs, all of which are barriers to compliance; and motivational factors such as social support which can enhance long-term compliance. This now considerable body of research clarifies a number of obvious and important issues for compliance research. For example, it is clear that good experimental research requires randomization to treatments (Byar et al., 1976) as well as multiple measures, both behavioral and medical, to assess compliance (Green et al., 1975; Leventhal, Safer, Cleary and Gutman, 1980). But it also makes clear the shortcomings of a technological-empirical approach to the compliance problem, as many of the major research findings fail to generalize from study to study. For example, the extraordinarily high level of compliance achieved at a work-site clinic in a retail establishment (Alderman and Schoenbaum, 1975) is not found when a work-site clinic is set up in a steel foundry (Sackett et al., 1975). Also, the use of individualized appointments may work in one setting (Finnerty et al., 1973), but not in another (Sackett et al., 1975).

Of course, findings can fail to generalize in theory-oriented, as well as in empirically-guided, research. But the two approaches will differ in the way they respond to such crises. The investigator using theory has an array of concepts to guide him in analyzing the situational and population factors which differentiate one study from another. But when the empirically-guided investigator encounters inconsistencies, his solution attempts are likely to appear random. The empirically-oriented investigator may reason that if an environmental factor, such as the location of the hypertension treatment clinic, fails to enhance compliance, an individual factor, such as knowledge of hypertension, will (Sackett *et al.*, 1975). If these individually directed educational efforts fail, the outlook is then bleak indeed until investigators can think of some other motivational factor to focus on, such as social support. By contrast, a theoretically-oriented investigator would never expect a particular treatment, such as work-site clinics or fear messages, to work the same way in all contexts (Leventhal, 1970, 1974). Theory leads us to aniticipate interactions.

The movement from one set of factors to another can take on the appearance of a search for the holy grail of compliance; all that is needed is to find the key factor. But, it may also take on the appearance of an eclectic collector's mansion with variables picked up by happy circumstance and lumped together as though each made an independent contribution to compliance. As Rogers (1975) has argued, one can account for differences between patients in compliance using complex descriptive models (e.g., multiple regression) and contribute relatively little to the understanding of the process by which compliance takes place. Finally, when we examine the description of variables with a theoretical eye, we cannot help but wonder if they have been adequately defined. Have the investigators testing the effectiveness of health education understood the educational process? Is the conceptual and operational definition of social support adequate? The theoretically inquisitive investigator may suspect that classes of variables were abandoned for hopefully greener pastures well before they were clearly understood.

2. THE ROLE OF EXPLANATORY THEORY

Can theory help solve problems posed by compliance? If so, where and how can such theory develop? It is clear that theory can be developed in any number of areas such as in compliance, delay, and doctor–patient communication, and in any number of disease categories such as cancer, heart disease, dental health, and so on. Theoretical work can also be conducted at the community, group, and individual level. It is important to recognize, however, that problem-solving broadly conceived need not lead to the development of explanatory theory. Neither our ability to predict outcomes nor our ability to generate *ad hoc* procedures for producing them ensures the presence of theoretical explanation. Explanation exists when we have a model or set of propositions that tells us how something takes place. Explanatory concepts underlie observations—they are not simply "abstract" descriptions (Hempel, 1966). If an explanatory model is powerful, it can be coordinated to measures in different settings or behavior in response to different disease problems. An explanatory model can direct us toward effective interventions by pinpointing causal processes which are amenable to change. But it would be foolish to expect an explanatory model to account for all of the variance observed in an applied problem such as compliance. After all, there are many reasons why a patient may fail to comply with a medical regimen. While we may find it convenient to picture the factors affecting compliance in a complex diagram (e.g., Becker and Maiman, 1975) and to use them as a set of predictors in a regression model, this does not mean the factors are components of a common, causal model.

3. AN EXAMPLE OF THEORETICALLY-BASED
COMPLIANCE RESEARCH

In our own research, we have attempted to blend theoretical and practical concerns in understanding how patients adapt to various medical treatments. We have developed a model of patient behavior that can be applied to different problem areas and that can be used to generate interventions which have practical significance. We are seeking to isolate sets of interacting variables that describe an underlying model of how patients comply or make use of specific treatments. We assume that people are motivated to avoid and to treat illness threats, and that people are active, self-regulating problem solvers in the health area. Our goal is to understand the self-regulatory process: How do people define or represent the illness threat? How do they proceed to cope with it? Our studies focus on understanding the patient's acceptance of medical treatment for hypertension and malignant lymphoma, and on understanding the patient's decision-making process in the use of medical care systems. Our strategy has been to try to understand the layman's perceptions or theories of medical problems. We assume the patient's ideas are shaped by information from various media and social sources (such as family, friends, and the medical care system), from the patient's past illness experience, and from his current symptomatic sensations. These theories play an important role in directing the patient's behavior because they set goals for coping. Why did we take this approach and what do we mean by a patient's theory of disease and treatment?

A. Starting Point for Current Research

To see why we undertook to understand compliance behavior by developing models of patients' theories of disease, it will help to examine briefly our prior research on fear communication and distress control. Our goal in the study of fear communication was to understand how people formulate persistent attitudes and how they construct lasting behavioral strategies for dealing with health threats. Understanding the persistence of behavior is critical in developing programs for health promotion, disease prevention, and risk reduction. Because these behaviors appeared to be motivated by the perception of danger, we attempted to understand how the arousal of fear contributed to the development of persistent preventive and compliance responses. Our experiments compared compliance with preventive health recommendations when these recommendations were presented after communication that aroused different (high or low) levels of fear. The experimental designs typically combined the fear factor with other variables, such as (1) action plans or instructions on how to take protective action, (2) information on the effectiveness of action, (3) manipulations of vulnerability, and (4) individual difference variables like self-esteem (see Leventhal, Singer and Jones, 1965; Leventhal and Singer, 1966; Leventhal, Watts and Pagano, 1967; Leventhal and Trembly, 1968). These experimental designs embodied the fundamental idea that information on the recommended action was insufficient to generate persistent protective health behavior—some level of threat and fear was essential. The fear component was conceptualized as adding to the crucial motivational power for action.

The results of our studies and those of other investigators (e.g., Kirscht and Rosenstock, 1977; Rogers and Mewborn, 1976; Rogers and Deckner, 1975), eventually convinced us that the additive assumption was incorrect. We could see little or no evidence that fear was necessary or even an essential ingredient for behavioral change. While fear did affect behavior—in some experiments it appeared to lead to avoidance of the recommended compliance behavior (e.g., Janis and Feshbach, 1953)—it seemed to have this effect only when the high fear message created fear of the recommended action itself. For example, although X-rays are the first step toward diagnosis and treatment, few people took X-rays after seeing a film on lung cancer. They did, however, try to stop smoking (Leventhal and Watts, 1966). A more common finding was that somewhat higher levels of compliance followed high fear messages. This general finding was true for tetanus inoculations (Leventhal, Singer and Jones, 1965; Leventhal, Jones and Trembly, 1966), willingness to use seat belts (Leventhal and Niles, 1965), desire to protect oneself against infectious disease (Chu, 1966), cigarette smoking (Leventhal and Niles, 1964; Leventhal and Watts, 1966), and attitudes and reported compliance with dental hygiene recommendations (Leventhal and Singer, 1966; Singer, 1965), etc. It is a waste of energy, however, to concentrate on counting how many studies show that high fear is superior to low fear for generating compliance. The important question is not whether high or low levels of fear are more effective in generating compliance, but how fear affects attitudes and behavior.

When we addressed the latter question, we found fewer answers than questions. We did, however, conclude the following:

(1) The effects of fear were relatively short-lived; fear is a relatively temporary state which can serve to motivate behavior.

(2) The avoidance responses motivated by fear seem to be automatic, rather than deliberate or volitionally planned.

(3) Fear leads to avoidance of the threatening source and can conflict with acceptance of preventive or protective recommendations when the recommendations are themselves threatening. For example, a chest X-ray exposes a smoker to the threat of surgery whereas quitting smoking does not; and a Tay–Sachs test is threatening to a pregnant woman, but not to a non-pregnant woman (Ben-Sira and Padeh, 1978).

(4) High levels of fear may disrupt the performance of preventive behaviors that would occur at low levels of fear. An overpowering threat can cause subjects low in self-esteem to feel helpless and vulnerable. These subjects do not manifest a denial reaction; they accept the threat, but experience a breakdown in coping.

Our most important conclusions, however, had little to do with fear. We concluded:

(a) Information about a health threat (smoking, tetanus) seems to be a necessary, but not sufficient condition for long-term adherence to a protective recommendation. The individual must be aware of the threat and its nature, but the level of fear stimulated by this information appears to be of little consequence in the formation of an awareness or representation of the threat—at least within rather wide limits of fearfulness.

(b) Information that stimulates action planning—which may involve identifying cues for specific initial actions, rehearsing these actions, and connecting the actions in a plan—seems to be a necessary but not sufficient condition for adherence to protective recommendations. In summary, long-term compliance with protective recommendations (stopping smoking or taking a tetanus shot) seems to require exposure to information about the danger and about a specific plan for action. The level of fear stimulated by the information at the time of exposure seems to be irrelevant, but exposure to information about threat can lead to action if accompanied by behavioral planning.

B. Development of the Current Model

The above conclusions represent the general view about how fear affects attitudes and protective health action (see Leventhal, 1970; Ley, 1977; Sternthal and Craig, 1974). But it leaves considerable ambiguity with respect to the role of fear in long-term compliance behavior. If fear plays a role in long-term action, it is probably because of its effects on memory. Fear may be coded in memory and re-stimulated whenever the individual confronts cues of danger (a conditioned fear hypothesis) and the re-activation of fear memory may be sufficient to sustain action. But processes of this sort are considerably more complex than those which were initially suspected to be involved in the arousal of states of fear. Because of this, we speculated that it was important to distinguish between the processes involved in the activation and control of fear and those involved in the perception and control of danger. Thus, we had two sets of questions. The first set addressed what makes subjects fearful and what they do (immediately and over a long term) to cope with fear; this is the fear control process. The second set addressed how the subject perceived and interpreted the threat, his representation of danger and how he went about coping with danger; this is the danger control process. This model was labeled the "Parallel Model" in recognition of the considerable degree of independence between fear and danger control. The two processes may share a number of mental mechanisms, but their internal calculus may lead to quite different response outcomes. It was also clear that each control process was comprised of steps or stages. In particular, there was a considerable degree of independence between the subject's perception and interpretation of danger and his ability to plan and act to cope with danger.

Although the fear study data pointed to the high degree of independence between danger and fear control processes, it soon became clear that the two processes can interact with one another. This was seen in our studies of distress control. We observed that ability to cope with stressful situations, such as swallowing a fiber optic tube during an endoscopic examination or pushing with each contraction during the latter stages of childbirth, was affected by fear. Fear interfered with coping, and the reduction of fear could facilitate the individual's ability to cope with objective situational demands. This was vividly illustrated in Johnson and Leventhal's (1974) study of patients undergoing an endoscopic examination. The patients were given information preparing them for the sensory experiences of the examination: the numbness to the throat caused by anesthesia, the gagging sensation generated by the fiber optic tube, the fullness of the stomach when inflated with air, etc. By preparing the patients to observe and objectify these specific sensory experiences, the sensations were converted to cues for coping, rather than as cues of threat. As a consequence, the prepared patients showed less heart rate acceleration, much less gagging, and exerted control over the rate at which they swallowed the fiber optic tube. For prepared patients, coping replaced less adaptive fear responses (see Leventhal and Johnson, in press).

In addition to showing that fear- and danger-control processes interact, this study made clear the importance of concrete sensory experiences for the control of behavior. Successful preparation for distress control appears to depend on the patient's readiness to interpret such cues as benign. Information that is more abstract in nature or that focuses on situational procedures divorced from the patient's direct sensory experience is far less effective in facilitating adaptation to stress.

4. PRINCIPLES OF BEHAVIORAL REGULATION

The findings of the distress control and fear studies suggested three important principles. First, both objective events—as understood by the individual—and subjective emotion establish goals for coping. Second, behavioral regulation requires the specification of goals in a picture or representation of danger, and the structuring and planning of action. Third, highly concrete information plays a central and critical role in the formation of both the representation and the plan for action. Both the studies on preventive health action and those on stress control demonstrated the need for concrete information on the threat and on methods of coping. To quit smoking or to take tetanus shots, one needs a concrete and clear image of the threat and a concrete and clear set of action instructions. To cope with swallowing an endoscopic tube, one needed concrete preparatory information describing the actual sensations. This information reduced fear. To generate effective coping during tube swallowing, the patients also needed concrete information and practice on how to breathe and swallow while the endoscopic tube was introduced into the pharynx. Both kinds of information are necessary for effective self-regulation.

The above principles suggested that efforts to enhance compliance with preventive and protective action might succeed or fail depending on whether health care providers presented the concrete information needed to generate a valid and believeable danger and an effective image of coping reaction—the two essential components of behavioral regulatory mechanisms. But they also raised the possibility that non-compliance may emerge because people generate their own representations of danger and their own coping reactions in order to deal with potential and present health threats. Many examples of this can be seen in the prevention literature. For example, smokers switched to filter and low tar and low nicotine cigarettes, because these seemed to be effective ways of coping with the health danger as *they* saw it (Leventhal and Cleary, 1979). Thus, to understand how communication affects patient compliance with preventive and protective action, it may be essential to understand how patients construct their own representations of these problems and how they construct behaviors to cope with the concrete goals embodied in these representations.

We will draw on two sources of data to illustrate the way people generate common-sense representations of illness episodes for self-regulation (Meyer, Reference Note 1; Nerenz, 1979). We will refer to these examples in later sections as we discuss representations in more detail. These common-sense models are of practical as well as theoretical interest as they "do not necessarily conform to scientific models, yet it is usually common-sense models that determine the use of medical facilities" (Mechanic, 1966, p. 17).

A. Representations of Danger for Self-regulation: Examples from the Study of Hypertension

Example 1. A 40-year-old black man was told at a neighborhood screening site that his blood pressure was elevated (150/102) and he was asked to return for a second reading. He reported that he had been "getting a lot of pressure at work and that's why it's up". At the second blood pressure reading two weeks later, his blood pressure was again high (155/105). He reported being surprised, since his work problems had largely resolved since the last reading. He had noticed several head-aches recently, and at the time he began treatment (after a third elevated reading), he reported that the headaches were probably the result of the elevated blood pressure. After a month of treatment, he reported a definite decrease in frequency and severity of headaches and after two months of good blood pressure control, the patient was lost to follow-up. He returned to the clinic after nine months when he presented himself at an emergency room with a severe headache and an elevated pressure reading (150/100). He said, "See, I knew it was back up when the headache came on. I need some more medicine to take the pressure off". This experience supported his use of headaches as indicators of elevations. While agreeing that "people in general can't tell when their blood pressure is up", he insisted that "since I'm the one who has it, I can tell when it's up".

Example 2. A 45-year-old white female R.N. (a nursing instructor) reported being diagnosed as hypertensive five years ago. She said, "I can tell my blood pressure is up when I get this funny little tension headache in my temples. It only happens every couple of months. When I feel it, I go get my cuff and you know, it's been up every time I had that headache. I take a diuretic that I keep at home until the blood pressure gets back to normal, usually a week or ten days. The headaches always go right away, and the next time the headaches come on, the pressure's back up". Unfortunately, she had never taken a blood pressure reading when she did not have the headache and was not taking the diuretic. Her headaches may be reliable and valid indicators of elevations, or they may just provide intermittent cues to take readings of pressure which had been elevated for weeks or months (examples from Meyer, Leventhal and Gutmann, Reference Note 4).

B. Representations of Danger for Self-regulation: Examples from the Study of Cancer Chemotherapy

Example 1. A 60-year-old man was diagnosed as having lymphoma after he came to his doctor with severe abdominal pains. The tumor was never easily palpable, so he relied on changes in the intensity of the pain to tell whether the chemotherapy was working. He now pays much more attention to aches and pains in his body, in order to detect any possible spread of disease. He has difficulty distinguishing between pains caused by the tumor and those caused by chemotherapy or other events, and thus is constantly dealing with what he perceives to be a possible spread or recurrence of his lymphoma.

Example 2. A 30-year-old male graduate student had had three periods of treatment for Hodgkins disease over the last 11 years. He stated that each episode of the illness had been preceded by a period of high stress, and that the episodes were also accompanied by a peculiar itching sensation on his legs and ankles. Based on this observed association he decided that his disease was caused by stress, and could be detected by this unusual itching. He now has learned to distinguish between the disease-induced itching and other itching that might be produced by dry skin, and has made clear efforts to control the disease by reducing stress—working part time and taking Valium occasionally.

5. PRINCIPLES OF DANGER CONTROL

These case examples were selected because they illustrate a number of important points about the ways in which patients regulate their illness behavior. We will list and discuss each of the points briefly and include other examples drawn from interviews of patients undergoing chemotherapy treatment for malignant lymphoma and breast cancer.

A. Patients Attempt to Understand and Regulate their Treatment

The first essential point is that patients attempt to understand and to regulate their medical treatment. It is incorrect to conceptualize the patient as a passive object who needs to be pushed to action by means of education and motivational devices. Patients *are* active. Patients take in and interpret information and cope with whatever problems arise. The perception of the patient as an object is a heritage of medical and behavioristic models which view patients as passive uninformed targets, and practitioners as active prescribing experts (see Engel, 1977; Parsons, 1951).

B. Symptoms Define Illness and Illness Defines Symptoms: there is a Symmetry of Relationship between Symptoms and Illness

Symptoms are typically the starting point for speculations as to whether one is ill (e.g., Mechanic, 1972; Leventhal, 1975; Pennebaker and Skelton, 1978; Safer, Tharps, Jackson and Leventhal, 1979). People seek information to label or define their body states (e.g., Schachter and Singer, 1962) and they use symptoms, or body states, to define labels. Our hypertensive respondents revealed the symmetry of this relationship. When a person is told he is hypertensive, he is likely to search for a symptom, a sensation, or some mood state that can serve as a concrete representation or indicator of his "illness" condition. The hypertensive male in Example A. above assumed that headaches were reliable indicators of blood pressure.

The generality of the above conclusion was illustrated by the respondents in four of the six groups of patients who were interviewed as part of an extensive investigation of hypertension: Group 1. Newly discovered hypertensives (interviewed at a screening site); Group 2. Newly treated hypertensives (interviewed at their first treatment visit); Group 3. Continuing treatment hypertensives (in treatment for at least six months and up to 15 years); Group 4. Re-entry patients (people who had dropped and then re-entered treatment when it was discovered that their blood pressure was still elevated). Two remaining groups (Groups 5 and 6) were nonhypertensive controls. When asked, "Do you think you can tell when your blood pressure is up?", 94 per cent of the patients who had dropped out of, and then re-entered, treatment reported a bodily sensation or symptom which allowed them to monitor changes in blood pressure. This response also occurred for 88 per cent of the actively treated group, 71 per cent of the newly treated group, and 52 per cent of the newly discovered patients. In the normotensive control group, 45 per cent of the people—patients and non-patients alike—believed they could monitor blood pressure change. On a six month follow-up interview, 92 per cent of the newly treated patients reported a symptom they believed allowed them to monitor blood pressure changes.

Two points are clear. First, people believe they can monitor pressure change. Second, the longer people are in the treatment system, the more likely they are to search for, and find, a symptom to represent their disorder. This occurs even though most patients believe (e.g., 80 per cent of the actively treated patients) that "people can't tell when their blood pressure is up". Finally, there was no association between individual differences in actual blood pressure (systolic or diastolic) and individual differences in reported symptoms. Thus, there was no evidence (at least on a between subject basis) that symptoms are valid indicators of blood pressure.

C. Symptomatic Representations Facilitate Attributional Analysis

What advantage could there be in representing illness by a concrete symptom? The answer may be that symptoms are highly available cues that can be experienced without complex instruments and give instant (and continuous) feedback about the progress of one's illness. The more intense the symptom, the more intense the illness. The less intense the symptom, the less intense the illness. Thus, symptoms are extremely convenient devices for determining the causes of a disease and for evaluating treatments. What other device can match these ever-present, highly recognizable and highly sensitive indicators? What else can so readily evaluate the impact of a wide range of specific life experiences and activities on one's illness state? If a heavy work schedule intensifies headaches (one commonly used indicator of hypertension), is it not plausible to conclude that work stress is the cause of hypertension? If medication reduces headaches, is it not plausible to conclude that medication can control, if not cure, hypertension? For example, the hypertensive nurse in Example A. concluded that medication was only necessary when a particular headache was present. It is important to recognize we are articulating the patient's logic, a logic which may be consistent and sensible even though its basic premises are completely invalid.

D. Symptoms and Attributions Form Organized, Implicit Theories of Illness and Treatment

The patient's symptoms, his beliefs about their determinants, and his beliefs about treatment form an organized and more or less coherent theory of illness. The degree of organization will vary from person to person as will the ability to verbalize the organization. The patient's statements may not be identical with his underlying beliefs.

Three basic types of models seemed to emerge from the analysis of the interviews with hypertensives. When asked how long they expected treatment to last and what its outcome will be, 30 per cent (71/233) expected short-term treatment followed by cure. This is an "acute episode model". Another 31 per cent (72/233) expected the symptoms to subside for a period of time and then recur. This is a cyclic model. Finally, 39 per cent (90/233) believed they would need continuing or long-term treatment. This is a chronic model. (A total of 56 hypertensive patients reported no symptoms (Meyer, Reference Note 1).)

The pattern of symptoms differed for the three models. Fifty-five per cent of the patients thinking in terms of an acute episode model pointed to a recent symptom and a specific time and place for the onset of their hypertension. Seventy per cent of this group attributed the onset of their high blood pressure to specific home or job stress. Their ideas about the underlying physiological changes focused on the increased speed of heart beat and "tightness of the blood vessels". Patients thinking in terms of cyclic models were more likely to report a random or repetitive symptom pattern, to attribute the onset of hypertension to diet or drinking (58 per cent), and to explain hypertension in terms of excess blood and clogging of veins. Patients thinking in terms of a chronic model saw symptoms as long term (70 per cent), believed that age or heredity caused onset (57 per cent), and explained the disease in terms of damage to the heart and blood vessels or the body being "run down".

It appears that a similar picture will emerge in our study of patients with malignant lymphoma (Nerenz, 1979). Many patients appear to generate an acute episode model of their disease and use it to evaluate the cause and course of their illness. The particular example is the belief that life stress is a determinant of the illness. Why this model should emerge is not yet clear. One possibility is that the onset of life stress increases the salience of the symptoms and thereby convinces the patient that life stress actually exacerbates disease (see Mechanic, 1974). The recurrence of tumors may also stimulate fear and memories of negative affect which lead to the recall of a large number of unpleasant and stressful life events (Leventhal, 1979). Whatever the sequence—and both seem plausible—there is a perceived contingency between symptomatology and life stress. This contingency becomes in thought, if not in reality, a causal linkage.

These belief systems may be implicit rather than explicit. For example, the cognitive structures comprising the representation may be nonverbal perceptual memories that are difficult (or impossible) to represent verbally (Leventhal, 1979). The ability to verbalize may emerge only with time, something observed years ago in the study of concept learning (Hull, 1920; Posner, 1973). Because their cognitive structures are implicit, patients become aware of all its parts simultaneously, including his beliefs about cause, cure, underlying mechanisms, and the effects of disease on his coping behavior.

Because these beliefs are implicit, it is often difficult to see that they do function as an organized system helping the patient to explain and interpret his experience. One clue which suggests that beliefs function as an organized system is their resistance to change. In response to the question, "Can you tell if you have high blood pressure?", virtually all patients respond, "My doctor says people can't tell", or

"Most people can't tell", and then spontaneously, or in response to probing, they will add, "But I can tell". Thus, they use a simple device: the segregation of their experience from that of other typical patients in order to protect their beliefs from contradictory information which they have obviously received from doctors, nurses, health booklets, magazines and other media. It would be unusual for a specific, isolated belief to be so resistant to influence (see Zajonc, 1968).

Many patients recognize they are committed to a belief system contrary to the physicians. When asked about taking medication, they will say, "Well, don't tell my doctor", and then describe the experimental procedures they use to appraise the frequency and amount of medication needed to control their high blood pressure, how they monitor symptoms and vary their medication. They even invent little white lies which allow them to confess to not taking medication while protecting and keeping secret the reasons for missing. One vivid example involved a patient who took medications after lunch and dinner to control the headaches he experienced at these times. On this same visit, the physician asked why his pill bottle was roughly one-third full. The patient responded that he had been away for a week and forgotten to take his pills with him.

We believe that patients hide the reason for noncompliance to avoid a confrontation between their private, implicit theories of illness (symptoms, causes and cures) and the practitioner's medical model. They may avoid confrontation, because they feel awkward about arguing, are concerned about looking foolish, fear losing the support and help of the doctor by challenging his authority, and do not wish to express fears which may be associated with their underlying interpretations of their illness (see Leventhal, 1975). Fear of loss of support by challenging medical authority was vividly illustrated in two of the twelve initial pilot interviews we conducted with patients receiving chemotherapy for breast cancer. Both patients believed they were on placebo treatment, though they had been given a detailed description of their regimen and its expected effects. They believed they were getting a placebo, because the treatment produced none of the severe symptoms which they expected from chemotherapy. They did not believe a chemical injected into their bodies could kill cancer cells if they did not feel aches and pain and experience nausea, vomiting, and hair loss. Killing cancer is supposed to hurt! However, they did not communicate these concerns to their doctor.

E. The Patient's Theory of Illness Changes with Experience

There are three basic sources of information which appear to shape the patient's theory of illness: (1) bodily experience, (2) information from the external social environment (from health care providers, family, media, etc.), and (3) information based on past experience with illness. The growth of theories is seen in the changing percentage of individuals who think they can detect blood pressure elevations—45 per cent in normotensive controls, 52 per cent in newly discovered hypertensives (at a state fair screening site), 71 per cent in newly treated (first visit for medication), 88 per cent in actively treated, and 92 per cent for those who are re-entry hypertensives (Meyer, Reference Note 1).

The patient's initial representation of his illness seems to be heavily influenced by semantic factors. When people are told they are hypertensive or have high blood pressure, they often interpret this to mean they are *emotionally* tense and have a problem with their heart. It is no surprise, therefore, to see them focus on signs of tension and cardiac activity (heart rate) as symptomatic indicators of disease. But, as new information comes in and they discover they have elevated blood pressure when they cannot feel rapid heart rate activity, they will shift toward other symptoms. Heart rate is very infrequently used as an indicative symptom for patients who have been in treatment for any period of time.

A variety of incidental factors may also influence symptom selection, as well as the use of an acute, cyclic, or chronic model of illness. For example, a highly salient environmental event may be influential. If one has recently engaged in heavy physical activity, experienced conflict with a spouse or work partner, or been subject to some other unusual job stress, it is likely the event will be seen as the cause of the pressure increase and the hypertensive reading interpreted as an acute episode (stress model). The expectation is that pressure will be normal after an appropriate waiting period. However, if a person has just eaten a distinctively flavored food such as salty soup or a large amount of potato chips, he may attribute his hypertension to the ingestion of salt, an hypothesis that is compatible with medical theories appearing in the mass media. Since salt can be ingested in fairly large amounts at picnics and parties, etc., the patient may expect his current hypertension to disappear, but believe that it will reappear at a later date. When no simple explanation is available and family history indicates "susceptibility" to hypertension, the individual may make a chronic attribution: he expects the disease to last. The directive influence of social opinions and the contingency between highly available external cues and specific body symptoms at the time a pressure is taken, may be critical in steering the patient's theory of illness.

Past experience with illness and injury seems to be a fundamental aspect in the symptom selection process and in the shift from one symptom indicator to another. Our experience with illness and injury make it difficult to conceive of an asymptomatic illness threat. Hypertension "must" have symptoms; cancer "must" be painful and symptomatic, etc. Furthermore, the disappearance of symptoms "must" reflect the disappearance of the underlying disorder and cure.

The richness of the material generated from these simple premises can be astonishing. For example, interviews with our malignant lymphoma patients show very substantial elaboration of their conception of the disease process over time. A patient may come to believe that lumps or growths on only one side of the body are cancerous, while those which are symmetrical are not. Or a patient may believe that pains in the original site are recurrences of disease, while pains at new sites are not. A patient may be shocked when tumors spread upward or to distant parts of the body rather than growing slowly out from their initial site or "falling downwards" by gravity. These assumptions reflect views of cancer as a mechanical, geographically isolated process. These beliefs appear to be a common-sense blend or integration of concrete body experiences with physician comments.

The process of theory development also appears to be highly influenced by positive instances, such as occasions on which pressure is elevated and symptoms present. Instances where events co-appear are used for theory building. Occasions where pressure is normal, or where no tumors are present, are less likely to be used to formulate or evaluate a theory of the illness process. The nurse instructor in

Example A2 from the hypertension study, illustrates how positive instances dominate thinking and theory construction. It never occurred to this medically trained woman to take her pressure when she did not have a headache. Thus, she did not generate the occasions critical for disconfirming her theoretical preconceptions.

F. The Symptomatic Representation is a Guide to Coping

Representing an illness as a concrete set of symptoms "caused" by a salient, antecedent, environmental event is a major step toward generating a plan for coping. Indeed, if the representation has a purpose, it is to guide coping. Representing the illness in palpable and highly available symptoms allows for ongoing analysis and ongoing selection and evaluation of specific coping efforts. Indeed, the more concrete and specific the symptom, the simpler it is to evaluate its antecedents and its response to treatments. It should come as no surprise, therefore, that Meyer found more elaborate representations of hypertension in patients who manifest clear coping competencies. Patients who can generate a detailed and specific plan for dealing with illness are the patients who are more likely to elaborate a detailed representation of the hypertensive process. Meyer (Reference Note 1) measured coping by asking patients what they would do if they were told of an abnormal X-ray or cholesterol test at a screening site. The responses were scored for specificity and appropriateness of plans to deal with the health threat. A common set of cognitive skills (positive self-esteem, imagination, goal setting, and anticipation of potential outcomes) appear to underlie both generation of the illness representation and creation of the plan for action.

G. Immediate, Concrete Goals Facilitate Coping and Outcome Appraisal: Abstract, Remote Goals Generate Uncertainty and Distress

A concrete representation of an illness provides a specific set of immediate goals for action. These cues provide a clear indicator of progress or failure. Clear concrete cues provide a reality-bound picture of a knowable threat and not a mysterious, remote, uncertain, and infinitely threatening view of the illness process.

The hypothesis heading this section has been tested numerous times in a series of studies demonstrating that preparatory information on sensory experiences can reduce pain and distress and increase adaptive coping during treatment. For example, preparatory information on the concrete sensations accompanying the swallowing of an endoscopic tube greatly reduced signs of emotional distress (Johnson, Morrisey and Leventhal, 1973). Combining sensation information with instructions on swallowing and breathing reduced distress and facilitated active coping (voluntary swallowing of the endoscopic tube (Johnson and Leventhal, 1974)). Attention to contractions facilitated coping during childbirth and delivery (Shacham, Leventhal, Boothe and Leventhal, Reference Note 3). Sensation information and training in post-surgical exercise combined to produce significant reductions in days of hospitalization and days taken to get back into a routine of daily activity upon returning home (Johnson, Rice, Fuller and Endress, 1978). These and other excellent field studies by Johnson and her colleagues (Fuller, Endress and Johnson, 1978; Johnson, Kirchoff and Endress, 1975), and by Sime (1976), Wilson (1977), and Mills and Krantz (1979), make clear the importance of concrete, immediate goals in facilitating adaptation. (For more detailed reviews see Leventhal and Everhart, 1979; and Leventhal and Johnson, in press.)

A striking finding for patients with malignant lymphoma can be added to this list. A sizable proportion of patients with malignant lymphoma can assess the progress of their disease by directly monitoring their tumors which may be visible or palpable. The impact of chemotherapy treatment on tumors is also highly variable. In some instances, the tumors disappear virtually instantly by the end of the second, if not the first, week-long cycle of treatments. (The cycle typically begins with an injection followed by several days of oral medication.) In other instances, the tumors slowly, but steadily, shrink over four, five, or six treatments. In still others, the rate of change is so slow as to be unnoticeable. Distress induced by chemotherapy was compared for patients who had no palpable tumors and for patients whose tumors disappeared abruptly, slowly, and not at all. Patients who experienced a complete, immediate remission reported much higher levels of distress than most other patients. Patients who showed slow, but consistent, tumor regression with treatment reported the very lowest level of distress. While it may seem paradoxical that patients who benefited most swiftly were most distressed, a moment's reflection makes clear that the immediate regression of the tumors left patients without the one concrete cue they could use to measure treatment effectiveness. They also lost their major justification—the steady remission of disease—for continuing this uncomfortable and distressing treatment. Somewhat similar logic appears to account for the high level of distress reported by breast cancer patients receiving chemotherapy treatments after apparently successful breast surgery. The cancer has been removed, the patient "cured", and it is impossible to monitor benefits directly and difficult to justify the distress induced by the noxious chemical agents used for this adjuvant treatment.

H. The Patient Uses his Symptomatic Representation of Disease to Evaluate and Regulate the Utilization of Treatment

The most dramatic examples of patient regulation of treatment are seen in hypertension. The persons in the hypertension examples used symptoms as cues to re-enter treatment (Example 1) and to regulate medication taking (Example 2). Where 58 per cent of newly treated patients remain in treatment for six months or longer, only 38 per cent of the group who present with a symptom remain in treatment. Of the actively treated patients (patients who stayed in treatment), those who believed treatment ameliorated their symptoms were far more likely to be taking their medications as prescribed (71 per cent) than those who reported no effect of the treatment on their symptoms (31 per cent).

A curious effect appears for patients who report a symptom and have re-entered treatment after previously dropping out. Of the patients who re-entered with the very same symptom they had on the prior occasion, 83 per cent (5/6) dropped out once again. Of the patients who re-entered treatment with a new symptom, an apparently different sign of hypertension, only 7 per cent (1/15) dropped out. While the sample size is small, the difference is very large. It seems that a new symptom undermines the patient's confidence in his ability to predict blood pressure levels and to monitor treatment effects. This may increase his dependence on the medical personnel who use direct measurement of pressure to assess the course of the disease and the efficacy of treatment.

I. The Representation of Illness Guides Coping that is an Adjunct to Medical Treatment

Patients' representations of illness, particularly their attributions of cause, naturally lend themselves to the construction of a variety of coping procedures which are perceived as additional means of fighting their disease. One elaborate pattern was seen in the patient who associated the initial onset and recurrences of his Hodgkin's disease to life stress (Example 2). Because the itching he used to gauge disease activity became more noticeable during times of stress, he concluded that stress caused the recurrences of his illness. The logic of his observations led him to cut back his work from full to half time, and to avoid stressful situations wherever possible. He hoped this would further retard the spread of his illness.

The above example is not unique. Both hypertensives and cancer chemotherapy patients use acute, episodic models of their illness in which stress is seen to be responsible for both the onset and recurrence of their disease. Cutting back on work commitments, seeking aid and assistance with work from friends and family, and obtaining rest to build strength are common coping patterns. Another very common coping pattern for distress control is to differentiate more sharply between life problems which are truly important and those which are trivial. Patients refuse to become emotionally upset and involved with the minor ones.

Patients who define cancer in more mechanical terms, as bad cells or tumors, may engage in intensive exercise, adopt health food diets, and make other changes to strengthen their bodies' defenses against illness. While patients differ in their degree of conviction in the effectiveness of these supportive or adjunct therapies, they often see the therapies as beneficial in controlling maladapative emotional reactions and in enhancing the quality of life. These latter effects, particularly on the quality of life, may be quite substantial, and it is not unusual to find enormous gains in self-control and feelings of ability to manage one's existence. Illness crises can promote growth. By providing a set of bodily symptoms for continuous disease and health monitoring, the patient finds a clear direction for immediate coping behavior and clear criteria (symptom minimization and feelings of increased wellness and enhanced level of energy) for evaluating positive coping outcomes. The patient's representation of illness provides a focus for self-regulating behaviors that may expand into a greater sense of self-determination and control over both emotional experiences and the quality of life (see Bandura, 1977).

J. Unpredictable and Uncontrollable Effects of Treatment Can Induce High Levels of Distress and Hopelessness

To the outside observer, it may seem remarkable that a patient can adapt to a chemotherapy regimen consisting of a massive injection of noxious chemicals followed by a series of pills, particularly when these medications can lead to pain, fatigue, hair loss, nausea, and vomiting every 20 minutes for 12 to 18 hours. Yet, some patients adapt by developing a number of minor tactics for coping with these effects. They may rest when tired or suck lozenges to kill the taste and odor of the chemical agents. The majority of patients gradually adapt, showing less severe and less prolonged side effects with repeated treatment cycles (treatment may involve as many as 12 or 18 two-week cycles). Indeed, coping with side effects may become quite automatic. The patient goes to the bathroom to vomit every 20 minutes as though he were doing nothing more dramatic than urinating, and he describes this experience in a matter-of-fact way.

In sharp contrast to the above pattern, there are a small number of cases where emotion continues to run at high levels. Distress blends into feelings of hopelessness. In these cases, the side effects of the drugs may be unpredictable and apparently random in onset. The nausea and vomiting may start immediately or three to four hours after the injection. The vomiting spells may last 5 minutes or 40 minutes. The patient who cannot predict when his nausea will begin and how often it will recur, and when he will or will not vomit, may describe his symptoms in words and tone of voice that suggest a high level of distress. Yet the impact of chemotherapy on his system may be objectively less severe than that seen for most other patients. For example, he may have less frequent and shorter episodes of nausea and vomiting.

Unpredictability not only results from a lack of precise temporal rhythm, but can also appear when symptoms are vague and lacking in precision (Leventhal, 1975). Tiredness and general aching are less clear sensory and symptomatic effects than hair loss and vomiting. The more vague symptoms of tiredness and fatigue are more likely to be seen as signs of disease, rather than as signs of treatment. On the other hand, nausea, vomiting, and hair loss are more readily attributed to treatment. Vague, non-specific symptoms are also the hallmark of hypochondriacal, stress-induced concern about the body (Mechanic, 1972), and hypochondriasis tends to be a personal and permanent attribution.

6. THE RELATIONSHIP OF DANGER CONTROL TO OTHER PROCESSES

We have hypothesized a variety of processes involved in the generation of a representation of illness dangers. These representations are guides to coping with treatment, illness, and life problems. Representations guide coping and are constructed to permit coping. Though we used case studies to support many of our formulations, the cases appear to represent findings emerging from a more systematic analyses of three large scale studies: Meyer's (Reference Note 1) investigations of reactions during treatment for hypertension, Nerenz's (1979) study of reactions during treatment for malignant lymphoma, and Ringler's (Reference Note 2) as yet incomplete study of reactions to chemotherapy treatment for the control of metastatic breast cancer and for the prevention of recurrence of breast disease (adjuvant chemotherapy). The representation of the illness, the coping responses, and the mechanism for the evaluation of coping outcomes, make up the complete self-regulatory system for the control of danger.

The symmetrical relationship of body sensations (symptoms) and disease labels are at the core of these processes. It is customarily argued that people seek verbal labels to define their body status (e.g., Schachter and Singer, 1962; Leventhal, 1975;

Mechanic, 1966). Our data presents an equally persuasive case for the opposite conclusion: people define abstract body states with sensations and symptoms. From such meagre beginnings, elaborate cognitive systems bloom. We suggest that cognitive systems of this sort determine much illness and sick-role behavior (Mechanic, 1972; Kasl and Cobb, 1966a, 1966b). We also believe this conceptualization of the danger control process is very different from that suggested by more traditional decision theories such as the health belief model (e.g., Becker, 1974; Becker and Maiman, 1975; Hochbaum, 1958; Leventhal, Hochbaum, Carriger and Rosenstock, 1960; Rogers, 1975). Our model differs from these decision models because it attempts to conceptualize the processes involved in the construction of judgments of vulnerability, severity, and effectiveness. We believe that it offers, therefore, a rich array of suggestions for potential interventions.

There are, however, two key issues we have not yet discussed. The first concerns the relationship of these processes to fear and fear control. The second concerns the outcome of self-regulatory attempts and the factors that focus evaluations on specific coping reactions (this response was good or bad), the self (I am a good or bad coper), or the representation of the illness (I thought cancer curable—it is not). Though we cannot address these issues at length in the present chapter, they are important with respect to the process of intervention and require at least minimal attention.

A. Interactions of Danger and Fear Control

The process of selecting a symptom, delving into causal antecedents, and constructing and evaluating coping responses is affected by fear. Fear of pain, injury, loss of control, and death may appear at any number of points during the ongoing process of danger control. Observations of a symptom and a fleeting question—"Could it be a cancer?"—can send a shiver up the spine. A diagnosis of hypertension can generate fear, bewilderment, and questions as to why one might "deserve" an illness, and can lead to a search for contingencies between presumed symptoms of disease (hyperactivity and tension) and environmental stress. The appearance of a splitting headache after several days of experimentation with variations and reductions in drug regimen can stimulate fear of the inadequacy of the self-generated treatment, fear of stroke, guilt at having departed from the prescribed regimen, and so forth. Such fleeting feelings of fear may have little overall impact, other than to add a bit of urgency to the danger control process of problem-solving. Fear may also strengthen the commitment to pursue treatment more effectively and consistently, and intensify the desire not to forget taking medication.

When fear functions in the ways described above, it will be of relatively little significance for the process of danger control, because it merely adds to the intensity of coping and does relatively little to steer or direct decisions. Thus, decisions are primarily under the control of the individual's model of danger, and fear will facilitate or interfere with participation in the medical care system, depending on the overlap of the patient's model with his treatment needs. Fear stimulated by threat can direct behavior in ways that are antagonistic to effective coping. Thus, an ex-cardiac patient who is frightened and has never adequately mastered his images of surgery and fear of death, may respond to chest pain with fright and denial. He may insist it is indigestion and refuse to believe it could be a recurrence of heart disease (Hackett and Cassem, 1969). A cancer patient experiencing pain in lymphatic sites may attribute the pain to muscular distress rather than accept the possibility of the recurrence of malignancy. Examples of this sort are commonly described as instances of denial, or as coping with fear by avoiding awareness of, and contact with, signs of threat. Coping activity of this sort is, of course, maladaptive, as it prevents affective, realistically oriented danger-control activity (see Janis and Leventhal, 1967). But efforts to cope with fear need not conflict with danger control processes. One could make the "rational" decision to cope with fear by visiting the physician as soon as one notices cues of danger. Behaviors of this sort can avoid hours of worry and enhance the effectiveness of living. More severe forms of these behaviors resemble the hypochondriacal hypervigilance observed in the so-called worried well who over-utilizes both screening facilities and doctors' services (Mechanic, 1972).

Emotionally grounded hypervigilance (Janis, 1958; Janis and Leventhal, 1967) can generate exquisite sensitivity to bodily sensations and can lead to elaborate illness representations. An example of this was observed in a hypertensive drug study conducted by Meyer, Jackson and Gutmann at Mount Sinai hospital. A middle-aged female patient who was exceptionally anxious about her hypertensive disorder was so observant of bodily cues that she detected even minor increases in edema when switched from a diuretic to a placebo. After only three days on placebos, she systematically measured her own pressure and noticed it increasing. After a week of anxious days and sleepless nights, she went back to her original medication. While this instance of behavior reflected a valid analysis of her condition, there were many instances where fear motivation directed her attention to invalid symptoms and led to sharp increases in medication when symptomatic and decreases when asymptomatic. These coping reactions, valid or invalid were exceptionally resistant to influence.

The above examples of denial and hypervigilance provide important examples of two quite contrasting ways in which fear can interact with danger control processes. First, fear can operate quite independently of the danger control process. The patient can be so strongly motivated to eliminate fear that he cares little about confronting, manipulating, and learning about the elements which comprise danger. This is seen in Zborowski's (1952) example of the traditional, ethnic Italian patient's reaction to pain. The second and more important way that fear can operate is by affecting the representation of danger. By increasing sensitivity to body cues, and by altering the patient to causal events and coping possibilities, fear constructs a phenomenological image of disease and coping that is experienced as a valid representation of external reality. When fear makes use of, or operates through, the individual's experience of external reality, its phenomenological base becomes a powerful bulwark against counterintuitive (though medically valid) argument.

B. Outcome Appraisals: Who Failed and Who Succeeded

Having coped, one appraises impact: Did the response produce the desired effect? Can I generate an effective response? Is the illness (representation) other than what I thought? Lazarus (1966) called this "a secondary appraisal" to distinguish it from the initial representation (primary appraisal) of the threat. The critical issue, however, is not merely to distinguish the two forms of appraisal—they will undoubtedly prove similar in many ways—but to identify the factors that direct evaluation of feedback to one or another of these questions: Is the response adequate? Is the representation of the threat adequate? Is the self adequate?

In most instances, feedback will first address the issue of the adequacy of the response, next that of the representation of the threat, and last, that of self-effectiveness. This ordering is a guess at typically expected empirical outcomes; while it is not a theoretical hypothesis, it is based on a number of theoretical hypotheses. One hypothesis is that change probably occurs in the *least* differentiated and *least* well-anchored of the three components—this component is likely to be the coping response. Life teaches us the need for trial and error to test the most effective means of coping with specific problems. Thus, we anticipate a degree of experimentation and usually do not overcommit ourselves to a particular means for reaching a desired goal. The representation of a threat, however, is likely to be more firmly anchored. Once grounded in symptoms, it is anchored to a palpable reality. This reality is further supported by a lifetime of experience with symptoms and illness and with social mythologies about symptomatology and illness. Fear may further anchor the representation, for adherence to a particular model provides hope of escape from the threat. The self-system is likely to be most solidly anchored and, in most people, this anchoring will be positive (e.g., Aronson, 1969). Most people's histories are filled with abundant examples of successful coping, a point which lends support to the hypothesis that one's actions control the environment (Seligman, 1975; Masserman, 1957).

A host of variables will contribute to the stability of each of the components and to their respective openness of resistance to feedback. These will include *situational sets* involving anticipation of outcome and specific information about particular responses, symptoms, and the self; *social comparisons* in which the patient compares himself to those with similar difficulties and in which he questions the uniqueness of his problems; *personality factors* such as self-esteem; and many *other variables* which direct attributions of outcome either to the coping response, to the representation of illness, or to the self. Because of their complexity, we will forgo further discussion and direct the reader to other sources which review these processes (e.g., Abramson, Seligman and Teasdale, 1978; Wortman and Dintzer, 1978; Leventhal, 1975).

7. CONCLUSION

We have argued in this chapter that a patient's behavior, both in preventing and dealing with illness, can be studied in the context of the patient's own representation of his illness. This representation is largely based on concrete symptom experience. It acts as part of a regulatory system to guide coping efforts and to set goals through which coping efforts are evaluated. We have attempted to illustrate the value of this approach using examples from our current research. We suggest that the focus on patient representations is valuable both in leading to fruitful areas of inquiry and in organizing a range of diverse empirical findings.

The study of patient illness representations and their contribution to self-regulation offers a challenge to clinical, personality, and social psychologists. The problems and the data may illuminate issues fundamental to theories of regulatory processes (e.g., Powers, 1973) and to theories on the contribution of the self-system to regulation. The data also offer insight into the relationships between representations of external reality (danger control processes) and subjective emotional experiences (fear control processes or representations of affective responses to object representations). These findings and models will also relate to a host of theoretical models of judgement processes (e.g., Tversky and Kahneman, 1973), attribution (Kelley, 1967; Nisbett and Wilson, 1977), and emotion (Leventhal, 1974, 1979, 1980; Schachter and Singer, 1962).

Our emphasis on the self-regulatory process contrasts sharply with more traditional medical–sociological approaches which focus on descriptive demographic and test data (personality traits, social class, etc.) which, for the most part, are resistant to intervention (Rogers, 1968). Our approach also contrasts with that which emphasizes common public representations of illness (e.g., Herzlich, 1973). We believe that public representations are important, but as patients experience an illness in themselves, shared public beliefs will be substantially modified to fit the patient's own concrete experience.

There are, however, two additional reasons for studying representations of danger in self-regulation. First, models depicting how the individual builds his understanding of disease process and how his coping is directed by (and, in turn, constructs) the representation of illness, are rich in suggestions for patient education. There is great potential for developing effective methods of intervention, methods which would help patients to develop valid self-regulatory processes. This would be a primary source of satisfaction for investigators working on real-world problems.

The second, and perhaps most important reason for studying these problems is to build substantive theories of social–psychological processes. Chemistry, for example, would not have developed as a science without the discovery of elements. The discovery of elements (of basic substantive units) was an essential step for developments in dynamics and resulted in laws of fixed proportion which led to notions of atomic weight, structural models of elements, bonding, and so on. The cognitive psychology of illness may likewise offer fundamental insights, because it will yield a description of fundamental units of meaning: for example, the three models of disease (acute, cyclic and chronic) and the sub-varieties (stress, dietary, hereditary) within each category. With stable meaning units we can raise exciting questions regarding structures, combinations of structures, and the impact which external information (body cues, social inputs, etc.) has on concrete images and on more abstract representational thought systems.

REFERENCE NOTES

1. Meyer, D. The effects of patients' representations of high blood pressure on behavior in treatment. Doctoral dissertation in progress, University of Wisconsin—Madison.
2. Ringler, K. Processes of coping with cancer chemotherapy side effects. Doctoral dissertation in progress, University of Wisconsin—Madison.
3. Shacham, S., Leventhal, H., Boothe, C. S. and Leventhal, E. The role of attention in distress control during childbirth. Unpublished manuscript, University of Wisconsin—Madison, 1978.
4. Meyer, D., Leventhal, H. and Gutmann, M. (1979) Symptoms in hypertension: How patients evaluate and treat them. Unpublished manuscript, University of Wisconsin—Madison.

ACKNOWLEDGEMENTS

This work was supported in part by NIH grant No. HL24543-01 to the first author.

The authors wish to thank collaborators at Mt. Sinai Medical Center, Milwaukee: Mary Gutmann, Ph.D., Thoman Jackson, M.D. and Frank Gutmann, M.D., and collaborators at University of Wisconsin—Madison School of Medicine: Richard Love, M.D. and Elaine Leventhal, M.D.

REFERENCES

Abramson, L., Seligman, M. E. P. and Teasdale, J. (1978) Learned helplessness in humans: Critique and reformulation, *Journal of Abnormal Psychology*, **87**, 49–74.

Alderman, M. and Schoenbaum, E. (1975) Detection and treatment of hypertension at the work site, *New England Journal of Medicine*, **293**, 65–68.

Aronson, E. (1969) The theory of cognitive dissonance: A current perspective, in L. Berkowitz (Ed.), *Advances in experimental social psychology*, Vol. 4, Academic Press, New York.

Bandura, A. (1977) Self-efficacy: Toward a unifying theory of behavioral change, *Psychological Review*, **84**, 191–215.

Baranowski, T. (1979) Cognitive-emotional social learning theory aspects of regimen compliance, Paper presented at 1979 Annual Convention of the American Psychological Association.

Becker, M. (Ed.) (1974) The health belief model and personal health behavior, *Health Education Monographs*, **2**, 324–508.

Becker, M. H. and Maiman, L. A. (1975) Sociobehavioral determinants of compliance with health and medical care recommendations, *Medical Care*, **13**, 10–24.

Ben-Sira, Z. and Padeh, B. (1978) "Instrumental coping" and "affective defense": An additional perspective in health promoting behavior, *Social Science and Medicine*, **12**, 163–168.

Byar, D. P., Simon, R. M., Friedewald, W. T., Schlesselman, J. J., Demets, D. L., Ellenberg, J. H., Gail, M. H. and Wave, J. H. (1976) Randomized clinical trials: Perspectives on some recent ideas, *New England Journal of Medicine*, **295**, 74–80.

Chu, G. C. (1966) Fear arousal, efficacy, and imminency, *Journal of Personality and Social Psychology*, **4**, 517–524.

Engel, G. (1977) The need for a new medical model: A challenge for biomedicine, *Science*, **196**, 129–136.

Finnerty, F., Mattie, E. and Finnerty, F. (1973) Hypertension in the inner city: 1. Analysis of clinic dropouts, *Circulation*, **47**, 73–75.

Fuller, S. S., Endress, M. P. and Johnson, J. E. (1978) The effects of cognitive and behavioral control on coping with an aversive health examination, *Journal of Human Stress*, **4**, 18–25.

Green, L. W., Levine, D. M. and Deeds, S. (1975) Clinical trials of health education for hypertensive outpatients: Design and baseline data, *Preventive Medicine*, **4**, 417–425.

Gutmann, M., Meyer, D., Leventhal, H., Gutmann, F. and Jackson, T. (1979) Medical versus patient oriented interviewing. Paper presented at National meeting, American Federation for Clinical Research, Washington D.C.

Hackett, T. P. and Cassem, N. H. (1969) Factors contributing to delay in responding to the signs and symptoms of acute myocardial infarction, *American Journal of Cardiology*, **24**, 651–658.

Hempel, C. G. (1966) *Philosophy of Natural Science*, Prentice–Hall, Englewood Cliffs, N.J.

Herzlich, C. (1973) *Health and Illness: A Social Psychological Analysis*, Academic Press, New York.

Hochbaum, G. M. (1958) *Public participation in medical screening programs: A sociopsychological study*, Public Health Service Publication No. 572, U.S. Government Printing Office, Washington, D.C.

Hull, C. L. (1920) Quantitative aspects of the evolution of concepts: An experimental study, *Psychological Monographs*, **28**, (1, whole No. 123).

Janis, I. L. (1958) *Psychological Stress*, Wiley, New York.

Janis, I. L. and Feshbach, S. (1953) Effects of fear-arousing communications. *Journal of Abnormal and Social Psychology*, **48**, 78–92.

Janis, I. L. and Leventhal, H. (1967) Human reactions to stress, in Borgatta, E. and Lambert, W. (Eds.), *Handbook of Personality Theory and Research*, Rand McNally, Boston.

Johnson, J. E. and Leventhal, H. (1974) Effects of accurate expectations and behavioral instructions on reactions during a noxious medical examination, *Journal of Personality and Social Psychology*, **29**, 710–718.

Johnson, J. E., Kirchoff, K. and Endress, M. (1975) Deferring children's distress behavior during orthopedic cast removal, *Nursing Research*, **75**, 404–410.

Johnson, J. E., Morrisey, N. and Leventhal, H. (1973) Psychological preparation for an endoscopic examination, *Gastro intestinal Endoscopy*, **19**, 180–182.

Johnson, J. E., Rice, V. H., Fuller, S. S. and Endress, M. P. (1978) Sensory information, instruction in a coping strategy and recovery from surgery, *Research in Nursing and Health*, **1**, 4–17.

Kasl, S. V. and Cobb, S. (1966a) Health behavior, illness behavior, and sick-role behavior, I, Health and illness behavior, *Archives of Environmental Health*, **12**, 246–266.

Kasl, S. V. and Cobb, S. (1966b) Health behavior, illness behavior, and sick-role behavior, II, Sick-role behavior, *Archives of Environmental Health*, **12**, 531–541.

Kelley, H. H. (1967) Attribution theory in social psychology, *Nebraska Symposium on Motivation*, **14**, 192–241.

Kirscht, J. and Rosenstock, I. (1977) Patient adherence to antihypertensive regimens, *Journal of Community Health*, **3**, 115–124.

Lazarus, R. (1966) *Psychological Stress and the Coping Process*, McGraw–Hill, New York.

Leventhal, H. (1970) Findings and theory in the study of fear communications, in L. Berkowitz (Ed.), *Advances in experimental social psychology*, Academic Press, New York.

Leventhal, H. (1974) Emotions: A basic problem for social psychology, in C. Nemeth (Ed.) *Social psychology*, Rand McNally, Chicago.

Leventhal, H. (1975) The consequences of depersonalization during illness and treatment, in Howard, J. and Strauss, A. (Eds.), *Humanizing Health Care*, Wiley, New York.

Leventhal, H. (1979) A perceptual–motor processing model of emotion, in P. Pliner, K. Blankstein and I. M. Spigel (Eds.) *Advances in the study of communication and affect: Perception of emotion in self and others*, Plenum, New York.

Leventhal, H. (in press) Toward a comprehensive theory of emotions, in L. Berkowitz (Ed.) *Advances in experimental social psychology*, Vol. 12.

Leventhal, H. and Cleary, P. (1979) Behavioral modification of risk factors: Technology or science, in Pollock, M. *et al.* (Eds.), *Heart Disease and Rehabilitation: State of the Art*, Houghton–Mifflin, New York.

Leventhal, H. and Everhart, D. (1979) Emotion, pain, and physical illness, in Izard, C. (Ed.), *Emotion and Psychopathology*, Plenum, New York.

Leventhal, H., Hochbaum, G., Carriger, B. and Rosenstock, I. (1960) Epidemic impact on the general population in two cities, in Rosenstock, I., Hochbaum, G. and Leventhal, H. (Eds.), *The Impact of Asian Influenza on Community Life*, Public Health Service Publication No. 766, U.S. Government Printing Office, Washington D.C.

Leventhal, H. and Johnson, J. E. (in press) Laboratory and field experimentation: Development of a theory of self-regulation, in Woolridge, P. H. and Schmitt, M. H. (Eds.), *Behavioral Science and Nursing Theory*.

Leventhal, H., Jones, S. and Trembly, G. (1966) Sex differences in attitude and behavior change under conditions of fear and specific instructions, *Journal of Experimental Social Psychology*, **2**, 387–399.

Leventhal, H. and Niles, P. (1964) A field experiment on fear arousal with data on the validity of questionnaire measures, *Journal of Personality*, **32**, 459–479.

Leventhal, H. and Niles, P. (1965) Persistance of influence for varying durations of exposure to threat stimuli, *Psychological Reports*, **16**, 223–233.

Leventhal, A., Safer, M., Cleary, P. and Gutmann, M. (in press) Cardiovascular risk modification by community based programs for life style change: Comments on the Starford 8 study, *Journal of Consulting and Clinical Psychology*.

Leventhal, H. and Singer, R. (1966) Affect arousal and positioning of recommendations in persuasive communications, *Journal of Personality and Social Psychology*, **4**, 137–146.

Leventhal, H., Singer, R. and Jones, S. (1965) Effects of fear and specificity of recommendations upon attitudes and behavior, *Journal of Personality and Social Psychology*, **2**, 20–29.

Leventhal, H. and Trembly, G. (1968) Negative emotions and persuasion, *Journal of Personality*, **36**, 154–168.

Leventhal, H. and Watts, J. (1966) Sources of resistance to fear arousal communications on smoking and lung cancer, *Journal of Personality*, **34**, 155–175.

Leventhal, H., Watts, J. and Pagano, F. (1967) Effects of fear and instructions on how to cope with danger, *Journal of Personality and Social Psychology*, **6**, 313–321.

Ley, P. (1977) Psychological studies of doctor–patient communication, in Rachman, S. (Ed.), *Contributions to Medical Psychology*, Vol. 1, 9–42, Pergamon Press, Oxford.

Masserman, J. H. (1957) Evolution versus "revolution" in psychotherapy: A biodynamic integration, *Behavioral Science*, **3**, 89–100.

Mechanic, D. (1966) Response factors in illness: The study of illness behavior, *Social Psychiatry*, **1**, 11–20.

Mechanic, D. (1972) Social psychological factors affecting the presentation of bodily complaints, *New England Journal of Medicine*, **286**, 1132–1139.

Mechanic, D. (1974) Discussion of research programs on relations between stressful life events and episodes of physical illness, in Dohrenwend, B. and Dohrenwend, B. (Eds.), *Stressful Life Events: Their Nature and Effects*, Wiley, New York.

Mechanic, D. (1978) *Medical sociology*, 2nd Ed., The Free Press, New York.

Mills, R. T. and Krantz, D. S. (1979) Information choice, and reactions to stress: A field experiment in a blood bank with laboratory analogue, *Journal of Personality and Social Psychology*, **37**, 608–620.

Nerenz, D. R. (1979) Control of emotional distress in cancer chemotherapy, Unpublished doctoral dissertation, University of Wisconsin.

Nisbett, R. E. and Wilson, T. D. (1977) Telling more than we can know: Verbal reports on mental processes, *Psychological Review*, **84**, 231–259.

Parsons, T. (1951) *The social system*, The Free Press, New York.

Pennebaker, J. and Skelton, J. (1978) Psychological parameters of physical symptoms, *Personality and Social Psychology Bulletin*, **4**, 524–530.

Posner, M. I. (1973) *Cognition: An Introduction*, Scott, Foresman, Glenview, Ill.

Powers, W. T. (1973) *Behavior: The Control of Perception*, Aldine, Chicago.

Rachman, S. (Ed.) (1977) *Contributions to Medical Psychology*: Vol. 1, Pergamon Press, Oxford.

Rogers, E. S. (1968) Public health asks of sociology, *Science*, **159**, 506–508.

Rogers, R. W. (1975) A protection motivation theory of fear appeals and attitude change, *Journal of Psychology*, **91**, 93–114.

Rogers, R. W. and Deckner, C. W. (1975) Effects of fear appeals and physiological arousal upon emotion, attitudes, and cigarette smoking, *Journal of Personality and Social Psychology*, **32**, 222–230.

Rogers, R. W. and Mewborn, C. R. (1976) Fear appeals and attitudes change: Effects of a threat's noxiousness, probability of occurrence, and the efficacy of coping responses, *Journal of Personality and Social Psychology*, **34**, 54–61.

Sackett, D. and Haynes, R. (1976) (Eds.) *Compliance with Therapeutic Regimens*, Johns Hopkins University Press, Baltimore.

Sackett, D., Haynes, R., Gibson, E., Hackett, B., Taylor, D., Roberts, R. and Johnson, A. (1975) Randomized clinical trial of strategies for improving medication compliance in primary hypertension, *The Lancet*, **1**, 1205–1207.

Safer, M., Tharps, Q., Jackson, T. and Leventhal, H. (1979) Determinants of three stages of delay in seeking care at a medical clinic, *Medical Care*, **17**, 11–29.

Schachter, S. and Singer, J. E. (1962) Cognitive, social, and physiological determinants of emotional state, *Psychological Review*, **69**, 379–399.

Seligman, M. E. P. (1975) *Helplessness*, W. H. Freeman, San Francisco.

Sime, A. M. (1976) Relationships of preoperative fear, type of coping, and information received about surgery to recovery from surgery, *Journal of Personality and Social Psychology*, **34**, 716–724.

Singer, R. P. (1965) The effects of fear-arousing communications on attitude change and behavior, Unpublished doctoral dissertation, University of Connecticut.

Sternthal, B. and Craig, C. (1974) Fear appeals: Revisited and revised, *Journal of Communications Research*, **1**, 22–34.

Tversky, A. and Kahneman, D. (1973) Availability: A heuristic for judging frequency and probability, *Cognitive Psychology*, **5**, 207–232.

Wilson, J. F. (1977) Determinants of recovery from surgery: Preoperative instruction, relaxative training and defensive structures. Unpublished doctoral dissertation, University of Michigan.

Wortman, C. B. and Dintzer, L. (1978) Is an attributional analysis of the learned helplessness phenomenon viable?: A critique of the Abramson–Seligman–Teasdale reformulation, *Journal of Abnormal Psychology*, **87**, 75–90.

Zajonc, R. B. (1968) Cognitive theories in social psychology, in Lindzey, G. and Aronson, E. (Eds.), *The Handbook of Social Psychology*, Addison–Wesley, Reading, Mass.

Zborowski, M. (1952) Cultural components in responses to pain, *Journal of Social Issues*, **8**, 16–30.

Zifferblatt, S. M. and Wilbur, C. S. (1977) Maintaining a health heart—Guidelines for a feasible goal, *Preventive Medicine*, **6**, 514–525.

2

BEHAVIOURAL TREATMENT OF DEPRESSION IN HISTORICAL PERSPECTIVE

VICKY RIPPERE

Institute of Psychiatry, University of London

Theories come and go, but practices, good or bad, have a surprising way of surviving and of being rationalised differently according to the fashionable theories of the day.

Ackerknecht (1957)

CONTENTS

1. INTRODUCTION

The new medical psychology is basically an attempt to apply psychology to the solution of problems previously considered to fall within the scope of medicine. Depression represents a relatively recent addition to their number. Until about 15 years ago, psychologists had little to say about it and, apart from those engaged in dynamic psychotherapy, they left treatment to the doctors, who mainly dispensed drugs and other forms of physical treatment. Properly psychological conceptualizations of depressive disorders—as opposed to occasional experimental studies of people labelled depressed by psychiatrists—did not exist. However, since the early 1960s, psychologists have enthusiastically discovered depression; and we now have a great variety of psychological paradigms for organizing both thought and clinical actions on behalf of the depressed (see, e.g. Friedman and Katz, 1974; Becker, 1977, for reviews).

The present study is proposed as an adjunct to these developments. It does not offer a new modern paradigm for construing depression and its treatment; neither does it review the paradigms currently under development, nor does it contrast

31

them with contemporary medical approaches. Rather, the aim here is to look back at what was said about depression in the period before the medical model, which until recently was more or less universally taken for granted and is only now being challenged by psychological models, came to predominate. To keep things manageable, we will be restricted to discourse in English-language printed books; we will be examining what writers had to say about depression—or melancholy, as it was called—in the period from the early sixteenth to the end of the nineteenth century, by which time the medical model was pretty firmly entrenched. In particular, we will be concerned with the original form in which the classical tradition of advice to the melancholy came to be transmitted to the readership of early English-language printed books and the subsequent transformations which it underwent over the course of the next 400 years. Within this broad area, we will be most concerned with that aspect of the tradition which was designated as *Regimen*, or health practices to be carried out by the individual in the course of daily life, as opposed to *Physic*, or practices carried out upon people by physicians. Considerations of space preclude examining either pre-English language developments or further ones since 1900; these latter may form the basis of a later study. Meanwhile, both psychologists and doctors who deal with depressed people may broaden their perspectives from viewing the practices of the more distant past and as a result may be less willing to accept current views as the only possible ways of thinking about the problems of the depressed.

The tradition of thought on melancholy is said to begin with Hippocrates in the fifth century B.C., to have been systematized by Galen in the second century A.D., thereafter to have been preserved and elaborated by Arabic and other Eastern physicians in the millennium between the end of the classical period and its reintroduction into the West, mainly in Latin translations, in the late Middle Ages, when it was adopted into the curriculum of the new medical schools attached to mediaeval universities and passed on from there, also in Latin, with relatively few changes, well into the Renaissance. In the late fifteenth century, a new development occurred which, though it was not itself part of the ancient tradition of thought on melancholy, was to contribute more to its transformation than probably any other single event since its earliest origins. This development was William Caxton's introduction of the printing press into England in 1477. Within less than half a century, the Graeco-Roman heritage of advice on the nature and treatment of melancholic disorders had begun an entirely new phase of its development, as the traditional materials were translated into English and disseminated further as a popular vernacular tradition. It is at this point, in the early decades of the 16th century, that our story begins.

Prominent amongst the earliest English printed books were translations of ancient medical writings and philosophical treatises of spiritual consolation. In addition to classical works, translators also turned their hand to contemporary Latin works and others in European vernaculars. Besides these classical and modern translations, there was a third pathway along which the received ideas were transmitted, in the form of a popular medical literature written directly in English.

Not all such books were the work of physicians. The earliest manual of domestic medicine in English, which appeared in 1534, was written by the diplomatist and translator, Sir Thomas Elyot, who, though he had studied medicine, was not himself a qualified "doctour of physicke". Elyot presents *The Castel of Helth* as "gathered ... out of the chiefe Authors of Physycke", but the compilation and ordering of the received materials is his own. The same is true of one of the first medical works in the vernacular by an English physician, the *Breviary of Helthe* (written 1542, published 1547) and its companion volume, the *Dyetary of Helth* (1542), by Dr Andrew Boorde. The *Breviary* is an alphabetical 2-volume compendium of classical and Eastern medical terms, listed under their English equivalents, and includes chapters on the entire universe of complaints as well as melancholy. Before the end of the century, such compilations had been superseded by more specialized offerings, such as Philip Barrough's medical textbook, *The Methode of Physicke* (1583), Thomas Cogan's manual of student health, *The Haven of Health* (1584), and finally, by the first work in English to be devoted entirely to the problem of melancholy and its vicissitudes, Dr Timothy Bright's *Treatise of Melancholie* (1586).

The spirit in which the sixteenth century popularizers set about importing the ancient medical tradition into contemporary English culture was both a sign of the times and an important factor contributing to its rapid assimilation and further development. From the first, the popularizers proposed the teachings of the ancients as a many-splendoured curriculum in self-preservation. The benefits promised to those who followed the course were potentially great. Boorde, in the *Breviary*, declared as his aim in writing "to do sycke men pleasure and whole men profyte, that sicke men may recuperate their helthe and whole men may preserve their selfe from sickenes (with goddes help)..." Underlying this statement was a network of assumptions about the readership which included the beliefs that people could, should, and moreover were highly motivated to take an active part in maintaining, preserving, and restoring their own health. The opportunity to do so was considered to be both ubiquitously and universally available, since it was, as Dr Bright put it in his *Treatise*, in the "use of those familiar things which every one daily putts in practise, without the advise of a physician"—such as eating, sleeping, and activity—that the most suitable occasions for the practice of hygiene were to be found. All that people were thought to be lacking was the necessary knowledge, both of themselves and of the rules of right living. In the preface of *The Touchstone of Complexions*, Lemnius (1576) spoke for many when he said that it was "by ignoraunce or not knowing our own selves, and by negligente looking to the state of our own bodyes and mindes" that we are "throwen into sondry diseases and innumerable affections". It was this knowledge which the popularizers sought to provide.

The salience of the classical rules for health was of course enhanced by the enormous risks to life with which the readers of the time were constantly confronted: high infant and maternal mortality, widespread infectious diseases, epidemic plagues, nutritional disorders, and mad dogs, among others. Physicians were in short supply and the treatments they supplied were often drastic, often ineffective, and sometimes positively harmful, not to mention costly. In the case of melancholic afflictions, the general prudence of healthful living was even greater than usual, since these conditions were held to be both difficult to cure and eminently preventable by rational means. As this view differs from the contemporary view of affective disorders as readily treatable on an empirical basis but not yet sufficiently well understood to be preventable on a rational one, it is well to survey briefly the theoretical basis on the sixteenth century popularizers' advice. This survey of the theory of the four elements and the four humours will prepare us to consider certain continuities and discontinuities in the tradition of advice as it developed over the next three centuries.

By the time it was popularized in English, the theory had enjoyed a history of some 2000 years. Briefly, the theory of elements held that all matter consisted in fire, water, earth, and air, in varying proportions. These "elements" represented the basic qualities of heat, dryness, moisture, and cold, each element combining two. The human body contained four humours—blood, phlegm, yellow bile or choler, and black bile or melancholy—which were analogous to the elements comprising the physical world. Melancholy, like earth, was cold and dry, and had its seat in the spleen. Humours were formed in the body, each being derived from a different part of the *chylus* or digested food, melancholy being formed from the dregs. The balance of the humours determined both health and disease. When they were in balance, the individual enjoyed a state of health. Imbalance in proportion or quantity or a qualitative alteration led to disease. This theory of humoral pathology was the basis for so-called constitutional theory, which held that people differed in constitutional type, whose characteristics—physical appearance, stature, tempo, and psychological qualities—were determined by their predominant humour. The individual's complexion or temperament derived from the combination of elemental qualities resulting from his proportions of the various humours and was named after the predominant one. The terms sanguine, phlegmatic, choleric, and melancholy, could thus refer either to the humour itself or to the associated temperament. Complexion also played a role in pathology, in that the form of disease to which a person was susceptible was held to be largely determined by his temperament or type. Each type had certain negative features which, though not pathological *per se*, could, if exaggerated, readily become so. The melancholy were at greatest risk and it is for this reason that the authors wrote so much more for and about them than about the other types.

The line between the natural melancholic temperament and its major disorder, melancholy or melancholia, was often a thin one. The characteristic "signes" of the melancholy complexion were listed by Elyot as follows:

> Leannesse with hardnesse of skynne
> Heare playne and thinne
> Colour duskysh, or white with leannes
> Moche watche (e.g. wakefulness)
> Dremes fearefull
> Stiffe in opinions
> Digestion slow and yll
> Tymerous and fearefull
> Anger longe and frettinge
> Pulse lytle
> Seldome lawghynge
> Urine watry and thynne

Melancholia proper differed from the manifestations of the natural melancholic temperament in both quantitative and qualitative ways. The normal characteristics of fearfulness, gloominess, and anger were exaggerated, but there were also new departures from normal behaviour and experience, in the form of delusions and suicidal wishes. ". . . some think themselves vessels of earth, or earthen pottes, therefore they withdrawe themselves from them that they meet, lest they should knocke together", wrote Barrough in *The Methode of Physicke*. "Moreover," he added, "they desire death, and do verie often behight and determine to kill themselves..." Such extreme states, carrying a certain risk of mortality, were obviously worth avoiding, if at all possible. How were they thought to be caused?

A state of melancholia, which was thought to reflect some form of humoral disturbance, could be brought on by a range of environmental, behavioural, and psychological precipitants. Inappropriate diet, consisting of foods with a propensity to engender black bile ("melancholy meates") or foods difficult to digest and hence likely to leave more dregs, was considered a chief cause. Lack of exercise and excessive sedentariness were also implicated, since they caused stagnation of body fluids. Particular sedentary activities, such as study, philosophical reflection, and abstruse reading were also held culpable, as they led to one-sidedness and imbalance. Psychological causes included fear, sadness, and other extreme emotions including anger, excessive joy, unrequited love, remorse for past misdeeds, and afflictions of conscience. These causes, the concept of humoral pathology, and the general principles of constitutional theory provided the rationale for the corpus of advice on melancholy and its management which the sixteenth century popularizers transmitted.

Their paradigm comprised a broad-based, multi-modal, rational approach to both prophylaxis and therapy. It comprised three main headings:

Physic: consisting of medicinal and physical forms of remedial treatment, usually prescribed by a physician;

Regimen: consisting of rules of conduct in matters of diet, aimed either at preserving the harmonious balance of humours from disturbance or restoring it when disequilibrium occurred; and

Spiritual consolation: consisting of aids to reflection to prepare the mind for adversity and to help it accommodate misfortune when it occurred.

As the methods of *Physic* correspond to contemporary physical treatments rather than to psychological and behavioural approaches, we need not dwell upon them further, except to point out that they shared a common theoretical basis with the non-medical treatments we will be considering under the heading of *Regimen*.

The notion of diet comprised by *Regimen* was taken by the majority to mean Galen's six "non-naturals", so-called because, with the exception of air, they were not part of a natural body, essential though they were for the maintenance of its health. The standard schema included: air, meat and drink, sleep and wakefulness, exercise or activity, both physical and mental, and rest, repletion and excretion of superfluities, and the regulation of the affects and passions of the mind. Advice on housing, apparel, and sexual activity might also be included, according to the writer's particular interest. In *The Haven of Health*, for example, Cogan argued in favour of a five-fold classification derived from an aphorism of Hippocrates: *Labor, Cibus, Potio, Somnus, Venus*, a sixth clause being moderation in all things. This framework, he maintained, was "more evident for the common capacitie of men, and more convenient for the diet of an English Nation". His justification illustrates the effort of many writers to adapt their traditional materials to contemporary circumstances.

The most significant innovations, however, occurred in the third branch of treatment for melancholy, Spiritual Consolation. From the first, the treasury of aids to reflection upon the misfortunes and disappointments that might befall a person, which the classical moral philosophers—Aristotle, Cicero, Seneca, Plutarch—and mediaeval writers such as Boethius had bequeathed to the West, was supplemented by the Christian *Bible* as a source of spiritual preparation for adversity and comfort after its occurrence. Elyot refers the melancholic reader to "the holesome counsayles found in holy Scripture, and in the bokes of morall doctrine", and Bright adds "to the godly instructions of the divines" as well as "the comfort of their friends". The inclusion of the burgeoning Puritan literature of piety and salvation (see Wright (1958) for discussion) amongst the means a melancholic individual might adopt in attemptimg to subdue his unruly—and pagan—humours is a development whose import will become more evident when we reach the seventeenth century. Meanwhile, it illustrates another early adaptation of the traditional Graeco-Roman material to the dominant preoccupations of the receiving sixteenth century culture.

The three branches of treatment were applied according to a common therapeutic philosophy, the doctrine of contraries. In his *Treatise on Melancholie*, Bright expressed the doctrine as follows: "the ordinarie cure of all diseases & helps of infirmities are to be begun with removing of such causes as first procured the infirmitie (except they be removed of themselves, through their nature, neither stable nor permanent) by succession of a contrarie cause of the same kinde". In prevention, application of the principle consisted in active avoidance of such causes as would procure infirmity with active approach to alternatives that would promote a desirable state of affairs. Since prevention was recommended wherever possible, much of the popularizers' advice took the form of instructions about what to avoid.

Now that the basic paradigm is clear, we may examine its contents under the headings of the six non-naturals.

2. REGIMEN IN THE SIXTEENTH CENTURY

A. Air

The rules regarding air derived from the characteristic coldness and dryness of the melancholy complexion. Instructions were based on the doctrine of contraries and could be either positive—"...let them tarie in an aire hot and moist" (Barrough) or negative—"...Going into aire intemperately hotte, colde, or drie, all these thinges do annoye them that be greved with any melancolye" (Elyot). Du Laurens (1599) in his *Discourse of Melancholike Diseases* offered practical advice on domestic air conditioning. A suitable air, he wrote,

> may be made by such an art, casting abroad in your chamber good store of flowers, or Roses, Violets, and water Lyllies. Or else you may have a great vessel full of warme water, which will keepe the ayre moyst continually. It will be needful to perfume the chamber with Orange flowers, Citron pilles, and a little Storax...

Air was not, however, the major matter about which the popularizers sought to instruct the public, since, apart from avoiding "a grosse, dark, gloomish, stinking ayre" (Du Laurens), there was not really much of a practical nature that they could do about it.

B. Meat and Drink

The extensive rules about meat and drink were grouped under six traditional headings: substance, quantity, quality (e.g. whether hot or cold), custom, time, and order. Substance received most attention, advice about quantity reduced to restatements of the principle of moderation, and the rest, if included at all, were normally dealt with in summary fashion. Substance was most important because foods differed in their likelihood of engendering melancholy. The worst offenders in this respect were known. Elyot summarized them in a convenient table:

> *Meates ingendrynge melancoly.* Biefe/Gotes fleshe/Hares fleshe/Bores fleshe/Salte fleshe/Salte fyshe/Cole wortes/All pulses, except whyte peason/Browne breadde course/Thycke wyne/Black wyne/Old chese/Olde fleshe/Great fyshes of the Sea.

Besides these, he urged those with a tendency to melancholy also to avoid "meates harde, dry, very salt, or sowre, bourned meate, fried meat" and "all thynges, which heateth to moche, keleth to moch, or drieth to moche..." The doctrine of contraries also dictated choice of suitable foods. Boorde in the *Dyetary* advised:

> And use these thynges, Cowe mylke, Almon mylke, Yolkes of rere egges. Boyled meate is better for Melancoly men then rosted meate. All meate the which wylbe soon dygested, & all meates the which doth ingender good blode, And meates the which be temperately hote, be good for Melancoly men. And so be all herbes the whiche be hote and moyste.

Although most of the advice was highly stereotyped, there was not universal agreement about all minor details and sometimes authors disagreed openly with their classical sources. Du Laurens, for instance, in his discourse *Of the Diseases of Melancholie* (1599), noted that "Galen forbiddeth the flesh of hee-goates, Buls, Asses, Dogs, Camels and Foxes, but he might have spared this his inhibition, for their daintines is not such, that men should delight in, much less doat upon them". The critical tendency again reflects the writers' efforts to adapt their materials to local conditions.

C. Sleep and Wakefulness

Positive advice about sleep tended to be sketchy. Lemnius, for example, exhorted, "let them lye in very soft beds and sleepe wel & longe". The melancholy were thought to require more sleep than others, because of its beneficial effects on the bodily functions most involved in the production of humours—digestion, the state of the blood, and body heat. Its power of "restoring nature" (Boorde) and "comforting the spirits" (Elyot) were often noted. In view of this, all agreed that the melancholy should avoid excessive wakefulness at night: "Watching is altogether enemie to those that are troubled with this disease" (Du Laurens). The most extensive advice, therefore, concerned ways to procure sleep. Boorde in the *Dyetary* gave homely and straightforward counsel: at bedtime, be merry or have merry company about "so that to Bedward no anger nor hevines, sorow nor pencyfulnes do troble or dysquiet you". Du Laurens enumerated a large number of remedies, both inward and outward. The inward means included "mundified barlie, a Condite, an Opiate, a Tart, a Restaurative, a Potion, a bole, and masse of Pils", all given with recipes for home preparation, and a caveat:

> But in the use of all these stupefactive medicines taken inwardly wee must take heed to deale with very good advise, for feare that in stead of desiring to procure rest unto the sillie melan-cholike wretch, wee cast him into an endless sleepe.

The outward remedies, which were "not althogether so dangerous", included "head powders, frontlets, bags, emplasters, oyntments, epithemes, nosegaies, pomanders, and lotions for the legs". "Blood suckers or horse leaches" were also mentioned as a method used by some; these were applied behind the ears and when they were taken away the sufferer was to "put by little and little a graine of Opium upon the hole". The method was said to have been used "with good successe"— which is one of the very few evaluative remarks to be found in the entire literature.

D. Exercise and Rest

Advice pertained to mental as well as physical activity. Moderate exercise was indicated prophylactically because, Lemnius noted, "as maryshes & standing waters become dampish and stynking: so likewise the body, lacking exercise, gathereth fulsoments & pestilent savours". In established pathology, particularly if caused by excessive study, exercise had therapeutic implications as well. First, harmony of body and mind required active restorative efforts. Bright explained: "... as the mind by speculation, after a sort disioyneth it selfe from the bodie: so the bodily exercise may revoke it again into the former fellowship..." The melancholic's exercises were to be "corporall actions of grosser sort" (Bright). Barrough gave as examples, "let them ride or walke by places pleasant and greene, or use sailing on water". Cogan followed Galen in commending tennis as an exercise of great virtue, "because it may be easily used of al estates, as being of little cost" and because "it doth exercise all partes of the body alike". The less energetic, of those for whom "violent motion & exercise be ... painful and laborious" Lemnius advised to be "recreat and exercise themselves with pleasaunt singing, Musical instruments and delectable walkinges". A second indication for exercise was to disrupt the mental organization resulting from preoccupation with abstruse matters. "Runnyng to farre in fantasies or musynge or studienge upon thynges that his reason can nat comprehende", Boorde wrote in the *Breviary*, could readily lead to "a sicknes full of fantasies, thynkyng to here or to se that thynge that is not harde nor sene". Such folk were to "use company and nat to be alone nor to muse of this thynge nor of ye matter, but to occupy him selfe in some manual operacion or some honest pastyme". Likewise, Barrough noted that "the sick must labour that the false and wicked imaginations, and great sadness may be driven away by all meanes that can be invented".

But prevention was preferable to allowing pathology to become established. Elyot gave a veritable catalogue of things to be avoided by those with a tendency to melancholy:

> Avoyde all thynges that be noyous in syghte, smellynge, and heryng, and imbrace al thinge that is dilectable. Flee darknes, moche watche, and busynesse of mynde, moche companieng with women, the use of thinges very hote and drie: often purgations, immoderate exercise, thirst, moche abstinence, dry wyndes and colde.

Lemnius, counselling avoidance of "solitarynesse, abstinence & lassitude" was more laconic, but the message was essentially similar. As an alternative to activity, people might be advised to seek the company of others. "... durynge the time of that passion", wrote Elyot, "eschewe to be angry, studyous or solitarie, and reioyce the with melody, or els be al way in such company, as beste may contente the". Besides providing comfort, others had specific therapeutic tasks to perform. Du

Laurens explained that one was occasionally to *humour* the sufferer: "... sometimes they must bee flattered, and yeelded unto in some part of that which they desire, for feare least this humour which is rebellious by nature, and given to selfe wilfulnes, should grow raging and furious". But it was recognized that such indulgence required moderation. Bright remarked that "agreing with humour, it may be meanes of increase thereof, and augmenting the fancie". Sometimes, others were to discourage pathological thinking and behaviour directly. Du Laurens continued: "Some whiles they must be chid for their foolish imaginations, as also reproached and made ashamed of their cow-hardiness". At the same time, by the doctrine of contraries, a positive attitude and behaviour were to be encouraged: "they must be imboldned to the uttermost that we can, and praised in their actions". Distressing ideas were to be replaced by reminders of past achievements and amusing anecdotes: "... and if they have in some cases done something worthie of praise wee must put them oft in minde thereof, uphold them with merrie tales". Finally, he said "we may not call to their minds any thing that might cause them to feare, nor yet bring them any unpleasant tidings". The programme of intervention may be said to represent a broad-based cognitive therapy.

E. Repletion and Evacuation of Superfluities

The popularizers had practically nothing to say about repletion; of evacuation they wrote more copiously, but mainly under the heading of *Physic* rather than *Regimen*. Some included lists of "Purgers of Melancoly" and recipes for home preparation, but most regarded it as preferable for the melancholic to keep themselves "laxative and soluble" by attention to diet than to expose themselves to the risks inherent in the "forcible meanes" (Du Laurens) that might be administered by physicians.

F. Affects and Passions of the Mind

Authors varied most in their coverage of the passions, probably because, in contrast to the other non-naturals, where general instructions could apply to everyone much of the time, effects tended to require rather particular and specialized advice. Thus, although everyone might act on Elyot's remark that "the ofte recordynge of myserie, prepareth the mynde to fele less adversitie" by meditating upon Scripture or a suitable classical consolatory text in advance of personal disaster, once stricken, individuals might need special advice, according to the type of event that had precipitated them into their melancholy affliction.

In dealing with grievous afflictions, people were advised to seek social support. Elyot commends "the counsell of a many wyse and well lerned in moral philosophye"; Bright refers people to "the comfort of their Friends". In some cases, the individual might be unable or unwilling to do what was necessary on his own behalf; then friends would have to intervene. The main strategy for dealing with perturbing griefs was, according to Lemnius, "to take away the headspryng of the whole mischiefe & pluck up by the rootes that inconvenience which distempereth the mynde". When this was not practicable, the aim shifted to mitigating the emotional effects of the event upon the sufferer. The strategy is best exemplified in the case of the love melancholic, where, if "the inioying of the thing beloved" (Du Laurens) were not possible, persuasion that "the subiect of that he liketh is not so lovely" might be required and "whatsoever iustly may be alleadged to the parties disgrace" would need to be spelled out to him (Bright) in an attempt "to draw him with fayre words from these fond and foolish imaginations" (Du Laurens). Setting forth the dangers which he was courting with examples of "such as have been overthrowne thereby" (Du Laurens) might also be called for. If such tactics did not suffice, friends might try to excite another, opposite, passion, such as anger or fear, or remove the sufferer to new surroundings and distract him "to bring into his mind a hundred and a hundred sundrie things, to the end he may have no leisure to think of his love" (Du Laurens).

In most cases, however, the main responsibility for regulating the passions fell upon the individual himself. The most important thing he could do was to try to avoid extremes of affect, both generally, as a precautionary measure and particularly when in a melancholic state. The popularizers were not, however, explicit in their instructions as to how the reader was to go about trying to keep "tranquility and constancy of mynde" (Lemnius) within himself.

3. THE SEVENTEENTH CENTURY

In the seventeenth century, this corpus of received ideas about melancholy was disseminated so widely and became so firmly assimilated into English culture that a modern commentator on the period has called it "the Elizabethan malady" (Babb, 1951). The continued spread of English printed books, the continuing flood of translations of relevant classical and contemporary continental works, and the emergence of modern English as a literary language with its own corpus of writings all contributed to the development of melancholy as a fashionable literary theme. The saturation of seventeenth century literature with melancholy (Babb, 1951, Veith, 1970) attests the success of the sixteenth century popularizers' efforts. All manner of approaches to the topic were taken, ranging from more medical popularizations to light verse, as for example Nicholas Breton's (1600) *Melancholike Humours* and Samuel Rowland's (1607) *Democritus, or Doctor Merry-man his Medicines against Melancholy Humours*. Melancholy lovers, cynics, villains, and scholars appeared as stock characters in drama and fiction (Spencer, 1948; Saagpakk, 1968). The doctrines of the ancients also figured prominently in subject matter and imagery of the serious poetry of the time. Burton's (1621) *Anatomy of Melancholy* both reflects and consolidates the fashion; he wrote within an established vernacular genre—the English language treatise on melancholy—for the knowledgeable public which his predecessors had created. Besides representing a definitive consolidation of what had gone before, in its elaboration of religious melancholy as a distinct entity, Burton's *Anatomy* gave shape to what was to come.

Under the developing influence of Puritanism as the dominant force in English culture, the tradition of advice on melancholy underwent several changes. First, illness took on a theological dimension of meaning. Thus Dr Tobias Venner wrote in 1623:

> When yee are visited with Sicknesse, yee must consider that it is a symptome of your sinne, and therefore first by humble confession and a penitential heart, make peace between God and your conscience, and then send for the Physician (*Via Recta ad Vitam Longam*, Pars Secunda).

Second, the theory of humoral pathology receded in importance and the Galenic doctrine of animal, vital, and natural spirits, which previously had been accorded only a minor role in explaining bodily derangements, advanced. Whereas humours were fluid, spirits, which arose from them, were airlike substances—vapours— which were thought to give strength and power to bodily members. If disturbed, they could, like the humours, give rise to disorder. Third, the emphasis which Reformation Christianity placed upon the individual's efforts on his own behalf (Thomas, 1971) led to the self-help ethos that had been implicit in the sixteenth century popularizers' writings becoming fully explicit. In his popular medical hand-book *ΥΓΙΕΝΗ or a Conservatory of Health* (1650) Humphrey Brooke asks the reader of the section on "Remedies against Sadness" to consider "that... *what is without thy power to help, ought not to afflict thee, for tis utterly vain; if it be within thy power, then greive (sic) not, but help thy self*". The *locus classicus* of this code is, of course, found in *The Pilgrim's Progress* (1678), where Bunyan represents Help extending a hand to pull Christian from the Slough of Despond. Fourth, some changes occurred in what was actually transmitted; writers were more openly and extensively critical of their classical sources; classical prescriptions were increasingly tailored to local conditions; and writers increasingly tended to specialize, thus breaking up the original comprehensive package of doctrines. However, despite this trend towards division, some comprehensive works continued to appear; Brooke's *Conservatory* was one and Everard Maynwaring's (1683) *Method and Means of Enjoying Health, Vigour and Long Life* another. Despite these changes, much of the advice actually offered to melancholic readers remained much the same as before, though the physical aspects received less emphasis. Let us now survey how *Regimen* fared in the seventeenth century writers' accounts.

Regimen in the Seventeenth Century

Air

Regarding air, most authors, apart from Burton (1621), who wrote a chapter on it, had little to say. Gideon Harvey (1672) in his *Morbus Anglicus* repeated Galen's advice about the choice of "a serene, thin, dry, temperate, sweet, and pleasant air", which differed somewhat from the standard sixteenth century advice that the preferred air should be hot and moist. Otherwise "change of air" was recommended (Harvey, 1672, Maynwaring, 1683). Brooke (1650) advised against taking the counsels of *Regimen* too literally, as that in itself could breed disorder. He warned people:

> not to be oversolicitous in the choise of Aire, or to judg that they cannot have their healths except in some few places of best and excellent Aire, for they do thereby very much deject *Nature, and opinionate themselves into Sickness*. Such imaginations keep the mind in continuall doubts & perplexities, and make *us sickly*, out of a *fear of being sick*.

His comment suggests the seriousness with which the advice of the popularizers was taken.

Meat and Drink

Previous instructions to "abstain from all obstructive, melancholique, and dreggish Victuals" (Harvey 1672), "all meats hard of digestion" and "excess both in eating and drinking" (Culpeper, 1652) still stood, though Harvey (1672, 2nd Edition) added the proviso that "a small excess committed now and then is in no wise hurtful". Lists of prescribed food, though still in evidence, were rarer and shorter. Harvey (1672, 2nd Edition) advised against overmuch worry about the substance of diet "for if every objection against this or that sort of meat, will cause you to refrain, there you must resolve to live without Victuals, there being no meat in the world, but what may be excepted against". With the exception of Burton (1621) dietary recommendations were less often couched in specifically antimelancholic terms; prudence and moderation were for everyone, regardless of constitutional type.

Sleep

Again, with the exception of Burton, seventeenth century authors were taciturn. "Cherish sleep" advised Maynwaring; Venner repeated the old advice about the melancholy requiring more sleep than the phlegmatic and sanguine; whilst Harvey (1672, 2nd Edition) noted that "what concerns their proportion of sleep, every one knows best what his nature requires". The virtues of sleep continued to be enumerated and the perniciousness of "too much watchfulnesse" (Venner) or "tiresome waking in the night" (Maynwaring) was stressed. Sleeping draughts were less commonly mentioned, and behavioural techniques scarcely at all.

Exercise and Rest

Activity occupied an important place in the seventeenth century canon of advice. But instructions to engage in gross bodily movements aimed at stirring stagnant humours were largely replaced by counsels to undertake purposive activity aimed at warding off Idleness, alias "the devil's cushion" (Burton). As William Vaughan (1630) expressed it in *The Newlanders Cure*:

> The Mind on Labour fixed Sure
> Stops wandring thoughts from Sathans lure.

Whereas sixteenth century authors had tended to emphasize recreational activities, their successors more often recommended "some serious employment or other" (Ferrand, 1640). Thus Moore (1692), in his sermon *Of Religious Melancholy*, urged sufferers not to "leave your Callings, nor forsake the Post wherein Providence hath placed you". And when it came to distracting their thoughts from "the desperate Condition, wherein their disturbed Phancy hath placed their Souls", his emphasis was on "vertuous and cheerful Conversation, innocent Recreation, and moderate Business".

Despite the prominence of the Christian influence, the older advice survived virtually unchanged in less specialized and more derivative works, up to midcentury and beyond. Brooke (1650) with minor modifications, simply repeated Elyot's counsel to "avoid all things that be noyous in sight, smelling, hearing" up to and including the "dry Winds and very Cold". And Maynwaring (1683) repeated the standard sixteenth century advice to:

> walk in green Fields, orchards, Gardens, Parks, by Rivers, and variety of Places...avoid solitariness, and Keep merry Company. Be frequent at Musick, Sport and Games. Recreate the

spirits with sweet, fragrant and delightful smells... Give not your self to much study, nor nightwatchings: two Great Enemies to a melancholy person.

In contrast to the more highly developed diction of less derivative seventeenth century writers, these "traditional" passages sound archaic.

Counsels to the friends of the melancholy continued to be fairly similar to what had gone before, but there were signs of the tempering influence of direct experience. Burton enjoined the friends of a melancholy discontented person never to leave him alone or idle, but "set him about some business, exercise or recreation, which may divert his thoughts, and still keep him otherwise intent", lest he "melancholize". Equally conventional was his advice that if the sufferer "cannot discern what is amiss... it behoves them by counsel, comfort, or persuasion, by fair or foul means, to alienate his mind, by some artificial invention, or some contrary persuasion, to remove all objects, causes, companies, occasions, as may anyways molest him, to humour him, please him, divert him". But to this catalogue of standard instructions he added one which adds an entirely new dimension to the enterprise: "... and, if it is possible, by altering his course of life, to give him security and satisfaction". This sort of comment contrasts with the rather mechanical instructions to distract the sufferer at all costs in its psychological, as opposed to logical, view of what needed to be done.

Excretion

With the exception of Burton's chapter on "Retention and evacuation rectified", instructions concerning excretions were practically nonexistent as a part of *Regimen*, though, of course, accounts of *Physic* continued to focus on means of reducing the humours and redistributing the spirits by mechanical means. When Brooke (1650) advised avoiding "often and violent purgations", he did so in the context of the passage he had borrowed practically verbatim from Elyot.

Regulation of the Passions

Seventeenth century advice on regulating the passions was heavily permeated with Christian influence. Wright (1601), for example, advised, "when thy passions are most vehement, then seeke for succour from Heaven, flie under the wings of Christ". And as a suitable course of action in such a "disease of the soul", Burton in his chapter on "Perturbations of the Mind rectified" repeated Comineus's counsel to Charles, Duke of Burgundy, "first pray to God, and lay himself open to Him, and then to some special friend, whom we hold most dear, to tell all our grievances to him".

Nonetheless, much of the advice given was the same as when it was only a question of keeping one's humours in order. Venner (1623) urged people to "bridle all irrational notions of the minde by the reason and understanding, and labour by all meanes to observe a mediocritie in their passions", Harvey (1672, 2nd Ed.) urged them to "avoid all occasions of anger, fretting, and peevishness" and Maynwaring (1683) to "banish all passions as much as in you lies". Reynolds (1640) noted with Plutarch, that "we should have a prepared Minde, which when any Evill falleth out, might not be surprised by it". Brooke (1650) counselled people, "fortifie thy self

against all accidents before they come, by frequent reading, and rightly understanding the Scriptures and other Religious and Moral Writings" and Burton (1621)
included a whole chapter on consolations "gleaned out of our best orators, philosophers, divines, and fathers of the Church, tending to this purpose".

But, especially in specialized works dealing with the passions, methods and techniques came in for more attention than in the previous century. Wright (1601), for
instance, presented nine general remedies, including the avoidance of provocative
occasions, the mortification of the body, and the diversion of thoughts to another
matter. Whatever other methods they recommended, most authors had something
to say about distraction and diversion of thoughts; their recommendations were
more often cognitive and less often behavioural than those of their predecessors,
who had also commended distraction. The seventeenth century writers' cognitive
orientation also extended to their analysis of the various affects and passions.
Whereas sixteenth century authors had focused upon the sorts of external events
that might commonly give rise to grief, sorrow, and the like, their successors
included in their analysis the cognitive appraisal required for an untoward event to
give rise to emotional distress. Thus Charron (1608) described sadness as "a kind of
discouragement ingendered by the opinion that we have of those evils that afflict
us" and Reynolds (1640) extended the appraisal to include the mind's view of its
own resources: grief and sorrow, he said, were "nothing but a perturbation and
unquietnesse wrought by the pressure of some present evill, which the mind strugg-
leth in vain with, as finding it selfe alone too impotent for the conflict". There were
even instructions to melancholics for appropriate higher-order cognitive processing
of their first-order thoughts. Moore (1692) advised sufferers that "when you find
these Thoughts (e.g. of damnation) creeping upon you, be not mightily dejected, as
if they were certain Tokens of your Reprobation" but to follow him in attributing
them instead to "the indisposition of the Body". Thus, within the course of the
century, Venner's modern advice to regard one's sickness as a symptom of sin came
in for the same sort of criticism as impracticable aspects of the advice of the
Ancients.

4. THE EIGHTEENTH CENTURY

In the eighteenth century, the transformation of the corpus of advice continued.
Although much of the basic schema and many of the specific recommendations
remained recognizable, there were a number of changes with far-reaching implications for the future of the tradition. The new watchwords, replacing Ancient
Authority and the Divine Spirit, were Reason, Observation, and Experience. Under
these new auspices, the enterprise became increasingly medicalized, and, under the
conventions of the time, scientific. Though the literary fashion for melancholizing
showed no signs of abatement, the practical literature on the nature and treatment
of melancholy disorders was increasingly written not only by, but also for, physicians. The practices recommended, in *Regimen* as well as in *Physic*, were increasingly meant to be administered to sufferers under supervision, often within an
asylum, rather than adopted by the sufferers themselves of their own initiative.
While the spirit of self-help which had informed the writings of the sixteenth

century popularizers and had become explicit in seventeenth century texts was still alive as the century opened, by its end the days of this ethos were numbered.

By contrast to works of early days when the tradition of advice was first being imported into England, eighteenth century writings on melancholy were characterized by great profusion, idiosyncrasy, and growing pessimism. John Haslam (1798) remarked in his *Observations on Insanity* that "in our own Country more books on Insanity have been written than in any other". A major concern of the authors of this burgeoning literature was to classify mental pathology. There was little standardization, and classifications and terminology multiplied, so that what had previously been designated as a few recognized types of melancholy disorder were variously termed Melancholy, Vapours, the Spleen, Low Spirits, and Hypochondriasis (so-called because the site of difficulties was the hypochondriac region of the abdomen); some distinguished these from Lunacy, Madness, and Insanity, and some did not.

Along with different nomenclature, different authors adopted different theories to explain the phenomena. Perhaps the most common was an updated chemical version of humoral pathology based on the acid or alkaline properties of various bodily fluids, which, by the operation of mechanical principles upon bodily fibres, especially the nerves, engendered symptoms of mental disorder. But theories, whatever their nature, were not held with the same enthusiastic conviction as formerly. Thus Thomson (1795) wrote in his *Enquiry into the Nature, Causes, and Method of Cure of Nervous Disorders* that "we know too little of the physiology of the nerves, to be immediately acquainted with the nature and modification of their diseases". As he suggested, theory no longer provided a secure base from which rational practices could be deduced. "Our theory", he continued, "is conjectural, and our practice, if not founded on principles too vague, is frequently indiscriminate". As Andrew Harper (1789) wrote in his *Treatise on the Real Cause and Cure of Insanity*, there was "no doubt, much labour yet remaining in the field of medical science" where mental disorder was concerned.

Under these conditions, it is hardly surprising that the original tightly-knit canon of prophylactic and therapeutic ideas concerning melancholy continued the fragmentation which had begun in the previous century. But, by contrast to the specialized treatment of particular aspects of the canon typical of seventeenth century writings, eighteenth century texts effected their contribution by aiming to be comprehensive, on the one hand, but reflecting mainly the individual author's personal views on the other hand. The formal headings of the six non-naturals soon fell by the wayside. There was a loss of emphasis on the individual sufferer and more concern with problems of regulating the behaviour of numbers of—often refractory—institutionalized people. The doctrine of types gave way to a concept of constitutional individual differences, which many authors took as a contraindication for attempting to prescribe universally applicable rules of conduct. Thus Thomson (1795) noted that "the infinite diversity of temperaments renders it impossible to deliver rules accommodated to every individual". Nonetheless, writers continued to prescribe.

Let us now examine eighteenth century versions of Regimen.

Regimen in the Eighteenth Century

Air

If comments on climate may be taken as constituting views on air, eighteenth century writers, following upon Cheyne's establishment of "the English Malady" in 1733, had more to say about the matter than earlier English writers. The moisture and variableness of English weather came in for adverse comment (Cheyne, 1733, Anon., 1750). "A dry temperate air" was to be preferred, "change of air" sought, and "the extremes of heat and cold" avoided (Harper, 1789). Observations were couched in local terms; Hill (1766), for example, remarked: "It is common to think of the air of high grounds best; but experience near home shows otherwise: the Hypochondriac patient is always worse at Highgate even than in London". However, it was still recognized that the air and climate he inhabited might "not be in every Persons Power to change" (Anon., 1750).

Meat and Drink

Attention to diet continued to be held important in both prophylaxis and treatment of melancholic disorders. "...a proper Regimen of Diet may, in a great Measure, prevent (the) Effects (of climate)" wrote the author of an anonymous *Treatise ... on Low Spiritedness* (Anon., 1750). "In no other chronic disorder", wrote Thomson (1795) "is a dietetic restriction equally indispensable: for the person who would either stop the complaint, or obtain a recovery, must be not only temperate, but circumspect, in all convivial gratifications". Foods to be preferred were "of easy Digestion" (James, 1745), those which "enrich and comfort the Blood, and supply it with Plenty of wholesome Juices" (Blackmore, 1725) or which were "loosening and gently stimulating but not acrid" (Hill, 1766). Those to be avoided were "offensive to the Stomach by its Bulk" (James, 1745), required "a strong Digestion" (Anon., 1750) or "acids and all things that are in a state of fermentation" (Hill, 1766). Lists of particulars were infrequent, but James (1745) kept tradition alive when he noted that:

> ... Patients subject to Melancholy or Madness ought carefully to abstain from smoked Fleshes, whether Pork or Beef; from Shell-fish; from Fish of an heavy or noxious Quality; and from vaporous Substances, and Aliments prepared with Onions and Garlick ...

Hill (1766) listed "Veal, lamb, fowls, lobsters, crabs, craw-fish, fresh water fish and mutton broth, with plenty of boiled vegetables" as being "always right". Raw vegetables, he said, were "all bad: sour wines, old cheese, and bottled beer" were "things never to be once tasted". The modern dietary features of tea, sugar, alcohol, and tobacco were also mentioned, mostly unfavourably.

Sleep

Most of what the eighteenth century writers had to say of sleep was fairly global and traditional. Strother (1718) declared bluntly that it "cures all Distempers of the Mind". It was one area where moderation did not apply: "let him indulge it freely", wrote Hill (1766). Some authors did offer practical advice for its attainment, however. Thomson (1795) recommended Benjamin Franklin's practice of getting out of bed and sitting "for some time, with no other covering than the shirt". He also commended the habit of rising early, since this implied an early retirement the night before. He regarded sleep in the country as particularly beneficial, since the beauty of the morning landscape would "conspire to regale the senses with innocent delight, and sooth that irritability which accompanies nervous affection". His recommendation was accompanied by a rhapsodical description of the delights of the English countryside that could hardly have appeared in a medical textbook of any other time and place.

Exercise

Exercise was held to be of great importance. Cheyne (1733) wrote that "There is not any one Thing more approv'd and recommended by all *Physicians*" for nervous distempers. The exercise recommended by eighteenth century writers was characteristically "gentle exercise" which could be "used with least exertion on the part of the patient" (Walker, 1796); it was to be "frequent; but not violent" (Hill, 1766) and its main purpose was to distract the sufferer's attention from his preoccupations whilst avoiding fatigue. Most authors favoured riding on horseback, found carriage-riding a second-best, and regarded walking as a poor substitute for either. Travelling (James, 1745, Whytt, 1765, Cullen, 1777) and other activities performed on horseback, such as hunting, and also "the various kinds of sport" (Cullen, 1777), including "Shooting, Bowls, Billiards, Shuttlecock, and the like" (Cheyne, 1733), attending spas (Purcell, 1702, Leake, 1781) and nature study (Hill, 1766, Leake, 1781) were all promoted. More traditional pastimes continued to be mentioned: "chearful Company, Poetry, Music and Dramatic Entertainments of the comic Kind" (Leake, 1781), "agreeable Conversation" (Shaw, 1728), "taking the Air in the Parks" (Purcell, 1702) and "Application to some kind of Business" (Anon., 1750). Cheyne (1733) recommended reading of "light, entertaining, and diverting material".

Advice about avoidance was similarly traditional: Solitude (Baxter, 1713, James, 1745, Fawcett, 1780), "Study of difficult and intricate matters" (Cheyne, 1733), Idleness (Baxter, 1713, Blakeway, 1717, Cullen, 1777), "excessive watching" (Arnold, 1782), "all Concerns, Anxieties, Passions" (Purcell, 1702), "vexation, grief, and despondence" (Thomson, 1795), and "all disagreeable and shocking sights" (Whytt, 1765) continued to be mentioned as bad for the melancholic. Arnold's (1782) mention of "the avoidance of the occasional causes . . . so far as they may, by our care and diligence, be avoided" reflects the new circumspection of advice meant to be based on Experience and Observation.

Excretion

As in the seventeenth century, authors had very little to say on the topic of evacuations as a part of *Regimen*. Strother (1718) mentioned briefly that evacuation "cures all Distempers of the Mind"; and for the most part his contemporaries said even less. The subject still remained prominent in accounts of *Physic*, however.

Regulation of the Passions

The Age of Reason held the regulation of the passions in high esteem. Although fewer, if any, ancient authorities were cited, the broad outlines of traditional advice remained clearly discernible. Advice took three major forms: long and short-term preservative strategies, on the one hand, and, on the other hand, defensive tactics for use when prophylaxis failed. Long-range strategies included "cultivating Habits of Equanimity and Firmness", mainly through Education (Harper, 1785), cultivating competing emotions, such as "benevolence … and the art of contentment" (Arnold, 1782) and to accustom the mind "frequently to ruminate on Misfortunes, and to be in a kind of constant Expectation of the Worst that may happen" (Anon., 1750). Short-term preventatives consisted mainly in avoidance manoeuvres aimed at both internal and external provocations. The avoidance of extreme emotional states generally (Robinson, 1729; James, 1745) and especially of the "selfish and malevolent" (Arnold, 1782) was regarded as desirable. Robinson (1729) recommended that people "never too anxiously pursue Objects that may give us too great Pain and Uneasiness, or that are out of our Reach to attain". The situations provoking such extreme states were also to be avoided, either by the sufferer acting freely on his own initiative or—if he could not or would not—by others incarcerating him in an asylum "at some distance from his home" (Battie, 1758). This was, of course, a new development. Finally, once disorder had arisen, eighteenth century writers recommended "the Creation of new and opposite Impressions" (Harper, 1785), a strategy formulated either in terms of "Contraries" (Strother, 1718) or of diversion of the mind to other objects than its own feelings (Cullen, 1777). Harper (1785) noted that it might be more effective to "endeavour to supersede (passions) by means of other, pleasant Sensations, than to attempt, all at once, to stifle and restrain them". The techniques most usually recommended to these ends were a change of objects and a change of scene.

One topic which is conspicuous by its absence from eighteenth century accounts is advice to friends of the melancholy. In his *Treatise on Madness*, Battie (1758) specifically prohibited "the visits of affecting friends" as likely to be detrimental to the welfare of the unfortunates in institutional care. His prohibition marked the end of an era.

5. THE NINETEENTH CENTURY

In the nineteenth century, the term *melancholia* was reinstated in order to facilitate psychiatric discourse, but its re-establishment was accompanied by a progressive decline in advice about what the individual could do to prevent it. The idea that a person's life style could contribute significantly to prevention was promulgated at intervals in Bakewell's (1805) *Domestic Guide in Cases of Insanity*, Barlow's (1843) *On Man's Power Over Himself to Prevent or Control Insanity*, and the chapters on auto-prophylaxis in Tuke's (1878) *Insanity in Ancient and Modern Life*. But the view that was to prevail was that of Henry Maudsley (1874), who in his *Responsibility in Mental Disease* advocated social rather than individual personal initiative in prevention.

Numerous factors contributed to the decline of the idea of self-help in prophylaxis. The spread of a deterministic philosophy led writers to regard men's unhealthy modern living habits as immutable. "… we may, with equal prospect of success," wrote Johnson in 1818, "attempt to arrest the tides of the ocean, as turn (man) from the habits in which he is now naturalized; or emancipate him from various morbific causes, which necessarily flow from the state of society in which he lives." A new theory of mental pathology, which held that melancholia was attributable to depletion of nervous substance, presupposed lack of the energy that such self-help efforts would require. A change in asylum population, from the select few gentlefolk who could afford private madhouses to the unwashed hordes of pauper lunatics, whose containment in public institutions Scull (1979) has recently described, meant that certain former assumptions about the inner, as well as the material, resources of sufferers were no longer easy to make. Moreover, there was increasingly widespread acknowledgement that the causes of mental disorder were too complex to be reduced to simple formulae and recognition that some factors, such as hereditary endowment, were not within the individual's power to change.

These conditions led to a new phase in the criticism of the tradition of advice. Whereas in the past authors had taken issue with particular items of advice but had not questioned the concept of advising, they now ceased to quibble with particulars and instead questioned the rationality of the whole enterprise. In his *Responsibility in Mental Disease*, Maudsley (1874) effectively declared the tradition bankrupt:

> ... when we consider deeply what advice should be given to a person who fears that he may become insane, we too often discover that we have none to give which will be of any real use to him ...

But despite the demise of prophylactic advice, the recommendations which authors made about treatment recognizably derived from tradition. Even here, however, there are anticipations of the decline of the therapeutic counterpart which was to occur in our own century under the influence of the medical model and psychoanalysis.

Regimen in the Nineteenth Century

Air

Up until the end of the century, writers continued to comment on air as a factor in mental disorder. Early on, Hill (1814) and Johnson (1818) noted the effects of atmospheric changes on the nervous. Esquirol, whose *Mental Maladies* appeared in English in 1845, recommended "a dry and temperate climate" as "well-adapted to melancholics". And, as late as 1892, Clouston declared:

> ... If I were as sure of everything else in therapeutics as this, that fresh air ... (is) good for melancholic people, I should have saved myself many medical questionings. Such patients cannot have too much fresh air ... It is the best sleep-producer, the best hunger-producer, and the best aid to digestion and alimentation. Without it, all the rest is totally useless in most cases.

Such an extreme statement would be most unlikely to be made in our own times; it may be said to reflect a final burst of vitality before the tradition of advising on the air fit for melancholics lapsed into obsolescence.

Diet

Throughout the nineteenth century, writers agreed that diet was a major consideration in treating the insane. Maddock (1854) declared that "the *regulation of diet* is a subject of the highest importance in ... treatment ... of (complaints) connected with any impairment of the mental faculties", and, as late as 1892, Tuke placed the administration of food "first among the restorative means". But despite consensus at a general level, writers disagreed amongst themselves about particulars, both of foods to administer and foods to avoid. Hill (1814), for example, noted that the solids should be "principally vegetable"; by contrast, Johnson (1818) remarked that "most vegetables disagree". Though the majority of writers continued to favour temperance, they disagreed about who—whether the individual himself (Maddock, 1854) or the physician (Haslam, 1809)—was to decide how much was enough. Alcohol consumption occasioned even more dissent. Hill (1814) regarded "the avoidance of all stimulation drinks as a *sine quâ non*"; Dickson (1874) said that because of their poor circulation melancholic "patients all require stimulants". The writers' lack of consensus foreshadows the disappearance of dietary recommendations from later writings on the subject of treatment for melancholics.

Sleep

The nineteenth century physicians had relatively little to say of sleep as a matter of *Regimen*; was rapidly becoming purely a medical matter; and most discussions concerned medical means of procuring it for institutional inmates, since lack of it was still regarded as a contributory factor in precipitating insanity. Tuke's (1878) counsel to the sleepless exemplifies the medicalization of advice: "If unable to discover any special cause for sleeplessness, or knowing it, a man removes it and is still no better, I cannot too strongly advise him to lose no time in consulting his physician and rigorously obey his prescription."

Exercise and Rest

Exercise and rest held pride of place in nineteenth century accounts of *Regimen*. As late as 1890, Beard declared that "the hygiene of nervous diseases has three gospels—rest, work, and change of work". Advice on mental as well as physical exercise was given. Tuke (1813) regarded "regular exercise (as) perhaps the most generally efficacious" and particularly recommended "those kinds ... which are accompanied by considerable bodily action; that are most agreeable to the patient, and which are most opposite to the illusions of his disease". Authors gave differing emphases to these three components, and some disagreed strenuously about the amount of bodily action that ought to be encouraged. Dickson (1874) insisted on bed rest, rather than exertion, in the first instance and added that the patient should be "strictly watched if necessary".

Despite disagreements, however, most of the advice was fairly stereotyped and traditional: employment; change of activity, scene, topic, or objects; social contact; travelling, variety; music; riding on horseback; carriage riding; walking, especially "in the open air" or "in fields or woods" (Prichard, 1835); drawing; reading; the study of science, the fine arts, and nature; outdoor games such as bowls, shuttlecock, tennis, billiards, and shooting, were all recommended. A sprinkling of new recreations was introduced: swing exercise, quoits, rowing, digging, cricket, draughts, ninepins, chess, football, fishing, mountaineering, cycling, card playing, and "the feeding of a bird" (Dickson, 1874). "Useful labour" (Knight, 1827) was also promoted in a way that would have been largely foreign to earlier writers, since the activities recommended mainly represent work for lunatics in the fields and kitchens of the institutions they inhabited. Ellis (1838) also mentioned "making little articles, from which profit may be derived...(for) religious or benevolent purposes". Separate activities for female inmates were sometimes specified.

Advice on what melancholics should avoid remained traditional: intemperance in food and drink; physical exhaustion; solitude; intense and protracted thinking, all continued to be banned. The continuity of advice on avoidance in the face of numerous changes in theory and increasing disagreement in other spheres of advice is striking, but it too was shortly to vanish from accounts of treatment for melancholic disorders.

Excretion

The nineteenth century authors had little to say of excretion as a part of *Regimen*. Few followed Bakewell (1805) in recommending "opening medicines" to be taken at the sufferer's own discretion. Dickson (1874) was more typical in regarding "the regulation of the excretory organs" as one of the essentials of treatment, to be applied by the physician to the bowels of the patient. The impersonal language of organs characterizes nineteenth century writing on the topic.

Regulation of the Passions

The nineteenth century authors were less convinced than their predecessors that excesses of passion were a cause of madness and melancholia. Some argued, with Maddock (1854), that the relationship went the other way, viz., "that the morbid emotions of the lunatic are more generally *results*, rather than *causes*, of his ailment". Although a fair amount of the original canon of advice survived in the face of this reversal, it is to be found scattered in various texts rather than occurring in one piece in any one work. Thus Mayo (1838) Spoke of "education rendering the effects of calamity less intense, by cultivating antagonistic states of mind" and Esquirol (1845) put forward the notion of substituting one passion for another, Maddock (1854) warned against indulgence of passions, caprices, and selfish feelings, and Tuke (1878) commended the cultivation of a cheerful frame of mind. But on the whole, by midcentury writers were more concerned with providing for the occupation and feeding of their charges than with encouraging them to know themselves and apply their knowledge. Even the function of knowing the sufferer was to be taken over by the physician. Thus Esquirol (1845) noted that:

> Each melancholic should be treated on principles resulting from a thorough acquaintance with the tendency of his mind, his character and habits, in order to subjugate the passions which, controlling his thoughts, maintain his delirium.

His words constitute a sort of epitaph for the spirit of the neoclassical tradition of advice on melancholy.

6. CONCLUSION

This brief survey does not do justice either to the wealth of historical material or to the finer details of many of the older writers' ideas. The final submergence of the tradition of advice in psychiatric writings of the early twentieth century, its survival outside the professional literature of psychiatry, and piecemeal reemergence in contemporary writings, have not been dealt with. The present account should suffice, however, to suggest that many of the apparently new notions that are coming to be discovered in the current debate on behavioural approaches to depression are really rediscoveries of ideas and practices that have been long established, on different bases. Perhaps this survey of historical approaches may prompt contemporary theorists and therapists to re-examine their own theories and therapies in the light of centuries, rather than decades, of previous experience. Even though we might not choose to agree with all the particulars of the traditional canon, the extreme hardiness of its broad outlines might make us pause to reflect whether certain of its features, which are not well represented, if at all, amongst current orthodox approaches to treating depression, might not deserve reconsideration. The basic notion of circumspect, temperate living, based on knowledge of one's own individual and constitutional susceptibilities, the focus on enhancing efficient biological functioning through attention to diet, sleep, and exercise, the strategy of deliberately avoiding known physiological and psychological precipitants, the notion of the individual as a member of a supportive social network, the practice of systematically preparing to face adversity, and, finally, the concept of personal responsibility and initiative in choosing to live with care, would seem to be a heritage worth conserving.

REFERENCES

Anonymous (1750) *A Treatise on the Dismal Effects of Low-Spiritedness*, W. Owen, London.

Arnold, T. (1806) *Observations on the Nature, Kinds, Causes and Prevention of Insanity*, 2nd Ed., 2 Vols., R. Phillips. London (1st Ed. 1782).

Babb, L. (1951) *The Elizabethan Malady: A Survey of Melancholia in English Literature from 1580 to 1642*, Michigan State College Press, East Lansing.

Bakewell, T. (1805) *The Domestic Guide in Cases of Insanity, Pointing out the Causes, Means of Preventing, and Proper Treatment of that Disorder*, T. Allbut, London.

Barlow, J. (1843) *On Man's Power Over Himself to Prevent or Control Insanity*, William Pickering, London.

Barrough, P. (1590) *The Methode of Physicke*, London (originally published 1583).

Battie, W. (1758) *A Treatise on Madness*, Whiston & White, London.

Baxter, R. (1713) *Preservatives against Melancholy and Overmuch Sorrow, Or the Cure of both by Faith and Physic*, London.

Beard, G. M. (1890) *A Practical Treatise on Nervous Exhaustion (Neurasthenia): Its Symptoms, Nature, Sequences, Treatment*, H. K. Lewis, London.

Becker, J. (1977) *Affective Disorders*, General Learning Press, Morristown, N. J.

Blackmore, R. (1725) *A Treatise of the Spleen and Vapours: or, Hypocondriacal and Hysterical Affections, with Three Discourses on the Nature and Cure of the Cholick, Melancholy, and Palsies*, London.

Blakeway, R. (1717) *An Essay Toward the Cure of Religious Melancholy, In a Letter to a Gentlewoman afflicted with it*, London.

Boorde, A. (1547) *The Breuiary of Helthe*, London.

Boorde, A. (1870) *The Fyrst Boke of the Introduction of Knowledge/A Compendyous Regyment or A Dyetary of Helth*, edited ... by F. J. Furnivall, Early English Text Society, Extra Series No. 10, London (originally published 1542).

Breton, N. (1929) *Melancholike Humours*, edited with an Essay on Elizabethan Melancholy by G. B. Harrison, Scholartis Press, London (originally published 1600).

Bright, T. (1940) *A Treatise of Melancholie*, reproduced from the 1586 edition printed by Thomas Vautrollier, with an Introduction by Hardin Craig, Columbia University Press, New York.

Brooke, H. (1650) *ΥΓΙΕΝΗ or a Conservatory of Health*, London.

Bunyan, J. (1903) *The Pilgrim's Progress*, The Religious Tract Society, London (originally published 1678).

Burton, R. (1972) *The Anatomy of Melancholy*, edited with an introduction by Holbrook Jackson, J. M. Dent, London (originally published 1621).

Charron, P. (1608) *Of Wisdome Three Bookes...* translated by Samson Lennard, London.

Cheyne, G. (1733) *The English Malady*, Or, A Treatise of Nervous Diseases of all Kinds, as Spleen, Vapours, Lowness of Spirits, Hypochondriacal, and Hysterical Distempers, G. Strathan, London.

Clouston, T. S. (1892) *Clinical Lectures on Mental Disease*, 3rd. Ed., J. & A. Churchill, London.

Cogan, T. (1584) *The Haven of Health*, London.

Cullen, W. (1827) *Works*, 2 Vols., T & G. Underwood, London (Vol. 2 contains his *First Lines of the Practice of Physic* (1777)).

Culpeper, N. (1652) *The English Physitian: or An Astrologo-Physical Discourse of the Vulgar Herbs of the Nation*, Peter Cole, London.

Dickson, J. T. (1874) *The Science and Practice of Medicine in Relation to Mind*, H. K. Lewis, London.

Du Laurens, A. (1938) *A Discourse of the Preservation of the Sight: of Melancholike Diseases: of Rheumes, and of Old Age* (1599), translated by Richard Surphlet, with an Introduction by Sanford V. Larkey, The Shakespeare Association/Oxford University Press, London.

Ellis, W. C. (1838) *A Treatise on the Nature, Symptoms, Causes, and Treatment of Insanity*, Samuel Holdsworth, London.

Elyot, T. (1936) *The Castel of Helth* (1541), Scholars' Facsimile Reprints, New York.

Esquirol, J. E. D. (1965) *Mental Maladies: A Treatise on Insanity*, A Facsimile of the English Edition of 1845, with an Introduction by Raymond de Saussure, Hafner, New York & London.

Fawcett, B. (1780) *Observations on the Nature, Causes, and Cure of Melancholy, Especially of that which is commonly called Religious Melancholy*, Shrewsbury, London.

Ferrand, J. (1640) *Erotomania or A Treatise Discoursing of the Essence, Causes, Symptomes, Prognosticks, and Cure of Love, or Erotique Melancholy*, Oxford.

Friedman, R. J. and Katz, M. M., Eds. (1974) *The Psychology of Depression: Contemporary Theory and Research*, John Wiley, London.

Harper, A. (1785) *The Oeconomy of Health, or A Medical Essay: Containing New and Familiar Instructions for the Attainment of Health, Happiness and Longevity*, Ludgate-Hill.

Harper, A. (1789) *A Treatise on the Real Cause and Cure of Insanity*, C. Stalkes, London.

Harvey, G. (1672) *Morbus Anglicus, or a Theoretick and Practical Discourse of Consumptions, and Hypochondriack Melancholy*, London.

Harvey, G. (1672) *Morbus Anglicus, Or the Anatomy of Consumptions*, 2nd Ed., London.

Haslam, J. (1798) *Observations on Insanity*, F. & C. Rivington, London.

Haslam, J. (1809) *Observations on Madness and Melancholy*, 2nd Ed., J. Callow, London.

Hill, G. N. (1814) *An Essay on the Prevention and Cure of Insanity*, Longman, London.

Hill, J. (1766) *Hypochondriasis: A Practical Treatise on the Nature and Cure of that Disorder, Commonly called the Hyp and Hypo*, London.

James, R. (1745) *A Medicinal Dictionary*, 3 Vols, T. Osborne, London.

Johnson, J. (1818) *A Practical Treatise on Derangements of the Liver, Digestive Organs, and Nervous System*, To which is added an Essay on the Prolongation of Life, and Conservation of Health (Adapted to General Perusal), London.

Knight, P. S. (1827) *Observations on the Causes, Symptoms, and Treatment of Derangement of the Mind*, Longman, London.

Leake, J. (1781) *Medical Instructions Towards the Prevention and Cure of Chronic Diseases Peculiar to Women*, 2 Vols., Baldwin & Payne, London.

Lemnius, L. (1576) *The Touchstone of Complexions*, Thomas Barth, London.

Maddock, A. B. (1854) *Practical Observations on Mental and Nervous Disorders*, Simpkin–Marshall, London.

Maudsley, H. (1874) *Responsibility in Mental Disease*, Appleton, New York & London.

Maynwaring, E. (1683) *Method and Means of Enjoying Health, Vigour and Long Life*, London.

Mayo, T. (1838) *Elements of the Pathology of the Human Mind*, John Murray, London.

Moore, J. (1692) *Of Religious Melancholy*, A Sermon Preach'd before the Queen at Whitehall, March the 6th 1692, London.

Prichard, J. C. (1835) *A Treatise on Insanity and Other Disorders Affecting the Mind*, Sherwood, Gilbert & Piper, London.

Purcell, J. (1702) *A Treatise of Vapours, or Hysterick Fits*, Newman & Cox, London.

Reynolds, E. (1640) *A Treatise of the Passions and Faculties of the Soule of Man*, London.

Robinson, N. (1729) *A New System of the Spleen, Vapours, and Hypochondriack Melancholy*, Bettesworth, Innys & Rivington, London.

Rowlands, S. (1607) *Democritus, or Doctor Merry-man his Medicines against Melancholy Humours*, London.

Saagpakk, P. F. (1968) A Survey of Psychopathology in British Literature from Shakespeare to Hardy, *Literature & Psychology*, **18,** Nos. 2–3, 135–165.

Scull, A. T. (1979) *Museums of Madness: The Social Organization of Insanity in Nineteenth-Century England*, Allen Lane, London.

Shaw, P. (1728) *A New Practice of Physic*, 2nd Ed., 2 Vols., Osborn & Longman, London.

Spencer, T. (1948) The Elizabethan Malcontent, in J. G. McManaway, G. E. Dawson and E. E. Willoughby (Eds.) *Joseph Quincy Adams Memorial Studies*, pp. 523–535, The Folger Shakespeare Library, Washington.

Strother, E. (1718) *EUODIA: Or a Discourse on Causes and Cures*, C. Rivington, London.

Thomas, K. (1971) *Religion and the Decline of Magic: Studies in popular beliefs in sixteenth and seventeenth century England*, Weindenfeld & Nicolson, London.

Thomson, A. (1795) *An Enquiry into the Nature, Causes, and Method of Cure of Nervous Disorders*, 4th Ed., Cadell & Davies, London.

Tuke, D. H. (1878) *Insanity in Ancient and Modern Life, with Chapters on its Prevention*, Macmillan, London.

Tuke, D. H. (1892) *A Dictionary of Psychological Medicine*, 2 Vols., J. & A. Churchill, London.

Tuke, S. (1964) *Description of the Retreat* (1813), Reprinted . . . with an Introduction by Richard Hunter and Ida Macalpine, Dawsons, London.

Vaughan, W. (1630) *The Newlanders Cure*, London.

Veith, I. (1970) Elizabethans on Melancholia, *Journal of the American Medical Association* **212,** 127–131.

Venner, T. (1623) *Via Recta ad Vitam Longam*, Pars Secunda, London.

Walker, S. (1796) *A Treatise on Nervous Diseases*, J. Phillips, London.

Whytt, R. (1765) *Observations on the Nature, Causes, and Cure of those Disorders which have been Commonly called Nervous, Hypochondriac, or Hysteric*, Edinburgh.

Wright, L. B. (1958) *Middle-Class Culture in Elizabethan England*, Methuen, London.

Wright, T. (1601) *The Passions of the Minde*, London.

3

STRESS AND MEDICAL DISORDERS

ANDREW STEPTOE

St. George's Hospital Medical School, University of London

CONTENTS

1. INTRODUCTION

Stress is a term that apparently absorbs common sense and experience into an empirically valuable framework of explanation. Unfortunately, as with many general formulas, it may conceal more than it reveals. Stress has become an umbrella for discussions of emotional and behavioural influences on physical disorders, referring to almost every method by which personality, actions or environment affect illness. The massive range of experimental, clinical, and anecdotal literature brought under the rubric of stress testifies to the appeal of the concept; in his monumental compilation of research, Selye (1976a) cites more than 7,500 references published over the last half-century. Yet, it will be argued here that, as far as psychosomatic dysfunctions are concerned, general stress theory has outgrown its usefulness—it is both theoretically confusing and empirically deficient. The involvement of psychological factors in organic disorders will only be clarified when stress is replaced by narrower, but more precise, hypotheses.

The discussion will focus on the role of behaviour and emotion in non-psychiatric disorders, including some traditionally psychosomatic complaints, and other forms of organic pathology. Thus cardiovascular dysfunctions, gastro-intestinal lesions, immunity and infection are considered. In addition, the autonomic and neuroendocrine pathways that mediate psychological influences will be outlined.

Some confusion has been caused by terminological inconsistencies in stress research. Selye (1976b) uses the word to describe the "nonspecific response of the body to any demand", but also refers to people being "under stress", implying that stress is a stimulus rather than a reaction. Others define the expression as the interaction or transaction between person and environment (Lazarus and Cohen, 1977). The introduction of the phrase "psychological stressor" to describe stimuli has done little to clarify ambiguities, since stressors cannot be specified by their physical characteristics, only by their consequences. For instance, electrical shock is perhaps an archetypal experimental stressor; yet the responses to shock depend not simply on qualities such as intensity and duration, but on predictability, prior experience, behavioural response requirements, pattern of presentation, cognitive appraisal, the availability of coping strategies and other factors. Under such circumstances, labelling shock as a stressor conveys very little information.

These are not merely semantic problems, since they introduce a vagueness into discussions of the area that can inhibit serious analysis. Stress may be used as a glib explanation of phenomena that are poorly understood, discouraging the search for other causes of disturbance. Each generation invariably considers the "stresses of everyday life" to be greater than ever before, with the spread of alienation, materialism, and the destruction of the family. It is, of course, difficult to appraise contemporary society dispassionately, yet empirical studies of earlier social structures and customs indicate that notions of progressive deterioration in the quality of life cannot pass unqualified (Laslett, 1977; Stone, 1977).

There are other limitations to the explanatory value of stress. Arguments based on the concept are frequently irrefutable, as almost any effect may be "understood" in these terms. For example, it has been argued that church attenders are protected from stress, since they have access to social supports, group cohesion, and strategies for coping with life that are backed by religious tenets (Kaplan, 1976). On the other hand, the religious may be under more stress than nonbelievers; the bases of the faith are increasingly challenged by cultural changes, while the contradictions between the demands of a religious life and the means of achievement in contemporary materialist society widen. Similarly, stress theory might predict that immigrants to a new country who persist in their traditional practices are at risk. Alternatively, those who modify their behaviour and try to adapt may be vulnerable. The fluidity of stress diminishes its utility, and unless hypotheses are generated before investigations, almost any health variation with psychosocial or cultural factors can be "explained".

A further problem is that unwarranted generalizations about reaction patterns are made. Although stress is used to describe responses in the cognitive, emotional, behavioural, neuroendocrine and physical domains, it cannot be assumed that reactions are congruent. The experience of psychological stress, however defined, is not consistently associated with disturbed physiological functions, nor does it always lead to the same alterations in overt behaviour. Conversely, physical stress can be produced by haemorrhage or cold in anaesthetized preparations, where behavioural and mental parameters are unaffected. It is often assumed that a manipulation which attenuates some aspect of stress will be beneficial for all components. An example particularly relevant to physiological reactions is control over the source of aversive stimulation. While control may reduce some responses, the phenomenon is not universal, and other reactions may actually be more severe when the individual engages in active coping behaviours.

The empirical strengths and limitations of stress will be traced through four distinct research fields, each of which has contributed hypotheses relating psychological disturbance to organic dysfunction. Firstly, the investigation of animals in the laboratory. Here a major problem lies in fixing on dependent variables. Many workers have concentrated on end-organ responses; thus restraint, conflict, and motor activity may all induce gastric lesions. Yet the relevance of such models for human pathology is limited, unless the pathways mediating reactions parallel human pathology. In some cases, it is more useful to explore autonomic and neuroendocrine responses, rather than target organ dysfunction. Accordingly, short-term psychophysiological studies of humans, and reactions to the natural hazards of everyday life, will be considered. Finally, space will be given to psychosocial disturbances in patients with clinical disorders. It is becoming apparent in all these areas that stress responses are not uniform, but that different components of pathophysiology are sensitive to different factors.

2. STRESS AND THE PATTERN OF PHYSIOLOGICAL RESPONSE

The concept of non-specificity is central to Selye's notion of stress and has been incorporated into his definition of the term (Selye, 1976b). Selye showed that the General Adaptation Syndrome is elicited by a wide range of stimuli, including anoxia, immobilization, cold and X-rays. The reaction pattern passes through stages of alarm, resistance, and exhaustion, but the major pathological consequences are predominantly due to sustained overstimulation of neuroendocrine systems. Selye argued that responses could be divided into specific changes dependent on the particular tissue damage or stimulation imposed, and residual general reactions; the latter might include adrenal cortical enlargement, gastro-intestinal ulcers, myocardial necrosis and thymal atrophy.

However, there is considerable doubt about the non-specificity hypothesis (Mason, 1972). The pituitary–adrenocortical tract, which is the principal pathway discussed by Selye, does not respond indiscriminantly to all stressors. The generality of reactions observed in early investigations may have been due to the common element of psychological disturbance; for, although many of the stimuli used by Selye provoked peripheral tissue damage or homeostatic imbalance, they were also likely to inspire considerable fear and distress in the animals studied (Mason et al. 1976). When the behavioural disturbance is minimized, stressors such as fasting and exercise do not elicit corticosteroid responses. It is probable that no single physiological variable monitors stress reliably, and that the pattern of neuroendocrine and autonomic responses should be evaluated. This implies that the biological components of stress responses are selectively activated by different forms of stimulation.

In contrast with Selye's emphasis on the adrenal cortex, Cannon (1915) explored the role of the sympathetic nervous system in reactions to behavioural disturbance.

He argued that responses are organized to promote mobilization and preparation of the body for muscular work. Sympathetic fibres have direct effects on cardiac performance and vasomotor tone, and also stimulate the adrenal medulla to secrete catecholamines. Stored energy supplies are released by enhancing lipolysis in adipose tissue, while pulmonary, renal, and haemostatic mechanisms are modified.

These different response patterns are relevant to the discussion of psychosomatic dysfunctions, since it is probable that the pathways contribute selectively to pathology. Thus the cardiovascular adjustments underlying early essential hypertension may be associated with sympathetic/adrenomedullary stimulation (Steptoe, 1979). On the other hand, many of the psychological influences on bronchoconstriction are mediated through the vagal (parasympathetic) fibres (Weiner, 1977). Disturbances of immune response, leading to increased risk of infection and malignancy, may be dependent on the immunosuppressive effects of high corticosteroid concentrations, although there is also evidence that autonomic pathways are involved (Bourne et al. 1974; Rogers et al. 1979). No general agreement has been reached on the tracts mediating psychological influences on ulcers, although it is unlikely that sympathetic stimulation promotes lesions (Mikhail et al. 1978). In view of the role of the vagus in the regulation of gastric acid, these fibres may be involved in the translation of central influences on duodenal ulcer formation (Rehfeld and Amdrup, 1979).

There is abundant evidence that experimental stressors do not have equal impacts on all these autonomic and neuroendocrine systems. One of the problems in animal research lies in distinguishing responses to behavioural manipulations from those contingent on physical strains; comparisons of animals exposed to electric shock, immobilization or intense sensory stimulation with unstressed controls cannot be used to demonstrate psychological effects. Consequently, yoked control procedures have been employed, in which pairs of animals are subject to identical physical discomfort, while behavioural contingencies are varied. Thus one animal may perform responses that attenuate or eliminate aversive stimulation, while a second endures the same conditions without being able to respond. Parameters such as predictability can also be explored with this strategy. Such investigations tend to show that corticosteroid output is reduced in escape/avoidance conditions. Corum and Thurmond (1977) compared rats escaping shock in a shuttle box with animals yoked for shock, but unable to avoid. Corticosteroid concentration increased in both groups, but the rise was significantly greater in the inescapable condition. Hanson et al. (1976) exposed rhesus monkeys to high intensity noise for 13-minute bursts. At the end of each period, one group could terminate the noise by pressing a lever. The plasma cortisol levels of escape animals remained lower than those in yoked condition. Long-term shock avoidance experiments confirm that behavioural control over the source of stimulation reduces adrenocortical activation. After avoidance responses are learned, so that few shocks are actually administered, neither rats nor rhesus monkeys show sustained corticosteroid reactions (Coover et al. 1973; Brady, 1965; Feldman and Brown, 1976).

These data emphasize the deleterious effects of helpless exposure to stressors, and the benefits of control. But the pattern is reversed when cardiovascular reactions, in particular those associated with β-adrenergic sympathetic pathways, are monitored. Monkeys, or rats with genetic susceptibility for hypertension, fail to show increased blood pressure with inescapable shock (Dahl *et al.* 1968; Forsyth, 1968). Leenen and Shapiro (1974) monitored plasma renin activity (PRA) in rats subjected to regular inescapable shock. During prolonged sessions of 8 or 24 hours, PRA (which is stimulated by catecholamines and sympathetic fibres) soon fell to control levels. The adrenocorticol hormone corticosterone, on the other hand, remained at high concentrations.

Sympathetically mediated cardiovascular responses are promoted not by inescapable conditions, but by circumstances in which stimulation may be modified by the animal's behaviour. Long-term shock avoidance schedules elicit persistent increases in heart rate and arterial pressure, and lead to stable hypertension in some species (Forsyth, 1969; Harris *et al.*, 1977). Figure 1 summarizes the cardiovascular responses to prolonged free operant (Sidman) avoidance in a single monkey; after several months of this intense stimulation, sustained elevations in arterial pressure were recorded.

The responses of the immune system during avoidance conditioning are inconsistent. In mice, susceptibility to infection with *herpes simplex* and other viruses is increased, while passive anaphylactic reactions are reduced (Rasmussen, 1969). Yet monkeys subjected to shock avoidance schedules similar to that in Fig. 1 were actually more resistant to poliomyelitis virus than controls (Marsh *et al.* 1963). Other behavioural manipulations, such as restraint and crowding, alter immune

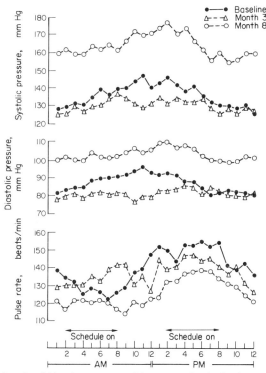

FIG. 1. Diurnal cycle of blood pressure and heart rate in single rhesus monkey during baseline (12 values averaged in each hour), month 3 and month 8 (30 values for each hour). After the baseline, the monkey performed a 20-sec Sidman avoidance task for two periods each day. (From Forsyth, 1969.)

responses, although reactions are again not uniform (Rogers *et al.* 1979). Thus mice injected with encephalomyocarditis virus were more vulnerable when housed singly rather than in groups, while the opposite was the case for the rodent malarial parasite *Plasmodium berghei* (Friedman *et al.* 1970; Plaut *et al.* 1971).

Nor may clear conclusions be drawn about the relationship between experimental ulcers and avoidance conditioning. The influential "executive monkey" studies, reported by Brady (1958), indicated that avoidance animals developed more ulcers than yoked controls, and implicated the deleterious effects of active responding. However, the results were not replicated by Foltz and Millett (1964), while Weiss's data in rats suggests that the reverse is the case—helpless, yoked animals appear more vulnerable (Weiss, 1968; 1977). These effects too have not been reproduced consistently; and it is evident that the association of ulceration with behaviour is fragile (Desiderato and Testa, 1976; Mikhail *et al.* 1978).

The implications of experimental studies in animals for psychosomatic connections are therefore complex and depend on a number of interrelated factors:

(a) The neural or endocrine pathways involved in the dysfunction must be considered. Parallels cannot necessarily be drawn between reactions in different target organs, since the efferent tracts mediating central influence are differentiated. Reactions may not be uniform across species.

(b) The behavioural contingencies are crucial, and have selective effects on efferent pathways. Sustained sympathetic and catecholamine release may be evoked when active responding is required to cope with noxious stimulation. Other tracts are activated in passive or helpless situations. These distinctions are relative rather than absolute, since all systems generally respond to very severe or acute stimulation; but parallels with medical disorders are more likely to emerge from consideration of prolonged noxious conditions.

These different patterns are rarely observed in single experiments, since most research is confined to particular physiological parameters. Even responses that are superficially similar may be sustained by distinct mechanisms according to the contingencies imposed. For example, blood pressure increases in dogs both during shock avoidance and in the period preceding each stress session (Anderson and Brady, 1972). Yet the pathways mediating the response are different in the two cases. Prior to avoidance, pressure rises without tachycardia, due to elevations in total peripheral resistance. When the avoidance schedule starts, however, there is a rapid increase in cardiac output, stimulated by β-adrenergic tone to the heart; cardiac mechanisms then serve to maintain the pressor response (Anderson and Tosheff, 1973; Galosy *et al.* 1979).

(c) All behaviours have metabolic concomitants, and the activities provoked during stimulation may generate their own physiological costs. Consequently, some of the variations in reaction are due to differences in motor output. It is too readily assumed that changes reported during behavioural experiments must be due to the "stress" effect rather than the associated physical actions (Langer *et al.*, 1979).

3. STRESS AND PERSONAL CONTROL

It has been argued that generalizations about stress reactions are unwarranted—a behavioural manipulation may reduce responses in some psychological or physiological systems without being universally beneficial. This is illustrated by recent studies of control over stressors. Many authors have suggested that control, or the belief in control, over sources of stress is protective, and that loss of control with its attendant experience of helplessness is deleterious. Helplessness has been implicated in such diverse disturbances as sudden cardiac death (Richter, 1957), depression (Seligman, 1975) and Type A coronary prone behaviour (Glass, 1977).

Control is a much abused term, and may refer to the availability of behavioural escape or avoidance responses, the self-administration of noxious stimulation, or the cognitive strategy adopted when confronting threat (Averill, 1973; Miller, 1979). However, data from animals suggest that sympathetic and catecholamine reactions may actually be heightened when certain types of avoidance are permitted. Similar patterns have been recorded in psychophysiological studies of man.

Groups of healthy volunteers were subjected to three experimental conditions by Obrist et al. (1978). The cold pressor test (hand immersion in iced water) and an explicit pornographic movie were stimuli for which no behavioural responses were required. The third condition was a reaction-time task, in which fast reactions allowed participants to avoid severe electric shock; alert responding was therefore needed in order to avert pain. Different patterns of cardiovascular response were recorded in the passive and active cases. Systolic pressure increased during the reaction-time test, together with rises in heart rate and indices of cardiac contractility—this suggested that β-adrenergic tone to the heart was elevated. The passive conditions provoked large diastolic pressure responses with less cardiac stimulation, reflecting adjustments dependent on high peripheral vascular resistance. These mechanisms were confirmed by running subjects under β blockade, since the heightened cardiac responses during the reaction-time task were attenuated. Light and Obrist (1980) replicated the pattern using shock as the source of threat in both active and passive conditions, while similar manipulations have been shown to provoke differential heart rate responses (Houston, 1972; Thackray and Pearson, 1968). Although cardiovascular reactions do occur under passive stresses such as classical conditioning with electric shock, they are not mediated by β-adrenergic mechanisms (Gliner et al. 1977). Carruthers and Taggart (1973) reported that heart rate actually fell during the observation of violent films, while inconsistent adrenomedullary and cardiovascular adjustments may be provoked by other passive stressors (Sapira and Shapiro, 1966).

The mechanisms eliciting responses are important, since the β-adrenergic tracts are implicated in the early stages of essential hypertension (Steptoe, 1978a; 1979). Obrist et al. (1978) were able to clarify the contingencies provoking sympathetic pathways by manipulating the reaction-time criteria required for shock avoidance. One group was given an "Easy" criterion of 400 msecs, while those in the "Impossible" condition were obliged to respond within 200 msec in order to avert shock. This criterion was rarely met. A third group were subject to intermediate "Hard" contingencies, in which fast responses were demanded without a criterion being fixed. The number of shocks in the Hard and Impossible conditions were matched, and Fig. 2 outlines the changes in systolic pressure and heart rate evoked under these circumstances. Initially, substantial responses were observed in all cases, but cardiovascular arousal was maintained to a greater extent in the Hard condition. Thus, although subjects in the Impossible group consistently failed to avoid and

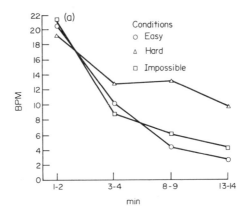

FIG. 2a. Change from baseline in heart rate during shock avoidance as a function of task difficulty (Obrist *et al.*, 1978).

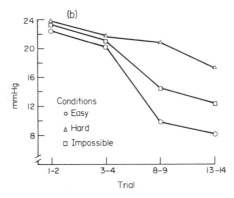

FIG. 2b. Change from baseline in systolic blood pressure during shock avoidance as a function of task difficulty (Obrist *et al.*, 1978).

(Figures 2a and b: Copyright © 1978, The Society for Psychophysiological Research. Reprinted with permission of the publisher from "The Relationship Among Heart Rate, Carotid d*P*/d*t*, and Blood Pressure in Humans as a Function of the Type of Stress", by P. A. Obrist *et al.*, *Psychophysiology* **15**, 102–115.)

were consequently under repeated threat of shock, they did not sustain high pressure or heart rate. The correlations of cardiovascular responses and indices of somatic activity and movement were inconsistent, and average reaction times did not differ between groups; hence the patterns of cardiovascular adjustment were not simply functions of varying motor-activity levels.

Cardiovascular reactions appear to be greater when partial control can be exerted over the source of aversive stimulation, when active or alert coping is required, and when the outcome of behaviour is uncertain. The Impossible group experienced failure and had little control, yet reactions in these autonomic pathways rapidly declined. Elliot (1969) reached similar conclusions about the availability of active coping responses, after a series of experiments on heart rate changes during cognitive and perceptual tasks. Yet these data stand in contrast to reports of the positive, stress-reducing aspects of control. Two features may account for the variation.

The first is the type of physiological reaction recorded. Alert coping behaviours have not been shown convincingly to attenuate responses mediated by the sympathetic nervous system. Frankenhaeuser and Rissler (1970) monitored catecholamine excretion while varying the degree of behavioural control, but their study is uninterpretable, since avoidance manipulations were confounded with habituation and the number of electric shocks administered. Geer et al. (1970) found that volunteers who were told that fast reaction times would reduce shock duration (perceived control) shared lower skin-conductance responses than no-control groups receiving equivalent shock. However, the skin conductance effects were not replicated, although the benefits of control for behavioural outcomes appears to be robust (Glass et al., 1973).

The second important consideration is the type of behaviour required. Cardio-vascular and sympathetic reactions may be reduced by instrumental control when response demands are low, and not actively challenging (as in the Easy condition of Fig. 2). This is seen in studies of systolic pressure and catecholamine reactions, where the "control" responses are trivial and easy to carry out (Hokanson et al. 1971; Lundberg and Frankenhaeuser, 1978). Manuck et al. (1978) tested these hypotheses by varying both control over aversive noise and the difficulty of successful avoidance. Systolic blood pressure was highest in subjects who could gain control by performing concept-formation tasks under difficult conditions; when the controlling response was easy, cardiovascular reactions were less marked.

Laboratory studies of man parallel research on animals in showing that components of stress responses are differentially influenced by experimental contingencies. When noxious stimulation is administered so that alert energetic coping will reduce threat, sympathetic and catecholamine pathways are activated. Other physiological indices of disturbance (possibly including the corticosteroids) may be less aroused under such circumstances, but may be more responsive when the individual is helpless and cannot avoid threat.

4. STRESS AND CHRONIC PHYSIOLOGICAL REACTIONS

Psychophysiological response patterns may be short-term adjustments, and their relevance to the aetiology of clinical dysfunctions is not self-evident. Yet the study of long-term biological reactions to distress is a laborious business. Laboratory stressors cannot be used in man, so it is necessary to rely on the experiences of everyday life. Unfortunately, confounding factors such as exercise, diet, or smoking may not be precisely controlled. Two strategies have been used in the field studies of chronic stimulation.

(a) Individuals are followed through periods of particular anguish or life experience. Thus groups of men being made redundant, and the parents of leukaemic children, have been monitored over long periods (Cobb and Kasl, 1977; Friedman et al. 1963). Such surveys may take several years to complete and are costly to run. Additionally, control groups are difficult to devise. Thus an alternative methodology is frequently adopted.

(b) Cross-sectional rather than longitudinal measures are taken during everyday behaviour; if circumstances are typical of the normal experience of subjects, the reactions measured may reflect chronic patterns of adjustment. Assessments of this type have been made on motorcar drivers, aircraft pilots, soldiers, factory workers, and other groups. Individuals need not be kept under surveillance for extended periods, so there are large savings in expenditure and research effort. However, reactions can only be considered representative if the recording procedures themselves are unobtrusive; unless this condition is fulfilled, responses to measurement may equal those to the stressor. Cardiovascular and neuroendocrine systems are extremely sensitive to the techniques of recording and to the circumstances surrounding monitoring. Buhler *et al.* (1978) showed that tonic catecholamine levels in both animals and man were very much lower than frequently noted, when readings were taken in undisturbed conditions. Inconsistent results may therefore be due to differences in technique.

Both strategies have yielded patterns of chronic reactivity that vary with the physiological or biochemical parameter monitored. Sustained oversecretion of corticosteroids is not consistently observed. A sequence of studies in the 1960s focused on the excretion of the metabolite 17-hydroxycorticosteroid (17-OHCS) from the parents of children with severe leukaemia (Friedman *et al.*, 1963). Most were followed for several months, both before and after their children died. Parents showed a wide range of 17-OHCS outputs, yet levels within individuals remained relatively uniform. When extra traumas occurred, such as infections or deaths on the ward, excretion rose above that seen during chronic distress (Teece *et al.*, 1966). However, sustained reactions were not recorded, many of the parents showing rather low outputs in comparison with other adults. Furthermore, measures taken at 6 months, and 2 years after the death of children were no lower on average than those recorded before the loss; but the grouped data disguised large individual variations during the recovery period (Hofer *et al.*, 1972).

Longitudinal surveys of neuroendocrine responses have revealed marked individual differences in cortisol output, but few gross changes with everyday experience (Rahe *et al.*, 1974). Adrenocortical function has also been studied during dangerous or taxing tasks, such as landing airplanes on an aircraft carrier. Marked elevations in serum cortisol and urinary 17-OHCS occurred on landing compared with control days, with increases in pilots exceeding 250 per cent (Miller *et al.*, 1970). Yet a rather different pattern was registered from helicopter ambulance men during combat in the Vietnam War (Bourne *et al.*, 1967). Urine was analysed from flight days when the men were exposed to extreme danger while picking up casualties, and days back at the base. Despite the episodic stress, there were no systematic differences in adrenocortical activity between flying and non-flying days. No matched control group was assessed, but excretion values were considered to be rather low in comparison with expected levels. There were no signs of adrenal exhaustion.

The data from field studies thus suggests that while the adrenal cortex may remain reactive in the long term, chronic hyperactivity is rare (Mason, 1968). Investigations of the adrenal medulla and catecholamines have uncovered more consistent patterns of activation. Frankenhaeuser and Gardell (1976) measured catecholamine excretion from different groups of workers in a sawmill. The high risk group were employed on machine-paced jobs, with short work cycles and continuous,

repetitive demands that were largely outside personal control. Lower risk maintenance men performed more varied jobs and operated at their own pace, but otherwise work and domestic status were similar. Increases in adrenalin excretion were
greater in machine-paced men, particularly early and late in the work shift.

Positive correlations have been found between life-change scores, recorded from
the Schedule of Recent Events, and catecholamines in patients with ischaemic heart
disease (Theorell et al. 1972). Another Swedish study indicated that even the mild
discomfort of crowding on a commuter train provoked catecholamine responses
(Singer et al. 1978). Catecholamine reactions may therefore be maintained when
conditions become very familiar; recordings from groups such as airline crew,
night-shift workers, and urban motor car drivers are compatible with this conclusion (Carruthers et al., 1976; Theorell and Åkerstedt, 1976; Bellet et al., 1969).

Similarly, blood pressure and heart rate are responsive not only to harrowing
environmental traumas, but also to everyday perturbations. Studies in North Africa
and Finland during the Second World War suggested the incidence of high arterial
pressure increased amongst people exposed to battle conditions (Graham, 1945;
Ehrström, 1945). War, of course, brings a variety of chronic deprivations and restrictions in addition to emotional strain, but similar patterns have been seen after
unexpected disasters in civilian populations (Ruskin et al., 1948). The haemodynamic effects of less dramatic disturbances have been amply documented with ambulatory monitoring techniques (Werdegar et al., 1967; Littler et al., 1973). Large
changes in heart rate and myocardial performance are also recorded during acute
harassments such as public speaking, and may be attenuated by β-adrenergic blockade (Taggart et al., 1973).

Circulating metabolites that are partially under the control of neural or neuroendocrine mechanisms, including plasma cholesterol, free fatty acids and factors
involved in blood coagulation, have also been studied. Here interpretation is more
problematic, since these variables may be influenced by diet, exercise, medication
and other parameters that are themselves not stable; it is not surprising, therefore,
that relationships with psychological threats are inconsistent (Friedman et al., 1958;
Theorell et al., 1972; Arkel et al., 1977; Palmblad et al., 1977).

This brief survey indicates that the tracts likely to modulate stress-related pathology behave in different ways, some showing shifts in reactivity, while others produce tonic adjustments in output. Failure to observe reactions to threat or challenge may be due to several factors:

(a) Some pathways may be incapable of continued overactivity on behavioural
stimulation, and will adapt after a time. If this is the case, the significance of such
mechanisms for chronic dysfunctions is doubtful, and their involvement in clinical
disorders can only be acute.

(b) The environmental conditions that have been studied may not be appropriate
for the pathway in question. If the distinctions suggested by acute laboratory investigations are valid, differences between the various neural and neuroendocrine systems may emerge according to the nature of stimulation, and the coping responses
required.

(c) A third factor that can contribute to low reactivity is the ability of people to
adapt to sustained perturbation. Certain conditions will not remain sufficiently
stressful to provoke responses; individuals may become accustomed to task re-

quirements or to the presence of risks and so experience little distress after the initial novelty has worn off. This explanation would gain credibility, if successful forms of mental coping or defence were associated with low physiological reactivity. However, consistent correlations of this type have not yet been recorded (Teece *et al.*, 1966; Wolff *et al.*, 1964; Bourne *et al.*, 1967).

These possibilities would be clarified by simultaneous monitoring of several physiological parameters during chronic threat, and extensive research on parachutists suggests how response patterns might fractionate. During the first stages of parachute training, large reactions are recorded in most of the pathways commonly associated with psychological stress, including the corticosteroids, catecholamines, heart rate, blood pressure, free fatty acids and growth hormone (Ursin *et al.*, 1978). Adrenocortical reactions rapidly diminish, so that after some training this system fails to respond. Yet sympathetic pathways are consistently activated, even amongst experienced parachutists (Bloom *et al.*, 1963; Fenz, 1975). Although responses are smaller than those recorded at the start of training, modifications in catecholamines, cardiovascular and electrodermal parameters persist (Hansen *et al.*, 1978). Figure 3 illustrates changes in PRA from three groups of parachutists (Langos *et al.*, 1976). Measures were taken from novices, men in training and from experienced sportsmen. There was no difference on rest days, yet differential reactions followed jumps. All groups showed a rise immediately after the jump, but the increase was smaller amongst the more experienced performers. Urinary adrenaline and noradrenaline were also elevated after the jump. The PRA peak was not only smaller in sportsmen, but the return to baseline was more rapid. However, it is significant that these β-adrenergic reactions persisted even in people with considerable task experience. Parachuting is an activity where physical demands are associated with mental alertness, and some of the responses may be potentiated by the metabolic requirements of exertion. It is an active rather than passive stressor, in that the threat of disaster is dependent on the individual's behaviour.

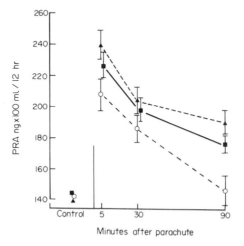

FIG. 3. Average plasma renin levels $\pm$ S.E. (mg/100 ml/12 hr) after parachuting in three groups: ▲---▲, beginners ($n = 10$); ■——■, trainees ($n = 9$); ○---○, sportsmen ($n = 6$). Control values were recorded during a rest day. (From Langos *et al.*, 1976.)

Unfortunately, most field stressors are not easy to classify on dimensions such as behavioural response requirements, so physiological reactions are complex. The responses of men losing their jobs through factory closure illustrate these problems (Cobb and Kasl, 1977). Changes in blood pressure, catecholamines, serum cholesterol, uric acid and other parameters were recorded, with some variables rising in anticipation of redundancy, while others responded to factory shut-down itself or to subsequent unemployment. Returns to baseline were also modulated by several factors, including social support. Although relationships with hypertension, arthritis, ischaemic heart disease and other disorders were observed, the links were not straightforward. Such variations emphasize the need to go beyond simple stress concepts to more detailed predictions.

5. STRESS AND CLINICAL DISORDERS

Psychological studies of disease states share a number of problems.

(a) Reporting bias. Patients may ascribe their disorders to earlier experiences retrospectively, exaggerating minor harassments and disturbances. Life-event techniques are frequently used to try to circumvent this difficulty. Yet, while the survey methods introduced by. Holmes and Rahe (1967) confirm some associations between life events and illness in general, they have been criticized on the grounds of reliability and definition (Brown, 1974). Extensive assessments of life events in ischaemic (coronary) heart disease have yielded disappointing results, and little relationship is found in polyarthritis (Hendrie et al., 1971; De Faire and Theorell, 1976). However, links have been shown retrospectively between life stress and subarachnoid haemorrhage (Penrose, 1972), while intriguing associations with streptococcal infections were recorded by Meyer and Haggerty (1962). Life events may also influence disturbances in the clinical stability of chronic disorders such as diabetes mellitus (Bradley, 1979).

(b) Changes with onset. Diagnosis of severe disorder is itself a traumatic and harrowing experience, and may precipitate profound adjustments in self-evaluation, ambitions and lifestyle. Characteristics present after the recognition of a dysfunction may not be typical either of the premorbid state, or of the condition before diagnosis. Thus Robinson (1964) collected psychological ratings and blood-pressure recordings from hypertensive outpatients, psychiatric outpatients and participants in a cardiovascular screening survey. The diagnosed essential hypertensives had higher neuroticism scores than the population sample, but did not differ from psychiatric outpatients. Within the screening group, there were no significant correlations between neuroticism and arterial pressure. Similarly, differences have been found between patients with diagnosed ischaemic heart disease, and those identified through screening (Segers et al., 1974). The personality profiles of cancer patients may in part be products of the pain experienced (Bond, 1976).

(c) Long-term aetiology. Many diseases pass through prolonged asymptomatic periods before coming to clinical attention. Thus, even though stress is monitored on a prospective basis, the possibility that associations are products rather than causes cannot be ruled out. The relationships between serum immunoglobins and emotional expression in women admitted for breast cancer biopsy may be compromised in this manner (Pettingale et al., 1977).

(d) Selective survival. Prospective studies of ischaemic heart disease indicate that the psychological profiles of survivors differ from those who die at early stages (Lebovits *et al.*, 1967; Bruhn *et al.*, 1969). It is not however known whether this is typical of other disorders.

Further methodological difficulties arise in the case of stress. Since definitions are vague, measurements of intensity may be ambiguous. Work-related stress, for instance, cannot simply be defined in terms of workload, amount of responsibility, or physical conditions. It depends on the social supports available in an outside work, work strategy, the ability to delegate, and other factors. Furthermore, variattions in stress may be associated with other risks that themselves have an impact on health; the hardworking executive in a competitive profession may not only work obsessively, but may smoke and drink heavily, take little exercise, and eat rich foods. These behaviours will affect physical disease processes independently.

These problems are reflected in the thorough assessment of occupational stress amongst factory workers carried out by House *et al.* (1979). Comprehensive questionnaires tapped the many aspects of "work-related stress", including responsibility, role conflict, concern for quality, job satisfaction and conflict between work and leisure activities. Striking differences were observed, however, between health as indexed by symptom questionnaires and medical examinations. Self-report data suggested close associations of occupational stress with dermatological, respiratory, psychiatric, cardiovascular, and gastro-intestinal disorders. Yet only the relationship with cardiovascular risk was confirmed by physical tests. It is possible that the tendencies to complain of life stress and physical symptoms are connected, irrespective of the observable state of health.

Cross-sectional data relating stress to physical disorders have been collected in comprehensive reviews elsewhere (Weiner, 1977; Selye, 1976a). Some investigators have resolved measurement problems by selecting groups considered *a priori* to differ in stress experience—for example, the bereaved and those who have suffered severe life events. The increased morbidity and mortality of bereaved people has been generally confirmed (Parkes, 1975), while Bartrop *et al.* (1977) showed depression of lymphocyte (T cell) function in this group. Variations of health and disease incidence in different societies and cultures have also been interpreted in terms of stress (Henry and Stephens, 1977); however, such groups tend to differ on a number of factors, so fluctuations in illness experience cannot be ascribed unambiguously to psychosocial factors.

Comparisons within populations are more valuable. The survey of air traffic controllers and airmen reported by Cobb and Rose (1973) assessed two groups that live and operate under similar conditions. However, controllers carry out work with heavy responsibilities, requiring constant alertness. High arterial pressure was four times as prevalent amongst controllers than airmen. Some difference may have been due to licensing practices, since airmen were more likely to be rejected as unfit because of hypertension. Cobb and Rose therefore collected data over another year, and calculated an incidence rate that was less biased by licensing variations. The essential results are summarized in Table 1. Annual incidence was over five times higher in controllers, being greater in all age strata. The mean age of onset of hypertension was 41 amongst controllers, compared to 48 in airmen; thus the taxing occupation was associated with more high blood pressure and an earlier

TABLE 1.
High Blood Pressure in Air Traffic Controllers and 2nd-Class Airmen

Annual incidence of hypertension per 1,000 men		
Age	Controllers	Airmen
20–29	2	1
30–39	12	2
40–49	17	4
50+	15	4

Air traffic controllers in high- and low-stress towers		
Age	High stress	Low stress
20–29	4	1
30–39	18	12
40–49	77	36
50+	—	36

(From Cobb and Rose, 1973.)

onset. An additional analysis was performed on controllers working at airfields with high and low traffic densities (designated high stress and low stress towers in Table 1). The prevalence rates suggest that men working at busy terminals were prone to develop hypertension at a younger age. Prevalence of peptic ulcers was also higher amongst controllers than airmen, and was significantly greater in workers from high stress control towers.

Recent studies of psychological factors in physical disorders have generally abandoned non-specific stress concepts in favour of more limited hypotheses. This has permitted a greater reliability in measurement of environmental and behavioural characteristics, together with the testing of specific predictions. Examples from ischaemic heart disease alone include the social incongruities confronting Japanese Americans, the job-related problems of Swedish building workers, and Type A coronary-prone behaviour (Marmot and Syme, 1976; Theorell and Floderus-Myrhed, 1977; Rosenman and Friedman, 1974). Limitations of space prevent detailed evaluation of these trends, but it is significant that issues investigated experimentally re-emerge. For example, it has been suggested that Type A behaviour is related to control over sources of stress (Glass, 1977). This may reflect the growing interdependence of psychosocial epidemiology and laboratory psychophysiological strategies.

Psychological factors do not operate either through personality or behavioural predisposition alone, or solely through the experience of objective stimulation and trauma. An interactional model, in which these elements combine with physical risks, may be most fruitful. This is apparent in the case of cardiovascular disorders. There is little support for the notion that life events in isolation predispose individuals to ischaemic heart disease (De Faire and Theorell, 1976; Connolly, 1976). On the other hand, Type A coronary-prone behaviour is not an inherent characteristic that will inevitably be expressed, but depends on exposure to appropriate eliciting environments. Rosenman (1978) has argued that the materialist societies of urban developed countries encourage aggressive ambitions and foster Type A behaviours. Thus the psychological risk may depend both on behavioural disposition and environment.

Theorell (1976) investigated this interaction in a prospective study of ischaemic heart disease amongst middle-aged Swedish men in the construction industry. Only individuals who both displayed coronary-prone response styles, and had experienced many life events, showed elevated arterial pressure; those scoring high on one characteristic only did not have raised levels. In a different context, Harburg and his associates (1973, 1979) have identified interactions between external stress (living conditions in urban Detroit), constitutional vulnerability (race and sex), and response or coping style (expression or inhibition of anger and hostility), in the modulation of blood pressure levels.

Most research on physical disorders has focused on particular dysfunctions to the exclusion of others. However, the same elements of experience or behaviour are associated with different illnesses. Bereavement, for example, has been connected with cardiovascular death, depressed lymphocyte function, symptoms of depression, and general deteriorations in health. Men facing redundancy may sustain reactions that promote arthritis and gout as well as cardiovascular vulnerability (Cobb and Kasl, 1977). The air traffic controllers studied by Cobb and Rose (1973) not only manifest frequent hypertension, but also developed more peptic ulcers than airmen. Even Type A coronary-prone behaviour may not be exclusively related to heart disease, since groups with high Type A scores are also at risk for a variety of other physical and social pathologies (Eliot et al., 1977). Many psychosocial pressures may increase health vulnerability in general. Some homogeneity might be predicted, if dysfunctions are modulated by similar neural and neuroendocrine pathways. But research is urgently required into the manner in which psychological factors interact with biological and constitutional dispositions in the aetiology of physical disorders.

6. THE MANAGEMENT OF PHYSIOLOGICAL STRESS RESPONSES

The aim of this chapter is not to assess techniques of stress control; nevertheless, an important implication of the foregoing discussion is that procedures designed for the general management of psychological stress may not attenuate biological reactions. The divergence between physiological, endocrine, and behavioural responses suggests that methods focusing on some aspects may not transfer to others.

Distinctions can be drawn between programmes aimed specifically at physiological reactions, and those concerned with psychological appraisal and coping. The latter have attracted much interest in the relief of psychological distress, but have not yet been applied extensively in the modification of biological responses. However, several reports have confirmed the favourable consequences of psychological preparation for surgery; not only is personal discomfort relieved, but changes are measured in objective indices of recovery (see Chapter 10, this volume).

Cognitive and behavioural interventions have also been directed at Type A coronary-prone individuals. Some components of this behaviour pattern, including chronic time urgency, aggressiveness, and hard drive may, in part, be responses to particular environments and cultural demands. Suinn and Bloom (1978) adapted the methods of Anxiety Management Training to a group of middle-class Type A males recruited by advertisement. No significant alterations in arterial pressure or plasma lipids followed treatment, although fewer Type A responses were recorded on questionnaire measures. A stress management programme was compared with cognitive therapy and waiting list controls by Jenni and Wollersheim (1979). Anxiety decreased in both active conditions, but these gains were not translated into reliable modifications of physiological risk. In contrast, Roskies's comparison of brief psychotherapy with behavioural intervention did produce lowering of arterial pressure and cholesterol levels amongst Type A volunteers (Roskies et al., 1978). Effects were sustained more reliably at follow-up by the behavioural group (Roskies et al, 1979).

Psychophysiological reactions have been modified more impressively with biofeedback and relaxation. Other contributions to this volume make detailed consideration superfluous here (Young and Blanchard, this volume). Although conventionally applied to resting subjects in low states of arousal, biofeedback and relaxation have recently been used to train people to overcome physiological reactions under disturbing conditions. This approach may promote greater degrees of voluntary control that have previously been recorded (Steptoe, 1979); preliminary data suggest that both exteroceptive feedback and relaxation or meditation procedures, may assist in the reduction of cardiovascular reactions to psychological and physical challenge (Patel and North, 1975; Victor et al., 1978; Steptoe, 1978b).

Patel and her associates have shown how biofeedback and relaxation may be employed on a large scale in the modification of physical risk factors (Patel et al., Reference Note 1). Over 1,100 industrial workers were screened, and those found to be moderately vulnerable on two of the three major cardiovascular risks—blood pressure, plasma cholesterol, and smoking—were recalled. Participants were allocated to biofeedback and control groups, matched for age, sex and proportion of

TABLE 2.
Modification of Cardiovascular Risk Factors

Variable	% of group at risk		Reduction: Pre-post treatment Mean ± S.E.		Reduction: Pre-6-month follow-up Mean ± S.E.	
	Biofeedback ($n = 99$)	Control ($n = 93$)	Biofeedback	Control	Biofeedback	Control
Blood pressure						
Systolic (mm·Hg)	64	62	18.0 ± 1.72†	8.8 ± 1.42	20.2 ± 1.99†	11.2 ± 1.70
Diastolic (mm·Hg)			10.6 ± 1.37†	3.8 ± 1.04	11.5 ± 1.43†	3.2 ± 1.32
Serum cholesterol (mmol/l.)	82	87	0.90 ± 0.12*	0.52 ± 0.12	0.77 ± 0.10	0.56 ± 0.11
Cigarette smoking (average cigs/day)	82	70	5.8 ± 0.73†	2.6 ± 0.75	4.8 ± 0.77	2.3 ± 0.74

† Significant difference between groups (t-test), P 0.01–0.001.
* Significant difference between groups (t-test), P 0.05.
(From Patel et al., Reference Note 1.)

members with raised arterial pressure and cholesterol. The biofeedback group participated in eight weekly sessions of relaxation, meditation and electrodermal feedback, while controls received only brief counselling and health literature. Some of
the important results are summarized in Table 2. Amongst individuals with initially
high levels of each risk factor, reliable decreases were recorded after treatment.
Changes also occurred in controls, but these were less substantial. After six months
follow-up, the biofeedback group continued to show larger reductions in blood
pressure and smoking. These data suggest that psychological methods may be
applicable on a large scale to sub-groups of the general population that are not
specially motivated for change.

However, it should be emphasised that the control of physiological reactions is
not the only method by which behavioural scientists may contribute to the management of medical disorders. An alternative strategy is to intervene at the level of risk
behaviour, rather than stress response. The impact of eating, smoking, and physical
exercise on health is well established; although these activities contribute to "physical" risk through influencing weight, blood pressure, plasma lipids, and immunity,
they are not themselves pathophysiological conditions. The value of altering behaviours, both in the prevention and management of non-psychiatric complaints, is
being increasingly recognized. Thus progressive structured exercise programmes are
recommended for the rehabilitation of coronary patients, and improvements in
circulatory function have been documented (Wenger and Hellerstein, 1978). Impressive reductions in arterial pressure may be produced by introducing hypertensives
to low salt diets (Morgan et al., 1978; Shibata et al., 1979). Patient compliance with
medication may be improved by self-monitoring and special attention, with consequent gains in the treatment of many medical complaints (Sackett and Haynes,
1976).

Multiple cardiovascular risk factor management through behaviour modification
was explored by Meyer and Henderson (1974). Thirty-six men, considered to be at
high risk for cardiovascular disease, participated in programmes aimed at increasing physical activity, reducing smoking, losing weight and altering diet. Twelve
attended a behaviour modification group with their spouses, while a further ten
were given individual counselling in which health information was provided without specific behaviour recommendations. A control group had only one single
consultation with a physician. Weight loss was recorded in all groups, with significantly greater changes in the two treatment conditions. Similarly, modifications in
diet, smoking, and exercise occurred, the adjustments being somewhat larger in the
behavioural group. Decreases in serum cholesterol were recorded across the treatment period in all conditions, but only the behaviour modification group maintained change at 3 month follow-up.

These approaches may become increasingly attractive in preventive medicine. It
may be hoped that specific recommendations about altering activities will be
backed with procedures that capitalize on laboratory experiences of attitude and
behaviour change.

7. CONCLUSIONS

The concept of stress has been important in demonstrating to sceptical medical
scientists that cognitive, behavioural, and environmental factors contribute to the

aetiology of non-psychiatric disorders. However, its value may now be exhausted, since the neural and endocrine pathways that translate central influences have been extensively documented. The general formula of psychological stress can now be dissected, so that the specific roles of different environmental conditions, coping behaviours, and personal capabilities may be identified.

This chapter has set out to describe some of the reaction patterns that emerge from laboratory studies of animals and man. Activation of the mediating autonomic and neuroendocrine tracts is selective, and responses vary with behavioural demands and individual characteristics. These distinctions are less easy to observe in naturalistic settings, but clearer patterns may emerge with the refinement of psychosocial research strategies. The prime implication for management is that programmes of intervention may need to be formulated with greater attention to the biological processes underlying each separate problem area.

REFERENCE NOTE

1. Patel, C., Marmot, M., Terry, D., Carruthers, M. and Sever, P., Coronary risk factor reduction through biofeedback aided relaxation and meditation, Unpublished paper.

ACKNOWLEDGEMENTS

The author is grateful to Andrew Mathews for his comments on earlier drafts of this chapter.

REFERENCES

Anderson, D. E. and Brady, J. V. (1976) Cardiovascular responses to avoidance conditioning in the dog: effect of β-adrenergic blockade, *Psychosomatic Med.*, **38**, 181–189.

Anderson, D. E. and Tosheff, T. G. (1973) Cardiac output and total peripheral resistance changes during preavoidance period in dogs. *J. Applied Physiol.*, **34**, 650–654.

Arkel, Y. F., Haft, J. I., Kreutner, W., Sherwood, J. and Williams, R. (1977) Alteration in second phase platelet aggregation associated with an emotionally stressful activity, *Thrombosis Haemostasis*, **38**, 552–561.

Averill, J. R. (1973) Personal control over aversive stimuli and its relationship to stress, *Psychol. Bull.*, **80**, 286–303.

Bartrop, R. W., Luckhurst, E., Lazarus, L., Kiloh, L. G. and Penny, R. (1977) Depressed lymphocyte function after bereavement, *Lancet*, **1**, 834–836.

Bellet, S., Ronan, L. and Kostis, J. (1969) The effect of automobile driving on catecholamine and adrenocortical excretion, *Amer. J. Cardiol.*, **24**, 365–368.

Bloom, G., Von Euler, U. S. and Frankenhaeuser, M. (1963) Catecholamine excretion and personality traits in paratroop trainees, *Acta. Physiol. Scand.*, **58**, 77–89.

Bond, M. R. (1976) Pain and personality in cancer patients, in *Advances in Pain, Research and Therapy*, 1, Eds. J. Bonita and D. Albe-Fessard, Raven Press, New York.

Bourne, H. R., Lichtenstein, L. M., Melmon, K. L., Henney, C. S., Weinstein, Y. and Shearer, G. M. (1974) Modulation of inflammation and immunity by cyclic AMP, *Science*, **184**, 19–28.

Bourne, P. G., Rose, R. M. and Mason, J. W. (1967) Urinary 17 OHCS levels—data on seven helicopter medics in combat, *Arch. General Psychiatry*, **17**, 104–110.

Bradley, C. (1979) Life events and the control of the diabetes mellitus, *J. Psychosomatic Research*, **23**, 159–162.

Brady, J. V. (1958), Ulcers in executive monkeys, *Scientific American*, October, 95–100.

Brady, J. V. (1965) Experimental studies on psychophysiological responses to stressful situations, in *Symposium on Medical Aspects of Stress in the Military Climate*, Walter Reed Army Institute of Research, Government Printing Office, Washington, D.C.

Brown, G. W. (1974) Meaning, measurement and stress of life events, in *Stressful Life Events: Their Nature and Effects*, Eds. B. S. and B. P. Dohrenwend, Wiley, Chichester.

Bruhn, J. G., Chandler, B. and Wolf, S. (1969) A psychological study of survivors and non-survivors of myocardial infarction, *Psychosomatic Med.*, **31**, 8–19.

Buhler, H. V., DaPrada, N., Haefely, W. and Picotti, G. B. (1978) Plasma adrenalin, noradrenalin and dopamine in man and different animal species, *J. Physiol.*, **276**, 311–320.

Cannon, W. B. (1915) *Bodily Changes in Pain, Hunger, Fear and Rage*, Routledge and Kegan Paul, London.

Carruthers, M., Arguelles, A. F. and Mosovich, A. (1976) Man in transit: biochemical and physiological changes during the intercontinental flights, *Lancet*, **1**, 977–981.

Carruthers, M. and Taggart, P. (1973) Vagotonicity of violence: biochemical and cardiac responses to violent films and T.V. programmes, *B.M.J.* **3**, 384–389.

Cobb, S. and Rose, R. M. (1973) Hypertension, peptic ulcer and diabetes in air-traffic controllers, *J. Amer. Med. Assoc.*, **224**, 489–492.

Cobb, S. and Kasl, S. V. (1977) *Termination: the consequences of job loss*, NIOSH Research Report, DHEW Publ. N. 77–224.

Connolly, J. (1976) Life events before myocardial infarction, *J. Human Stress*, **2**, Part 4, 3–17.

Coover, G. D., Ursin, H. and Levine, S. (1973) Plasma corticosterone levels during active avoidance learning in rats, *J. Comp. Physiol. Psychol.*, **82**, 170–174.

Corum, C. R. and Thurmond, J. B. (1977) Effects of acute exposure to stress on subsequent aggression and locomotor performance. *Psychosomatic Medicine*, **39**, 436–443.

Dahl, K., Knudson, K. D., Heinem and Leitl, G. (1968) Hypertension and stress, *Nature*, **219**, 735–736.

De Faire, U. and Theorell, T. (1976) Life changes and myocardial infarction: How useful are life change measurements? *Scan. J. Soc. Med.*, **4**, 115–122.

Desiderato, O. and Testa, M. (1976) Shock stress, gastric secretion and habituation in the chronic gastric fistula rat, *Physiology and Behaviour*, **16**, 67–73.

Ehrström, M. C. (1945) Psychogene Blutdruckssteigerung—Kriegshypertonien. *Acta. Med. Scand.*, **122**, 546–570.

Eliot, R. S., Clayton, F. C., Pieter, G. M. and Todd, G. L. (1977) Influence of environmental stress on pathogenesis of sudden cardiac death, *Federal Proc.*, **36**, 1719–1724.

Elliott, R. (1969) Chronic heart rate: experiments on the effects of collative variables lead to a hypothesis about its motivational significance, *J. Personal. Soc. Psych.*, **12**, 211–228.

Feldman, J. and Brown, G. (1976) Endocrine responses to electric shock and avoidance conditioning in the rhesus monkey—cortisol and growth hormone, *Psychoneuroendocr.*, **1**, 231–242.

Fenz, W. D. (1975) Strategies for coping with stress, in *Stress and Anxiety*, 2, Eds. I. Sarason and C. Spielberger, Wiley, New York.

Foltz, E. L. and Millett, S. E. (1964) Experimental psychosomatic disease state in monkeys, 1. Peptic ulcer—executive monkeys, *J. Surg. Research*, **4**, 445–453.

Forsyth, R. P. (1968) Blood pressure and avoidance conditioning, *Psychosomatic Med.*, **30**, 125–133.

Forsyth, R. P. (1969) Blood pressure responses to long-term avoidance schedules, *Psychosomatic Med.*, **31**, 300–309.

Frankenhaeuser, M. and Rissler, A. (1970) Effects of punishment on catecholamine release and efficiency on performance, *Psychopharmacologia*, **17**, 378–390.

Frankenhaeuser, M. and Gardell, B. (1976) Underload and overload in working life: outline of a multidisciplinary approach, *J. Human Stress*, **2**, 35–46.

Friedman, M., Rosenman, R. H. and Carroll, V. (1958) Changes in serum cholesterol and blood clotting time in men subjected to cyclic variations of occupational stress, *Circulation*, **17**, 852–861.

Friedman, S. B., Mason, J. W. and Hamburg, D. A. (1963) Urinary 17-hydroxycorticosteroid levels in parents of children with neoplastic disease, *Psychosomatic Med.*, **25**, 364–376.

Friedman, S., Glasgow, L. and Ader, R. (1970) Differential susceptibility to a viral agent in mice housed alone or in groups, *Psychosomatic Med.*, **32**, 285–299.

Galosy, R. A., Clarke, L. K. and Mitchell, J. H. (1979) Cardiac changes during behavioural stress in dogs, *Amer. J. Physiol.*, **236**, H750–H758.

Geer, J. H., Davidson, G. T. and Gatchel, R. I. (1970) Stress effect of perceived control of aversive stimulation, *J. Person. Soc. Psych.*, **16**, 731–738.

Glass, D. C. (1977) *Behaviour Pattern, Stress and Coronary Disease*, Lawrence Erlbaum, Hillsdale.

Glass, D. C., Singer, J. E., Leonard, H. S., Krantz, D., Cohen, S. and Cummings, H. (1973) Perceived control of aversive stimulation and the reduction of stress responses, *J. Personality*, **41**, 577–595.

Gliner, J. R., Browe, A. D. and Horvath, S. M. (1977) Haemodynamic changes as a function of classical aversive conditioning in human subjects, *Psychophysiology*, **14**, 281–286.

Graham, J. D. P. (1945) High blood pressure after a battle, *Lancet*, 239–240.

Hansen, J. R., Stoa, K. F., Blix, A. F. and Ursin, H. (1978) Urinary levels of epinephrine and norepinephrine in parachutist trainees, in *Psychobiology of Stress*, Eds. H. Ursin, H. Baade and S. Levine, Academic Press, London.

Hanson, J. D., Larson, M. E. and Snowdon, L. T. (1976) Effects of control over high intensity noise on plasma cortisol levels in rhesus monkeys, *Behav. Biol.*, **16**, 333–340.

Harburg, B., Erfurt, J. C., Hauenstein, L. F., Chape, C., Schull, W. J. and Schork, M. A. (1973) Socioecological stress, suppressed hostility, skin colour, and black–white male blood pressure: Detroit *Psychosomatic Med.*, **35**, 276–296.

Harburg, B., Blakelock, E. H. and Roeter, P. J. (1979) Resentful and reflective coping with arbitrary authority and blood pressure: Detroit, *Psychosomatic Med.*, **41**, 189–202.

Harris, A. H., Goldstein, B. T. and Brady, J. V. (1977) Viseral learning: cardiovascular conditioning in primates, in *Biofeedback and Behaviour*, Eds. J. Beatty and H. Legewie, Plenum Press, New York.

Hendrie, H. C., Paraskevas, F., Baragar, F. D., and Adamson, J. D. (1971) Stress, immunoglobulin levels and early polyarthritis, *J. Psychosomatic Research*, **16**, 327–342.

Henry, J. P. and Stephens, P. M. (1977) *Stress, Health and the Social Environment*, Springer-Verlag, New York.

Hofer, M. A., Wolff, E. T., Friedman, S. B. and Mason, J. W. (1972) A psychoendocrine study of bereavement, Part 1, 17-OHCS excretion, *Psychosomatic Med.*, **34**, 481–491.

Hokanson, J. S., Degood, D. E., Forrest, M. S. and Brittain, T. N. (1971) Availability of avoidance behaviour in modulating vascular stress responses, *J. Personal. Soc. Sci.* **19**, 60–68.

Holmes, T. H. and Rahe, R. H. (1967) The social readjustment rating scale, *J. Psychosomatic Research*, **11**, 213–218.

House, J. S., McMichael, A. J. Wells, J. A., Kaplan, B. H. and Landerman, L. R. (1979) Occupational stress and health among factory workers, *J. Health Social Behaviour*, **20**, 139–160.

Houston, B. K. (1972) Control over stress, method of control, and response to stress, *J. Person. Soc. Sci.*, **21**, 249–255.

Jenni, M. A. and Wollersheim, J. P. (1979) Cognitive therapy, stress management training and the type A behaviour pattern, *Cognitive Therapy Research*, **3**, 61–73.

Kaplan, B. H. (1976) A note on religious beliefs and coronary heart disease, *J. S. Carol. Med. Assoc. Supplement.*, 60–64.

Langer, A. W., Obrist, P. A. and McCubbin, J. A. (1979) Hemodynamic and metabolic adjustments during exercise and shock avoidance in dogs, *Amer. J. Physiol.*, **5**, H225-H230.

Langos, J., Kvetnansky, R., Blazicek, P., Novotny, J., Vencel, P. Burdiga, A. and Mikulaj, L. (1976) Plasma renin activity and dopamine–hydroxylase activity and catecholamine excretion in man during stress, in *Catecholamines and Stress*, Eds. E. Usdin, R. Kvetnansky and I. J. Kopin, Pergamon Press, Oxford.

Laslett, P. (1977) *Family life and illicit love in earlier generations*, Cambridge University Press.

Lazarus, R. S. and Cohen, J. B. (1977) Environmental Stress, in *Human Behaviour and Environment*, Vol. 2, Eds. I. Altman & J. S. Wohlwill, Plenum Press, New York.

Lebovits, B. Z., Shekelle, R. E., Ostfeld, A. and Paul, O. (1967) Prospective and retrospective studies of coronary heart disease, *Psychosomatic Med.*, **29**, 265–272.

Leenen, F. H. and Shapiro, A. P. (1974) Effect of intermittent electric shock on plasma renin activity in rats, *Proc. Soc. Exp. Biol. Med.*, **46**, 534–538.

Light, K. C. and Obrist, P. A. (1980) Cardiovascular response to stress: effects of opportunity to avoid shock experience and performance feedback, *Psychophysiol.*, **17**, 243–252.

Littler, W. A., Honour, A. J. and Sleight, P. (1973) Direct arterial pressure and ECG recording during motor car driving, *B.M.J.*, **2**, 273–277.

Lundberg, U. and Frankenhauser, M. (1978) Psychophysiological reactions to noise as modified by personal control over noise intensity, *Biological Psych.*, **6**, 51–59.

Manuck, S. B., Harvey, A. H., Lechleiter, S. L. and Neal, K. S. (1978) Effects of coping on blood pressure responses to threat of aversive stimulation, *Psychophysiol.*, **15**, 544–549.

Marmot, M. G. and Syme, S. L. (1976) Acculturation and coronary heart disease in Japanese Americans, *Amer. J. Epidemiology*, **104**, 225–247.

Marsh, J. T., Lavender, J. F., Chang, S. and Rasmussen, A. F. (1963) Poliomyelitis in monkeys: decreased susceptibility after avoidance stress, *Science*, **140**, 1414–1415.

Mason, J. W. (1968) A review of psychoendocrine research on the pituitary–adrenal cortical system, *Psychosomatic Med.*, **30**, 576–607.

Mason, J. W. (1972) A re-evaluation of the concept of non-specificity in stress theory, in *Principles, Practices and Positions in Neuropsychiatric Research*, Eds. J. Brady and W. J. H. Nauta, Pergamon Press, Oxford.

Mason, J. W., Maher, J. T., Hartley, L. H., Mougey, E. H., Perlow, N. J. and Jones, L. G. (1976) Selectivity of corticosteroid and catecholamine responses to various natural stimuli, in *Psychopathology of Human Adaptation*, Ed. G. Serban, Plenum Press, New York.

Meyer, A. J. and Henderson, J. B. (1974) Multiple risk factor reduction in the prevention of cardiovascular disease, *Preventive Med.* **3**, 225–236.

Meyer, R. and Haggerty, R. (1962) Streptococcal infections in families, *Paediatrics*, **29**, 539–549.

Mikhail, A. A., Kamaya, V. A. and Glavin, G. B. (1978) Stress and experimental ulcer critique of psychological literature, *Canad. Psych. Rev.*, **19**, 296–303.

Miller, R. G., Rubin, R. T., Clarke, B. R., Crawford, W. and Arthur, R. J. (1970) The stress of aircraft carrier landings, 1. Corticosteroid responses in naval aviators, *Psychosomatic Med.*, **32**, 581–588.

Miller, S. M. (1979) Controllability and human stress: method, evidence and theory, *Behaviour Research Therapy*, **17**, 287–304.

Morgan, T., Adam, W., Gillies, A., Wilson, M., Morgan, G. and Carney, G. (1978) Hypertension treated by salt restriction, *Lancet*, **1**, 227–230.

Obrist, P. A., Gaebelein, C. T., Teller, E. S., Langer, A. W., Grignolo, A., Light, K. C. and McCubbin, J. A. (1978) The relationship among heart rate, carotid dP/dT and blood pressure in humans as a function of the type of stress, *Psychophysiol.*, **15**, 102–115.

Palmblad, J., Blomback, M., Egberg, N., Froberg, J., Karlsson, C. and Levi, L. (1977) Experimentally induced stress in man: effects on blood coagulation and fibronolysis, *J. Psychosomatic Research*, **21**, 87–92.

Parkes, C. M. (1975) *Bereavement*, Penguin, London.

Patel, C. H. and North, W. R. S. (1975) Randomized control trial of yoga and biofeedback in the management of hypertension, *Lancet*, **2**, 93–95.

Penrose, R. J. J. (1972) Life events before subarachnoid haemorrhage, *J. Psychosomatic Research*, **16**, 329–333.

Pettingale, K. W., Greer, S. and Tee, D. E. H. (1977) Serum IgA and emotional expression in breast cancer patients, *J. Psychosomatic Research*, **21**, 395–399.

Plaut, S. M., Friedman, S. B. and Grota, L. J. (1971) Plasmodium berghei resistance to infection in group and individually housed mice, *Exp. Parasitology*, **29**, 47–52.

Rahe, R. H., Rubin, R. T. and Arthur, R. J. (1974) Three investigators study: Serum uric acid, cholesterol and cortisol variabilities during stresses of everyday life, *Psychosomatic Med.*, **36**, 258–268.

Rasmussen, A. F. (1969) Emotion and immunity, *Ann. New York Acad. Sci*, **164**, 458–461.

Rehfeld, J. F. and Amdrup, E. (1979) *Gastrin and the vagus*, Academic Press, London.

Richter, C. T. (1957) On the phenomenon of sudden death in animals and man, *Psychosomatic Med.*, **19**, 191–198.

Robinson, J. O. (1964) A possible effect of selection on the test scores on a group of hypertensives, *J. Psychosomatic Research*, **8**, 239–243.

Rogers, M. T., Dubey, D. and Reich, P. (1979) The influence of the psyche and the brain on immunity and disease susceptibility: a critical review, *Psychosomatic Med.*, **41**, 147–164.

Rosenman, R. H. and Friedman, M. (1974) Neurogenic factors in pathogenesis coronary heart disease, *Med. Clin. North America*, **58**, 269–279.

Rosenman, R. H. (1978) The interview method of assessment of the coronary prone behaviour pattern, in *Coronary Prone Behaviour*, Eds. T. M. Dembroski, S. M. Weiss, J. L. Shields, S. G. Haynes and M. Feinleib, Springer-Verlag, Berlin.

Roskies, E., Spevack, M., Surkis, A., Cohen, B. and Gilman, S. (1978) Changing the coronary prone (type A) behaviour pattern in a non-clinical population, *J. Behav. Med.*, **1**, 201–216.

Roskies, E., Kearney, H., Spevack, M., Surkis, A., Cohen, C. and Gilman, S. (1979) Generalizability and durability of treatment effects in an intervention programme for coronary-prone (Type A) managers. *J. Behavioral Med.*, **2**, 195–207.

Ruskin, A., Beard, O. W. and Schaffer, R. (1948) Blast hypertension, *American J. Med.*, **4**, 228–236.

Sackett, B. L. and Haynes, R. E. (1976) *Compliance with therapeutic regimens*, Johns Hopkins University Press, Baltimore.

Sapira, J. D. and Shapiro, A. P. (1966) Studies in man on the relationship of adrenergic correlates to pressor responsivity, *Circulation*, **34**, 226–241.

Segers, M. J., Graulich, P. and Mertens, C. (1974) Relations psycho-biocliniques dans un group de coronariens: étude preliminaire, *J. Psychosomatic Research*, **18**, 307–313.

Seligman, M. E. P. (1975) *Helplessness*, W. H. Freeman, San Francisco.

Selye, H. (1976a) *Stress in Health and Disease*, Butterworth, London.

Selye, H. (1976b) *The Stress of Life*, McGraw-Hill, New York.

Shibata, H. and Hatano, F. (1979) A salt restriction trial in Japan, in *Mild Hypertension: Natural History and Management*, Eds. F. Gross and T. Strasser, Pitman Medical, Bath.

Singer, J. E., Lundberg, U. and Frankenhaeuser, M. (1978) Stress on the train: a study of urban commuting, in *Advances in Environmental Psychology*, Vol. 1: *The Urban Environment*, Eds. A. Baum, J. E. Singer and S. Valins, LEA, Hillsdale.

Steptoe, A. P. A. (1978a) New approaches to the management of essential hypertension with psychological techniques, *J. Psychosomatic Research*, **22**, 339–354.

Steptoe, A. P. A. (1978b) The regulation of blood pressure reactions to taxing conditions using pulse transit time feedback and relaxation, *Psychophysiol*, **15**, 429–438.

Steptoe, A. P. A. (1979) Cardiovascular reactivity and its management with psychological techniques, in *Research in Psychology and Medicine*, Vol. 1, Eds. D. J. Oborne, M. M. Gruneberg and J. R. Eiser, Academic Press, London.

Stone, L. (1977) *The Family, Sex and Marriage*, Weidenfeld & Nicholson, London.

Suinn, R. N. and Bloom, L. J. (1978) Anxiety management training for pattern A behaviour, *J. Behavioural Med.*, **1**, 25–35.

Taggart, P., Carruthers, M. and Somerville, W. (1973) ECG, plasma catecholamines, and lipids, and their modification by oxprenolol when speaking before an audience, *Lancet*, **2**, 341–346.

Teece, J. J., Friedman, S. B. and Mason, J. W. (1966) Anxiety, defensiveness and 17-hydroxocorticosteroid excretion, *J. Nerve. Ment. Disease*, **141**, 549–554.

Thackray, R. I. and Pearson, P. W. (1968) Stress, heart rate and performance, *Perc. Motor Skills*, **27**, 651–658.

Theorell, T. (1976) Selective illnesses and somatic factors in relation to two psychosocial stress indices—a prospective study on middle-aged construction building workers, *J. Psychosomatic Research*, **20**, 7–20.

Theorell, T., Lind, E., Froberg, J., Karlsson, C. and Levi, L. (1972) A longitudinal study of 21 subjects with coronary heart disease: Life changes, catecholamine excretion and related biochemical reactions. *Psychosomatic Med.*, **34**, 505–516.

Theorell, T. and Åkerstedt, T. (1976) Day and night work: changes in cholesterol, uric acid, glucose and potassium in serum and in circadian pattern of urinary catecholamine excretion, *Acta. Med. Scand.*, **200**, 47–53.

Theorell, T. and Flodens-Myrhed, B. (1977) Work load and risk of myocardial infarction—a prospective psychosocial analysis. *Int. J. Epidemiology*, **6**, 17–21.

Ursin, H., Baade, E. and Levine, S. (1978) *Psychobiology of Stress*, Academic Press, London.

Victor, R., Mainardi, A. and Shapiro, D. (1978) Effects of biofeedback and voluntary control procedures on heart rate and perception of pain during the cold pressor test, *Psychosomatic Med.*, **40**, 216–225.

Weiner, H. (1977) *Psychobiology and Human Disease*, Elsevier, Amsterdam.

Weiss, J. M. (1968) The effects of coping responses on stress, *J. Comp. Physiol. Psychol.*, **65**, 251–260.

Weiss, J. M. (1977) Psychological and behavioural influences on gastro-intestinal lesions in animal models, in: *Psychopathology: Experimental Models*, Eds. J. D. Maser and M. E. P. Seligman, W. H. Freeman, San Francisco.

Wenger, M. K. and Hellerstein, H. K. (1978) *Rehabilitation of the coronary patient*, Wiley, Chichester.

Werdegar, D., Sokolow, M. and Perloff, D. E. (1967) Portable recordings of blood pressure: A new approach to assessment of the severity and prognosis of hypertension, *Trans. Ass. Life Ins. Med. Dir. America*, **51**, 93–115.

Wolf, C., Friedman, S., Hofer, M. and Mason, J. (1964) Relationship between psychological defences and urinary 17-OHCS excretion rates, *Psychosomatic Med.*, **26**, 576–591.

4

UNDERSTANDING PAIN PHENOMENA

MATISYOHU WEISENBERG

Bar-Ilan University, Ramar-Gan, Israel

CONTENTS

1. INTRODUCTION

Although sensory perception has long been recognized as a psychological process, it is only recently that the perception of pain has come to be recognized as a significant psychological problem of clinical concern. This recognition has come from within psychology itself as well as from the medical profession (cf., Brena, 1978).

Early work on pain concentrated upon pain as a sensation. This has led to the development of a finely controlled methodology for the explorations of pain phenomena (cf., Hardy, Wolff and Goodell, 1952). Nerve pathways have been studied, a variety of pain-inducing stimuli have been defined, measurement procedures have been developed and sensitivity of body zones has been mapped. However, as Beecher (1959), Melzack (1973), Chapman (1978) and others have shown, laboratory study of pain as a simple sensation is not adequate for the understanding of clinical phenomena. Pain perception is a complex process involving emotional arousal, motivational drive, and cognition. Sensory transmission of stimuli is but one component. Activation of nociceptive fibers that respond to tissue damage, is not synonymous with pain perception and reaction. Perception, the means by which a person becomes aware of his environment, especially where pain is concerned, is subject to a great deal of processing from the moment of nociceptive stimulation at the periphery to the point of awareness (cf., Chapman, 1978). Many psychological variables can influence the final perception.

Some of the complexity of understanding pain phenomena can be seen in attempts at its definition. Sternbach (1968), for example, defines pain as an abstract concept that refers to "(1) a personal, private sensation of hurt; (2) a harmful stimulus which signals current or impending tissue damage; (3) a pattern of responses which operate to protect the organism from harm" (page 12). Examination of pain phenomena, however, indicate that this or any other definition is inadequate. It is not always possible to specify the stimulus input in clinical pain. Furthermore, there are many examples of pain that begin not prior to the tissue damage but rather after healing has taken place e.g., causalgia. Certainly, when dealing with chronic pain, the tissue-damage notion is inadequate.

The environment and conditions under which the nociception and tissue damage occur can at times be more important in determining pain reaction than the harmful stimulus itself, as seen in the classic study of Beecher (1956). Of 215 men seriously wounded in battle, only 25 percent wanted a narcotic for pain relief. In comparison, in civilian-life with a similar surgical wound made under anesthesia, over 80 percent of the group wanted relief. Beecher attributes the difference in reaction to the significance assigned to the wound rather than to the extent of tissue damage. In battle, the wound meant a ticket to safety, while in civilian life the surgery meant disaster.

To deal with problems of a simplistic stimulus–response definition of pain, Merskey (1968) views pain as an unpleasant experience primarily associated with tissue damage, or described in tissue-damage terms, or both associated and described in tissue-damage terms. Psychogenic pain is caused mainly or wholly by psychological factors, while organic pain is pain caused mainly or wholly by physical causes. Psychogenic pain occurs under three main circumstances: (1) in hallucinations, e.g., schizophrenia, (2) pain due to muscle tension caused by psychological factors, e.g., myofascial pain dysfunction, tension headache, (3) conversion hysteria. From the patient's view, the subjective experience of psychogenic or organic pain may not be different.

Importantly, pain reactions often convey a great deal more than a signal that tissue damage is occurring. As Szasz (1957), Zborowski (1969), and others have pointed out in discussing human reactions to pain, communication aspects are frequently overlooked. Pain reactions can mean "Don't hurt me," "Help me," "It's legitimate for me to get out of my daily responsibilities," "Look, I'm being punished," "Hey, look, I'm a real man," "I'm still alive," Woodforde and Fielding (1970) have argued that cancer has a great deal less pain associated with it than is commonly assumed. Much of the prescribing of potent analgesics and narcotics is based on the feeling of hopelessness, helplessness, and a desire to have a reason to maintain doctor–patient contact.

Pain and anxiety are usually associated with each other. The general conclusion is that the greater the anxiety, the greater the pain (Sternbach, 1968). Therefore, control and reduction of anxiety can help reduce pain. However, the exact relationship of pain and anxiety is not fully understood. Thus, prescribing diazepam or teaching muscular relaxation will not automatically result in the absence of pain.

Although anxiety is prevalent in chronic pain, it is much more apparent in acute pain, that is, pain of recent onset (Sternbach, 1968, 1974, 1978b). Acute pain is associated with autonomic reactions that may be proportional to stimulus intensity. These include increases in heart rate, blood pressure, pupilary diameter, and striated muscle tone. In brief, these are the signs commonly associated with flight or fight reactions and anxiety. Anxiety techniques help a great deal.

Chronic patients with pain of several months duration seem to show an habituation of autonomic signs. Sternbach (1974, 1978b) has stressed depressive reactions such as disturbance of sleep, appetite, and libido. Use of antidepressive medication or otherwise treating the depression can help reduce the pain (Spear, 1967; Taub, 1975).

Brena (1978) has expanded upon the phenomena of chronic pain referring to the "Five D's" syndrome. Chronic pain patients are usually involved in a cycle of (1) *drug* misuse, changes and decreases in physical activity that result in (2) *dysfunction*, resulting in (3) *disuse* lesions such as frozen joints. These pain patients as a consequence are (4) *depressed*. Depression, in turn, makes the chronic pain patient more pain prone. The end point becomes (5) *disability*, for which western societies provide compensation. The compensation in turn reinforces reduced activity, disuse, dysfunction and drug use, ultimately leading to unbearable suffering.

Thus, when examining the reaction to pain and pain control, it becomes vital to consider the complexity of the phenomenon. Pain is a sensation. However, its perception involves a range of motivational, emotional, and cognitive variables. Therefore psychological intervention can have a great impact upon pain perception. The principles of learning and social influence processes have been applied to pain control. Behavioral techniques include greater use of stress- and anxiety-reducing procedures, such as relaxation, desensitization, hypnosis, biofeedback, modeling, and a variety of cognitive strategies. In other instances, patients are taught that they can control and contain the influence of pain on their lives, even when the sensation of pain itself cannot be eliminated completely. The amount of general anesthesia, surgical intervention, and the number of pills prescribed and consumed for pain- and anxiety-control have consequently gone down with the use of such behavioral approaches.

Even when pharmacological means are used to control pain, the psychological status of the patient will often determine their chemical effectiveness. Beecher (1959, 1972) has cited many examples supporting this assertion. The greater the stress, the more effective are placebos. There are certain drugs such as morphine that work for pain of pathological origin (which is usually accompanied by anxiety), but which fail to work for experimentally-produced pain (which has little anxiety). "Thus, we can state *a new principle of drug action*: some agents are effective only in the presence of a required mental state" (1972, p. 178).

This chapter will briefly examine some of these phenomena by first looking at some of the theoretical approaches to pain and its measurement. Following this, some of the behavioral intervention strategies will be described. It readily becomes apparent that understanding and controlling pain phenomona requires a multi-faceted view to which psychology has much to contribute.

2. THEORETICAL APPROACHES TO PAIN:
PSYCHOPHYSIOLOGICAL APPROACHES

Theories of pain ideally should account for the range of pain phenomena. However, as with definitions, no single pain theory is currently adequate to account for all pain phenomena. Each approach still leaves a great many unknowns. Many theories have focused upon the neurophysiological structures related to pain. Two main approaches that are still current are the specificity and pattern theories of pain.

Specificity theory refers to a pain system based upon a specific set of peripheral nerve fibers that are nociceptive in function (cf., Mountcastle, 1974). At the periphery are sets of free nerve endings, A-delta and C fibers associated with two qualities of pain, short-latency pricking pain and long-latency burning pain, respectively. Although temporal and spatial patterns may contribute to what is perceived, afferent impulses in A-delta and C fibers are both necessary and sufficient peripheral input to evoke painful sensations in the human being. Pricking-pain impulses enter the dorsal spinal cord, where they synapse and ascend via the anterolateral system to thalamic centers and from there to somatic sensory areas of the cerebral cortex. Burning-pain impulses follow a similar course into the anterolateral system, but project to different thalamic and cortical areas. These latter projections seem to account for the affective, autonomic reaction to pain impulses. The nature, location, and interactions of higher pain centers are still not clearly spelled out (Mountcastle, 1974).

The pattern theory opposes the notion that pain has its own set of specialized receptors despite the recent accumulation of a great deal of evidence (cf., Bonica and Albe-Fessard, 1976; Liebeskind and Paul, 1977; Sternbach, 1978a). It proposes that pain perception is based upon stimulus intensity and central summation (Goldsheider, 1894). Crue and Carregal (1975), recent advocates of this approach, argue that there is no need to speak of pain as a primary sensory modality. Therefore, there are no pain endings, pain fibers, or pain neurons in the peripheral nervous system. There is no such thing as a pain stimulus, only stimuli that are painful. Pain is a result of the summation of a spatial and temporal pattern of input.

Melzack and Wall (1965, 1970) and Melzack (1973) after critically examining specificity and pattern theories, rejected both notions. Specificity is viewed as making unwarranted psychological assumptions and not adequately accounting for pain phenomena, while pattern theory is described as running counter to physiological facts. They reject specificity, but accept specialization. Specialization can be found at receptor sites as with A-delta and C fibers, that respond to particular types and ranges of physical energy. However, specialization is not specificity. Specificity implies responding to one and only one given kind of stimulus. Calling specific receptors pain fibers implies a direct connection from the receptor to a brain center where pain would always be perceived. This is an unwarranted psychological assumption concerning perception. There are a small number of fibers that respond only to intense stimulation. However, this does not mean that they are pain fibers that always produce pain when stimulated. At various levels of energy stimulation, there are many things happening. Aside from the activation of specific fibers, changes occur in the total number of neurons responding, as well as in their temporal and spatial relationships. However, a pattern theory of pain by itself appears to contradict physiological evidence.

The gate-control theory of pain contains elements of both specificity and pattern theories. It attempts to account for psychological influences on pain perception, as well as such clinical findings as spread of pain and persistence of pain after tissue healing. Conceptually, gate-control theory proposes a dorsal spinal gating mechanism in the substantia gelatinosa that modulates sensory input by the balance of activity of small-diameter (A-delta and C) and large-diameter fibers (A-beta). Activity of large fibers closes the gate and prevents synaptic transmission to centrally-projecting T (transmission) cells, while small-diameter fibers open the gate and facilitate T cell activity once a critical level is reached. Small-fiber activity is believed responsible for prolongation of pain and spread to other parts of the body. A central control trigger can also influence the gate. Thus, cognitive processes can either open or close the gate.

The exact mechanism involved in gate-control is still not clear. Mendell and Wall (1964) and Hillman and Wall (1969) speak of pre- and post-synaptic effects. A single electrical stimulus delivered to small fibers produces a burst of nerve impulses followed by repetitive discharges in the spinal cord. Successive electrical stimuli produce a burst followed by discharges of increasing duration after each stimulation. Successive electrical stimulation of large fibers produces a burst of impulses followed by a period of silence after each pulse. These studies form much of the mechanical basis of the gate-control theory.

More than with any other theory, Melzack and Wall (1970) have emphasized the different aspects of pain perception. Pain has a sensory component similar to other sensory processes. It is discriminable in time, space, and intensity. However, pain also has an essential aversive–cognitive–motivational and emotional component that leads to behavior designed to escape or avoid the stimulus. Different neurophysiological mechanisms have been described for each system. The fibers that project to the ventrobasal thalamus and somatosensory cortex are partly involved in the sensory-discriminative aspects of pain. Fibers that project to the reticular formation, medial intralaminar thalamus, and limbic system are related to the aversive–cognitive–motivational and emotional component of pain that leads to escape behavior. Higher cortical areas are involved in both discriminative and motivational systems influencing reactions on the basis of cognitive evaluation and past experience. More than any other approach, gate-control emphasizes the major role of psychological variables and how they affect the reaction to pain. Especially with chronic pain, successful control often involves changing the motivational component, while the sensory component remains intact. Hypnosis, anxiety reduction, desensitization, attention distraction, as well as other behavioral approaches can be effective alternatives and supplements to pharmacology and surgery in the control of pain. Their effect is felt mostly on the motivational component of pain.

In a more recent statement of gate-control theory, Melzack and Dennis (1978) have emphasized differences between chronic and acute pain. With acute pain, there is usually a well-defined cause and a characteristic time course whereby the pain disappears after the occurence of healing. The rapid onset of pain is referred to as the *phasic* component. The more lasting persistent phase is referred to as the *tonic* component. The tonic component serves as a means of fostering rest, care, and protection of the damaged area, so as to promote healing.

However, with chronic pain the tonic component may continue, even after healing has occurred. Melzack and Dennis (1978) refer to low-level abnormal inputs that produce self-sustaining neural activity. These inputs seem to be memory-like mechanisms related to pain. They can occur at any level of the nervous system. Normally, these so-called inputs referred to as *pattern generating systems* are inhibited by a central control biasing system. Where neuronal damage occurs, such as after amputation or after peripheral nerve lesions, the central inhibitory influence is diminished, thus allowing sustained activity to occur even as a result of non-noxious input. Thus, for example, Loeser and Ward (1967) demonstrated abnormal bursts of firing in dorsal horn cells as long as 180 days after the sectioning of dorsal roots in the cat.

Melzack and Dennis (1978) propose that the abnormal, prolonged bursting activity that occurs in deafferented or damaged neuron pools can be modulated by somatic, visceral, and autonomic inputs, as well as by inputs from emotional and personality mechanisms by means of the activation of descending inhibitory input. Short-acting local blocks of trigger points or intense stimulation by dry needling, cold, injections of saline or electrical stimulation can interrupt the abnormal firing and produce relief beyond the duration of the treatment.

On the other hand, memories of prior pain experiences at spinal or supraspinal levels can also trigger abnormal firing patterns. Thus, once the pain is under way the role of neuromas, nerve injury, or other physical damage begins to be of lesser importance. What is needed is therapy to affect the pattern-generating mechanisms. Once the person is free from the influence of the pattern-generating mechanisms even temporarily, he can begin to maintain normal activity which in turn would foster patterns of activity that inhibit abnormal firing. These abnormal firing mechanisms can be affected by multiple inputs. It is therefore preferable to use simultaneous multiple therapies such as antidepressant drugs, electrical stimulation, anesthetic blocks, and realistic goals for the patient to achieve to make life worth living.

However, the gate-control theory has come under harsh criticism. "I think, therefore, that one ought at this stage to strongly support Schmidt in his attempt to prevent the Gate hypothesis from taking root in the field of neurology" (Iggo, 1972, p. 127). A key element in the gating mechanism is the differential response of large and small fibers. Investigators have failed to confirm the Mendell and Wall (1964) study whereby C fibers produce hyperpolarization of presynaptic terminals with resulting presynaptic facilization. Instead, both A and C fibers have been found to produce depolarization which is the accepted mechanism of presynaptic inhibition (Franz and Iggo, 1968; Zimmerman, 1968; Vyklicky, Rudomin, Zajac and Burke, 1969). "With a natural painful stimulus, we have found no evidence for the existence of a presynaptic gating mechanism activated by painful stimuli such as that proposed by Melzack and Wall" (Vyklicky, *et al.*, 1969, p. 186).

Dyck, Lambert and O'Brien (1976) have presented clinical evidence that fiber size does not control, facilitate, or inhibit pain as proposed by gate-control theory. Frederich's ataxia involves a markedly decreased number of large diameter fibers, without the production of neuropathic pain. Patients with inherited amyloidosis and sensory neuropathy have a selective decrease or absence of A-delta and C fibers potentials, with pain as a common feature. Pain seems to be related more to the rate of fiber degeneration, rather than to the selective loss of large or small fibers as hypothesized by Melzack and Wall (1970).

Wall (1976), in an attempt to counter criticism of gate-control theory, has argued that the 1965 presentation contained much speculation and was never intended to be a complete and final theory. Recent evidence does lend support to the theory. Although Burgess (1974) and Iggo (1974) discovered fibers in the A-delta group and in the C group which responded only to tissue damaging high-intensity pressure, this does not resolve the problem of how an individual perceives pain. Other fiber categories also respond to injury producing stimuli. Even the specific nociceptive A-delta and C fibers respond to stimuli that are not usually nociceptive in character. Light pressure stimulation produces a nociceptive reaction once fibers have been sensitized by damage, heat, or a particular chemical environment. Therefore, understanding specificity in simple terms is still not possible. In terms of the balance of large and small fibers, recent evidence, Wall argues, does not show that a preferential loss of large-diameter fibers leads to pain. However, it does seem that pain is not felt, if small fibers are missing. Functional predictions, Wall claims, should not be made only on the basis of morphological observations. Small fibers really could be regenerated large fibers. Secondly, although fibers may appear intact morphologically, there can be disturbance at the receptors, in transmission, or at central endings. For example, no agreement yet exists regarding morphological changes that occur in peripheral fibers with trigeminal neuralgia. Yet, it is known that a specific low-threshold afferent stimulus evokes pain.

Regardless of the accuracy of the specific wiring diagrams involved, the gate-control theory of pain has been the most influential and important current theory of pain perception. It ties together many of the puzzling aspects of pain perception and control. It has had a profound influence on pain research and the clinical control of pain. It has generated new interest in pain perception, stimulating a multidisciplinary view of pain for research and treatment. It has been able to demonstrate the importance of psychological variables. Still, there is little doubt that research will produce changes in the original gate-control conceptions.

3. THEORETICAL APPROACHES TO PAIN: BIOCHEMICAL AND NEURAL MECHANISMS OF PAIN CONTROL

Several of the most exciting findings in recent years relate to a neural humoral system of control of pain. These findings are the discovery of zones such as the midbrain periaqueductal gray matter from which stimulation produced analgesia (SPA) can be obtained (Reynolds, 1969; Liebeskind, Mayer and Akil, 1974; Liebeskind and Paul, 1977). These same zones seem to be closely associated with the opiate binding sites and mechanisms of action of morphine in the nervous system (Liebeskind, Mayer and Akil, 1974; Simon and Hiller, 1978). Furthermore, it appears that the body produces its own group of endogenous morphine-like substances called endorphins (Simon, Hiller and Edelman, 1975; Hughes, Smith, Kosterlitz, Fothergill, Morgan, and Morris, 1975).

SPA, as reviewed by Cannon, Liebeskind and Frenk (1978), has been reported to produce blocking of behavioral responses even to intense pinch, tissue damaging heat, and subcutaneous application of painful chemical substances. Results have been obtained in cats, monkeys, and in man for both acute and chronic pain. Pain relief lasts significantly beyond the time of stimulation. Analgesic effects are localized, depending upon the brain site stimulated.

SPA seems to share common sites and mechanisms of action with the opiates. As with SPA, strong analgesic effects for opiates are found when injected into the periaqueductal gray matter or in the more caudal or rostral periventricular structures. Both SPA and morphine are blocked by narcotic antagonists such as naloxone. Both SPA and opiate analgesia seem to produce an effect by inhibiting pain in a descending direction to lower centers in the spinal cord, in a selective manner. As Cannon, Liebeskind and Frenk (1978) describe it, there is a strong suggestion of an endogenous pain suppressive system that is activated by electrical stimulation and drugs.

The endogenous mechanism has been viewed as an active one depending upon the release of neurotransmitters, such as substance P (Terenius, 1978). Serotonergic neurons, in particular, seem to be important. Messing and Lytle (1977) reviewed evidence to show that increase in activity of the brain and spinal cord serotonin neurons is associated with the analgesic effects of opiate narcotics while decreases in the activities of these neurons is associated with diminished analgesic drug potency.

The discovery of endogenously produced endorphins has led to a series of studies relating a variety of pain-control strategies to the production of these endogenous substances. Thus, it has been reported that the pain-control effects of acupuncture, but not of hypnosis, have been blocked by naloxone (Mayer, Price, Barber, Rafii, 1976). Terenius (1978) reviewed evidence that lumbar cerebrospinal fluid from patients with chronic pain showed lower concentrations of endorphin. In turn, congenital insensitivity to pain may be related to a tonic hyperactivity of an endogenous pain system (Dehen and Cambier, 1978). Naloxone has been reported to have no effect (Mihic and Binkert, 1978) or a significant effect (Levine, Gordon, and Fields, 1978) in blocking the effects of placebos.

A great deal is still unknown. However, studies dealing with the endogenous pain-control system provide a neurohumoral basis for the behavioral and psychological control of pain. Ultimately, it might be possible to achieve the ideal non-addicting pain-control strategy, with the fewest side effects and complications, when we will be capable of behaviorally unlocking the body's own endogenous pain-control system.

Among the recent views of pain and its control, Lindahl (1974a, b) has proposed a biochemical theory. Since nerve function involves a metabolic mechanism, so too must pain have a metabolic background. The pain receptor may not be specific, but the stimulus should be. Lindhal proposes that pain is caused by an elevated hydrogen-ion concentration or acid pH in a nerve, or in the vicinity of a nerve or nerve-ending. In systematic laboratory tests, Lindahl found that the only factor found in concentration that elicited marked pain was the hydrogen-ion. In Lindhal's literature review, evidence was found to show that pus from painful septic abscesses was acid, while pus from painless turberculoces was neutral. Injection of alkaline or acid solutions into these abscesses could either abolish or provoke pain. Clinically, gastric ulcers, painful hematomas in fractures, malignant and aching tumors, and ischemic pain all have an acid pH or tissues with an acid pH. In rheumatoid arthritis, there probably is damage to cell membranes, so that acid metabolites escape extracellularly. This biochemical approach implies that pain control can be achieved by changes in pH.

Lindahl (1974b) has attempted treatment of rheumatoid arthritis type pain by changing the pH from acidic to alkaline. In one group of 81 patients, 69 percent showed marked improvement. In a second group of 50 patients, 52 percent showed improvement. In the latter group, urine acid pH was monitored. Subjective reports of improvement were found to shift with changes in urine acid pH.

These studies are not without their problems, however. It takes quite a long time (and it is not easy) to change acid pH. At this point, no double blind tests have yet been performed. Yet, this approach offers some promising new avenues in the understanding and control of pain.

4. THEORETICAL APPROACHES TO PAIN: PSYCHOLOGICAL APPROACHES

Following Sternbach (1968), no specific view is taken regarding monistic–dualistic views of the body. Linguistic paralellism is used instead. Sometimes it is easier to talk of pain in neurological–physiological terms, while at other times it is easier to talk of pain in psychological terms. Psychologically oriented theories have been written mainly to account for reactions to chronic pain that have been refractory to routine medical/dental treatment.

Engel (1959) has spoken of "psychogenic" pain and the pain-prone patient, based to a large extent upon his experience with atypical facial pain patients. In Engel's view, although pain can be viewed in neurophysiological terms, it is a psychological phenomenon. Pain perception may require an external stimulus at an early stage of development. However, with the development of a psychic organization for pain perception, the experience of pain no longer requires external stimulation, just as visual or auditory sensation can occur without sensory input. Such pain without external stimulation can be felt in some part of the body and from the patient's view is no different from pain based on external stimulation. Pain has special interpersonal meaning related to concepts of good and bad and success and failure. Pain becomes an important way of dealing with guilt.

According to Engel, pain-prone patients may show some or all of the following: (1) Conscious or unconscious guilt with pain providing atonement, (2) a background predisposing to use of pain as punishment, (3) a history of suffering, defeat, and intolerance of success, large numbers of painful injuries, operations, and treatment, (4) pain as a replacement for loss, or threat of loss of relationship, (5) a tendency toward a sado-masochistic type of sexual development, with pain occurring over sexual conflict, (6) pain location related to unconscious identification with a love object in which the pain either is the one suffered by the love object or is aroused by conflict with the love object, (7) psychiatric diagnoses include conversion hysteria, depression, hypochondriasis, or, occasionally, paranoid schizophrenia.

Szasz (1968) talks of pain as arising as a consequence of threatened loss of or damage to the body. The communication aspects of the pain are extremely important in understanding reactions to pain. At the first level, are the straightforward facts which the clinician requires to evaluate the physical symptom. The second level involves use of the pain complaint as a cry for help. It is tied to the first level. At the third level of communication, pain can be viewed as a symbol of rejection where the request for help has been frustrated. Pain complaints can become a form of aggression and a means of atoning for guilt.

In a later publication, Szasz (1968) refers to *l'homme douloureux* who has made a career out of his pain. Such individuals give up their former careers as attorneys, businessmen, models, etc., when they fail or are no longer sustained by them, to take on a career of suffering. It is the caretakers' responsibility to recognize such people and refrain from treating them, for the doctor can also help in the creation of a sick man. The career, chronic-pain patient does not wish to give up his suffering.

Merskey and Spear (1967) reviewed and evaluated these, as well as other psychiatric theories of pain, pointing to the difficulties involved in obtaining evidence to support them. They conclude that each approach has some value, but none of them is adequate to explain pain phenomena.

Based upon his own research, Merskey (1968) describes the modal psychiatric patient with pain as a lower-class married woman that possibly once was, but no longer is, pretty, has never been keen on sexual intercourse, has a history of repeated negative physical findings, and in many cases with conversion symptoms in addition to pain—a sad tale of a hard life and depression that does not respond to antidepressant drugs.

Anxiety, Hysteria, Hypochondriasis, Depression

Spear (1967) reported on the results of a study of pain in psychiatric patients. Pain as a symptom appeared with the highest incidence in patients with anxiety states. Pain is found in some 45–50 percent of psychiatric patients. Pain is associated with a history of surgical operations, other somatic symptoms, and overt anxiety. No association was found between pain and overt depression, overt agitation, and, in females, no association between pain and dysmenorrhea. Patients were grouped into those suffering from depressive illness and those suffering from anxiety/hysteria. Pain associated with depression showed a positive prognosis, while pain associated with anxiety/hysteria showed a poor prognosis, at least on a short-term basis.

Anxiety is a complex concept. It has been used to refer to a state based upon the particular environment in which the person finds himself at the moment (state anxiety). It has also been used to refer to a trait (trait anxiety), that is, to a personality attribute reflecting the status of the person generally (Spielberger, Gorsuch and Lushene, 1970). Paul and Bernstein (1973) refer to anxiety as a complex response involving subjective feelings of apprehension and tension, associated with sympathetic physiological arousal. Arousal can be due to an external source or to the memory of a past experience. In common with pain, anxiety is perceived as uncomfortable and it leads to behavior that will reduce it. When avoidance of the source of arousal is used as the means to reduce the anxiety, the anxiety reaction is usually strengthened (Mowrer, 1950; Bandura, 1969). If a patient, for example, has successfully avoided treatment because of anxiety, his avoidance response becomes strengthened and his anxiety reaction is likely to be greater when treatment can no longer be avoided.

Anxiety as a trait has been looked at in the laboratory, as well as the clinic. Sternbach (1968) has reviewed some of these studies and concluded, as have others, that the greater the anxiety, the greater will be the reaction to painful stimulation. However, anxiety is an ambiguous concept. It undoubtedly relates to the reaction to pain. How it relates to pain perception and reaction is still not clear.

In Merskey's (1965a, b) studies of psychiatric patients, pain was associated most frequently with neurosis, especially hysteria. It was relatively rare in schizophrenia or endogenous depression. Nearly all the pain patients were married, came from large families, had problems of frigidity and unsatisfactory sex lives, and showed a great deal of resentment toward others. They had an excess of bodily symptoms and a special concern with their bodies.

Pilling, Brannick and Swenson (1967) suggest that pain seems to function in place of anxiety and depression. Patients with pain presented less often with depression and anxiety. These patients may use pain or other organic symptoms in place of depression and anxiety.

Pilowsky, Chapman and Bonica (1977) found that pain-clinic patients yielded a low degree of depressive affect, with few patients showing a depressive syndrome. Perhaps the pain does function in place of depression. Pilowsky *et al.* (1977), however, prefer to emphasize the importance of a greater conviction of disease and somatic preoccupation, a reluctance to consider health problems in psychological terms, and a denial of life's problems. The Pilowsky *et al.* pattern is referred to as abnormal illness behavior (see later section).

These findings raise questions concerning the widespread use of antidepressant medication in pain control (cf., Sternbach, 1974). It is possible as Taub (1975) has argued, that although the medication is called antidepressant, its effectiveness in pain control has little to do with classically defined depression. Sternbach (1978) has suggested that the antidepressant medication affects pain indirectly, by working on the emotional concomitants of chronic pain. However, chemical agents that promote brain serotonin activity such as chlorimipramine may directly affect pain tolerance (Sternbach, Janowsky, Huey and Segal, 1976).

Sternbach (1974) deals with both psychogenic pain patients as well as with patients with organic lesions for whom surgery is not appropriate or from whom expressions of pain are greater than would be expected. Sternbach disagrees with Szasz regarding *l'homme douloureux*. Contrary to Szasz, Sternbach feels that the career pain patients do suffer terribly and would like to give up their suffering. Four classes of patients have been defined by Sternbach (1974) on the basis of their Minnesota Multiphasic Personality Inventory Profiles (MMPI). (1) The *hypochondriasis* pattern (highest on the Hypochondriasis scale) displays extreme somatic preoccupation. It is more common among somatogenic than psychogenic patients. It is possible that Szasz's *l'homme douloureux* would fit into this group. It should also be noted that hypochondriacal patients were classed as treatment failures in the pain-clinic program. (2) *Reactive depression* profiles consist of patients with high

Depression scores that are willing to admit that the pain has gotten them down. These patients respond well to antidepressant medication. (3) *Somatization* reaction profiles are associated with patients that present the psychosomatic V. They are high on the Hypochondriasis and Hysteria scales and relatively low on the Depression scale. These patients focus on bodily symptoms to avoid latent depression. This pattern occurs in both psychogenic and somatogenic pain patients. Such patients have adjusted to their pain and derive satisfaction from the sick role. Moderate treatment success has been obtained in this group. (4) *Manipulative reaction* profile patients have clear physical findings. They show an elevated Psychopathic Deviate scale. The patient uses his symptoms deliberately to manipulate others. This pattern was observed in a group of patients who have litigation pending.

Approaches that have tried to rely upon personality traits to predict a variety of pain syndromes have not been overly successful. The personality-trait approach suffers from lack of replication, use of similar nomenclature, but different measures, and often conflicting results. Many of these studies have been reviewed previously (Weisenberg, 1975; 1977).

Abnormal Illness Behavior

To deal with the various, and at times ambiguous, psychiatric terms used to describe the chronic-pain patient, Pilowsky and Spence (1975, 1976a, 1976b, 1976c) introduced the concept of *abnormal illness behavior*. Illness behavior refers to the way an individual perceives and reacts to symptoms of all kinds. Psychiatric syndromes such as hypochondriasis, conversion reaction, neurasthenia, malingering, etc. are all included under the concept *abnormal illness behavior*. There is an inappropriate reaction by the patient to his symptoms and to the careful explanation of his doctor. A factor analytic study of an Illness Behavior Questionnaire (IBQ) has yielded seven main factors. The first factor relates to a phobic concern about one's state of health. There is also an element of interpersonal alienation blaming others for difficulties. The second factor relates to a conviction of disease to the point of rejecting the doctor's opinion. Other factors relate to a somatic versus a psychological perception of illness, difficulty in expressing feelings, acknowledgement of anxiety and depression, admission of life problems and irritability. Chronic-pain patients can be classified according to their responses on this 62 Yes–No item scale. Patients with pain that did not respond to conventional treatment were found to be more convinced as to the presence of disease, more somatically preoccupied, and less likely to accept reassurance from the doctor. There was no relationship found between abnormal illness behavior and degree of organic pathology (Pilowsky and Spence, 1976a).

Pilowsky and Spence (1976b) demonstrated how the IBQ can be applied to sort patients with intractable pain who had reported to the pain service. Such a sorting can have important implications for treatment. Pilowsky and Spence's Group 1 patients may not be utilizing enough analgesics, while their Group 5 "masochistic depressives" might be better managed by the therapist using a pessimistic, rather than an optimistic approach.

Although none of these theoretical statements concerning pain is complete in and of itself, they all point to factors to be considered in evaluating a patient who presents for treatment. As Chapman (1977b) has pointed out, complaints of pain reflect not only tissue damage but a variety of dimensions of human suffering. With chronic pain, life problems and secondary gain for the invalid role become very important. Treatment is not usually accomplished by simple, technical intervention alone. Other considerations include medication habits, physical and social activity, and disturbed circadian or othe biological rhythms.

Cultural and Racial Reactions to Pain

Differences in the reaction to pain among cultural and social groups have received a substantial amount of study. They are important for many reasons. They indicate, first of all, that there is no "correct" way in which an individual should react to pain. They can affect clinical diagnosis and choice of treatment, as well as add to our understanding of pain processes. Zola (1966) and Marbach and Lipton (1978), for example, have shown that different cultural social groups present similar problems in a different manner. Differences in cultural attitudes also can affect psychophysical and autonomic functioning as demonstrated by Tursky and Sternbach (1967) and Sternbach and Tursky (1965) in their studies of reactions to the pain of electric shock.

The study of cultural reactions to pain can affect *stereotypes* based on lack of research or poor methodology. For instance, Chapman and Jones (1944) conducted a study of a "group of Norther European stock; the remainder included 25 Southern Negroes, 15 Ukrainians and 30 of Jewish and other Mediterranean races" (1944, page 81). All subjects were tested for pain perception and pain reaction threshold using radiant heat. Eighteen of the 25 Negroes perceived pain at a lower level and had tolerance levels closer to pain perception level than the Northern Europeans. The "Mediterranean races" were closer to the Negroes, although they were more apt to protest being subjected to so intense a stimulus.

These findings, or "myths" as Zborowski (1969) calls them, seem to have persisted for many years despite the obvious over generalizations made on the basis of "18 Southern Negroes" and an unspecified, but small, number of "Mediterranean types." More recent studies show different results. Merskey and Spear (1964) found no difference in pain reactions of 28 White and 11 Afro–Asian male medical students using the pressure algometer. Winsburg and Greenlick (1968) found no difference in rated pain reaction between Black and White obstetrical patients.

Many groups have been studied. These include Italians, Irish, Jews and Yankees (Zola, 1966; Zborowski, 1969; Sternbach and Tursky, 1965), Blacks (Chapman and Jones, 1944; Merskey and Spear, 1964; Woodrow, Friedman, Siegelaub and Collen, 1972; Weisenberg, Kreindler, Schachat and Werboff, 1975), Eskimos and Indians (Meehan, Stoll, and Hardy, 1954), Puerto Ricans (Weisenberg et al., 1975) and an assortment of anthropological studies of groups around the world (cf., Wolff and Langley, 1968).

Major differences among these groups seem to be related to the reactions or tolerance component of pain rather than to the threshold discrimination of the pain sensation as demonstrated in the Sternbach and Tursky (1965) study. Using magnitude estimation procedures, they found that ethnic group differences disappear (see section on measurement). Underlying attitudes and anxiety reactions appear to be a major source of these differences in pain tolerance. In a study of Black, White and Puerto Rican dental patients (Weisenberg et al., 1975), for example, use of four variables in a multiple discriminant analysis, two anxiety and two attitudinal, were adequate to permit correct groupings of 18 out of 24 Puerto Ricans, 12 out of 25 Blacks, and 16 out of 24 Whites. Significant differences among these groups were obtained on trait anxiety (Spielberger, Gorsuch and Lushene, 1970) and dental anxiety (Corah, 1969). Attitude differences were also obtained reflecting relative willingness either to deny or avoid dealing with the pain or to get rid of the pain. This is shown by response to such items as, "The best way to handle pain is to ignore it," or "It is a sign of weakness to give in to pain," or "When I am sick I want the doctor to get rid of the pain, even before he finds out what the trouble is." Puerto Rican patients showed the strongest endorsement of these items, the Whites the weakest; Blacks were in-between.

Weisenberg (in press) reviewed these studies and placed them into a theoretical framework. Differences in social–cultural reactions to pain can be viewed from a theory of social comparisons (Festinger, 1950, 1954). Basically, the theory states that there exists a drive to test the validity of a person's judgment and opinions of the outside world. When outside sensory means for evaluation are reduced, the individual turns toward his social environment for validation of his judgements. Since pain is a private ambiguous situation, comparison with others helps to determine what reactions are appropriate and how pain is to be communicated. Is it permissible to cry? Does one have to "grin and bear it"? When is it permissible to ask for help? When is it appropriate to mask the pain with analgesics? People learn to express their reactions by observing the reactions of others. The models chosen are those who are similar to oneself, while those too divergent are rejected (Bandura and Whalen, 1966). Craig (1978) has demonstrated how pain tolerance is subject to the social influence of models in a laboratory situation (see later section). Within cultural and racial groupings there is a greater similarity in the manner in which individuals communicate with each other.

Different meanings to stimuli can be fostered through social and cultural environmental factors. The social-influence process in turn can have a great effect on reactions to pain. Pain reactions can become reinforced independently of the original physiological sensation and tissue damage connotation. Members of cultural groups learn some sensations are to be tolerated; others are not. Some are labeled as painful; others are not. Knowledge of the different meanings of pain can serve as the basis for effective control and therapy.

5. MEASURING PAIN PHENOMENA

Whether referring to the laboratory or to the clinic, it is still vital to be able to measure pain phenomena. If an intervention occurs, its significance can only be properly assessed through sound measurement. In the clinic, physicians often ask the question, "Is the pain reaction appropriate to the presumed physical damage?" The latter question also implies an ability to measure separately individual components of the pain reaction.

Two points in the process of measurements have been singled out: (1) threshold and (2) tolerance. *Threshold* refers to the point where an individual first perceives the stimulation as painful. *Tolerance* refers to the point where the individual is not willing to accept stimulation of a higher magnitude or to continue to endure stimulation at a given level of intensity. Threshold has been associated mainly with physiological factors, whereas tolerance has been associated with psychological factors such as attitutde and motivation (Gelfand, Gelfand and Rardin, 1965).

Much of the data and many of the techniques used to elicit pain reactions has come from laboratory study. These techniques have clinical limitations. For example, laboratory type tests of pain threshold and pain tolerance preoperatively do not predict postoperative need for analgesics (Parbrook, Steel and Dalrymple, 1973). Beecher (1959, 1963, 1972) even has argued that it is not possible to equate laboratory pain with clinic pain produced by pathological processes. Whereas, in the clinic, morphine can be extremely effective in reducing pain reactions, in the laboratory, morphine cannot be distinguished from saline. Whereas, in the clinic, placebos are effective with approximately 35 percent of the cases, in the laboratory, this percentage is reduced to 3.2. The missing ingredient, in the laboratory, is the anxiety associated with the disease process and the threat of disfigurement or death. Reducing pain reactions in the clinic often involves reducing anxiety. The laboratory presents a different context in which the complexity of the pain response is partially ignored. It may not, thus, be possible to generalize results from the laboratory to the clinic.

However, even Beecher (1966) has admitted that there are laboratory procedures that he can accept. The slowly building-up pain of ischemia (Smith, Egbert, Markowitz, Mosteller, and Beecher, 1966; Smith, Lowenstein, Hubbard, and Beecher, 1968) or the use of the Tursky, Watson and O'Connell (1965) electrodes in electric shock stimulation have been accepted as effective pain stimuli (Smith, Parry, Denton and Beecher, 1970).

Sternbach (1974) has combined an ischemic pain measure with a verbal rating as part of his routine, clinical assessment of pain patients. The verbal scale asks the patient to rate his pain on a scale of 0 to 100, in which 0 is no pain at all and 100 is pain so severe that the patient would commit suicide, if he had to endure it for more than a minute or two. Submaximum tourniquet pain ratings are obtained for the point at which the pain equals the patient's current levels and for the maximum pain he can tolerate. A tourniquet ratio score is computed by dividing the time to reach clinical pain by the time to reach maximum tolerance and multiplying by 100. This score is compared to the verbal rating. Differences between ratings are shown to the patient and used as a part of the therapeutic procedure. A health provider is thus able to say with a little more confidence, "The pain really isn't that bad." Treatment can scmetimes increase the tourniquet pain ratio score by increasing patient activity and reducing drug intake; but the verbal rating could indicate successful treatment, as the patient learns to accept his pain condition. Recently, Timmermans and Sternbach (1976) have demonstrated that the verbal rating scale is associated with the perceived interference of pain with normal daily activities such as sleep, sex, etc. The ischemic measure of pain was found to be related to depression.

Electrical stimulation as developed by Tursky (1974, 1976, in press) offers several advantages over ischemic pain. The shock is easy to apply to any part of the body, without constraining the subject. The stimulus can be instantly turned off or on, at any level in the range, without going through lower levels of intensity. Extremely painful levels can be used, without causing irreversible tissue damage. Intensity of shock stimulation can be compared with intensity of clinical pain. Consistency of pain judgments is obtained by controlling skin impedance and using a constant stimulator. The Tursky approach distinguishes between the sensory and reactive components on the basis of the way the shock is rated.

To measure the sensory component a *magnitude estimation* procedure is used, in which a standard electric shock of say 30 volts is presented and given a numerical rating of 10. Other presentations of shock stimuli above and below the standard are rated by the subject who provides a numerical estimate in comparison to the standard. Results indicate that, with skin impedance anchored at 5,000 ohms, perceived shock intensities yield a power function.

To assess the reactive–motivational components of pain, Tursky asks subjects to indicate four levels of intensity as the shock intensity is raised: (1) sensation threshold, (2) discomfort, (3) pain and (4) tolerance.

The results of these procedures can be seen in the Sternbach and Tursky (1965) study of ethnic differences in reaction to pain. The reactive measures, in which subjects were asked to identify the points of sensation threshold, discomfort, pain, and tolerance, did yield ethnic differences. However, the magnitude estimation approach did not yield ethnic differences, thus showing that the sensory evaluation of the shocks did not differ as a function of ethnic grouping.

The recent application of *signal detection* or *sensory decision* theory to the measurement of pain reactions is another method of sorting out the sensory component (d') from the criterion used to judge the stimulus as painful (Lx) (Clark, 1974, Chapman, 1978). In assessing pain control techniques, it becomes possible to know whether the effects are on the basic sensory component, or on the attitudinal–motivational component of pain. The analysis developed to sort signal from noise requires many more stimuli than the magnitude estimation procedure of Tursky and is mainly useful in the laboratory where the stimulus input is clearly defined. Clark (1974) has hypothesized that pain thresholds raised by placebos, redirection of attention, hypnosis and such, represent a response bias based on a reluctance to report pain (Lx) rather than a change in the sensory perception of the pain stimulus (d'). By contrast, a mixture of nitrous oxide administered for a duration sufficient to produce analgesic properties produces a change in the neural activity of the sensory system (d').

Clinically, attitude change can be very important. As indicated earlier, Beecher (1972) has argued that analgesic drugs work mostly by affecting attitude and subject predisposition to complain about pain. Morphine, for example, is described as not affecting the sensation of pain as much as the reaction to it. The patient may feel the pain, but is unconcerned. In chronic-pain treatment, the practitioner may be at a loss regarding his ability to eliminate the patient's pain. Treatment consists of teaching the patient to live and function despite the pain (cf., Fordyce, 1976).

The application of signal detection theory to pain phenomena has become a source of controversy. Rollman (1976, 1977, 1979) has argued that d' does not measure sensory pain phenomena such that a reduction in d' need not indicate a reduction in experienced pain. In turn, a reduction of experienced pain need not indicate a reduction of d'. Lx cannot be said to be a measure of emotional change associated with pain. Rollman argues that signal detection theory at best can tell whether one stimulus is discriminable from another, but this is not the same as measuring sensitivity. Furthermore, a powerful analgesic need not cause a lack of discrimination of adjacent stimulus levels to be effective from a sensory point of view. It is possible for both stimuli to shift downward. In turn, inability to discriminate adjacent levels does not mean severe pain has been relieved. Pain cannot be equated with discrimination.

Chapman (1977a) dismisses much of Rollman's criticism as based upon an inaccurate view of how pain researchers have used signal detection theory. Differences in results between laboratories using signal detection theory are related to differences in methodology, as well as to other different parameters studied, more than to the inconsistency of signal detection theory. Despite Chapman's strong defense of signal detection theory, Wolff (1978) is of the opinion that Rollman raises questions showing the need for further clarification of the meaning of d' and Lx especially at high levels of pain intensity.

Clinically, pain is described mostly in verbal terms. Pain can be described as burning, aching, stabbing, splitting, pounding, nagging, cramping, etc. Pain can also be intolerable, unbearable, awful, distressing, excruciating, severe, etc. To understand the relationships between these different expressions of pain, Melzack and Torgerson (1971) and Melzack (1975) developed a pain scale, the McGill Pain Questionnaire. They categorized 102 pain terms into three classes: (1) Sensory quality descriptors in terms of temporal, spatial, pressure, thermal, and other properties, e.g., pounding, spreading, crushing, burning, aching, etc. (2) Affective quality descriptors in terms of tension, fear and autonomic properties, e.g., exhausting, awful, nauseating, etc. (3) Evaluative terms that describe the intensity of the total experience, e.g., agonizing, excruciating, miserable, etc.

Each term was judged by groups of 20 judges to determine the degree of agreement of classification. Intensity relationships within classes were then judged by 140 students, 20 physicians and 20 patients. Substantial agreement was obtained in classifying the many different terms used to describe pain.

Development of descriptor scales can make possible meaningful clinical questionnaires using terms that are spaced appropriately. It becomes possible to say a *strong* pain is almost twice as great as a *moderate* pain, while an *excruciating* pain is more than four times as great (Tursky, 1976). Melzack and Torgerson (1971) and Melzack (1975) suggest that, when used with spatial and temporal variables, it should be possible to categorize reliably distinct pain syndromes, as found in the various disease classifications, so that more appropriate diagnosis and treatment could be performed. Dubuisson and Melzack (1976), using the McGill Pain Questionnaire, were able to demonstrate differences among constellations of words for eight clinical syndromes. Eight diagnostic categories were developed on the basis of which 77 percent of the patients were correctly classed. When information such as sex, age, spatial location of pain, and analgesic drugs was added to the verbal descriptions, 100 percent of the patients were correctly classed.

A variety of studies have been performed using the McGill Pain Questionnaire or techniques similar to it. Agnew and Merskey (1976) examined the complaints of patients with chronic pain of organic or psychiatric origin. Sensory–thermal descriptions (hot, burning) were more frequently used by patients with organic diagnoses. Female patients with pain complaints attributed to anxiety used more sensory–temporal words (throbbing, beating) than other female patients. Those with a mixed psychiatric–organic pain complaint, compared to organic patients, used more affective–tension words (nagging, tiring). Boyd and Merskey (1978) found that most adjectives used by psychiatric patients to describe their pain were primarily sensory, rather than affective or evaluative. Reading and Newton (1977) were able to separate patients with dysmenorrhea from those with IUD related pain. A larger sensory component was found to be prominent among IUD users while an affective component predominated among patients with dysmenorrhea. Crockett, Prkachin and Craig (1977) studied low back patients and a group of volunteers. They demonstrated overlap with the three major dimensions of pain found by Melzack and Torgerson (1971). However, Crockett et al. obtained five dimensions, suggesting a finer breakdown of categories.

Van Buren and Kleinknecht (1979) examined pain reports following oral surgery. The McGill Pain Questionnaire was found to reflect accurately recovery time and increased use of narcotics. Overlap was found among the sensory, evaluative and affective subscales. State anxiety was found to be more strongly related to the evaluative and sensory subscale than to the affective subscale that was designed to measure fear, tension, and autonomic aspects of the pain experienced.

Baily and Davidson (1976) have shown that the intensity rating of pain accounts for far less of the variance than has previously been assumed. Once more, sensory adjectives were found to be related to the affective–evaluative adjectives. A physician may therefore have difficulty determining pain intensity by simply relying upon intensity terms alone.

Contrary to earlier assumptions (cf., Melzack, 1975), Hunter, Philips and Rachman (1979) were able to demonstrate using the McGill Pain Questionnaire that recall of pain by neurosurgical patients was accurate over a five-day period. Those who made errors were women with initially high levels of pain and affect. In general, overall intensity was more accurately recalled than the more subtle sensory and affective qualities.

Studies of the McGill Pain Questionnaire or instruments similar to it are an encouraging step in the right direction. Additional research obviously will be required to clarify, sort, and replicate findings. There are, however, those who might argue that use of scales such as the McGill Pain Questionnaire would be most appropriate for patients with good verbal skills, but not for those without such skills (cf., Wolff, 1978).

One approach that has been used to overcome language barriers is the visual analogue scale. As described by Wolff (1978), a visual analogue scale is a straight line whose ends are fixed by a statement of the extreme limits of the sensation to be measured e.g., No Pain–Excruciating Pain. The visual analogue scale has been found to be sensitive to changes in pain as a result of anesthetic. Scott and Huskisson (1976) report that visual analogue or graphic rating scales can readily be used by patients without any previous experience. These authors recommend these scales as the best available method for measuring pain or its relief.

Related Clinical Measures

Factors other than the description of the pain itself enter into the evaluation of the patient. Merskey (1974) recommends inclusion of an assessment of patient personality, as well as an assessment of severity of pain and responses of the patient to stimuli. For chronic-pain patients a widely used personality measure is the MMPI mentioned earlier (Sternbach, 1974). Test administration is easy, although it requires time on the part of the patient. Computer scoring and interpretation are also readily available for it. Even hand scoring requires no more than twenty minutes. The Pilowsky and Spence (1976) measure of illness behavior (see earlier section) is another easily administered scale that can be extremely useful in guiding choice of clinical treatment.

When dealing with the chronic-pain patient, Sternbach (1974) recommends careful observation of the manner in which the patient responds, as well as attention to what is said. Does the patient demand, whine, flatter, etc.? What emotional response does the patient elicit from the interviewer—bravery, sympathy, irritation, etc.? Major areas of information that are useful in understanding the role of the pain in the patient's life and secondary gain related to the pain include: (1) Evaluation of the patient's home and work environment. (2) A careful assessment of the patient's medication history. (3) Involvement of litigation and an evaluation of how the patient would live if he did not have the pain.

Chapman (1977b), in addition, asks the patient to maintain a diary of what he does at home, hour by hour, for several days. Important aspects of the diary are the amount of active versus passive (resting, reclining) time, changes in sleep patterns, sexual activity, and social activity.

6. INTERVENTION STRATEGIES

A number of approaches have been effectively demonstrated for reducing the reactions both to acute and chronic pain. Much of this literature has been reviewed earlier (cf., Weisenberg, 1975; 1977). Some of these strategies will be briefly mentioned in this section.

Suggestion and Placebo Phenomena

Placebo responsiveness has been well documented throughout the literature. Beecher (1972) has shown that 35 percent of patients with pathological pain will obtain pain relief with placebos. The greater the anxiety, the greater is the relief from placebo medication. Placebo relief seems to be based partially on the unwritten contract between doctor and patient that states the doctor is going to do all he can to relieve the patient's suffering. If he (the doctor) believes the treatment will work and the patient leaves with the expectation that it will work, the anxiety is relieved and the patient seems to heal himself.

Evans (1974a) has analyzed placebo treatment data collected by McGlashan, Evans and Orne (1969) as a function of chronic or state anxiety. Placebo reaction that resulted in increased pain tolerance was associated with state anxiety reduction. This result was especially notable for chronic anxiety subjects. Increased anxiety following the ingestion of the placebo drugs resulted in decreased pain tolerance. In an earlier paper, Evans (1967) did not find placebo reactors to be associated with personality measures of suggestibility.

Evans (1974b) reports the relative efficiency of placebos to drugs such as morphine, Darvon or aspirin as 0.54–0.56. That is, a placebo is 56 percent as effective as morphine. The effectiveness of a placebo is directly proportional to the active analgesic agent to which it is being compared. Placebo is usually more effective in relieving severe pain, The properties of the placebo mimic the drug to which it is being compared. Effects of the placebo and the comparison drug usually interact and are additive. Higher placebo dosages are more effective than lower doses. Injections are more effective than orally given placebos. Placebos are also more effective when described to patients as a powerful drug than when described as an experimental drug. They are more effective when given by a health provider who is more likely to use drugs.

Laskin and Greene (1972) demonstrated the effectiveness of a placebo capsule dispensed by prescription and enhanced by a suggestive name. Twenty-six of fifty patients (52 percent) with myofascial pain dysfunction (MPD) syndrome reported improvement in their condition, with symptoms of pain and tenderness affected most. Long-term (6 months to 8 years) evaluation of patients indicated no difference between those who positively responded to placebo therapy or other forms of therapy. Only six out of a hundred patients followed-up for a variety of different therapies reported that their MPD problem was not under control (Greene and Laskin, 1974).

The doctor–patient relationship is an important element in the effectiveness of placebo therapy. It is important to realize, however, that placebos do not depend only upon drugs. Goodman, Greene and Laskin (1976) demonstrated that two mock tooth equilibrations for MPD were effective in producing total or near total remission of symptoms in sixteen (64 percent) out of twenty-five patients. Thirteen of the patients for whom follow-up was possible remained symptom free 6–29 months later. Successfully treated patients actually did have a variety of tooth occlusal surface disharmonies that remained untreated. Goodman, Greene and Laskin argue that it is the strong positive suggestion that is likely to be responsible for the success of those who provide routine occlusal therapy for MPD.

That expectation of relief influence outcome was demonstrated in a controlled study of audioanalgesia. Melzack, Weisz and Sprague (1963) were able to demonstrate that auditory stimulation did not abolish cold pressor pain. They compared three groups of subjects. Group 1 received strong auditory stimulation, but no suggestion about the purpose of the music and noise. Group 2 received strong auditory stimulation, together with strong suggestions of effectiveness. Group 3 received strong suggestion, but only a low-frequency hum rather than strong auditory stimulation. Each group served as its own control, having received cold pressor stimulation without any sound prior to group assignment. Group 2 produced a substantial increase in pain tolerance while neither Group 1 or Group 3 did in comparison to their control stimulation periods. What the audio stimulation did was divert attention away from cold pressor pain, when accompanied by strong suggestion. Therefore, in the hands of a practitioner who could relate well to his patients, it was effective. For practitioners who could not build up expectations of effectiveness, it did not work.

Melzack and Perry (1975) built upon these results in a clinical study of alpha training, hypnosis, and suggested benefits. Three groups of chronic-pain patients were compared. Group 1 was provided with alpha training, with explicit suggestions that it would help control pain. Patients were also given hypnotic training that included progressive relaxation and ego strengthening instructions. Group 2 was provided with the hypnotic training only, while Group 3 was given the alpha training only. Results indicated that the combination hypnosis–alpha training significantly relieved pain from the baseline measures. Fifty-eight percent of the patients reported a decrease in pain of 39 percent or greater. Hypnosis alone achieved substantial, but statistically insignificant, change from baseline while alpha alone was ineffective. The authors interpret the combined procedure as consisting of alpha training as a distractor of attention, combined with relaxation, suggestion, and a sense of control over pain. The increase in percentage alpha production alone, a measure often used to indicate relaxation, was not adequate.

Hypnosis

How do suggestion and placebo phenomena relate to hypnosis? To answer this question requires a clarification of the meaning and effects of hypnosis. There is little doubt that, regardless of the theoretical arguments concerning the reality of hypnosis, it is an effective technique to be used for pain control.

Chaves and Barber (1974) have stressed that many of the claims of hypnosis are based on a readiness on the part of the individual to accept suggestions and not on some magical trance powers that certain individuals possess to influence others. Many experimental studies of hypnosis do not assess the contributions of the separate variables they use in obtaining effects. There are suggestions that certain physiological effects will occur. Instructions are given to maximize motivation to accept suggestion. Suggestions are given for relaxation. Subjects are asked to close their eyes, etc. Each of these variables contributes to produce a person who is highly motivated to accept suggestion, without postulating that a separate state has been attained. Much of what is done under hypnosis could also be done with the waking individual.

Barber and Hahn (1962), for example, asked subjects to immerse their hands in 2°C water for three minutes. One group received hypnotic induction and suggestions of hand anesthesia. A second group was asked to imagine a pleasant situation. A third group was simply exposed to the painful stimulation, while a fourth group was asked to immerse in water at room temperature. The hypnotic or pleasant-imagery groups did not yield differences either on subjective reports of pain on four physiological measures. Both were equally effective in reducing subjective pain reports, respiratory irregularities, and forehead muscle tension compared to the non-instructed controls. However, compared to the room-temperature group the hypnotic-analgesia and pleasant-imagery groups reported higher levels of pain and showed elevated levels of skin conductance and faster heart rates.

Although Barber and Chaves have accomplished a great deal in changing hypnosis from the status of magic to science, many investigators disagree with their conclusions and regard hypnosis as a real phenomenon.

Hilgard (1973) has approached hypnosis on the basis of different levels of consciousness. There seem to be different systems of cognitive functioning, so that, even
though the pain stimulus is able to reach one level of consciousness, it is blocked
from the more immediate level of awareness. That is, the person does perceive the
pain stimulus at some lower level, when the "hidden observer" is asked if it is
painful. However, he is capable of keeping it from coming to the level of awareness
that makes it distressing.

From a Melzack and Wall (1970) point of view, both Barber and Hilgard stress
the effects of hypnosis on the motivational–affective system of pain control. Both
view hypnosis as producing an increased readiness to respond to suggestion.
Chaves and Barber feel that there is no such thing as a trance state. Little is to be
gained over the "waking" state by use of hypnotic induction techniques. Hilgard,
however, does feel that there is a state called hypnosis and that there are response
differences in the individual when he is hypnotized or awake. Orne (1974), too, feels
that hypnosis is a phenomenon which cannot be explained away by saying that
subjects are trying to please the experimenter. Clinically, inducements would be
hard to find to convince unhypnotizable subjects to undergo major surgery merely
to please the surgeon.

Hypnosis seems to be most effective when there is the presence of anxiety. Shor
(1962) found that without anxiety he could not distinguish between hypnotic and
faking subjects in reaction to electric shock on six physiological variables. Both
placebo and hypnotic treatments seem to involve suggestion, expectation of successful outcome and anxiety relief. It would seem, therefore, that they might be the
same. However, McGlashan, Evans and Orne (1969) have demonstrated that hypnotic reactions contain placebo reactions plus something more. A group of highly
hypnotically susceptible subjects and a group of non-hypnotizable subjects were
each exposed to three separate treatments while undergoing ischemic muscle pain.
The first session involved baseline reactions. The second session involved hypnotic
analgesia, while the third was a placebo drug given under double-blind conditions.
Placebo and hypnotic reactions were uncorrelated for the highly susceptible subjects, while for the non-hypnotized subjects they were highly correlated. Hypnosis
has a placebo component. However, it also produces a greater effect in response to
the suggestion that subjects will not experience pain.

Relaxation, Biofeedback, Desensitization

Both relaxation and desensitization procedures have become widely accepted as
a means of reducing anxiety and eliminating fear. Desensitization, or systematic
desensitization as referred to by Wolpe (1969), involves the pairing of anxiety-
arousing stimuli with relaxation or other anxiety-countering procedures. These
countering procedures serve to reduce the anxiety arousal. The attempt is to substitute relaxation for arousal, one response for another, and is referred to as *counter-
conditioning*. To the extent to which anxiety and pain are related, reducing anxiety
also reduces the reaction to pain. Wolpe (1969) has suggested further that relaxation is antagonistic to the elicitation of anxiety. A person cannot be relaxed and
anxious at the same time. It would follow, therefore, that relaxation should increase
pain tolerance.

Folkins, Lawson, Opton and Lazarus (1968) demonstrated that both cognitive rehearsal and relaxation were effective in reducing reactions to a stressor film, but cognitive rehearsal was slightly superior. Paul (1969) found that both hypnosis and relaxation training reduced anxiety. Similarly, Bobey and Davidson (1970) also found relaxation yielded increased tolerance for radiant heat and pressure algometer pain.

Gessel and Adlerman (1971) have taught relaxation to patients with myofascial-pain-dysfunction syndrome (MPD). MPD patients, who have facial pain because of overactivity of the masticatory muscles, appear to have higher chronic levels of muscle tension. Jacobsonian relaxation was taught in from one to twenty-seven sessions. Six out of eleven patients, those with an absence of depression, showed good results. Patients with depression were not helped.

Sherman, Gall and Gormly (1979) reported that fourteen out of sixteen phantom limb patients were either completely or partially relieved from pain, following a combined treatment of reassurance, progressive muscle relaxation, and biofeedback from the stump and forehead. Follow-up studies of up to three years indicated that the treatment remained effective.

Relaxation can be an effective procedure for increasing pain tolerance. However, experimental results indicate that it is not always an effective procedure (cf., Lehrer, 1972). The conditions under which it should optimally affect pain reaction must be clarified. A better understood definition of how anxiety affects pain will probably also clarify the role of relaxation.

Cognitive Dissonance, Attribution Theory and the Principles of Learning

Zimbardo, Cohen, Weisenberg, Dworkin and Firestone (1966, 1969) tested derivations from the theory of cognitive dissonance to show how commitment choice and justification can affect pain reactions. The theory states that when an individual experiences one or more behaviors or cognitions that are dissonant with each other a tension state is established that motivates the person to reduce dissonance (Festinger, 1957). When a person knows that electric shock is painful and yet of his own free choice commits himself to endure more electric shock, he has acted to create dissonance. Dissonance can be reduced by increasing the justification for the commitment or by reducing the perception of the shock as not being so painful. Subjects were tested in a two-part experiment. All subjects were asked to learn lists of words by serial anticipation. Part I consisted of the learning task with painful electric shock given randomly to all subjects, except those in one control group. Part II involved commitment to continue the study for either high justification (lo dissonance) or low justification (hi dissonance). Control subjects were either given shock at the same painful level in Part I or were given shock at a lower level. A third control group received a low level of shock in both Parts I and II. Dependent measures consisted of verbal ratings of shock, skin conductance, and number of learning trials to criterion. On all three measures, hi dissonance subjects performed comparably to the control group that was given shock at a lowered level, while lo dissonance subjects performed like the control group that had high shock levels maintained in Part II. Cognitive controls, thus, acted in the same way as physically changing the stimulation.

Attribution theory states that people seek causes or explanations for the observed events that take place around them. Davidson and Valins (1969) showed how pain tolerance can be increased when subjects are taught to attribute pain-tolerance changes to their own efforts as opposed to the effects of a pill. Subjects were first tested for shock pain tolerance after which they were given a "drug" and retested with the shock physically reduced. Half the subjects were told that they had been given a placebo. All subjects were then retested. Those subjects who were told that they had received a placebo and hence were able to attribute their behavior change to their own efforts, tolerated more shock on the last trial than those who thought they had received a drug and thus attributed their improved ability to tolerate pain to the medication.

Attribution of control as due to internal rather than external factors has been used as a key factor in the treatment of low back pain patients (Gottlieb, Hockersmith, Koller and Strite, 1975). Patients with low back pain exhibit a learned helplessness, as a result of their disability, which tends to become reinforced by masses of medication and dependency on others. Patients are taught self-regulation rather than drug regulation for dealing with their problems as part of a comprehensive treatment program.

Fordyce (1976, 1978) utilized techniques based on learning principles to deal with pain reactions based on learned helplessness in their treatment program for chronic pain. Verbalizing by means of moans asking for help, bodily movements etc. are all behaviors that can be affected by learning. Major changes in behavior and life style can occur as a consequence of the length of time people endure chronic pain. The program is aimed at the elimination of pain behavior and the restoration of effective well-behaviors. Emphasis is placed upon increased activity levels, reduction of pain behavior leading to protective actions by others, reduced pain medication consumption, remediation of social skills and interpersonal problems, and a modification of the reinforcing contingencies to pain and well-behavior. On a 22-month follow-up of thirty-one patients treated, Fordyce, Fowler, Lehmann, Delateur, Sand and Treischman (1973) found that measures of reduction in perceived pain, interference of pain with normal activities, and the reduction in reclining time remained significantly changed from preadmission, but not significantly changed from time of discharge.

Control and Choice

A variety of studies have shown how control over the pain situation can reduce subject stress and pain reactions. Bowers (1968) has argued that lack of control increases anxiety and hence results in larger pain and stress reactions. Subjects informed prior to shock-tolerance measurement that they would be able to avoid electric shock tolerated it at a level of more than twice as high as those who thought shock was random. Post-experimental ratings of shock painfulness did not differ for each group.

Staub, Tursky and Schwartz (1971) related control to predictability. Uncertainty increases anxiety and results in less pain-tolerance, while reduction of uncertainty increases tolerance. Subjects given control over the intensity and timing of shocks tolerated higher levels of shock before rating them as uncomfortable, compared to no-control subjects. Loss of control, after it had been given to subjects, resulted in lower intensities of shock being rated as uncomfortable. No-control subjects produced large heart-rate responses at all levels of intensity, while control subjects made more differentiated responses, reacting mainly to the most intense shocks.

Clinically, Keeri-Szanto (1979) has described a technique whereby post-surgical patients are permitted to control the administration of their own narcotic medications. Demand analgesia avoids the difficulties that occur clinically. The required prescription has to be written, once the patient indicates a need for pain relief, The nurse must be summoned and convinced the patient "really" is in pain and the drug must be signed out from the locked cabinet. The time it takes for the drug to be absorbed after injection also must be included. By the time all of the above has occurred, the drug level for which relief was originally requested is no longer the same and the pain has intensified. In contrast, with a demand system patients do not abuse the amount of drug used. It was also possible to identify approximately 20 percent of the patients who were placebo responders and for whom lesser concentrations of narcotic were indicated.

The issue of control and predictability as with other areas of pain perception is not entirely clear. Corah (1973) tried to replicate a study showing that a control device introduced into the dental operatory would produce more cooperative behavior. Twenty-four children ages 6–11 were provided with a two button green–red light device to use during treatment. The control-device group showed less response to high arousal procedures as measured by GSR and slightly more response during low arousal procedures compared to a no-control group. Behavioral ratings of each group did not differ. These results are not entirely clear regarding the effectiveness of control.

In an analysis of control as a variable, Averill (1973) shows that it has been used to refer to behavioral control, cognitive control or decisional control. He states that it is difficult to conclude that there is a direct relationship between stress and control. Other factors that must be considered include the presence or absence of feedback that tells the subject how well he is controlling, the subject's ability to tolerate the information necessary for control, and what appears as larger short-term stress reactions but long-term adaptation.

It seems that control is an important variable in pain reduction. However, who should be given the control e.g., patient or health provider, may vary depending upon the goals or circumstances. Long-term gain may require greater immediate arousal as seen in the literature on preparation for surgery.

Advanced Preparation for Pain

Preparation for surgery has been credited with reducing severity of post-operative outcomes. Egbert, Battit, Welch and Bartlett (1964) prepared one group of patients by a pre-operative visit. They were told about the preparation for anesthesia, the time and approximate duration of the operation, and warned that they would wake-up in the recovery room. They were also told they would feel pain, how severe it might be, and how long it would last. The patients were reassured that feeling pain was normal after abdominal surgery and that there were ways by which they would be able to cope with the surgery through relaxation procedures, by use of a trapeze and by instructions on how to turn their bodies. They also could ask for medication if it was needed. Compared to a control group, the specially instructed patients requested significantly less narcotic following surgery and were sent home an average of 2.7 days earlier.

Baldwin and Barnes (1966) studied 8–14 year old patients who had to undergo dental extraction. One group of subjects was given from four to seven days between the time of the announcement of the extraction and the extraction itself, while a second group was not notified until the day of the event itself. While both groups showed a stress reaction, as measured by a figure-drawing constriction prior to surgery, the waiting-period group showed an increase in figure-drawing size post-surgery, while the no-waiting period group remained constricted and began to show an increase in figure size only in the follow-up period, one month later.

What are the crucial ingredients that go into patient preparation? Janis (1958) has emphasized anxiety. There is an optimal relationship between the amount of suffering expected and the amount obtained, which seems conducive to a feeling of mastery of a difficult situation and to speed of recovery. The optimal degree of worry or anxiety prior to the stressful event is best reached when the patient receives realistic information and is able to listen and accept what is being told to him. This occurs when the patient experiences a moderate level of anxiety. The credibility of the practitioner is enhanced and the patient is helped to prepare for the event. The moderate-fear group in the Janis study had been better informed prior to surgery and felt worried before surgery. Fewer in this group became angry, resentful, or emotionally upset, following surgery. They had time to build up psychological defenses prior to surgery. Without the "work of worrying," Janis describes a different sequence of events. There is little anticipatory fear. Thus, there is no mental rehearsal of the impending danger. Lack of rehearsal results in feelings of helplessness when the danger manifests itself. In turn, this results in feelings of disappointment in protective authorities, intense fear, anger, and "victimization"— the sense of deprivation, loss, and suffering from a stressful experience.

Unfortunately, subsequent studies have not supported Janis's emphasis on fear and anxiety. Cohen and Lazarus (1973) have emphasized the importance of coping strategies in dealing with the stress of surgery. Unlike Janis, they feel that denial would be a beneficial strategy to use, when the outcome is expected to be positive. Melamed (1977), in a recent review of the preparation literature, reports some support of the Janis hypothesis, but this support is not unequivocal.

What the critical ingredients are still requires greater clarification. A period of advanced notice with prior information and coping techniques, however, does seem to help (Johnson, Dabbs, Leventhal, 1970). The amount of detail, the temporal spacing of information, and the personality disposition of the subject will also affect the outcome (Andrew, 1970; DeLong, 1970). Copers (those who attempt to deal with stress) and those called non-specific defenders (those who use both coping and avoiding strategies) seem to be able to accept more detailed information than avoiders (those who try to deny or avoid dealing with stress) (DeLong, 1970).

Information regarding the sensations to be experienced seems to be more effective in reducing distress than information regarding the procedures to be used (Johnson, 1973; Johnson and Leventhal, 1974). For example, Johnson, Kirchoff and Endres (1975), in a study of cast removal, found that children exposed to a brief tape recording, which included the sound of the saw and a description of the sensations of heat, flying chalk, etc. showed less distress and resistance to the procedure, compared to a group only told of the procedure or not told at all.

Melamed (1977) has also stressed the need to consider variables such as the patient's age and the timing of the advanced preparation. Less time in advance is desirable for younger children. Reducing parental feelings of anxiety has also been found to have a positive effect on the child patient.

Modeling

Modeling refers to the notion that a person can anticipate the consequences of a behavior, without having to experience it personally. Bandura (1971) is of the opinion that most learning occurs via modeling, rather than on a trial and error basis. Craig (1978) has recently done an extensive analysis of social modeling influences on pain, presenting data both from the laboratory and from the clinical setting. Melamed (1977) has summarized evidence of the overriding influence of modeling processes in preparing children for surgery.

In a series of studies, Craig and his co-workers showed how modeling can be used to change the ratings subjects give to electric-shock stimulation. Craig and Weiss (1971) had subjects rate the intensity of incremental shocks when observing the rating of a confederate model. In one condition, the model tolerated a great deal of shock before labelling it as painful, while in a second condition he tolerated a great deal less before terming it painful. The high tolerance group of subjects rated as painful shock of a mean intensity of 8.65 milliamperes. The control subjects yielded a mean of 6.35 milliamperes. The low-tolerance group rated a mean of 2.50 milliamperes as painful, some 70 percent less intense than the high-tolerance group. Furthermore, Craig and Neidermayer (1974) were not able to demonstrate any heart-rate or skin-conductance differences between high- and low-tolerance groups. The authors claim that this shows that the subjects were not merely masking subjective discomfort. However, it is possible that the physiological indicators were not adequately discriminative to show differences. Yet, Craig (1978) has reviewed evidence suggesting that modeling procedures affect pain sensitivity as assessed both by sensory decision analysis and magnitude estimation. Further evaluation of these effects is in order.

Another study (Craig and Weiss, 1972) complemented the earlier work by using a constant nonaversive shock. Each one of a group of subjects was paired with a model who rated the nonaversive shocks as increasingly painful. Compared to a control group, the model-paired subjects began to report ratings of painful to shock levels usually judged as nonaversive.

From both the clinical and experimental literature it is clear that modeling is a potent method for affecting the reaction to pain. It is one way of providing advanced information as to what will occur during treatment. It also permits the patient to see how someone who is similar to himself can cope with the treatment without excess anxiety and stress reaction. Models should have some degree of similarity to the patient and should give a fairly realistic reaction, not suppress all response (Vernon, 1974).

7. CONCLUDING COMMENT

Recent years have seen an increased concern for the control of pain and anxiety. New techniques, as well as a variety of older available approaches, have received prominence. Current views perceive pain as a complex phenomenon that includes a sensory and a motivational component. The motivational component has the stronger association with suffering. It includes memories of past experiences and involves a strong element of interpersonal communication. Chronic and acute pain phenomena may require different approaches.

Chronic-pain control has been linked to depression and helplessness, while acute-pain control has been strongly linked to the presence of anxiety. Behavioral strategies mainly influence the motivational component of pain. They can effectively be used to deal with both pain and anxiety. Behavioral techniques include suggestion, relaxation, placebos, biofeedback, desensitization, hypnosis, distraction, advanced preparation, modeling, as well as a variety of cognitive strategies. Their effectiveness as techniques is lessened by automatic machine-like application and is greatly potentiated by interpersonal factors. It behooves the psychologist to take his role as a full partner on the pain-control team.

REFERENCES

Agnew, D. C. and Merskey, H. (1976) Words of chronic pain, *Pain*, **2**, 73–81.
Andrew, J. M. (1970) Recovery from surgery with and without preparatory instruction for three coping styles, *Journal of Personality and Social Psychology*, **15**, 223–226.
Averill, J. R. (1973) Personal control over aversive stimuli and its relationship to stress, *Psychological Bulletin*, **80**, 286–303.
Bailey, C. A. and Davidson, P. O. (1976) The language of pain: intensity, *Pain*, **2**, 319–324.
Baldwin, D. C. Jr. and Barnes, M. L. (1966) The psychological value of a presurgical waiting period in the preparation of children for dental extraction, *Transactions of the European Orthodontic Society*, 1–12.
Bandura, A. (1969) *Principles of Behavior Modification*, Holt Rhinehart and Winston, New York.
Bandura, A. (1971) Analysis of modeling processes, in Bandura, A., (Ed.) *Psychological Modeling*, Aldine-Atherton, Chicago, Ill.
Bandura, A. and Whalen, C. K. (1966) The influence of antecedent reinforcement and divergent modeling cues on patterns of self-reward, *Journal of Personality and Social Psychology*, **3**, 373–382.
Barber, T. X. and Hahn, K. W. Jr. (1962) Physiological and subjective responses to pain producing stimulation under hypnotically-suggested and waking-imaged "analgesia", *Journal of Abnormal and Social Psychology*, **65**, 411–418.
Beecher, H. K. (1956) Relationship of significance of wound to the pain experienced, *Journal of the American Medical Association*, **161**, 1609–1613.
Beecher, H. K. (1959) *Measurement of Subjective Responses: Quantitive Effects of Drugs*, Oxford University Press, New York.
Beecher, H. K. (1963) Quantification of the subjective pain experience, *Proceedings of the American Psychopathological Association*, **53**, 111–128.
Beecher, H. K. (1966) Pain: one mystery solved, *Science*, **151**, 840–841.
Beecher, H. K. (1972) The placebo effect as a non-specific force surrounding disease and the treatment of disease, in Janzen, R., Keidel, W. D., Herz, A., Steichele, C., Payne, J. P., and Burt, R. A. P. (Eds.) *Pain: Basic Principles, Pharmacology, Therapy*, Georg Thieme, Stuttgart.
Bobey, M. J. and Davidson, P. O. (1970) Psychological factors affecting pain tolerance, *Journal of Psychosomatic Research*, **14**, 371–376.
Bonica, J. J. and Albe-Fessard D. (Eds) (1976) *Advances in Pain Research and Therapy*, Vol. 1, Raven Press, New York.
Bowers, K. S. (1968) Pain, anxiety and perceived control, *Journal of Consulting and Clinical Psychology*, **32**, 596–602.
Boyd, D. B. and Merskey, H. (1978) A note on the description of pain and its causes, *Pain*, **5**, 1–3.
Brena, S. F. (Ed.) (1978) *Chronic Pain: America's Hidden Epidemic: Behavior Modification as an Alternative to Drugs and Surgery*, Atheneum, New York.

Burgess, P. R. (1974) Patterns of discharge evoked in cutaneous nerves and their significance for sensation, in Bonica, J. J. (Ed.) *Advances in Neurology: International Symposium on Pain*, Vol. 4, Raven Press, New York.

Cannon, J. T., Liebeskind, J. C. and Frenk, H. (1978) Neural and neurochemical mechanisms of pain inhibition, in Sternbach, R. A. (Ed.) *The Psychology of Pain*, Raven Press, New York.

Chapman, C. R. (1977a) Sensory decision theory methods in pain research: a reply to Rollman, *Pain*, **3**, 295–305.

Chapman, C. R. (1977b) Psychological aspects of pain patient treatment, *Archives of Surgery*, **112**, 767–772.

Chapman, C. R. (1978) Pain: the perception of noxious events, in Sternbach, R. A. (Ed.) *The Psychology of Pain*, Raven Press, New York.

Chapman, W. P. and Jones, C. M. (1944) Variations in cutaneous and visceral pain sensitivity in normal subjects, *Journal of Clinical Investigation*, **23**, 81–91.

Chaves, J. F. and Barber, T. X. (1974) Hypnotism and surgical pain, in Barber, T. X., Spanos, N. P. and Chaves, J. F. (Eds.) *Hypnosis, Imagination and Human Potentialities*, Pergamon Press, New York.

Clark, W. C. (1974) Pain sensitivity and the report of pain: an introduction to sensory decision theory, *Anesthesiology*, **40**, 272–287.

Cohen, F. and Lazarus, R. S. (1973) Active coping processes, coping dispositions, and recovery from surgery, *Psychosomatic Medicine*, **35**, 375–389.

Corah, N. L. (1969) Development of a dental anxiety scale, *Journal of Dental Research*, **48**, 596.

Corah, N. L. (1973) Effect of perceived control on stress reduction in pedodontic patients, *Journal of Dental Research*, **52**, 1261–1264.

Craig, K. D. (1978) Social modeling influences on pain, in Sternbach, R. A., (Ed.) *The Psychology of Pain*, Raven Press, New York.

Craig, K. D. and Neidermayer, H. (1974) Autonomic correlates of pain thresholds influenced by social modeling, *Journal of Personality and Social Psychology*, **29**, 246–252.

Craig, K. D. and Weiss, S. M. (1971) Vicarious influences on pain-threshold determinations, *Journal of Personality and Social Psychology*, **19**, 53–59.

Craig, K. D. and Weiss, S. M. (1972) Verbal reports of pain without noxious stimulation, *Perceptual and Motor Skills*, **34**, 943–948.

Crockett, D. J., Prkachin, K. M. and Craig, K. D. (1977) Factors of the language of pain in patient and volunteer groups, *Pain*, **4**, 175–182.

Crue, B. L. Jr. and Carregal, E. J. A. (1975) Pain begins in the dorsal horn–with a proposed classification of the primary senses, in Crue, B. L. Jr. (Ed.), *Pain: Research and Treatment*, Academic Press, New York.

Davidson, G. C. and Valins, S. (1979) Maintenance of self-attributed and drug-attributed behavior change, *Journal of Personality and Social Psychology*, **11**, 25–33.

Dehen, H. and Cambier, J. (1978) Congenital indifference to pain and endogenous morphine-like system, *Pain Abstracts: Second World Congress on Pain*, **15**.

DeLong R. D. (1970) Individual Differences in Patterns of Anxiety Arousal, Stress-Relevant Information and Recovery from Surgery. Unpublished doctoral dissertation, University of California, Los Angeles.

Dubuisson, D. and Melzack, R. (1976) Classification of clinical pain descriptions by multiple group discriminant analysis, *Experimental Neurology*, **51**, 480–487.

Dyck, P. J., Lambert, E. H. and O'Brien, P. (1976) Pain in peripheral neuropathy related to size and rate of fiber degeneration, in Weisenberg, M. and Tursky, B. (Eds.) *Pain: Therapeutic Approaches and Research Frontiers*, Plenum Press, New York.

Egbert, L. D., Battit, G. E., Welch, C. E., and Bartlett, M. D. (1964) Reduction of postoperative pain by encouragement and instruction of patients, *The New England Journal of Medicine*, **270**, 825–827.

Engel, G. L. (1959) "Psychogenic" pain and the pain-prone patient, *American Journal of Medicine*, **26**, 899–918.

Evans, F. J. (1967) Suggestibility in the normal waking state, *Psychological Bulletin*, **67**, 114–129.

Evans, F. J. (1974a) *Placebo Analgesia: Suggestion, Anxiety and the Doctor–Patient Relationship*. Paper presented at annual meeting of the American Psychosomatic Society, Philadelphia, Pa.

Evans, F. J. (1974b) The placebo response in pain reduction, in Bonica, J. J. (Ed.) *Advances in Neurology: International Symposium On Pain*, Vol. 4, Raven Press, New York.

Festinger, L. (1950) Informal social communication, *Psychological Review*, **57**, 271–282.

Festinger, L. (1954) A theory of social comparison processes, *Human Relations*, **7**, 117–140.

Festinger, L. (1957) *A Theory of Cognitive Dissonance*, Row Peterson, Evanston, Ill.

Folkins, C. H., Lawson, K. D., Opton, E. M. Jr. and Lazarus, R. S. (1968) Desensitization and the experimental reduction of threat, *Journal of Abnormal Psychology*, **73**, 100–113.

Fordyce, W. E. (1976) *Behavioral Methods for Chronic Pain and Illness*, C. V. Mosby, St. Louis, Mo.

Fordyce, W. E. (1978) Learning processes in pain, in Sternbach, R. A., *The Psychology of Pain*, Raven Press, New York.

Fordyce, W. E., Fowler, R. S., Lehmann, J. F. Delateur, B. J., Sand, P. L., and Treischmann, R. B. (1973) Operant conditioning in the treatment of chronic pain, *Archives of Physical Medicine and Rehabilitation*, **54**, 399–408.

Franz, D. N. and Iggo, A. (1968) Dorsal root potentials and ventral root reflexes evoked by nonmyelinated fibers, *Science*, **162**, 1140–1142.

Gelfand, D. M., Gelfand, S. and Rardin, M.W. (1965) Some personality factors associated with placebo responsivity, *Psychological Reports*, **17**, 555–562.

Gessel, A. H. and Alderman, M. M. (1971) Management of myofascial pain dysfunction syndrome of the temporomandibular joint by tension control training, *Psychosomatics*, **12**, 302–309.

Goldsheider, A. (1894) *Ueber den Schmerz in physiologishcher und klinischer hinsicht*, Hirschwald, Berlin.

Goodman, P., Greene, C. S. and Laskin, D. M. (1976) Response of patients with myofascial pain dysfunction syndrome to mock equilibration, *Journal of the American Dental Association*, **92**, 755–758.

Gottlieb, J. J., Hockersmith, V. W., Koller, R. and Strite, L. C. (1975) *A Successful Treatment Program for Chronic Back Pain Patients*, Symposium presented at the meeting of the American Psychological Association, Chicago, Ill.

Greene, C. S. and Laskin, D. M. (1974) Long-term evaluation of conservative treatment for myofascial pain-dysfunction syndrome, *Journal of the American Dental Association*, **89**, 1365–1368.

Hardy, J. D., Wolff, H. G. and Goodell H. (1952) *Pain Sensations and Reactions*, Hafner Publishing, New York.

Hilgard, E. R. (1973) A neodissociation interpretation of pain reduction in hypnosis, *Psychological Review*, **80**, 396–411.

Hillman, P. and Wall, P. D. (1969) Inhibitory and excitatory factors influencing the receptive fields of lamina 5 spinal cord cells, *Experimental Brain Research*, **9**, 284–306.

Hughes, J., Smith, T. W., Kosterlitz, H. W., Fothergill, L. A., Morgan, B. A., and Morris, H. R. (1975) Indentification of two related pentapeptides from the brain with potent opiate agonist activity, *Nature*, **258**, 577–579.

Hunter, M., Philips, C. and Rachman, S. (1979) Memory for pain, *Pain*, **6**, 35–46.

Iggo, A. (1972) Critical remarks on the gate control theory, in Janzen, R. *et al.*, (Eds.) *Pain: Basic Principles, Pharmacology, Therapy*, Georg Thieme, Stuttgart.

Iggo, A. (1974) Activation of cutaneous nociceptors and their actions on dorsal horn neurons, in Bonica, J. J. (Ed.) *Advances in Neurology: International Symposium on Pain*, Vol. 4, Raven Press, New York.

Janis, I. L. (1958) *Psychological Stress*, John Wiley, New York.

Johnson, J. E. (1973) Effects of accurate expectations about sensations of the sensory and distress components of pain, *Journal of Personality and Social Psychology*, **27**, 261–275.

Johnson, J. E., Dabbs, J. M. and Leventhal, H. (1970) Psychosocial factors in the welfare of surgical patients, *Nursing Research*, **19**, 18–29.

Johnson, J. E., Kirchoff, K. T. and Endres, M. P. (1975) Deferring children's distress behavior during orthopedic cast removal, *Nursing Research*, **75**, 404–410.

Johnson, J. E. and Leventhal, H. (1974) Effects of accurate expectations and behavioral instructions on reactions during a noxious medical examination, *Journal of Personality and Social Psychology*, **29**, 710–718.

Keeri-Szanto, M. (1979) Drugs or drums: What relieves postoperative pain? *Pain*, **6**, 217–230.

Laskin, D. M. and Greene, C. S. (1972) Influence of the doctor–patient relationship on placebo therapy for patients with myofascial pain-dysfunction (MPD) syndrome, *Journal of the American Dental Association*, **85**, 892–894.

Lehrer, P. M. (1972) Physiological effects of relaxation in a double-blind analog of desensitization, *Behavioral Therapy*, **3**, 193–208.

Levine, J. D., Gordon, N. C. and Fields, H. L. (1978) Evidence that the analgesic effects of placebo is mediated by endorphins, *Pain Abstracts: Second World Congress on Pain*, **18**.

Liebeskind, J. C., Mayer, D. J. and Akil, H. (1974) Central mechanism of pain inhibition: Studies of analgesia from focal brain stimulation, in Bonica, J. J. (Ed.) *Advances in Neurology: International Symposium on Pain*, Vol. 4, Raven Press, New York.

Liebeskind, J. M. and Paul, L. A. (1977) Psychological and physiological mechanisms of pain, *Annual Review of Psychology*, **28**, 41–60.

Lindahl, O. (1974a) Pain— a general chemical explanation, in Bonica, J. J. (Ed.), *Advances in Neurology: International Symposium on Pain*, Vol. 4, Raven Press, New York.

Lindahl, O. (1974b) Treatment of pain by changing the acid-base balance, in Bonica, J. J. (Ed.) *Advances in Neurology: International Symposium on Pain*, Vol. 4, Raven Press, New York.

Loeser, J. D. and Ward, A. A. Jr. (1967) Some effects of deafferentation on neurons of the cat spinal cord, *Archives of Neurology (Chicago)*, **17**, 629–636.

Marbach, J. J. and Lipton, J. A. (1978) Aspects of illness behavior in patients with facial pain, *Journal of the American Dental Association*, **96**, 630–638.

Mayer, D. J., Price, D. D., Barber, J. and Rafii, A. (1976) Acupuncture analgesia: Evidence for activation of a pain inhibitory system as a mechanism of action, in Bonica, J. J. and Albe-Fessard, D. (Eds.) *Advances in Pain Research and Therapy*, Vol. 1, Raven Press, New York.

McGlashan, T. H., Evans, F. J. and Orne, M. T. (1969) The nature of hypnotic analgesia and placebo response to experimental pain, *Psychosomatic Medicine*, **31**, 227–246.

Meehan, J. P., Stoll, A. M. and Hardy, J. D. (1954) Cutaneous pain threshold in native Alaskan Indian and Eskimo, *Journal of Applied Physiology*, **6**, 397–400.

Melamed, B. G. (1977) Psychological preparation for hospitalization, in Rachman, S. (Ed.) *Contributions to Medical Psychology*, Vol. 1, Pergamon Press, Oxford.

Melzack, R. (1973) *The Puzzle of Pain*, Basic Books, New York.

Melzack, R. (1975) The McGill Pain Questionnaire: major properties and scoring methods, *Pain*, **1**, 277–299.

Melzack, R. and Dennis, S. G. (1978) Neurophysiological foundations of pain, in Sternbach, R. A. (Ed.) *The Psychology of Pain*, Raven Press, New York.

Melzack, R. and Perry, C. (1975) Self-regulation of pain: the use of alpha-feedback and hypnotic training for the control of chronic pain, *Experimental Neurology*, **46**, 452–469.

Melzack, R. and Torgerson, W. S. (1971) On the language of pain, *Anesthesiology*, **34**, 50–59.

Melzack, R. and Wall, P. D. (1965) Pain mechanisms: a new theory, *Science*, **150**, 971–979.

Melzack, R. and Wall, P. D. (1970) Psychology of pain, *International Anesthesiology Clinics*, **8**, 3–34.

Melzack, R. and Weisz, A. Z. and Sprague, L. T. (1963) Strategies for controlling pain: contributions of auditory stimulation and suggestion, *Experimental Neurology*, **8**, 239–247.

Mendell, L. M. and Wall, P. D. (1964) Presynaptic hyperpolarization: a role for fine afferent fibres, *Journal of Physiology*, **172**, 274–294.

Merskey, H. (1965a) The characteristics of persistent pain in psychological illness, *Journal of Psychosomatic Research*, **9**, 291–298.

Merskey, H. (1965b) Psychiatric patients with persistent pain, *Journal of Psychosomatic Research*, **9**, 299–309.

Merskey, H. (1968) Psychological aspects of pain, *Postgraduate Medical Journal*, **44**, 297–306.

Merskey, H. (1974) Assessment of pain, *Physiotherapy*, **60**, 96–98.

Merskey, H. and Spear, F. G. (1964) The reliability of the pressure algometer. *British Journal of Clinical Psychology*, **3**, 130–136.

Merskey, H. and Spear, F. G. (1967) *Pain: Psychological and Psychiatric Aspects*, Bailliere, Tindall and Cassell, London.

Messing, R. B. and Lytle, L. D. (1977) Serotonin-containing neurons: their possible role in pain and analgesia, *Pain*, **4**, 1–21.

Mihic, D. and Binkert, E. (1978) Is placebo analgesia mediated by morphine? *Pain abstracts: Second World Congress on Pain*, **19**.

Mountcastle, V. B. (1974) Pain and temperature sensibilities, in Mountcastle, V. B. (Ed.) *Medical Physiology*, C. V. Mosby, Saint Louis.

Mowrer, O. H. (1950) *Learning Theory and Personality Dynamics*, Ronald Press, New York.

Orne, M. T. (1974) Pain suppression by hypnosis and related phenomena, in Bonica, J. J. (Ed.) *Advances in Neurology: International Symposium on Pain*, Vol. 4, Raven Press, New York.

Parbrook, G. D., Steel, D. F. and Dalrymple, D. G. (1973) Factors predisposing to postoperative pain and pulmonary complications, *British Journal of Anesthesia*, **45**, 21–33.

Paul, G. L. (1969) Physiological effects of relaxation training and hypnotic suggestion, *Journal of Abnormal Psychology*, **74**, 425–437.

Paul, G. L. and Bernstein, D. A. (1973) *Anxiety and Clinical Problems: Systematic Desensitization and Related Techniques*, General Learning Press, Morristown, N.J.

Pilling, L. F., Brannick, T. L. and Swenson, W. M. (1967) Psychologic characteristics of psychiatric patients having pain as a presenting symptom, *Canadian Medical Association Journal*, **97**, 387–394.

Pilowsky, I., Chapman, C. R. and Bonica, J. J. (1977) Pain, depression and illness behavior in a pain clinic population, *Pain*, **4**, 183–192.

Pilowsky, I. and Spence, N. D. (1975) Patterns of illness behavior in patients with intractable pain, *Journal of Psychosomatic Research*, **19**, 279–287.

Pilowsky, I. and Spence, N. D. (1976a) Pain and illness behavior: a comparative study, *Journal of Psychosomatic Research*, **20**, 131–134.

Pilowsky, I. and Spence, N. D. (1976b) Illness behavior syndromes associated with intractable pain, *Pain*, **2**, 61–71.

Pilowsky, I. and Spence, N. D. (1976c) Is illness behavior related to chronicity in patients with intractable pain? *Pain*, **2**, 167–173.

Reading, A. E. and Newton, J. R. (1977) A comparison of primary dysmenorrhoea and intrauterine device related pain, *Pain*, **3**, 265–276.

Reynolds, D. V. (1969) Surgery in the rat during electrical analgesia induced by focal brain stimulation, *Science*, **164**, 444–445.

Rollman, G. B. (1976) Signal detection theory assessment of pain modulation: a critique, in Bonica, J. J. and Albe-Fessard, D. (Eds.) *Advances in Pain Research and Therapy*, Vol. 1, Raven Press, New York.

Rollman, G. B. (1977) Signal detection theory measurement of pain: a review and critique, *Pain*, **3**, 187–211.

Rollman, G. B. (1979) Signal detection theory pain measures: empirical validation studies and adaptation-level effects, *Pain*, **6**, 9–21.

Scott, J. and Huskisson, E. C. (1976) Graphic representation of pain, *Pain*, **2**, 175–184.

Sherman, R. A., Gall, N. and Gormly, J. (1979) Treatment of phantom limb pain with muscular relaxation training to disrupt the pain–anxiety tension cycle, *Pain*, **6**, 47–55.

Shor, R. C. (1962) Physiological effects of painful stimulation during hypnotic analgesia under conditions designed to minimize anxiety, *International Journal of Clinical and Experimental Hypnosis*, **10**, 183–202.

Simon, E. J., Hiller, J. M. and Edelman, I. (1975) Solubility of a stereospecific opiate-macromolecular complex from rat brain, *Science*, **190**, 389–390.

Simon, E. J. and Hiller, J. M. (1978) The opiate receptors, *Annual Review of Pharmacology and Toxicology*, **18**, 371–394.

Smith, G. M., Egbert, L. D., Markowitz, R. A., Mosteller. F. and Beecher, H. K. (1966) An experimental pain method sensitive to morphine in man: the submaximum effort tourniquet technique, *Journal of Pharmacology and Experimental Therapeutics*, **154**, 324–332.

Smith, G. M., Lowenstein, E., Hubbard, J. H. and Beecher, H. K. (1968) Experimental pain produced by the submaximum effort tourniquet technique: further evidence of validity, *Journal of Pharmacology and Experimental Therapeutics*, **163**, 468–474.

Smith, G. M., Parry, W. L., Denton, J. E. and Beecher, H. K. (1970) Effect of morphine on pain produced in man by electric shock delivered through an annular-disc cellulose sponge electrode, *Proceedings of the 78th Annual Convention of the American Psychological Association*, **5**, 819–820.

Spear, F. G. (1967) Pain in psychiatric patients, *Journal of Phsychosomatic Research*, **11**, 187–193.

Spielberger, C. D., Gorsuch, R. L. and Lushene, R. E. (1970) *Manual for the State-Trait Anxiety Inventory*, Consulting Psychologists Press, Palo Alto, Calif.

Staub, E., Tursky, B. and Schwartz, G. E. (1971) Self-control and predictability: their effects on reactions to aversive stimulation, *Journal of Personality and Social Psychology*, **18**, 157–162.

Sternbach, R. A. (1968) *Pain: A Psychophysiological Analysis*, Academic Press, New York.

Sternbach, R. A. (1974) *Pain Patients: Traits and Treatment*, Academic Press, New York.

Sternbach, R. A. (Ed.) (1978a) *The Psychology of Pain*, Raven Press, New York.

Sternbach, R. A. (1978b) Clinical aspects of pain, in Sternbach, R. A. (Ed.) *The Psychology of Pain*, Raven Press, New York.

Sternbach, R. A., Janowsky, D. S., Huey, L. Y. and Segal, D. S. (1976) Effects of altering brain serotonin activity on human chronic pain, in Bonica, J. J. and Albe-Fessard, D., *Advances in Pain Research and Therapy*, Vol. 1, Raven Press, New York.

Sternbach, R. A. and Tursky, B. (1965) Ethnic differences among housewives in psychophysical and skin potential responses to electric shock, *Psychophysiology*, **1**, 241–246.

Szasz, T. S. (1955) The nature of pain, *Archives of Neurology and Psychiatry*, **74**, 174–181.

Szasz, T. S. (1957) *Pain and Pleasure*, Basic Books, New York.

Szasz, T. S. (1968) The psychology of persistent pain: a portrait of l'homme douloureux, in Soulairac, A., Cahn, J., and Charpentier, J., (Eds.) *Pain: Proceedings of the International Symposium on Pain*, Academic Press, New York.

Taub, A. (1975) Factors in the diagnosis and treatment of chronic pain, *Journal of Autism and Childhood Schizophrenia*, **5**, 1–12.

Terenius, L. (1978) Endogenous peptides and analgesia, *Annual Review of Pharmacology and Toxicology*, **18**, 189–204.

Timmermans, G. and Sternbach, R. A. (1976) Human chronic pain and personality: a canonical correlation analysis, in Bonica, J. J. and Albe-Fessard, D. *Advances in Pain Research and Therapy*, Vol. 1, Raven Press, New York.

Tursky, B. (1974) Physical, physiological and psychological factors that affect pain reaction to electric shock. *Psychophysiology*, **11**, 95–112.

Tursky, B. (1976) The pain perception profile: a psychophysical approach, in Weisenberg, M. and Tursky, B., (Eds.) *Pain: Therapeutic Approaches and Research Frontiers*, Plenum Press, New York.

Tursky, B. (in press) The measurement of pain reactions: laboratory studies, in Weisenberg, M. (Ed.) *The Control of Pain*, Psychological Dimensions, Inc., New York.

Tursky, B. and Sternbach, R. A. (1967) Further physiological correlates of ethnic differences to shock, *Psychophysiology*, **4**, 67–74.

Tursky, B., Watson, P. D. and O'Connell, D. N. (1965) A concentric shock electrode for pain stimulation, *Psychophysiology*, **1**, 296–298.

Van Buren, J. and Kleinknecht, R. A. (1979) An evaluation of the McGill Pain Questionnaire for use in dental pain assessment, *Pain*, **6**, 23–33.

Vernon, D. T. A. (1974) Modeling and birth order in responses to painful stimuli, *Journal of Personality and Social Psychology*, **29**, 794–799.

Vyklicky, L., Rudomin, P., Zajac, F. E. III and Burke, R. E. (1969) Primary afferent depolarization evoked by a painful stimulus, *Science*, **165**, 184–186.

Wall, P. D. (1976) Modulation of pain by nonpainful events, in Bonica, J. J. and Albe-Fessard, D. (Eds.) *Advances in Pain Research and Therapy*, Vol. 1, Raven Press, New York.

Weisenberg, M. (Ed.) (1975) *Pain: Clinical and Experimental Perspectives*, C. V. Mosby, Saint Louis.

Weisenberg. M. (1977) Pain and pain control, *Psychological Bulletin*, **84**, 1008–1044.

Weisenberg, M. (in press) Cultural and racial reactions to pain, in Weisenberg, M., (Ed.) *The Control of Pain*, Psychological Dimensions, New York.

Weisenberg, M., Kreindler, M. L., Schachat, R. and Werboff, J. (1975) Pain: anxiety and attitudes in black, white and Puerto Rican patients, *Psychosomatic Medicine*, **37**, 123–135.

Winsburg, B. and Greenlick, M. (1968) Pain responses in negro and white obstetrical patients, *Journal of Health and Social Behavior*, **8**, 222–227.

Wolff, B. B. (1978) Behavioural measurement of human pain, in Sternbach, R. A. *The Psychology of Pain*, Raven Press, New York.

Wolff, B. B. and Langley, S. (1968) Cultural factors and the response to pain: a review, *American Anthropologist*, **70**, 494–401.

Wolpe, J. (1969) *The Practice of Behavior Therapy*, Pergamon Press, New York.

Woodforde, J. M. and Fielding, J. R. (1970) Pain and cancer, *Journal of Psychosomatic Research*, **14**, 365–370.

Woodrow, K. M., Friedman, G. D., Sieglaub, A. B. and Collen, M. F. (1972) Pain differences according to age, sex and race, *Psychosomatic Medicine*, **34**, 548–556.

Zborowski, M. (1969) *People in Pain*, Jossey–Bass, San Francisco.

Zimbardo, P. G., Cohen, A. R., Weisenberg, M. and Firestone, I. (1966) Control of pain motivation by cognitive dissonance, *Science*, **151**, 217–219.

Zimbardo, P. G., Cohen, A. R., Weisenberg, M., Dworkin, L. and Firestone, I. (1969) The control of experimental pain, in Zimbardo, P. G., (Ed.) *The Cognitive Control of Motivation*, Scott, Foresman, Glenview, Ill.

Zimmerman, M. (1968) Dorsal root potentials after C-fiber stimulation, *Science*, **160**, 896–898.

Zola, I. K. (1966) Culture and symptoms: an analysis of patients' presenting complaints, *American Sociological Review*, **31**, 615–630.

5

RECENT DEVELOPMENTS IN TENSION HEADACHE RESEARCH: IMPLICATIONS FOR UNDERSTANDING AND MANAGEMENT OF THE DISORDER

CLARE PHILIPS

Institute of Psychiatry, University of London

CONTENTS

1. INTRODUCTION

In this article, recent psychophysiological findings will be reviewed and their implications discussed both with respect to our understanding of tension headaches and their management. It will be argued that psychologists are now in a good position to make a positive contribution to the study of tension headache. It is no longer possible to persist with the outmoded view that ties headache to muscular activity alone.

During the last decade, psychologists have become increasingly interested in the relevance of their discipline to medical problems. Tension headache has been among the disorders receiving considerable attention, and it is an appropriate focus. This type of complaint is one of the most pervasive chronic problems (Dunnell and Cartwright, 1972) and has evaded a medical/pharmacological solution.

The psychological contribution to the understanding of headache has taken two forms. First, there have been psychophysiological investigations of the differences between groups with tension headache, migraine headache, and headache-free controls (Bakal and Kaganov, 1977; Philips, 1977a; Martin and Mathews, 1978; Epstein and Abel, 1977; Cohen, 1978), Second, there have been a series of clinical treatment trials which have been concerned with assessing psychological methods of treating tension headache. Predominantly, these have entailed muscular biofeedback and general relaxation training (Budzynski *et al.*, 1973; Haynes *et al.*, 1975; Chesney *et al.*, 1976; Hutchings *et al.*, 1976; Cox *et al.*, 1975). But more recently an interest in cognitive restructuring (Holroyd *et al.*, 1977, 1978) and rational emotive therapy (Lake *et al.*, 1979) has emerged.

The underlying assumption of these studies (psychophysiological and treatment) is the same. Both make their starting point the prevailing medical view of tension headache: that these headaches are *caused* by sustained contraction of the skeletal muscles of the shoulders, neck, and head. Consequently psychophysiological studies have investigated the tonic activity of the appropriate muscles (frontalis, temporals, neck, trapezius) to document the pathophysiology of this disorder. Assuming abnormal muscle tension, biofeedback and general relaxation techniques have been used to reduce the presumed muscular basis. Unfortunately these two approaches have continued without influencing each other.

Investigations of muscular activity have undermined the traditional view of tension headache (Philips, 1978), and yet the therapeutic technique of reducing EMG levels flourishes, and costly EMG feedback instruments are purchased and used freely. In addition, there have been few attempts to deal with the conceptual and practical implications of the findings for our understanding of tension headache pain.

At least two conceptual shifts are necessary. First, it seems appropriate to shift to a conception of tension headache as a type of *pain* phenomenon, rather than as one of fifteen headache types (Friedman, 1962). This leads immediately to consideration of central determinants of the experience (Weisenberg, 1977; Melzack, 1973), to behaviour motivated pain and to the factors that sustain it, to the interrelation of subjective expressions of pain, and so on.

The second shift comes from taking more seriously the fact that tension headache is a stress-related dysfunction. Abnormality of muscular levels has been the predominant research interest. Little attention has been given to specifying the stress stimuli, or their phasic consequences.

This article will attempt to show why both the above shifts are advisable, and a start will be made in specifying how such changes in conceptualizing the headache problem may affect research methodology and the treatment of headache sufferers.

2. RECENT PSYCHOPHYSIOLOGICAL STUDIES

The prevailing medical (and psychological) view of tension headaches has remained closely aligned to the definition formalized in 1962 by the Ad Hoc Committee (Friedman, 1962). It differentiated the most common headache, "tension", from some 15 other types of headache by the following definition:

> Ache or sensation of tightness, pressure, or constriction widely varied in intensity, frequency and duration sometimes long-lasting and commonly sub-occipital. It is associated with sustained contraction of the skeletal muscles in the absence of permanent structural change, usually as part of the individual's reaction during life stress.

When using this conception of tension headache, researchers and clinicians are making a number of assumptions. Seven of those have been delineated elsewhere (Philips, 1978) but for the purpose of the present argument it is sufficient to look at only the key assumptions:

(1) Sustained contraction of the muscles of the head, neck, and shoulders is a *necessary* and *distinguishing* feature of tension headache.

(2) The muscular dysfunction takes the form of a sustained elevation of resting level, or a tonic abnormality, such that headache suffers will be distinguished irrespective of current state (headache or pain-free).

(3) The severity of the headache (intensity, frequency, duration, etc.), the elevation of the EMG in the key muscles, and the behaviour motivated by the pain, are highly (if not perfectly) associated.

The results from a number of psychophysiological investigations during the past four/five years have failed to support these assumptions. Each assumption will be considered below in turn. Table 1 summarizes the results with respect to the first assumption.

(1) Despite the obvious shortcomings (different dependent variables, selection criteria, etc.) the findings are clear. EMG levels at rest can no longer be depended upon to differentiate the two major types of headache: tension and migraine. Migraine sufferers have been found to have higher levels of tension in the key muscles than do tension cases (Pozniak-Patewicz, 1976; Philips. 1977; Bakal *et al.*, 1977; Philips and Hunter, 1980a). Although tension cases often have a higher group average EMG score on the key muscles, it does not always reach a statistically differentiable level from headache-free control (Martin and Mathews, 1978; Pearce, 1977). A proportion of "tension" headache cases show no tonic abnormality in the muscles assessed (Hart *et al.*, 1975; Martin and Mathews, 1978; Pearce, 1977; Bakal and Kaganov, 1977). In a replication and extension of an earlier investigation, Philips and Hunter (1980a) found that 40 per cent of their severe tension-headache sufferers showed no tonic abnormality, when compared to a control group. (Although psychiatric in-patients and out-patients were the samples, the non-headache controls were indistinguishable psychophysiologically, from a normal non-headache sample.) Overall, an elevated EMG resting level cannot be taken as a necessary and differentiating criterion of tension headache.

(2) It is assumed that tension headache sufferers will be distinguishable from others by virtue of an elevation of the tension of key muscles when at rest (i.e. unstimulated and without headache). This sustained elevation is known technically as a "tonic" abnormality. It is this abnormality that is being assessed in the group comparisons summarized in Table 1 and discussed above. It is also this type of presumed abnormality that has been the sole target of biofeedback and general relaxation treatment approaches.

Tonic abnormalities are distinguishable from "phasic" abnormalities, which refer to abnormal muscular reactions to *specific* stimuli (i.e. light, noise, anger, concentration, etc.). A possibility exists that a preoccupation with tonic state (assumed by the prevailing view of headache) may be misguided. The muscular abnormality may be *phasic*, occurring as excessive reactivity to certain stimuli/or reactivity that is slow to attenuate or decay.

TABLE 1.
Summary of Recent Psychophysiological Investigations of Headache

Authors	Groups	Selection Basis	Muscles	Results
Hart et al. (1975)	Tension $n = ?$ Headache free controls $n = ?$	?	?	Recorded headache free: Resting EMG. Significantly different between tension and controls, due to some headache cases having very high values, while others were indistinguishable from the controls.
Pozniak-Patewicz (1976)	Classical and common migraine Cervical migraine Tension headache Controls $n = 51$	132 "Patients" C: no headache	Neck Temporalis	Record without headache (57 cases) and with headache (75 cases). All headache cases showed more muscle tension than the controls. Tension headache cases showed *less* muscle tension than the migraine cases.
Philips (1977a)	Migraine $n = 20$ Tension $n = 17$ Controls $n = 20$ (few or no headache)	Random selection from G.P. and some neurologist referrals	Frontalis Temporalis Neck Trapezius	Recorded during headache-free period. No difference between the groups with respect to neck and trapezium tension. Migraine and Tension cases both showed significantly elevated frontalis resting tension, though they were not significantly different. The tension level rose across the groups in the following order: controls, tension, migraine. The same trend was evident in the temporalis muscle.
Pearce (1977)	Migraine $n = 6$ Tension $n = 6$ Controls $n = 6$	Neurologists referral C: colleagues	Frontalis	Recorded headache free. No significant differences in resting level, but clear increasing tension: controls, "tension", migraine.
Bakal et al. (1977)	Tension $n = 10$ Migraine $n = 10$ Controls $n = 10$	Neurologists referral C: headache free	Frontalis Neck	Recorded with and without headache. The results apply equally to both occasions. Tension did not differ from controls in frontalis tension but migraine significantly higher than tension cases. Both migraine and tension were significantly higher than controls re. neck tension, but not significantly different from each other
Martin and Mathews (1978)	Tension $n = 37$ Controls $n = 37$	Pain complaint to G.P. Controls: staff of psychiatric hospital. ? freq./intensity of headaches	Frontalis Neck	Recorded during headache-free and headache periods, and data combined. No significant differences in resting frontalis and neck tension, though muscle tension higher in headache cases (especially post-stress).
Philips and Hunter (1980a)	Migraine $n = 10$ Tension $n = 23$ Control (normal) $n = 10$ Control (psychiatric) $n = 10$	Selection from psychiatric IP OP sample	Frontalis Temporalis	No significant difference between controls on either muscle and replicates earlier control levels (1977a). No significant difference between tension and migraine on frontalis or temporalis, but migraine temporalis tension higher. Significant difference between headache and non headache groups on temporalis (0.02) and approaching on frontalis (0.07).

A start has been made in the last 3 years to explore this source of muscular abnormality (see Table 2).

In spite of the difficulties of comparing these studies (different stimuli, subject selection and muscles sampled etc.), it is apparent that phasic reactions to relevant stressors occur (concentrations: Boxtel et al., 1978; idiosyncratic stress: Philips, 1977a; Philips and Hunter, 1980a) and may be an important muscular abnormality in tension headache. The overreactivity is not a general dysfunction as it is not present for neutral auditory stimuli (Bakal and Kaganov, 1977; Philips and Hunter, 1980a). Consequently it is important to consider how relevant the stimulus is to the person assessed. Stress material identified by the subjects as being potent in exacerbating or producing headache (i.e. Boxtel et al., 1978; Philips, 1977a) seems a more rational approach to stimulus selection. Unfortunately, two of these studies lack appropriate controls (Vaughn et al., 1977; Philips, 1977a), so the diagnostic significance of the reactivity found was unclear.

In a recent study that extends the earlier finding (Philips and Hunter, 1980a), the reactivity of tension and migraine sufferers (psychiatric patients) was assessed utilizing an appropriate control group. Using potent imaginal stressors, Philips and Hunter have shown significant muscular responses in all headache sufferers, irrespective of headache type. This study unfortunately, like the others reviewed (Table 2), fails to assess recovery rate. However, there is an indication that tension cases, with repeated imaginal stress, show accumulated or incrementing tension. This did not occur in migraine cases. It is hoped that more studies will be completed in the near future to clarify the relevance of muscular reactivity in headache. The assumed reliance on resting "tonic" EMG abnormality may prove to be misguided.

(3) The prevailing view of tension headache depends upon a conception of pain which has now been superseded (review and discussion of this can be found in Rachman and Philips, 1975, and Philips, 1977a). In brief, the pain suffered by a headache sufferer is seen as a direct consequence of, and proportional to, the contraction of certain muscles. A one-to-one link is made between the putative physiological basis and the subjective experience. Accordingly, the behavioural expressions of pain (complaint, medication level, etc.) are expected to be highly associated with the level of pain experienced and the muscle implicated.

This conception of pain depends upon a "specificity" theory of pain, which has proved to be inadequate (Melzack 1973). Pain experiences can occur *without* physiological underpinning (Melzack 1973), while many psychological factors can affect both the behaviour motivated by pain (Weisenberg, 1977; Bond and Pilowsky, 1966; Fordyce, 1976, 1978), as well as the qualities and intensity of pain experienced (Beecher, 1959). In light of this, it would have been surprising, if the assumption of high correlations of the behaviour, subject, and physiological manifestation of tension headache had proved to be correct. In fact, marked discordances have been recorded (Philips, 1977a; Epstein and Abel, 1977; Martin and Mathews, 1978; Haynes et al., 1975), suggesting that the classic case of Sainsbury and Gibson (1954), in which the headache and EMG elevation followed a parallel course, may be rare. However, it is important to recognize that low correlations between components can be a consequence of utilizing inappropriate or restricted measures. Medication rate, for example, is clearly an inadequate measure of pain-

TABLE 2.

Summary of Psychophysiological Investigations of Reactivity to Stimulation

Authors	Groups (n)	Measures	Stimuli	Results
Bakal and Kaganov (1977)	Migraine (10) Tension (10) Non-headache (10)	EMG: frontalis and neck T.A. pulse velocity	Non-aversive passive auditory stimulus at 80 db, 5 sec duration (eyes open)	—No difference between groups or state (head-ache vs. headache-free) in reactivity to tone —Significant: decrease velocity in T.A. in head-ache cases —Significant: increase velocity in T.A. in controls for left artery only
Vaughn et al. (1977)	Tension High freq. (8) Low freq. (9)	EMG: frontalis	Serial subtraction, silent, no check, with time stress 1 min duration	—No significant response in High Frequency group though small change takes approximately 9 min to dissipate —Significantly larger task response in Low Frequency group, and approximately 4 min recovery rate.
Philips (1977a)	Tension (17)	EMG: frontalis temporalis neck trapezius	Subject-defined imaginal stress and non-stress material. One presentation for 45 sec	—Only frontalis and temporalis reactions —Significant difference between stress and non-stress on frontalis EMG only —Individual differences in size and presence of reactivity to imagined stress
Boxtel et al. (1978)	Students with severe study headaches (7) Students with no headaches (11)	EMG: frontalis temporalis trapezius forearm	Stress task: 20 min study period followed by questions	—Gradual task increment over 5 min for fron-talis EMG only in headache cases

Martin and Mathews (1978)	Tension (37) Controls (37)	EMG: frontalis neck	Nufferno level, timed and visually presented	—Headache sufferers had higher EMG during relaxation and lower during task. (Group × Occasions Interaction.) No differences between groups. —Difference in recovery rate apparent, but unanalysed. Controls show immediate recovery; headache sufferers fail to recover to basal level (frontalis)
Philips and Hunter (1980a)	Tension (23) Migraine (10) Controls (20)	EMG: frontalis temporalis	(a) Subject-defined imaginal stress and non-stress material. Two presentations of each (b) Loud tones (85 db) 2x (c) Quiet tones (60 db) Demanding active vigilance 6x	—State (Headache/Headache-free) irrelevant —Significant frontalis reactivity to stress (vs. non-stress) in both tension and migraine. No difference between tension and migraine in this respect. —Temporalis reactivity not significantly different for stress/non-stress material —Tension significantly differentiated from migraine with respect to the effect of repeated stress (stress × repetitions $P < 0.04$) suggests delayed recovery and/or incrementing reactions No effect of tones on any groups

motivated behaviour, it being greatly influenced by attitudes to doctors/drugs that may be independent of the pain suffered (Philips, 1977a). In a larger correlational study of concordance of pain components (Philips and Hunter, 1980b), various aspects of each of the three components were assessed in migraine and in tension. In tension-headache cases, medication rate was again found largely unrelated to the subjective and the physiological measures, or to other behavioural measures. Measures of behavioural complaint and avoidance related significantly to the subjective experience of pain (Melzack Pain Questionnaire), though not to the physiological measures. With adequate measures of the components, it seems likely that the discordances between aspects of headache pain may prove more informative than the concordances. Future concern will be to delineate the factors (chronicity, intensity, neuroticism, personality, headache type) that effect the degree of association. Treatment studies also suggest that reducing the EMG does not entail *synchronous* reductions in pain experience, or behaviour (Philips, 1977b; Martin and Mathews, 1978; Cox *et al.*, 1975). These pain components decline, but at a different rate and partially independent of the EMG levels.

In conclusion, it is evident that recent psychophysiological investigations of tension headache have undermined the key assumptions of the prevailing medical view of this disorder. Tension headache is not distinguished from migraine on the basis of underlying muscular tension. Although there is some evidence of raised tension in some groups of tension cases, a subgroup must be acknowledged who are without muscular abnormalities. The presumed one-to-one association of muscle tension and pain is thus fallacious. Discordance has been encountered, both in investigations and treatment studies, between physiological, behavioural and subjective components of headache.

3. ISSUES ARISING FROM PSYCHOPHYSIOLOGICAL INVESTIGATIONS

It is evident from the previous section that most of the progress made to date has been negative, in the sense that it is clearer what tension headaches are not. However, a number of issues arise as a consequence of the findings reviewed above (e.g. group comparisons, stimulus potency, the role of EMG in headache, responsivity, headache as pain) which may lead to more constructive research.

A. Group Comparisons

All investigations to date have followed the diagnostic grouping implied by the Ad Hoc Committee Definition (Friedman, 1962).[1] Comparisons are made between groups of headache cases (migraine, tension, or muscular contraction), and groups without headache (controls).

As the rationale for dividing the headache population into these groups has been undermined, it is necessary to reconsider the selection criteria. A proportion of tension headache cases will not have any muscular component associated with their

---

[1] (For a fuller account of the clinical procedure used for selection of tension headache and the issue of "negative diagnosis", see Philips, 1977a).

pain reports. The remaining cases will show individual differences in muscles implicated (frontalis or temporalis predominant), and its relation to pain locus. Frontalis and temporalis muscle have been found to be uncorrelated at rest ($r = 0.03$, Philips and Hunter, 1980a). A high degree of specificity in muscular activity has been reported between muscle groups (Alexander, 1975). The key muscle elevated at rest and when stimulated, and the locus of pain complaint, coincided in only 25 per cent of the cases studied (Philips, 1977a). If the research or treatment concern is for EMG activity, it is necessary to assess subjects on the relevant muscle at rest and when appropriately stimulated. Subjects can then be grouped into homogeneous groups (EMG normal/abnormal, EMG raised at rest and in reaction etc.). If the concern is for headache as a pain phenomena (as will be argued below), the physiological expression (muscular and/or vascular) needs to be assessed at rest and in reaction. It can no longer be assumed to be present or to take a certain form (i.e. tonic frontalis elevation).

B. The Role of Muscular Activity

It could be argued that retaining an interest in EMG levels may no longer be justified in discussions of tension headache. This extreme position has grown from the failure to find differences between tension levels of tension-headache cases and controls (Martin and Mathews, 1978). Although it is clear that muscle tension is not a necessary and sufficient condition of tension headache, it is unwise to disregard the muscular activity entirely. Although EMG levels may not differentiate tension from migraine, muscle tension may play different roles in the two groups. Statistically equivalent levels of frontalis and temporalis tension have recently been found in two groups of headache cases: migraine and tension (Philips and Hunter, 1980a), largely replicating an earlier study (Philips, 1977a). However when the correlations of this activity and the subjective component are studied, it becomes clear that the significance of muscular tension may be different for the two types of headache. In tension headache, there is a significant association of resting levels of tension and headache intensity ($r = 0.40$, $P < 0.03$ for tension).

In addition, although some tension cases have been found indistinguishable from controls with respect to EMG levels (Martin and Mathews, 1978; Pearce, 1977; Bakal and Kaganov, 1971), a sizeable group remain who have abnormal resting levels. In a current investigation of a psychiatric group, 60 per cent (approximately) show abnormal levels on one or both of the two muscles assessed (Philips and Hunter, 1980a).

Considering these points, it seems important to attempt to offer an explanation of tension headache that can explain these findings. One tentative hypothesis would be the following. Some other factor—such as "mental tension"—may be instrumental in producing tension headaches *and* muscular responses. The latter would occur only in individuals with a pronounced and persistent muscular response when stressed (mentally and/or emotionally).

Acknowledging two groups of tension-headache cases (with and without EMG abnormalities), it is possible to study the intercorrelations of the pain components in the two, as well as testing the predicted differences of the two with reference to personality and mood state. This approach will be a useful one in clarifying the role of EMG in tension headache (and migraine). It would be unjustifiable to disregard EMG activity. What seems in order is to demote it from a position of "cause" to one of a number of correlates. Such an approach leads to the search for factors influencing the degree of association between components.

C. Stimulus Potency

Muscular activity (at rest and in reaction) has been the focus of psychophysiological studies, in keeping with the view that it is the muscular level at rest (or when stimulated) that is abnormal. This focus on level has been at the expense of a concern for stimulus specificities and potency. In other psychophysiological studies, quite the opposite has often occurred (i.e. Lacey, 1967), with the effect of different stimuli on physiological activity being studied. Despite a number of suggestions to the contrary, this parameter has been neglected in headache research.

The close connection of headache occurrence and environmental events has always been acknowledged. Headache is believed to be provoked or exacerbated by stressful stimuli (Martin, 1967; Ostfeld, 1962). It is "part of the individual's reaction during *life stress*" (Friedman, 1962). Discussion with headache sufferers quickly provides one with situations and stimuli that are well established antecedents of *their* headaches (i.e. noise, bright lights, emotional excitement, driving a car, studying, or worry, etc.). The stimuli selected vary among sufferers, but, for almost all cases, a check list is easily completed.

However, in spite of this, interest has centred on response and not stimulus parameters. Preliminary work (Philips, 1977a; Philips and Hunter, 1980a) suggests that the selection of an appropriate provocative stimulus may be crucial in producing differential EMG reactions and in designing a treatment strategy (see below). The extent of subjective reaction and tolerance of certain potent stimuli may also prove a useful objective calibration of pain experience (Philips and Hunter, in progress).

D. Responsivity

Although the main response studied has been the tonic state, an interest in phasic responsivity is developing (Table 2). If the differential effects of certain stimuli on EMG are explored further, it will be important to record and examine in detail the muscular recovery curve, as well as the response itself. So far, there are no studies of recovery or of the cumulative effect of repeated stimulation on recovery. These problems are currently under investigation (James and Philips, 1980).

E. Headache as Pain

It looks increasingly useful to consider tension headache as a type of *pain phenomenon* in which a muscular component (tonic/phasic) may be implicated (Philips, 1977a, 1978). This view is distinct from the one we have been content to use to date, namely, that tension headache is one of fifteen types of headache distinguished by excessive sustained muscle tension. In tension head *pain*, a muscular component may not be present, or if present, may not correlate highly with subjective reports of suffering or behaviour motivated by the pain. This being so, the methodology used to assess the phenomenon (pain) must change. It will be necessary to look with more care and detail at the subjective and behavioural components. Psychophysiological studies of headache have been inadequate in this respect. Subjects are obtained from varied sources (see Table 1), but their homogeneity with respect to pain behaviour and degree/type of distress is assumed. No investigations of headache pain behaviour are available. The behavioural measure incorporated by Philips (1977b) to assess headache pain was medication rate. It proved a blunt and inadequate measure of behaviour motivated by the pain. There are distinguishable aspects of such behaviour: avoidance of certain stimuli, reduction or modulation of certain stimuli, non-verbal complaint or manifestations, verbal complaint etc. Current work shows these types of behaviour are not related to the medication rate, although they feature frequently in chronic pain behaviour (Philips and Hunter, 1980c). The extent to which these types of behaviour cohere in headache, and the influence of such factors as chronicity, personality, sex, etc. on the association, is being studied. The relationship between pain behaviour and the physiology and pain experience is also interesting. An example of some data using this approach will clarify this point. A current study (Philips and Hunter, 1980b) shows that, in tension headache, avoidance and complaint behaviour are unrelated to either the physiological indices or the subjective estimates of headache intensity, frequency, or duration. However, both are significantly associated with the affective quality of the pain experienced. This type of behaviour is best understood with respect to the emotional aspect of the headache pain experience.

The subjective evaluation of the pain also needs a separate assessment, as well as being related to the other expressions of pain (physiological and behavioural). The lack of sophistication in reported studies of headache pain experience is notable. The distress and pain are assumed to be equally present in groups referred or selected for headache. Details of frequency, intensity, and duration are usually missing (Hart et al., 1975; Pozniak-Patewicz, 1976; Martin and Mathews, 1978; Pearce, 1977; Bakal and Kaganov, 1977). No details of the pain experienced with respect to the sensory or affective qualities are available. Treatment studies suggest that it may be unwise to persist with an analysis that summates information about frequency, intensity, and duration (see 5C below). This is equally true in psychophysiological studies of headache pain. Intensity and duration of a tension headache may, for example, be more closely linked to the affective pain qualities (Harper et al., 1978; Hunter and Philips, 1980b). Further study of the subjective component in its own right, as well as its relation to other aspects of the phenomenon, is needed.

In conclusion, now that the presumption of a tight relationship between EMG tension and suffering and/or pain behaviour can be dismissed, it is necessary to explore the components in more detail. We find ourselves in an exciting position of having to widen our view and to measure and incorporate more ingredients, in an attempt to explain the patterns of behaviour and the reported suffering.

4. TREATMENT OF TENSION HEADACHE

Psychologists became interested in the treatment of headache when they recognized a possible application of the biofeedback methodology that had developed

(Miller, 1969, 1970). Learning from their medical colleagues of a specific disorder of the muscles that led to tension headache, they were eager to determine whether training sufferers to reduce tension in the underlying muscle would eliminate the suffering. There followed a rush of studies first comparing EMG biofeedback to no treatment (Budzynski *et al.*, 1973; Haynes *et al.*, 1975), to a pseudo-treatment (Budzynski, *et al.*, 1973; Philips, 1977b), and to a medical placebo (Cox *et al.*, 1975). The results were encouraging. More recently, the interest has turned to comparing EMG as a treatment to alternative approaches (general relaxation, Hutchings and Reinking, 1976; Haynes *et al.*, 1975; Cox *et al.*, 1975; rational psychotherapy, Lake *et al.*, 1979).

All the studies started from the same basis—the medical model of tension headache. It was argued that cases diagnosed as tension headache would, ipso facto, have abnormal and sustained muscle tension in head and neck. The level of pain suffered would be commensurate with the muscle tension. Biofeedback training to lower this tension was a justifiable intervention. The key issue has become whether reductions in EMG level would be sufficient to result in clinical improvements. This belief in the concordance of muscle activity and pain reports has been so strong that many researchers report on the efficacy of the treatment merely by assessing change in headache activity (i.e. Haynes *et al.*, 1975; Chesney *et al.*, 1976). The (muscular) homogeneity of the medical diagnosed group is also assumed, with no individual assessments, and the frontalis selected as the valid spokesman of the muscular dysfunctions. (The weaknesses of these assumptions are considered in Philips, 1977a). It should also be noted that none of the studies have incorporated measures of the vascular concomitants (i.e. temporal artery pulse).

The over-all result of the studies suggests that biofeedback and general relaxation training can both modify subjective reports of headache pain. However, the studies are methodologically weak. The results are not presented in a way which allows an assessment of the specificity of the treatment effect. It remains unclear to what extent, if at all, the subjective relief reported by patients is specifically due to EMG reductions during treatment. In addition, there is no attempt made to assess whether control of EMG levels has in fact been taught by the biofeedback procedure. An assessment of the specificity of learned control entails evaluating the capacity of each patient to raise and lower the muscular tension at will and without feedback aids. The significant improvement in this capacity, as a consequence of biofeedback training, is a minimal requirement of learned control. This has not been done. In many cases, EMG data were not analysed (Haynes *et al.*, 1975; Chesney *et al.*, 1976) and the reduction of EMG is merely assumed to have occurred. The failure to assess the muscular state of the subjects and select the most abnormal muscle complicates the issue. It is unclear who is being treated and if they are being treated on the appropriate muscle. The improved designs and measures that have tempered early B.F. studies in heart rate control and blood pressure (i.e. Steptoe, 1978, 1980; Lang and Twentyman, 1976; Surwit and Shapiro, 1978) have not been matched in headache research. Positive clinical results were accepted uncritically and the biofeedback modification of tension headache has been quoted as one of the best examples of the practical application of a new psychophysiological technique in medicine (Miller, 1978; Silver and Blanchard,

1978). However, Young and Blanchard's (1980) review in this volume is far more reserved (see Chapter 9).

Given the uncritical support, it is important to remember that, although bio-feedback and relaxation appear to help headache sufferers, we remain unclear *why* this improvement occurs and *how* it is mediated. Cheaper and less complicated management and treatment may prove equally or more efficacious.

5. IMPLICATIONS OF PSYCHOPHYSIOLOGICAL INVESTIGATIONS FOR TREATMENT RESEARCH AND MANAGEMENT

Treatment research has progressed with little notice being taken of the psycho-physiological results reviewed above. The two psychological approaches (psycho-physiological investigations and treatment) to headache have been distinct and unfortunately have been slow to affect each other. The most fruitful steps in our understanding of headache may come from an attempt to explore the implications of the psychophysiological studies on pain assessment and modification. It has been argued above that the medical assumptions concerning tension headache are chal-lenged by experimental results. A number of implications flow from this.

A. Treatment Rationale

The rationale for the use of B.F. and relaxation training for *all* tension cases is undermined. However, there remains a group of cases with high EMG levels who may be most appropriately treated by biofeedback. This possibility is currently being assessed (Philips and Hunter, in progress). But for those with normal EMG levels, biofeedback training is unjustified, and has proved to be impotent (Martin and Mathews, 1978).

B. Selection Criteria

Selection of headache cases using current diagnostic procedures (based on the *ad hoc* definition) will *not* provide a homogeneous group with respect to EMG, abnor-malities. It is necessary to assess the presence of, locus of, and type (tonic/phasic) of the muscular abnormality, to form groups suitable for specific treatments, and group comparison studies.

C. Treating Reactivity

Biofeedback and relaxation treatments are designed to effect tonic levels of EMG or produce general relaxation. No attempt has been made to treat the specific reactions to headache exacerbators (or provoking event). It is likely that training to lower tonic EMG levels teaches little about how to control the size of a muscular reaction and the speed of its attenuation. If these parameters prove important (especially in the initiation of a pain episode), different biofeedback procedures will have to be developed for over-reactors. These treatments will need to utilize the appropriate stress stimuli and train reduced reactions to them.

Cognitive treatments have been concerned with teaching alternative cognitive appraisals in order to "defuse" stress stimuli. They are clearly modifying reactivity—though from a different premise, using the subjective component only (beliefs, attitudes to self and others). Unfortunately, they have not attempted to validate the potency of certain beliefs about stimuli, using assessment of other aspects of the phenomenon (i.e. psychophysiological reactivity). But they show a timely concern for the interaction of the headache sufferer with specific stimuli and situations, i.e. his reactivity.

D. Assessing Efficacy of Treatment

It is necessary to consider adopting a different methodology for assessing headache in treatment studies. If the EMG level is poorly related to the subjective experience (Epstein and Abel, 1977; Philips, 1978), an exclusive dependence on measures of this experience (intensity, frequency, duration) will be an inadequate monitor of the headache phenomenon. It has been argued elsewhere (Philips, 1977a), that a more appropriate methodology is one that takes cognizance of the three major components of the headache (pain) phenomenon: the physiological, the subjective, and the behavioural. Rather than prejudging their relationship, we can examine the extent of concordance, as a step towards understanding the nature of headache pain. Factors such as severity, chronicity, personality, mood (i.e. depression), emotionality (anxiety), sex, etc. are likely to affect the degree of association of the three components. Separate evaluation of the components will be useful in assessing both the efficacy of treatment, as well as identifying mediators of the change.

Treatment success has depended predominantly on showing an improvement (reduction) in an headache index, usually derived by an arithemetic summation of subject-rated intensity and duration. It can be seen from Table 3 that no studies have assessed any other aspects of the pain experience e.g. affective reactions, evaluative reactions, or sensory qualities. These dimensions have been explored with success by Melzack (1975) in his Pain Questionnaire and have proved discriminable and useful parameters in other investigations of pain experience (Leavitt et al., 1978; Crockett et al., 1977). Consequently, the pain experience in headache (and its modification when treated) has not been studied to date. Even the judgements of frequency, intensity, and duration are often merged into headache scores (Budzynski et al., 1973; Bakal and Kaganov, 1977; Hutchings and Reinking, 1976). In this way the differential effect of a treatment on the three parameters is lost. There is some indication that frequency of headache may be shifted more readily (first and most) than intensity (Haynes et al., 1975; Chesney and Shelton, 1976) in biofeedback and relaxation. Duration is difficult to shift by biofeedback (Chesney and Shelton, 1976; Philips, 1977b), but seems to account for most of the improvements reported by cognitive treatments (Holroyd et al., 1977, 1978). These findings will be useful in understanding how therapeutic changes come about.

It can be seen in Table 3 that the behaviour motivated by pain has been almost ignored. Medication rate is sometimes used to supplement measures of treatment efficacy. It appears to be a poor candidate to assess the immediate behavioural effects of treatment. It is unrelated to either muscular levels or intensity/frequency

TABLE 3.
Summary of Assessments of Pain Undertaken in Major Treatment Studies

Authors	Pain components		
	Physiological	Subjective	Behavioural
Budzynski et al. (1973)	EMG: frontalis (tonic)	Headache Index—weekly average (incorporates frequency, intensity and duration)	Medication rate/type pre-treatment, during first half and last half of treatment
Haynes et al. (1975)	EMG: frontalis (tonic) (not assessed)	Headache Index—weekly Intensity (10–10 rating) Frequency weekly Duration average No. hours	None
Chesney et al. (1976)	EMG: frontalis (tonic) (not assessed)	Frequency Duration Severity (0–100) } Pre- and post-treatment	None
Hutchings et al. (1976)	EMG: frontalis (tonic)	Headache Index	None
Cox et al. (1975)	EMG: frontalis (tonic)	Headache Data (intensity and duration combined) Frequency Duration	Medication rate
Philips (1977b)	EMG: frontalis	Intensity, Duration, Frequency } weekly average	Medication rate
Bakal et al. (1977)	EMG: frontalis	Headache Index	None
Martin et al. (1978)	EMG: frontalis neck	Headache Index	None

of tension headaches (Philips, 1977b). In addition, it has currently been found unrelated to two other aspects of pain behaviour sampled (Philips and Hunter, 1980c). However, because of the role of pain behaviour in management and adjustment, it is important to assess this component in its own right, as well as to determine its relationships to the pain experience. By pain behaviour, I refer to withdrawal from certain stimuli, avoidance of certain stimuli, verbal and non-verbal complaint (moaning, holding head etc.), as well as ameliorative actions (seeking advice, pills etc.). Fordyce (1976, 1978) has been primarily concerned with operant pain behaviour in the form of inactivity and verbal complaint. But, there are many *active* behavioural patterns motivated by headache.

As yet, no one has investigated whether avoidance and withdrawal behaviour do reduce subjective judgements of pain, and whether exposure exacerbates pain. It is possible that *some* pain behaviour acts to increase subject vulnerability to headache in the longer run, though giving immediate relief. A more detailed approach to pain behaviour will allow some of these issues to be considered.

In summary, investigations of pain behaviour and subjective experience are needed. With these additional measures, and the physiological measures, the interrelatedness of the expression of pain can be studied in detail. A procedure designed to modify one component (i.e. EMG level in biofeedback) can be studied and the effect of this change on the subjective and behavioural component observed.

E. Treatment Choice

As tension-headache cases vary in the extent of EMG involvement, as well as in the amount of pain behaviour or pain experience, it becomes necessary to consider the problem of treatment choice. It is possible to select from a variety of treatment approaches, i.e. behavioural, psychophysiological, rational psychotherapy, cognitive, etc.; and a new concern must be to predict the best and most efficient treatment for an individual sufferer. In 1977a, I made a number of predictions in this respect, based on the assumption that the most pronounced aspect of the pain phenomenon would be the best initial focus. Some of these predictions are currently being tested in the hope of identifying prognostic indicators. It will be a useful step forward, if one can confidently predict the best procedure to follow from an assessment of the physiological, behavioural and subjective expressions of headache pain.

6. CONCLUSIONS

Although the psychophysiological research has largely provided clarity with respect to what tension headache is *not*, the contribution has not been all negative. It has laid the basis of at least two important contributions.

(1) It has forced a consideration of headache as a more complex phenomenon than the contraction of a set of muscle fibres. Headache must now be conceptualized as a type of pain experience, thus affected in its expression and course by a wide set of psychological factors as well as physiological ones.

(2) This conceptual change is closely linked to the second major contribution that has been made. The methodology for studying headache pain and its modifica-

tion is changing. It is no longer possible to assess the phenomenon by measuring muscle potentials. The subjective and behavioural expression of pain are as relevant (and possibly more so) than the physiological.

It is likely that these conceptual and methodological changes will have an important effect on treatment and management of tension cases. The treatment of choice may be better determined by assessing the individual expression of pain (behavioural, physiological and subjective), rather than relying upon headache diagnosis. In addition, it is clear that a greater attention needs to be given to the situational determinants of pain episodes, both in designing treatments and counselling management of headache. Specific muscular/vascular or mood control can be taught, in face of provoking stimuli. Alternative behavioural strategies can be evolved to cope with both trigger events and the pain itself. At present, we assume that strategies which bring immediate relief (avoidance etc.) are the best long-term policy. However, such advice could be as misguided as withdrawal proved to be to those with phobic anxiety. There are now a whole set of new research issues to be undertaken that have come directly from the last decade's work on headache. A number of misconceptions have been removed, and it seems likely that considerable progress can now be made in both the understanding of the disorder and in its treatment and management.

REFERENCES

Alexander, A. B. (1975) An experimental test of assumptions relating to the use of electromyographic biofeedback as a general relaxation training technique, *Psychophysiol.*, **12**, 656–662.

Bakal, D. A. and Kaganov, J. A. (1977) Muscular contraction and migraine headache: A psychophysiological comparison. *Headache*, **5**, 208–216.

Beecher, H. K. (1959) *Measurement of subjective responses*, Oxford University Press.

Bond, M. R. (1971) The relation of pain to EPI. Connell MI and Whitley Index of Hypochondriasis. *Br. J. Psychiat.*, **119**, 553.

Bond, M. R. and Pilowsky, I. (1966) Subjective assessment of pain and its relationship to administration of analgesics in patients with advanced cancer, *J. Psychosom. Res.*, **10**, 203.

Boxtel, Van A. and Van der Ven, J. R. (1978) Different EMG activity in subjects with muscle contraction headaches related to mental effort, *Headache*, **17**, 233–237.

Budzynski, T. H. Stoyva, J. M. and Adler, C. (1973) EMG biofeedback and tension headache: a controlled outcome study. *Psychosomatic Med.*, **35**, 484–496.

Chesney, M. A. and Shelton, J. L. (1976) A comparison of muscle relaxation and EMG biofeedback treatments for muscular contraction headache, *J. of Behav. Therapy and Exper. Psychiat.*, **7**, 221–225.

Cohen M. J. (1978) Psychophysiological studies of headache: Is there similarity between migraine and muscular-contraction headache? *Headache*, **18**, 189–196.

Cox, D. J., Freudlich, A. and Meyer, R. G. (1975) Differential effectiveness of EMG feedback, verbal relaxation instructions and medication placebo with tension headache, *J. consult. clin. Psychol.*, **43**(6), 892–898.

Crockett, D. J., Prkachin, K. M. and Craig, K. D. (1977) Factors of the language of pain in patients and voluntary groups, *Pain*, **4**, 175–182.

Dunnell, K. and Cartwright, A. (1972) *Medicine Takers, Prescribers and Hoarders*, Routledge & Kegan Paul.

Epstein, L. H. and Abel, G. G. (1977) An analysis of biofeedback training effects for tension headache patients, *Behav. Ther.*, **8**, 37–47.

Fordyce, W. E. (1976) *Behavioural methods for chronic pain and illness*, Mosley, St. Louis.

Fordyce, W. E. (1978) Learning processes in pain, in Sternbach, R. A. *The Psychology of Pain*, Raven Press.

Friedman, A. P. (1962) Ad Hoc Committee on classification of Headache, *J. Amer. Med. Assoc.*, **179**, 717–718.

Harper, R. G. and Steger, J. C. (1978) Psychological correlates of frontalis EMG and pain in tension headache, *Headache*, **18**, 215–218.

Hart, J. D. and Cichanski, K. A. (1975) Biofeedback as a treatment for headaches: Conceptual and methodological issues. Paper presented at Association for Advancement in Behavior Therapy, San Francisco.

Haynes, S. N., Griffin, P., Mooney, D., Parise, M. (1975) EMG biofeedback and relaxation instructions in the treatment of muscular contraction headaches, *Behav. Ther.*, **6**, 672–678.

Holroyd, K. and Andrasik, F. (1978) Coping and self-control of chronic tension headache, *J. consult. clin. Psychol.*, **46**(5), 1036–1045.

Holroyd, K., Andrasik, F. and Westbrook, T. (1977) Cognitive control of tension headache, *Cognitive Therapy and Res.*, **1**, 721–733.

Hunter, M. and Philips, C. (1980) An assessment of the subjective component in headache pain, In preparation.

Hutchings, D. F. and Reinking, R. H. (1976) Tension headache: what form of therapy is most effective? *Biof. and Self-regulation* **1**, 183–190.

James, P. and Philips, C. (1980) Muscular reactions and recovery in tension headache. In preparation.

Lake, A., Rainey, J. and Papadorf, J. D. (1979) Biofeedback and rational emotive therapy in the management of migraine headache, *J. appl. Behav. Anal.*, **12**, 127–140.

Lacey, J. J. (1967) Somatic response patterning and stress, In Appley, M. H. and Turnbull, R. (Eds.) *Psychological Stress*, Appleton–Century–Croft, New York.

Lang, P. L. and Twentyman, C. T. (1976) Learned control of HR: Effects of varying incentive and criterion of success on task performance, *Psychophysiol.*, **13**(5), 378–386.

Leavitt, F., Garron, D. C., Whisler, W. W. and Mitchell, B. (1978) Affective and sensory dimensions of back pain, *Pain* **4**, 273–281.

Martin, M. J. (1967) In, *Studies in Headache*, A. P. Friedman (Ed.), Vol. I, Karger, Basle.

Martin, P. R. and Mathews, A. M. (1978) Tension headaches: Psychophysiological investigations and treatment, *J. Psychosom. Res.*, **22**, 389–399.

Melzack, R. (1973) *The Puzzle of Pain*, Penguin.

Melzack, R. (1975) The McGill Pain Questionnaire: Major properties and scoring methods. *Pain*, **1**, 277–299.

Miller, N. E. (1963) Learning of visceral and glandular responses, *Science*, **163**, 434–445.

Miller, N. E. (1970) Learned modification of autonomic function, in T. X. Barber *et al.* (Eds.) *Biofeedback and Self-control*, Alding Pub. Co., pp. 351–359.

Miller, N. E. (1978) Biofeedback and visceral learning, *Ann. Rev. Psychol.*, **29**, 373–404.

Ostfeld, A. M. (1962) *The Common Headache Syndrome: Biochemistry, Pathophysiology, Therapy*, C. C. Thomas, Illinois.

Pearce, S. (1977) The relationship between physiological measurement of muscle activity and subjective report. M. Phil. dissertation, University of London.

Philips, C. (1977a) A psychological analysis of tension headache, in *Contributions to Medical Psychology*, S. Rachman (Ed.), Vol. 1, Pergamon Press, Oxford.

Philips, C. (1977b) The modification of tension headache pain using EMG biofeedback, *Behav. Res. & Ther.*, **15**, 119–129.

Philips, C. (1978) Tension headache: Theoretical problems, *Behav. Res. & Ther.*, **16**, 249–261.

Philips, C. and Hunter, M. (1980a) A psychophysiological investigation of tension headache. In preparation.

Philips, C. and Hunter, M. (1980b) An assessment of headache pain: the three component approach. In preparation.

Philips, C. and Hunter, M. (1980c) Pain behaviour in headache sufferers. In preparation.

Pozniak-Patweicz, E. (1976) Cephalic spasm of head and neck muscles, *Headache*, **15**, 261–266.

Rachman, S. J. and Philips, C. (1978) *Psychology and Medicine*, Pelican.

Sainsbury, P. and Gibson, J. G. (1954) Symptoms of anxiety and tension and accompanying physiological changes in the muscle system, *J. Neurol. Neurosurg. & Psychiat.*, **17**, 216.

Silver, B. N. and Blanchard, E. B. (1978) Biofeedback and relaxation training in the treatment of psychophysiological disorders: Or are the machines really necessary? *J. Behav. Med.*, **1**, 217–239.

Steptoe, A. (1978) New approaches to the management of essential hypertension with psychological techniques, *J. Psychosom. Res.*, **22**, 339–354.

Steptoe, A. (1980) Stress and medical disorders. This volume.

Surwitt, R. S. and Shapiro, D. (1978) Comparison of cardiovascular biofeedback, neuromuscular biofeedback and meditation in the treatment of borderline essential hypertension, *J. consult. clin. Psychol.*, **46**, 252–263.

Vaughn, R., Pall, M. L. and Haynes, S. N. (1977) Frontalis EMG response to stress in subjects with frequent muscular contraction headaches, *Headache*, **16**, 313–317.

Weisenberg, M. (1977) Pain and pain control, *Psychol. Bull.*, **84**, 1008–1044.

Young, L. D. and Blanchard, E. B. (1980) Medical applications of biofeedback training: A selective review, In *Contributions to Medical Psychology*, Vol. 2, S. J. Rachman (Ed.), Pergamon Press.

6

THE PROBLEM OF LOW BACK PAIN

MICHAEL HUMPHREY

St. George's Hospital Medical School, University of London

CONTENTS

1. INTRODUCTION

Common observation would suggest that by middle life many, if not most, adults have experienced pain or strain in the lumbar region, whether they refer to it as lumbago, slipped disc, or merely backache. It is one of the more important causes of absence from work, accounting for nearly five million lost days in a year according to one estimate (Troup, 1965). The heavy manual labourer is more prone to back strain and less likely to remain at work during periods of disability, while the risk of "chain injuries" is also greater (Jaffe *et al.*, 1964). It has been reported that as many as 65 per cent of industrial workers in the U.S.A. have back trouble (McBeath, 1970). Yet, even a sedentary job may involve activities from which the backache victim is effectively debarred, such as driving to work or chairing interminable committee meetings. It is reasonable to suppose that, even in our present strike-bound and clock-watching society with its diminished enthusiasm for work, leisure activities are still more vulnerable to the low back syndrome. Again, it is the more vigorous members of the community who are most likely to be affected.

Lumbar pain is among the more frequent reasons for consulting a general practitioner in adulthood regardless of whether a sickness certificate is required. Ward *et al.* (1968) in a survey of 16 practices covering a population of 45,000 in the North Midlands found an annual incidence of 22.8 per 1,000 in men and 15.3 per 1,000 in women. Dillane *et al.* (1966) found that 7.5 per cent of the population at risk in their South-east London practice presented with this complaint over a four-year period. The annual incidence was 24.3 per 1,000 in men and 20.3 per 1,000 in women, reaching a peak in the sixth decade for both sexes. Most episodes were transitory and of unknown origin; fewer than 10 per cent of patients were referred to hospital and none of the latter required surgery. The recurrence rate of 45 per cent was almost four times what might be expected in a group with the same age and sex distribution.

The condition has no established pathology or aetiology, and structural abnormalities seen on X-ray examination are difficult to correlate with clinical symptoms (Harrison, 1960; Hollander, 1960). It is probably as a consequence of this uncertainty that it often seems to produce "as much, if not more, discomfort in those treating the condition as in those suffering from it" (Silverman, 1977). The level of complaint and degree of manifest disability are liable to fluctuate in an unpredictable manner. Some patients exasperate their doctors by failing to recover when all the clinical indications suggest that they should; others are suddenly relieved of chronic handicap by fringe medicine, hypnosis, or a visit to Lourdes. Small wonder, then, that psychological factors have been invoked from time to time, especially in patients seen by psychiatrists and psychoanalysts (Paul, 1950). Whilst the case for a psychogenic aetiology may be rather tenuous, this does not mean that personal and social circumstances play little or no part in the prolongation of symptoms. The same consideration applies to all bodily complaints (even terminal cancer), and it is high time that the clinical psychologist brought his expertise to bear on the management of what Sternbach *et al.* (1973b) have christened the "low-back loser".

I was drawn into this field by an orthopaedic colleague (Mr Robin Bendall, FRCS). Over the past four years some fifty outpatients as well as a number of in-patients have been referred by Mr Bendall and other consultants for psychological evaluation, usually because they had responded poorly to conservative treatment and were being considered for surgery. On the strength of the psychologist's report, some patients received an operation which might otherwise have been postponed or withheld; and, in one or two instances, the surgeon was surprised by the extent of the lesion which standard investigations had failed to disclose. Other patients were spared surgical intervention, which was thought likely to prove unhelpful, if not positively harmful; and in some of these cases, there was a history of one or more previous spinal operations that had failed. Some patients were more dismayed than relieved when told that surgery had nothing to offer them, since they had pinned all their hopes on a dramatic rescue from their pain. While, in theory, this opened the way to a psychological approach, in practice this was seldom exploited. Either the patient would refuse to countenance the idea, or resistance would be expressed through cancelled or unkept appointments.

Recently I have studied a series of fifty patients admitted to the Wolfson Medical Rehabilitation Centre (part of the St. George's Hospital group) with a primary complaint of low back pain. The main object of this survey was to assess the frequency and importance of psychological factors in patients who had been selected for intensive rehabilitation on purely physical criteria. A programme based largely on physiotherapy and remedial exercises was scarcely optimal for patients who, in the opinion of the staff, were handicapped chiefly by "functional overlay".

This easily abused term had not infrequently crept into the Centre's case notes over the years, but only after much futile expenditure of therapeutic effort. If the unresponsive patient could be identified in advance, then he or she could be either excluded or managed on different principles, leading to better allocation of resources and improvements in staff morale. A follow-up interview and clinical examination of these fifty patients (in collaboration with the Medical Director, Dr David Jenkins) will be conducted a year after their discharge from the Centre, to determine whether the psychologist's contribution had any predictive value. Meanwhile, only preliminary findings can be reported here, but the problems to be anticipated from introducing an experimental regime into an orthodox medical rehabilitation centre will be discussed in the final section of the chapter.

What follows is divided into five sections. First, I shall review what is known of the demographic and other characteristics of sufferers from this condition, and then look at the results and predictive value of psychological testing, with special reference to the Minnesota Multiphasic Personality Inventory (MMPI), which has stolen the limelight in this context. Next, the question of treatment strategies drawing on psychological principles will come under scrutiny. Lastly, a possible role for the clinical psychologist will be adumbrated, in the light of personal experience and knowledge of the literature. Detailed discussion of therapeutic methods will not be attempted on the grounds that, as in any pioneering field, effective development rests on individual enterprise.

2. PERSONAL AND SOCIAL ATTRIBUTES OF SUFFERERS

Most of the published reports on victims of low back pain suffer from the drawback of being purely descriptive and lacking in adequate control data. There is not much point in calculating the proportion of patients who are poorly educated or unhappily married (even from a representative sample), unless one can be sure that those with other complaints are significantly different in these respects. Nevertheless, some useful hints can be gleaned, where the findings from diverse studies are both consistent and in tune with clinical experience.

An association between limited formal education and manual work in chronic back sufferers has emerged from a variety of studies (e.g. Sargent, 1946; White, 1966; Beals and Hickman, 1972; Wilfling et al., 1973; Nagi et al., 1973; Gentry et al., 1974; Maruta et al., 1976). The conclusions of Nagi et al. (1973) are among the more reliable, in having been derived from an epidemiological survey of 1,135 persons aged 18–64 in Ohio, of whom 18 per cent reported being often bothered by pain in the back. They found an inverse relationship between educational attainment and frequency of complaint; manual workers were predominant, and women outnumbered men in all occupational categories (21 per cent against 14 per cent). Having eliminated menstrual disturbance as a factor by showing that the sex difference held good above the age of 50, the authors went on to attribute at least some of it to the well known discrepancies between male and female anxiety levels and pain thresholds.

Gentry et al. (1974) had a sample of only fifty-six patients, of whom two-thirds were in "hard manual or routinised clerical jobs" and almost one-fifth were

housewives. They considered that the strenuous nature of the work was not necessarily the main factor, since most patients "had experienced unmet dependency
needs early in life. That is, they had begun work at an early age and had worked at
relatively hard jobs for a long time prior to symptom onset. In addition, they were
typically later born children from large families, who in turn married early and
quickly had several children of their own. Thus, by virtue of providing for others
and not being able to fully depend on their own parents as children they had
postponed gratification of such needs until a minor injury provided a rational and
socially acceptable means of depending on others for emotional and economic
support" (p. 176). This is certainly an interesting perspective; and although the
nature of the patient's family experience requires more statistical support than is
currently available, it is reflected in a substantial minority of the author's own
rehabilitation group. For example, fifteen out of thirty-nine married patients had
three or more children, and all but four of this subgroup came from sibships of
three or more.

The significance of marital status is uncertain, as compared with age, sex, and
occupation. Nagi *et al.* (1973), while acknowledging that the relative immunity of
unmarried persons and the greater vulnerability of the widowed in their sample
could be largely an effect of age, nevertheless speculated on a possible linkage
through anxiety and difficulty in coping with life. Thus, in an earlier study, it had
been found that back sufferers with a history of divorce, separation, or bereavement
responded less well to a rehabilitation programme than married persons with no
such history (Nagi *et al.*, 1965). This relationship cannot be tested on the author's
own series of fifty patients, since only two were separated or divorced and none
widowed (an unexpected finding, in view of the common assumption that patients
lacking social support are more likely to require specialized resources for the con-
quest of handicap).

Marital disharmony could be more relevant to the persistence of handicap than
separation or divorce to which some people will have adapted. The importance of
this factor has been noted by Kreitman *et al.* (1965) in relation to bodily complaints
with no detectable organic basis. Marriage counselling has occasionally proved
successful in the relief of backache where more direct approaches had failed (Silverman, 1977).

The influence of the family receives a further boost from the study of Gentry *et
al.* (1974). More than half of their patients reported at least one family member
(parent, grandparent, sibling) as having either low back pain or some other equally
debilitating physical disorder, such as diabetes, cancer, myocardial infarction, or
arthritis. Moreover, one patient in four had "significant others" with a history of
chronic back trouble, which had also proved unamenable to conventional treatment. The absence of a control group, once again, limits interpretation, but the
impact of family models on pain and illness behaviour is now well authenticated
(Craig, 1978).

Possibly, the medical profession must themselves take some of the blame for the
chronic nature of so much lumbar discomfort. There does not appear to have been
any systematic study of doctors' responses to complaints of low back pain; but
once the patient has been referred to the hospital service, events are apt to pursue
their own relentless course. Special investigations may be inconclusive and pallia-

tive treatment ineffective, yet, sooner or later, some suspicous finding may tip the scales towards surgery. If the patient is still no better, perhaps even more disabled, there will be further demands on medical resources. The same unhappy sequence has been described in regard to gynaecological complaints which may culminate in avoidable hysterectomy (Richards, 1973). This point will receive further discussion in due course.

3. PSYCHOLOGICAL TEST FINDINGS

Despite their prime allegiance to psychiatry, clinical psychologists have been actively involved in the assessment of medical and surgical patients over the past three decades. Few psychophysiological disorders have attracted more interest than low back pain, and Hanvik (1949, 1951) started a fashion that has continued to this day. He set out to determine whether the MMPI could be used to discriminate between cases with demonstrable organic pathology and those where, in the absence of such pathology, a psychogenic basis could be assumed.

This test is available either in a paper and pencil version or as a set of 550 statements on individual cards to be sorted into the categories True, False, or Cannot say. The statements embrace a wide variety of thoughts, feelings, attitudes, and behaviour. Scoring of abnormal responses contributes to a set of scales which, in accordance with the original standardization process, are tied to psychiatric categories such as depression, hysteria, paranoia, and psychopathic deviance. Other syndromes and more general concepts (such as ego strength) have been added over the years. Probably, its chief advantage over most other clinical self-report instruments is the fact that it incorporates four measures of test-taking attitude, so that the subject who is unduly defensive or inclined to overdramatize his feelings can be detected and some allowance made for the resulting distortion of the profile. Among its recognized disadvantages are the time taken in administration (usually, at least an hour for the full version) and scoring (say, half an hour), and for European users, the occasional mysteries of the American idiom (e.g. "At school I was sometimes sent to the principal for cutting up", or "When I take a new job I like to be tipped off on who should be gotten next to"). Whether for these or other reasons there seem to be few British psychologists still making regular use of the test, which has lost none of its popularity across the Atlantic. An example of a normal record from the author's own series is given below (number of statements left unclassified = 13, or 2 per cent).

Hanvik's two groups of thirty patients were matched for age, social class, marital status, intelligence, and race. The organic group had undergone surgery for the removal of a slipped disc, except in two cases where a disc lesion had been diagnosed from the history, clinical examination, and X-ray evidence. Their composite test profile revealed slightly raised scores on the Hypochondriasis (Hs), Depression (D) and Hysteria (Hy) scales (the "neurotic triad"). In contrast the non-organic group profile displayed a fairly clear-cut "conversion-V" or "depressive valley" configuration, as first described by Gough (1946). This pattern could be taken to reflect the essence of the hysterical conversion syndrome, in which physical symptoms fail to elicit the expected emotional reactions—so-called *belle indifference*. The patient is saying, in effect, "I have numerous bodily complaints but I am relatively

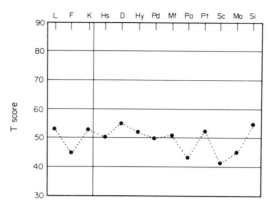

FIG 1. MMPI profile of case No. 12. Female, 30. Left school at 16, now working as receptionist. Married 8–9 years, no children. Onset 2–3 years ago, severe recurrence 2–3 months ago.

unworried, not depressed" (Hanvik, 1951, p. 351). The interest lies in the shape of the profile, rather than in the absolute magnitude of the scores; although it may be worth noting that the organic group obtained significantly lower scores on all but two of the eight clinical scales. A striking example of the conversion-V pattern from the author's own series is given below (number of statements left unclassified = 38, or 7 per cent).

In a study of fifty-eight back sufferers, seventy-two fracture patients, and a normal control group Phillips (1964) found evidence of a raised MMPI neurotic triad in the low back pain group, as compared with the fracture group, who in turn produced more abnormal scores than the controls. Female back patients were more overtly disturbed than male ones.

Sternbach et al. (1973b) gave the MMPI to 117 consecutive admissions to the San Diego University Hospital back clinic. This series included both acute and chronic patients (the latter defined as having been in pain for more than six months), patients with and without abnormal findings on clinical examination, and

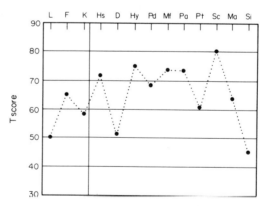

FIG. 2. MMPI profile of case No. 27. Male, 25, University graduate with chequered work record, now hoping for career in advertising. Unmarried. Onset 3–4 years ago after football injury, laminectomy a few months later. Recurrence within 9 months leading to gradual deterioration.

a subgroup of compensation cases. The composite profile showed a pronounced elevation of the neurotic triad (approximately two standard deviations above the normal mean), but here the D score was only slightly lower than the other two as one might expect from such a heterogeneous group. However, when the nineteen acute patients were studied separately, it was found that not only were they less disturbed, but there was a discernible tendency towards the conversion-V profile, which was interpreted by the authors as a sign of "masked depression". On the other hand, patients awaiting the outcome of a compensation claim emerged as *more* disturbed on all three scales. Rather unexpectedly, there were no significant differences between the group with physical findings and the group without them. Generally speaking, it was the men in this series who showed more disturbance (especially in the form of depression and passivity), which was taken to reflect the greater impact of physical impairment on the male breadwinner in a society which more readily condones weakness and absence from work in its female members.

The patients studied by Gentry *et al.* (1974) had all undergone surgery and thus, not surprisingly, were chronic in the sense already defined. Even so, they tended towards the conversion-V pattern which in Hanvik's experience occurred much less often in genuine surgical cases. In addition, their patients were apt to "fake good" on the evidence of the relationship between F and K scores (two of the validity indicators), which distinguished them from true malingerers—a category not often seen among the chronic backache population (Beals and Hichman, 1972). But the most interesting finding was the link between depression and chronicity that emerged when the data from Gentry *et al.*'s study were pooled with those from Hanvik and Beals and Hickman. Patients who had been in pain for more than 10 years produced a lower mean D score than those whose pain was of more recent origin. This suggests that the hysterical posture is more common among those who have defeated the best efforts of their physicians and surgeons, as clinical experience would lead one to expect.

Several other studies have reported on the use of the **MMPI** with back patients (e.g. Carr *et al.*, 1966; Shaffer *et al.*, 1972; Calsyn *et al.*, 1976; Freeman *et al.*, 1976; Maruta *et al.*, 1976; Bradley *et al.*, 1978). The one consistent feature is elevation of the neurotic triad. The normality or otherwise of the remaining clinical measures has varied from study to study, presumably owing to differences in the populations surveyed (acute vs. chronic, organic vs. functional, psychiatric vs. normal, etc.). Both Calsyn *et al.* (1976) and Freeman *et al.* (1976) have commented on the artificiality of the organic–functional dichotomy, since this ignores the reality of "functional overlay" in patients who persist in complaining long after their organic signs have receded. In comparing three small groups of patients matched for age and educational level—organic, functional and mixed—Freeman *et al.* found that the profiles of the functional and mixed groups could be distinguished from the organic group more sharply than from one another.

In one of the most elaborate studies to date, Bradley *et al.* (1978) gave the **MMPI** to 548 patients attending a large medical centre over a three-year period. All had been referred for evaluation, because of unresponsiveness to traditional medical or surgical treatment and/or a questionable physiological basis for their pain. By means of multivariate analysis, the authors were able to isolate three types of profile that appeared consistently in both men and women; but a fourth type—the by now familiar conversion-V—was confined to women. This supports the notion of hysteria as a predominantly female disorder and may help to explain the surfeit of women (typically in the ratio of 3:2) in most rehabilitation groups, which would include the more intractable cases. Oddly, the authors make no comment on this sex difference, but express the hope that their characteristic profiles may be associated with "distinct, pain-related behavioural attributes" which could have implications for treatment.

The author's own rehabilitation series comprised twenty-nine women but only twenty-one men, a reversal of the normal sex ratio in patients admitted to the Wolfson Centre. The age range was 17–56, most patients being in their 30s or 40s. The conversion-V profile appeared equally often in each sex—about one in four cases. In forty-one cases, a prediction was made from the interview data (which covered a wide range of topics, albeit superficially) as to whether the MMPI record would be normal or abnormal/borderline, and twenty-one out of twenty-four normal records were correctly predicted. Patients producing disturbed records were evidently more deceptive since only nine out of seventeen such records were correctly predicted. This may mean simply that patients were habitually given the benefit of the doubt; although it was not rare for a patient who appeared remarkably self-possessed in the interview to declare widespread abnormality on the test, just as patients presenting themselves as neurotic on interview might sometimes achieve a test profile that was both apparently reliable and well within normal limits. This is reassuring, in that it would be unsatisfactory, if such an elaborate self-report procedure were merely to duplicate the skills of an experienced interviewer.

In view of the not uncommon link between back pain and gynaecological disorders, it is worth noting that five women had undergone hysterectomy at ages ranging from 32–46; and in no case was this due to malignancy. A figure of 17 per cent seems high for such a relatively youthful group; and indeed fewer than 20 per cent of women in the general population suffer this indignity up to the age of 75 (Fairbairn and Acheson, 1969). Interestingly, their MMPI profiles were not among the more disturbed, all but one being within normal limits. The relative importance of physical and social pathology is illustrated by a comparison of the two oldest women in this small subgroup, who were 45 and 49 respectively at the time of interview. The first had marital problems that were as intrusive as her back complaint and of much longer duration; she was referred to the visiting psychiatrist for an opinion on her depression, which was thought not to require treatment in its own right. The profile indicated hysterical, rather than depressive, tendencies as her main problem; but she was defensive. The second behaved as if she was in agony, with palpable tension of the spinal musculature, yet had managed to keep going until recently with the support of a devoted husband and a rich family life. Her profile was fairly normal, despite an approach to the test that was anything but defensive.

Mention should be made at this point of attempts to develop special MMPI scales for discriminating between functional and organic patients. From his original data, Hanvik developed a twenty-five-item low back pain (Lb) scale. While few cross-validation studies have been reported from America, in France Pichot *et al.* (1972) have produced a rival sixty-three-item scale known as the Dorsales Fonc-

tionnelles (DOR). However, their criterion groups of eighty-four patients with functional back pain (including seventy-seven women) and 314 pain-free controls
(including 173 women) were quite different from those of Hanvik, who worked with
men only and used patients with pain-producing organic lesions as controls. Consequently, it need come as no surprise that the two scales were found to be relatively
independent and weakly correlated. In a cross-validation study reported in the
same paper, 57 per cent of patients were correctly classified on the DOR scale, as
compared with 43 per cent of patients on the Lb scale. When the two scales were
used in combination the proportion of correct assignments rose to 79 per cent, a
finding which has since been replicated by other workers (Calsyn et al., 1976;
Freeman et al., 1976). Even so, the fact that neither Hanvik nor Pichot et al.
reported base rates for their groups was bound to limit the clinical application of
these scales, which must remain experimental.

Although the MMPI has taken precedence over other measures, there have been
one or two attempts to introduce briefer self-report questionnaires in the evaluation
of patients with low back pain. For example, Nagi et al. (1973), in their epidemiological survey, found that back sufferers reported higher levels of anxiety than subjects with similar functional limitations but no back pain. Sternbach et al. (1973a)
devised a Health Index comprising fifty yes–no questions to explore various ideas
about the chronic backache victim: that he holds an extreme self-concept of himself
as an invalid, that he is depressed, and that he has an excessive reaction to pain,
and a hostile attitude towards the medical profession. The first ten items were taken
from the Cornell Medical Index (CMI) to measure invalidism (e.g. Does suffering
seem to be your way of life?). The next twenty items were adapted from the Self-
rating Depression Scale of Zung (1965) to tap feelings of hopelessness and helplessness (e.g. Are you dissatisfied with things you used to enjoy?). The final twenty
items were designed to assess the impact of pain on the patient's life and any
antagonism towards doctors (e.g. Do you find that all you can think about is your
pain? Do doctors seem to have failed you?). When this questionnaire was given to
twenty-six patients with low back pain and a control group of twenty-eight similarly disabled rheumatoid arthritics, the back patients more often responded positively on the invalidism, pain, and hostility items ($P < 0.01$), whereas on the manifest depression items, the difference fell just short of statistical significance. This
trend would repay further investigation, in view of the psychosomatic interpretations that rheumatoid arthritis has itself been known to attract.

4. THE PREDICTIVE VALUE OF PSYCHOLOGICAL TESTING

The use of the MMPI to delineate types of complainant has yielded some intriguing results, yet the practical value of the exercise is questionable, unless this extra
information can help to predict response to treatment. If the previous section seems
long-winded by comparison with the brevity of the present one, this is because of
an imbalance in the literature. Only three studies have been traced that deal explicitly with prediction.[1]

---

[1] A fourth study (Lloyd et al., 1979) has appeared since this section was written.

The earliest of these was retrospective. Wilfling *et al.* (1973) followed up a group of twenty-six men who had undergone spinal fusion. In addition to an intelligence test, the subjects were given three self-report instruments: the MMPI, the CMI, and the Mooney Problem Check List. Response to the operation was assessed on a three-point scale from a quantitative functional rating supplied by the orthopaedic surgeon. It was found that the best group endorsed significantly fewer CMI items referring to pain, deformity, and fatigue, as well as getting lower scores on the MMPI neurotic triad. However, this conclusion is of limited interest, since the inter-group differences could well have resulted directly from the presence or absence of post-operative pain and stiffness. It is to prospective studies that we must turn for a more valid appraisal of what psychological tests have to contribute.

Forrest and Wolkind (1974) gave the Middlesex Hospital Questionnaire (MHQ) to a series of fifty men with low back pain (but no evidence of disc lesion) on their first day at the rheumatology department of a general hospital. This forty-eight-item test was introduced by Crown and Crisp (1966) to provide a measure of general emotionality, along with a profile of six sub-test scores designed to measure free-floating anxiety, phobic anxiety, obsessionality, somatic concomitants of anxiety, depression, and hysterical personality. After six sessions of treatment (apparently physiotherapy), patients were asked to complete a self-rating questionnaire to describe their present clinical state. Treatment was usually spread over three weeks, and completed questionnaires were received from all but four patients, whose response was assessed from the case notes. The outcome was classified crudely as either good or poor. The twenty-seven "good" patients, who were relatively symptom-free, had a mean age of 35.1 whereas the twenty-three "poor" patients were significantly older with a mean age of 43.6 ($P < 0.05$). The latter obtained higher mean scores on all six scales, but significant differences were confined to the somatic scale ($P < 0.001$) and the obsessional and depressive scales ($P < 0.01$). When a cut-off score of seven points on the somatic scale was used to divide the patients into two groups of approximately the same size as the two outcome groups, it was found that proportionately three times as many of the higher scorers had a poor result ($P < 0.001$). When the scores of each group were compared with those from 1,288 men employed by the Atomic Energy Authority (Crown *et al.*, 1970) the superior outcome group differed on only two scales—free-floating anxiety ($P < 0.05$) and hysterical personality ($P < 0.01$)—whereas the inferior group differed on all six scales, at a significance level of at least $P < 0.01$.

On an item analysis, the two questions from the somatic scale that discriminated most sharply between the two outcome groups were as follows: (1) Has your appetite got less recently? (2) Has your sexual interest altered (lessened)? A positive response to either of these questions (which refer to symptoms commonly associated with depression) had more predictive value than the somatic scale as a whole. An advantage of the somatic over the depressive and obsessional scores in the present context is that the latter are more likely to rise with age (Crown *et al.*, 1970; Crisp and Priest, 1971).

In arguing that the poor outcome group could be suffering from unrecognized depression, the authors ask whether, in withdrawing interest from the outside world, these patients may have fallen in love with their physical symptoms. Even if this notion may appear somewhat whimsical, it does underline the need for a broader approach to the management of low back pain.

The other prospective study (Wiltse and Rocchio, 1975) involved a careful follow-up of 130 patients who had responded poorly to conservative measures over an average period of nearly three years. Prior psychological testing (MMPI and CMI) was used in an attempt to predict the efficacy of chemonucleolysis in the relief of low back pain. At the same time, the surgeons had rated their patients on a five-point scale recording (a) an opinion on suitability for this form of treatment, based on type and severity of objective findings, and (b) assessment of the probability of a psychogenic basis for the symptoms. At least a year later, the outcome was evaluated from both organic and functional standpoints, the latter being dependent on the patient's own report of symptom relief and activities engaged in.

Symptomatically, the best predictors proved to be the Hs and Hy scales of the MMPI, especially when used in conjunction with the surgeon's prior opinion regarding the psychogenic component. Only eleven out of forty-two patients (26 per cent) with T scores above seventy-five on these two scales achieved a good or excellent functional recovery, whereas prediction from the base rate yielded a figure of 48 per cent. Similar results were recorded for a small group of patients who were given the same tests and treated by laminectomy instead of chemonucleolysis.

The authors end by recommending the following policy as warranted by their results:

(1) If the patient has objective findings which point to surgery, but unfavourable findings on psychological testing, then counselling or operant conditioning should be offered before and after the event, in order to forestall the development of fixed pain behaviour that might lead to repeated operations.
(2) If the patient has few objective findings, but severe symptoms with a favourable test pattern, surgery could safely be contemplated.
(3) If the patient with severe symptoms but few objective findings has an *unfa*vourable test pattern the surgeon should proceed with the utmost caution, as the symptoms are likely to persist.

Further predictive studies are urgently needed, if the misery and wastage of inappropriate treatment is to be curbed. This last study was from California, but it is to be hoped that, as increasing numbers of British clinical psychologists venture into new fields, the scope for collaborating with physicians and surgeons will widen.

5. APPROACHES TO PSYCHOLOGICAL TREATMENT

In the treatment of patients with low back pain, some of the same general considerations will apply as in treating patients with any other source of pain, given that the standard repertoire of medicine and surgery is either inappropriate or has failed to bring relief. Readers looking for a broader perspective are advised to consult some of the standard texts, e.g. Merskey and Spear (1967), Melzack (1973), Sternbach (1968, 1974, 1978) and Fordyce (1976). The last author in particular has argued that medical treatment can be counterproductive rather than merely unhelpful, since the patient's belief in the purely physical nature of his symptoms is thereby reinforced. The same point was made earlier and in a much wider context by Balint (1957), who taught that doctors could hope to learn more from looking at the complainer than remaining fixated on the complaint.

Yet, for reasons mentioned in the introduction, there is something about the nature of back pain that predisposes to uncertainty, confusion, and sometimes wild empiricism. The pain of a genuine disc lesion can be excruciating, but the subjective experience of even a strained muscle may appear no less dramatic (as in an episode of *The Good Life* which some TV addicts will recall). In a general-practice setting, bed rest and other simple measures, combined with advice on posture and lifting, will suffice for the majority of patients, as Dillane *et al.* (1966) have convincingly shown. It is those requiring—or at any rate eliciting—more heroic measures who have featured in most of the literature so far reviewed. Here a cautionary note must be sounded, for, although adequate physical investigation is clearly essential, there are dangers in an undue reliance on the medical model. For example, thirty-two out of the fifty patients in the author's own rehabilitation series had received surgery at some time, yet, before admission to the Wolfson Centre, only one patient (see case No. 27, p. 000) had been referred to a psychiatrist and none to a psychologist specifically on account of intractable pain. This is all the more remarkable, in that half of these patients had been handicapped either constantly or intermittently for at least five years.

The alternative approaches to be considered now are (1) that for some patients low back pain is a "depressive equivalent", and (2) that for others it can be viewed as "learnt behaviour". In an earlier review of the literature, Sternbach (1968) noted that patients with chronic pain, but little in the way of organic findings, would often describe their problem in depressive terms. Fatigue, insomnia, loss of appetite, and decline in sexual interest would be reported almost as readily as by any group of psychiatric outpatients. Such were the findings of Forrest and Wolkind (1974) quoted in the previous section and confirmed in a further study along similar lines (Lloyd *et al.*, 1979). Yet, difficulty in management arises from the patients' denial of mood change and insistence that the backache has been causing all their troubles. This phenomenon of depressive symptoms without depressed mood (whether absent or denied) has led to the concept of "masked depression" (Lopez-Ibor, 1972). Theories of how and why depression should come to be translated into back pain have blossomed in the psychodynamic literature, e.g. Rangell (1953), Szasz (1957) and Engel (1959). Such theories, being neither precisely formulated nor supported by empirical evidence, will not be pursued further here. Also of interest in this connection are clinical studies of hypochondriasis, e.g. Kenyon (1964), Kreitman *et al.* (1965) and Ladee (1966). It would seem that patients with backache are not particularly well represented in these series, but shifting diagnoses and therapeutic failure are equally common.

Sternbach (1974, pp. 86–90) has compared the treatment implications of four typical MMPI profiles. The patient who admits to being disheartened by the pain ("reactive depression") is more likely to exhibit a definable organic basis and good premorbid adjustment; when the D score is borderline or above normal limits, and more especially when it is the highest peak, a favourable response to antidepressive medication may be anticipated. In contrast, the patient who practises denial as evidenced by high Hs and Hy and lower D scores ("somatization reaction") may or may not have a known physical basis for the pain, but is more likely to have derived major satisfaction from the invalid role. Such patients can be helped too, but not by medication. Patients in the other two categories respond less well to rehabilitation programmes. The patient whose highest peak is on the Hs scale must be suffering from a variety of somatic complaints, many of which do not relate to the specific pain problem. Such patients evidently cannot learn to ignore their symptoms for long, especially if there is a genuine physical cause. Sternbach (ibid., p. 31) quotes the definition of hypochondriasis offered by Ladee (1966) as a "fascinated absorption by the experience of a physical or mental impairment"—small wonder that the patient remains symptom-fixated, unless some equally powerful gratification can be substituted. The fourth type—happily rather rare, in Sternbach's experience—is the "manipulative reaction". Such patients, characterized by a high psychopathic deviation score as well as a raised neurotic triad, prevailed upon staff to "perform unnecessary operations, or write narcotics orders, or sign disability claims, and only long afterwards did we learn directly from the patients what they had done and why" (ibid. p. 89). Yet, these were not malingerers in the usual sense, and there were clear-cut physical findings in all six cases.

Overt depression was uncommon in the author's own series of fifty patients. Only three patients produced a sharply defined peak on the D scale, and one of these did so only on retesting after a wildly abnormal first record (she was reported to have cried continuously for hours after the psychological interview, and she was an obvious manipulator both on the test and in her day-to-day behaviour). The second patient, though described in the case notes as being in "severe mental and physical distress" on account of her pain, was not referred to the psychiatrist. Only the third patient, on the author's insistence, had a psychiatric evaluation. She was an Indian doctor at an awkward stage of her career, and the psychiatrist considered that her depression was realistic and therefore unlikely to respond to medication. So the over-all picture is that pronounced mood change was seldom recognized and never treated in its own right. As already indicated, Sternbach's "somatization reaction" was seen in four times as many patients.

Recent theories of depression have portrayed the victim's loss of self-esteem as governed by a sense of helplessness. According to the "learned helplessness" model (Seligman, 1975), individuals who are exposed to uncontrollable events come to believe that responding actively is futile. Such experience destroys the incentive to respond in other situations where events may be controllable, until the patient becomes totally apathetic. Seligman emphasizes that the concept of learned helplessness does not fit all depressed patients, but primarily those who are slow to initiate responses as a result of a perceived loss of control over gratification and relief from suffering (e.g. through physical illness, bereavement, or even the ageing process). Such patients can be helped by operant techniques that seek to restore a sense of control over the environment.

In fact, a variety of operant techniques have been used in an attempt to modify depressive behaviour, albeit usually in the form of inadequately controlled case studies. The method of "graded task assignments" (Burgess, 1969) is appropriate for those who have difficulty completing even very simple tasks. The therapist breaks down a target behaviour (e.g. writing a letter) into its component parts, praises the patient's completion of the first, simplest steps (no matter how remote from the final goal) and then continues to praise the more demanding manoeuvres that must follow, until eventually a normal level of activity is restored. This is what occupational therapists, for example, have been doing for years without benefit of any formal training in behaviour therapy. Sometimes it works quite well, but the real problem is that many depressed patients require constant reinforcement, if progress is to be maintained throughout the rehabilitation period—and what will happen when they return home?

Fordyce *et al.* (1968a,b, 1973) and Fordyce (1976) have suggested that chronic pain can sometimes be treated as learnt behaviour, even when it is *not* associated with latent or overt depression. A patient, whether deliberately or not, will signal pain to his associates through a set of "pain behaviours". Apart from complaining of pain, he or she will wince and grimace, ask for pain-killers, move guardedly, call for help, or even insist on remaining in bed. Such behaviour is liable to come under the control of its immediate consequences, being reinforced if the latter are favourable, but diminishing in frequency and ultimately disappearing if they are not. Tissue damage may have provided the original stimulus, but social experience has served to perpetuate a maladaptive response. Some patients, indeed, live in an environment which systematically rewards pain behaviour and either punishes or fails to reward more adaptive responses. A familiar example is the attention-seeking wife who uses her pain to recapture the interest of an erring, bored, or distracted husband. Thus, when the pain is due to a muscular strain that would normally resolve quite rapidly, it may persist simply as a new-found means of evoking sympathy. Pain may also be used as a means of avoiding unwelcome activities such as going to work, painting the kitchen, entertaining friends, or having sexual intercourse.

The treatment programme devised by Fordyce and his colleagues involves three phases:

(1) *Reduction of pain behaviour.* The inappropriately rewarded behaviour can be reduced, if not eliminated, by removing the positive consequences. In a hospital setting, this would require staff, as well as family members, to ignore all expressions of pain, reserving their approval for occasions when the patient is behaving in an acceptable manner.

(2) *Enhancement of activity level.* After an individual baseline has been established, a graduated programme of activities can be developed. Each new gain in endurance and capacity for exertion should elicit praise and encouragement from staff and family.

(3) *Promotion and maintenance of effective behaviour.* This last phase takes account of long-term interests, as well as daily goals prescribed during the treatment programme. In order to relinquish self-defeating behaviour, the patient must be helped towards a more rewarding, even if also more demanding, pattern of activities. To this end, he or she may need vocational or marital counselling and help with various practical arrangements. The initial motivation will come from the response of therapists, spouses, and others, yet, sooner or later, these pursuits will become self-reinforcing.

Although evidence for the efficacy of such training programmes is still fragmentary and far from compelling, preliminary reports give cause for optimism. Both Fordyce and Sternbach, however, have conceded that much less can be expected of an outpatient regime. An effective counter to the patient who is well versed in the art of "painmanship" (Szasz, 1968) calls for a coordinated effort on the part of diverse staff, not all of whom will be equally *au fait* with the principles of behaviour modification. An appraisal of some of the obstacles has been reserved for the final section.

6. THE ROLE OF THE PSYCHOLOGIST

Some of the literature on behavioural methods of treatment gives a rosy view of what can be accomplished by these means. The present author is perhaps fortunate in having embarked on his career at a time when clinical psychologists were less involved in treatment of any kind, so that he has remained committed to a sober realism about what should be attempted. Often enough there are barriers in a patient's life situation, sufficient to defeat even the most dedicated therapist, as the following two cases may help to demonstrate.

A divorced woman of 41 was referred for psychological evaluation with the following statement: "She has had a fairly long history of recurrent back pain probably due to mechanical instability. We have not been very successful with conservative measures and were beginning to think in terms of a spinal fusion". On enquiry, it soon became apparent that her symptoms were distinctly purposive. Her marriage to a Turkish Cypriot some 20 years earlier had ended, when he deserted her after three years of violence and promiscuity. She managed to bring up her daughter (now 19) without much support, but five years ago had met a "nice gentleman". with whom she lived but did not share a bed—"I suppose I'm old-fashioned!" She claimed to have led a chaste life since the end of her marriage, although the medical notes referred to an ectopic pregnancy 10 years earlier. She had been engaged for three years, but could not remarry while her back was in this state, and her fiancé was "most understanding".

She hobbled ostentatiously, except when confident of being unobserved, and generally acted the part of an invalid, having halved her hours of work as an estate agent's clerk. Her MMPI record was reliable and within normal limits, apart from a borderline Hy score. She emphatically refused any psychological approach to her problem, yet rather surprisingly agreed to appear before a group of clinical psychology students, as part of an exercise in interviewing skills.

Contact was then lost for two or three years, but she has recently overcome her scruples to the extent of remarrying and seeking further help from the surgeon, because the pain was interfering with her married life. He concluded that a degenerative lumbar disc lesion had led to mechanical instability, and offered to reconsider a spinal fusion in the light of further investigations. Should the case for surgery prove genuine it could be argued that she had at least partially faced up to her conflict by entering a new sexual relationship, but this is not to say that the conflict was resolved. It remains to be seen whether she will agree to another appointment with the psychologist.

A married man of 37 had been off work for eight months, after his back had suddenly given way on a shopping expedition. He had trained as a fitter and his work had always involved heavy lifting. Physically he was tall, but somewhat flabby, having put on more than a stone in weight during his period of

unemployment. His troubles had started 2–3 years earlier after a lumbar punc-
ture for suspected meningitis to which he had reacted rather dramatically—
when asked about his pain, he said it was hard to describe but felt "as if the
needle is still in me".

He took a long time to complete the MMPI, because of his poor literacy,
assessed on the Schonell graded word-reading test as at the 8–9 year level.
However, the record was apparently reliable and showed a marked Hs peak
with borderline D score. He appeared somewhat passive in the interview, and
recalled a traumatic experience at the age of nine, when he saw his seven year
old brother killed in a road accident while he himself was supposed to be in
charge (actually the brother, despite visual handicap, had tended to adopt a
protective role towards him). He had then suffered a complete breakdown and
been sent to recuperate with an aunt in the country. Though said to be timid
as a child, he maintained that he had always been capable of looking after
himself. At 22, he had married a woman of robust personality by whom he had
three children. She had propped him up during the occasional depressive
episode, when he had been weepy and helplessly dependent. Over the past 4–5
years, he had also suffered from migraine, especially during the month of
March.

The wife reported that he was domesticated and still easy to live with,
despite his frustration at the enforced idleness. He had been due to attend an
industrial rehabilitation unit, but this was cancelled when he fell during a bout
of migraine. The disablement resettlement officer (DRO) had suggested light
manual work, such as toy-making, and this appealed to him, especially as he
was convinced that his illiteracy would preclude an office job. (His story was
that he had never learnt to read at school, but had done a crash course in the
Army. The fact that he could tackle the MMPI was surely proof of some basic
competence.)

As no progress was being made towards finding a light job, he was referred
to another psychologist for a behavioural programme designed to increase his
activity and decrease his attention to pain. For two months he showed some
improvement in his ability to travel and work around the home, but he then
took to his bed complaining of increased pain and stiffness which he related to
the damp weather. Subsequent appointments were either missed or rendered
futile by his failure to carry out the programme, and he was later admitted to
the Wolfson Centre in order that his daily activities could be more closely
supervised. There his mental state improved in response to antidepressive
medication; and he was discharged after three months with an appointment to
see the DRO. Three years later he was still off work and described by his wife
as "no different".[2]

It would, of course, be wrong to espouse a nihilistic view of treatment by focusing
on patients who had either refused to cooperate or dropped out of a programme.
Nevertheless, situations of marital or occupational stalemate are by no means rare
in patients whose problems cannot be solved by physical methods, and the psycho-

---

[2] His attitude to work had always been positive, but his social security benefits were now a powerful
deterrent.

logist must be wary of putting his skills on trial. Even Sternbach (1974), for all his irresistible enthusiasm, was forced to acknowledge that some patients received no benefit from the vigorous and enterprising regime of his pain unit.

The advantages of a residential programme in terms of structure and supervision should by now have become apparent. Sternbach also advocates daily group therapy as a means of giving patients "an opportunity to express their concerns, to receive feedback from the staff and other patients about their behaviour, and to learn some of the elementary principles of pain psychology" (ibid., p. 103). The groups are run by the psychologist and attended by the surgeon once a week, as well as by nurses on duty. They enable patients to express personal anxieties (such as fear of cancer or paralysis), to become more aware of secondary gain from disability in the light of other patients' comments, and to develop an *esprit de corps*. One of the most crucial functions of the group is "to expose, by making explicit, the misuse of pain as a weapon of interpersonal control, or as a means of persuading a doctor to do what the patient thinks ought to be done, or as any of the other kinds of pay offs which may make pain too important for a patient to give up even after an organic lesion has been corrected, thus preventing his rehabilitation" (p. 104).

This third case illustrates the value of a planned programme of management:

A divorced woman of 28 was transferred to the Wolfson Centre from a psychiatric hospital where she had been treated for depression. There was a 3–4 year history of intermittent back pain which began after pushing a car and led to an emergency operation some months later, following an episode of urinary incontinence (the operative findings were consistent with a disc lesion although the actual disc was not found). It was at this stage that she decided to leave her husband whom she had married at 18 when already pregnant by him. The relationship had foundered, when his business took him away from home a great deal; and her frustration provoked him to violence when they were together. The two children remained with him in the family home. After further medical treatment had failed to relieve her persistent pain, she was referred to a psychiatrist. At this stage, she was fully mobile and able to dance, so that not surprisingly her symptoms were attributed to her personal problems.

Her progress continued to fluctuate; and after further inconclusive investigations in hospital, she spent five months in another rehabilitation centre, where her improvement was short-lived. She then had her first spell in the psychiatric hospital, but was soon transferred to a general hospital, because her pain was thought to have an organic basis. Here she was treated with a plaster jacket, which she tolerated poorly, and traction, which she tolerated well, mainly because she preferred to stay in bed and resisted all efforts at mobilization. It was during her second admission to the psychiatric hospital in the following year that she was referred to the psychology department for a behavioural programme, in which she was encouraged to walk for increasing lengths of time (in practice, these distances were relatively short), to sit rather than lie in the ward, and to carry out simple OT tasks. Shortly after her transfer to the Wolfson Centre, the psychologist wrote to the Medical Director as follows: "It was difficult for a number of reasons to achieve very much with this patient, although it is fair to say that her mobility increased significantly. The main reason for her refusal to carry out some of the programme set out for her was that she felt her problem was a purely physical one and could only be dealt with in a medical setting. Nursing staff were unwilling to press her beyond a certain point; and in view of her impending admission to your unit it was really not possible to operate any behavioural programme with any greater degree of success".

During her two months at the Wolfson Centre she made a modest improvement on the orthodox regime and was able to walk up to half a mile outside. The MMPI, completed in a non-defensive manner, revealed only borderline deviations, but the profile corresponds closely to Sternbach's "manipulative reaction". Some months later, she again took to her bed, and at her last follow-up appointment within a year of her discharge she still complained of being significantly handicapped in personal and household tasks. However, the consultant noted that on physical examination her range of movements was unrestricted, and he saw her symptoms as essentially depressive. She had meanwhile remarried, but her second husband was unemployed and had himself suffered from depression in the past. They lived in a rented room from which they were due to be evicted; but as the consultant optimistically remarked "this seems to be an improvement on her previous social position and they seem happy together".

Here, then, was a classical example of the "special" patient as described by Main (1957). She had an unhappy knack of persuading physicians to see her problems as psychiatric and psychiatrists to see them as physical, with the result that she oscillated between different styles of management and no consistent policy could be pursued. If her MMPI record is to be trusted, the prognosis may well have been doomed from the start; yet, if a behavioural programme was worth trying, how much better that it should have been tried at the first opportunity, rather than after a long period of therapeutic failure. Clearly, the psychiatric hospital was not geared to this approach in the context of pain and physical impairment; the Wolfson staff were used to this kind of patient, but unfamiliar with behavioural methods. Consequently, there was a repeated pattern of initial improvement followed by rapid decline, as each new regime was found wanting.

Any training programme, however carefully devised and competently executed, calls for judicious selection of patients. Here the psychologist can make a unique contribution by formulating a set of criteria and using agreed methods of assessment to ensure that as many patients as possible conform to them. The success rate will vary with the number of unpromising cases allowed to slip through the net; but considerations of cost effectiveness, to say nothing of staff morale, should dictate a cautious approach towards patients with gross personal and social problems. Over the 10 years that the author has been associated with the Wolfson Centre, certain lessons have been learnt, yet they need constant reinforcement. Among the present series of fifty patients were at least half a dozen who, from inspection of their case histories, ought probably to have been excluded, but much of the relevant information had not been secured before admission.

This chapter may have conveyed the impression of an undue reliance on the MMPI in the psychological assessment of patients with low back pain. There are simpler methods available; and, even if it is hard to escape from the limitations of self-report in dealing with such an interpersonal phenomenon as pain, there are other methods incorporating a behavioural element that would be easily introduced. For example, Sternbach *et al.* (1974) have adapted the submaximum effort tourniquet technique developed by Smith *et al.* (1966, 1968), whereby blood is drained from the non-dominant arm by a tight rubber bandage which is removed after a blood pressure cuff is inflated well above systolic pressure. The patient then squeezes a hand exerciser slowly 20 times, and a stopwatch is started. He reports when the pain corresponds to his usual clinical pain in intensity if not in quality, and the cuff is left on until he reports that the limits of his tolerance have been reached. The pain ratio score is computed by dividing the time taken to reach the clinical pain level by the time to reach maximum tolerance and multiplying the result by 100. This measure is reminiscent of what Wolff (1971) has called the pain endurance factor, and may be compared with the patient's rating of his average pain on a scale from 0–100 where 0 represents absence of pain and 100 pain of suicidal dimensions. The two tests can be repeated daily or weekly throughout a course of rehabilitation, and where there is a consistently large discrepancy between the two estimates (i.e. the patient habitually experiences much less pain than he can tolerate), the finding may be used therapeutically e.g. to promote stoicism.

The psychologist working at a rehabilitation centre can do much to influence the management of patients, even without recourse to individual treatment. By seeing his role as primarily one of evaluation and advice, and by using his many opportunities to counsel patients and staff, he will readily justify his place in the team. In the outpatient clinic, he can earn his keep merely by helping to ward off the surgeon's knife, although he may hope to be more actively employed in the long run. What matters ultimately is that he should contribute to the relief of human suffering, without investing too heavily in foreseeable failure.

ACKNOWLEDGEMENTS

I am grateful to Robin Bendall for introducing me to this fascinating field and for many stimulating discussions over the past four or five years. David Jenkins has encouraged me to pursue the research at the Wolfson Centre.

REFERENCES

Balint, M. (1957) The Doctor, his Patient and the Illness, Pitman, London.
Beals, R. K. and Hickman, N. W. (1972) Industrial injuries of the back and extremities, *J. Bone Joint Surg.*, **54A**(2), 1593–1611.
Bradley, L. A., Prokop, C. K., Margolis, R. and Gentry, W. D. (1978) Multivariate analyses of the MMPI profiles of low back pain patients, *J. behav. Med.*, **1**, 253–272.
Burgess, E. P. (1969) The modification of depressive behaviour, in Ruben, R. D. and Frank, C. M. (Eds.) *Advances in Behaviour Therapy*, Academic Press, New York.
Calsyn, D. A., Louks, J. and Freeman, C. W. (1976) The use of the MMPI with chronic low back pain patients with a mixed diagnosis, *J. clin. Psychol.*, **32**, 532–536.
Carr, J. E., Brownsberger, C. N. and Rutherford, R. S. (1966) Characteristics of symptom matched psychogenic and real pain patients on the MMPI, *Proceedings of the 74th Annual Convention of the American Psychological Association*, pp. 215–216.
Craig, K. D. (1978) Social modeling influences on pain, in Sternbach, R. A. (Ed.) *The Psychology of Pain*, Raven Press, New York.
Crisp, A. H. and Priest, R. G. (1971) Psychoneurotic profiles in middle age, *Brit. J. Psychiat.*, **119**, 385–392.

Crown, S. and Crisp, A. H. (1966) A short clinical diagnostic self-rating scale for psychoneurotic patients, *Brit. J. Psychiat.*, **112**, 917–923.

Crown, S., Duncan, K. P. and Howell, R. W. (1970) Further evaluation of the Middlesex Hospital Questionnaire, *Brit. J. Psychiat.*, **116**, 33–37.

Dillane, J. B., Fry, J. and Kalton, G. (1966) Acute back syndrome—a study from general practice, *Brit. med. J.*, **2**, 82–84.

Engel, G. L. (1959) 'Psychogenic' pain and the pain-prone patient, *Amer. J. Med.*, **26**, 899–918.

Fairbairn, A. S. and Acheson, E. D. (1969) The extent of organ removal in the Oxford area, *J. chron. Dis.*, **22**, 111–122.

Fordyce, W. E. (1976) *Behavioural Methods in Chronic Pain and Illness*, Mosby, St. Louis.

Fordyce, W. E., Fowler, R.S., Lehmann, J. F. and DeLateur, B. J. (1968a) Some implications of learning in problems of chronic pain, *J. chron. Dis.*, **21**, 179–190.

Fordyce, W. E., Fowler, R. S. and DeLateur, B. J. (1968b) An application of behaviour modification technique to a problem of chronic pain., *Behav. Res. Ther.*, **6**, 105–107.

Fordyce, W. E., Fowler, R. S., Jr., Lehmann, J. F., DeLateur, B. J., Sand, P. L. and Trieschmann, R. B. (1973) Operant conditioning in the treatment of chronic pain, *Arch. phys. Med. Rehabil.*, **54**, 399–408.

Forrest, A. J. and Wolkind, S. N. (1974) Masked depression in men with low back pain. *Rheumatol. Rehabil.*, **13**, 148–153.

Freeman, C. W., Calsyn, D. A. and Louks, J. (1976) The use of the Minnesota Multiphasic Personality Inventory with low back pain patients, *J. clin. Psychol.*, **32**, 294–298.

Gentry, W. D., Shows, W. D. and Thomas, M. (1974) Chronic low back pain: a psychological profile, *Psychosomatics*, **15**, 174–177.

Gough, H. E. (1946) Diagnostic patterns on the Minnesota Multiphasic Personality Inventory, *J. clin. Psychol.*, **2**, 23–37.

Hanvik, L. J. (1949) Some psychological dimensions of low back pain. Unpublished doctoral thesis, University of Minnesota.

Hanvik, L. J. (1951) MMPI profiles in patients with low back pain, *J. consult. Psychol.*, **5**, 350–353.

Harrison, T. R., ed. (1960) *Principles of Internal Medicine*, McGraw–Hill, New York.

Hollander, J. L. (Ed.) (1960) *Arthritis and Allied Conditions*, Ch. 71, Kimpton, London.

Jaffe, A. J., Day, L. H. and Adams, W. (1964) *Disabled Workers in the Labor Market*, Bedminster Press, New Jersey.

Kenyon, F. E. (1964) Hypochondriasis: a clinical study, *Brit. J. Psychiat.*, **110**, 478–488.

Kreitman, N., Sainsbury, P., Pearce, K. and Costain, W. R. (1965) Hypochondriasis and depression in outpatients at a general hospital, *Brit. J. Psychiat.*, **111**, 607–615.

Ladee, G. A. (1966) *Hypochondriacal Syndromes*, Elsevier, Amsterdam.

Lloyd, G. G., Wolkind, S. N., Greenwood, R. and Harris, D. J. (1979) A psychiatric study of patients with persistent low back pain, *Rheumatol. Rehabil.*, **18**, 30–34.

Lopez-Ibor, J. J. (1972) Masked depressions, *Brit. J. Psychiat.*, **120**, 245–258.

Main, T. F. (1957) The ailment, *Brit. J. med. Psychol.*, **30**, 129–145.

Maruta, T., Swanson, D. and Swenson, W. M. (1976) Low back pain patients in a psychiatric population, *Mayo Clin. Proc.*, **51**, 57–61.

McBeath, A. (1970) The problem of low back pain, *Wisc. med. J.* **69**, 208–210.

Melzack, R. (1973) *The Puzzle of Pain*, Penguin, Harmondsworth.

Merskey, H. and Spear, F. G. (1967) *Pain: Psychological and Psychiatric Aspects*, Bailliere, Tindall and Cassell, London.

Nagi, S. Z., Burk, R. D. and Potter, H. R. (1965) Back disorders and rehabilitation achievement, *J. chron. Dis.*, **18**, 181–197.

Nagi, S. Z., Riley, L. E. and Newby, L. G. (1973) A social epidemiology of back pain in a general population, *J. chron. Dis.*, **26**, 769–779.

Paul, L. (1950) Psychosomatic aspects of low back pain: a review, *Psychosom. Med.*, **12**, 116–124.

Phillips, E. L. (1964) Some psychological problems associated with orthopaedic complaints, *Curr. Pract. Orthop. Surg.*, **2**, 165–176.

Pichot, P., Perse, J., Lekeous, M. O., Dureau, J. L., Perez, C. I. and Rychewaert, A. (1972) La personnalité des sujets présentant des douleurs dorsales fonctionnelles: valeur de l'inventaire MMPI, *Revue de Psychologie Appliquée*, **22**, 145–172.

Rangell, L. (1953) Psychiatric aspects of pain, *Psychosom. Med.*, **15**, 22–37.

Richards, D. H. (1973) Depression after hysterectomy, *Lancet* **2**, 430–432.

Sargent, M. (1946) Psychosomatic backache, *New Engl. J. Med.*, **234**, 427–430.

Seligman, M. E. P. (1975) *Helplessness: on Depression, Development and Death*, Freeman, San Francisco.

Shaffer, J. W., Nussbaum, K. and Little, J. M. (1972) MMPI profiles of disability insurance claimants, *Amer. J. Psychiat.*, **129**, 403–407.

Silverman, L. (1977) Low back pain: a review of the psychological literature. Unpublished manuscript, Oxford Rehabilitation Research Unit.

Smith, G. M., Egbert, L. D., Markowitz, R. A., Mosteller, F. and Beecher, H. K. (1966) An experimental pain method sensitive to morphine in man: the submaximum effort tourniquet technique, *J. Pharm. exper. Therap.*, **154**, 324–332.

Smith, G. M., Lowenstein, E., Hubbard, J. H. and Beecher, H. K. (1968) Experimental pain produced by the submaximum effort tourniquet technique: further evidence of validity, *J. Pharm. exper. Therap.* **163**, 468–474.

Sternbach, R. A. (1968) *Pain: A Psychophysiological Analysis*, Academic Press, New York.

Sternbach, R. A. (1974) *Pain Patients: Traits and Treatment*, Academic Press, New York.

Sternbach, R. A. ed. (1978) *The Psychology of Pain*, Raven Press, New York.

Sternbach, R. A., Wolf, S. R., Murphy, R. W. and Akeson, W. M. (1973a) Aspects of chronic low back pain, *Psychosomatics*, **14**, 52–56.

Sternbach, R. A., Wolf, S. R., Murphy, R. W. and Akeson, W. M. (1973b) Traits of pain patients: the low back "loser", *Psychosomatics*, **14**, 226–229.

Sternbach, R. A., Murphy, R. W., Timmermans, G., Greenhoot, J. H. and Akeson, W. M. (1974) Measuring the severity of clinical pain, in J. J. Bonica (Ed.), *Advances in Neurology*, Vol. 4, *Pain*, Raven Press, New York.

Szasz, T. S. (1957) Pain and Pleasure: A Study of Bodily Feelings, Basic Books, New York.

Szasz, T. S. (1968) The psychology of persistent pain: a portrait of *l'homme douloureux*, in A. Soulairac, J. Cahn and J. Charpentier (Eds.) *Pain*, Academic Press, New York.

Troup, J. D. G. (1965) Relation of lumbar spine disorders to heavy manual work and lifting, *Lancet* **1**, 857–861.

Ward, T., Knowelden, J. and Sharrard, W. J. W. (1968) Low back pain, *J. Roy. Coll. Gen. Practit.*, **15**, 128–136.

White, A. W. M. (1966) The compensation back, *Appl. Ther.*, **8**, 871–874.

Wilfling, F. J., Klonoff, H. and Kokan, P. (1973) Psychological, demographic and orthopaedic factors associated with prediction of outcome of spinal fusion, *Clin. Orthop.*, **90**, 153–160.

Wiltse, L. L. and Rocchio, P. D. (1975) Pre-operative psychological tests as predictors of success of chemonucleolysis in the treatment of the low back syndrome, *J. Bone Joint Surg.*, **57A**, 478–483.

Wolff, B. B. (1971) Factor analysis of human pain responses: pain endurance as a specific pain factor, *J. abn. Psychol.*, **78**, 292–298.

Zung, W. W. K. (1965) A self-rating depression scale, *Arch. gen. Psychiat.*, **12**, 63–70.

7

PSYCHOLOGICAL ASPECTS OF EARLY BREAST CANCER AND ITS TREATMENT

COLETTE RAY

Brunel University

CONTENTS

1. INTRODUCTION

Breast cancer is the most common form of malignancy in the U.K., and in recent years there has been a considerable scientific involvement in determining the aetiology of the disease and methods for its control. Current approaches to the latter include radiotherapy, chemotherapy, and hormonal therapies; but surgical removal remains the central strategy in the treatment of primary breast cancer. Surgical procedures currently in use differ in terms of the extent of tissue which is taken away, with the more extensive operations usually being described as "radical" in contrast with less extensive or "conservative" operations. The most common procedures in this country today are the modified radical mastectomy in which the breast and the axillary contents are removed but not the pectoral muscles, and the simple mastectomy in which the breast is removed but the axilla are undisturbed.

There were few psychological investigations of mastectomy until the 1970s, in spite of some early evidence of the emotional distress experienced by some patients (Bard and Sutherland, 1955; Renneker and Cutler, 1952). Several factors have stimulated research. Firstly, there has been an increase in public awareness of breast cancer. The topic implicates illness and death on the one hand and sexuality on the other and, as the taboo status of these has weakened, so discussions of breast cancer have been taken up in the media. The issues discussed have included psychological, as well as physical, aspects of the disease and its treatment; indeed, it is often on the former rather than the latter that concern has been focused. The attitudes of many surgeons have also changed in recent years, with a greater emphasis on the care of the whole patient and a movement away from a purely technical approach which treats the disease in isolation. Thus it has been widely argued that the "quality of survival" as well as survival rate should be considered when assessing the success of any intervention; and there is now a widespread professional concern with the psychological impact of conditions such as breast cancer and with the implications of this impact for patient care. Another factor which has facilitated research has been the development of an extensive literature concerned with psychological reactions to crisis and stress. This has provided a research tradition and theoretical framework within which the problem may be considered. Studies in the area investigate particular situations as potential elicitors of stress, an approach which contrasts with much personality and clinical research where the concern is more often to trace the origins of an existing state of emotional disturbance. A number of situations have been investigated within this context, including several that are associated with illness or accident (Friedman et al., 1963; Hamburg et al., 1953; Visotsky et al., 1961). Breast cancer may similarly be regarded as a life crisis or stressor, and analysed with reference to the cognitive, emotional, and behavioural responses generally appropriate to such situations. One model of stress that can usefully be applied in this analysis is that of Lazarus (1966). Here emotional reactions are viewed as a function of the significance of the event for the individual and of the latter's ability to cope with the threat either by a re-evaluation of its significance or by direct action.

2. PSYCHOLOGICAL IMPLICATIONS OF EARLY BREAST CANCER

Any crisis or stressor will have unique characteristics which determine the precise nature of reactions to it; and these must be given special consideration. In the case of breast cancer, it is difficult to identify a single critical event or source of stress: the situation is a complex one in two respects. Firstly, not only will the patient's reactions change and develop as time progresses, but the situation is itself a dynamic one. If we take mastectomy as the "pivotal" event, the stressors to which the patient is exposed may be traced back into the past and forward into the future from the time of operation. To the extent that there is a crisis, it is one which unfolds over a period of time. Secondly, a number of potential sources of stress may be identified and should be distinguished within any detailed analysis. In the short term, there is the necessity for surgery; and this in itself poses a considerable threat for some individuals (Janis, 1958, Spielberger et al., 1973; Wilson-Barnett, 1978). Fears commonly voiced include that of one's complete vulnerability while under the anaesthetic and the anticipation of postoperative pain and discomfort (Ramsay, 1972; Ryan, 1975). Other aspects of hospitalization may also be stressful; the unfamiliarity of the surroundings, loss of independence, separation from family and friends, and submission to novel routines and procedures may combine to produce a feeling of helplessness and disorientation (Volicer and Bohannon, 1975). However, the sources of concern most commonly identified in the case of breast cancer are those which have longer term implications. These are the loss of the breast, which threatens the integrity of the patient's body image and her identity as a woman, and an awareness of the diagnosis of malignancy, which constitutes a threat to continued health and to life itself. A further addition to the list might be the ambiguity which characterizes the experience of many breast patients from the time when they first notice the symptom until long after the operation has taken place. This ambiguity cannot be considered independently of the other issues above, but its separate mention serves to emphasize the fact that much of the stress experienced by the breast cancer patient is associated with threats which may or may not materialize, and with apprehensions which may or may not be justified.

The Loss of the Breast

Any surgical procedure which produces mutilation will have some psychological implications, even after the period of postoperative recovery. In the case of mastectomy, the patient will not only be left with the scar of the incision, but will have to come to terms with the absence of the breast. She will normally be provided with a prosthesis to be worn inside her brassiere. This should make the outline of her bust look natural, but cannot fully substitute for her own breast. There will be some kinds of clothes which she can no longer wear and several situations, such as trying on clothes in a communal changing room, which she will now want to avoid. If she is married, concealment of the scar from her husband will be difficult and, even if it were possible, concealment in this context might have an adverse effect on the relationship. The woman herself will be forced to confront her disfigurement, by sight or by touch, whenever she dresses, undresses or bathes, and will be reminded of its existence in other practical situations such as buying clothes or caring for the prosthesis. Thus, she herself cannot help but be aware of her altered shape and appearance, whatever the extent to which this may or may not be apparent to others.

It is widely accepted that women should be more concerned with their appearance than are men; and studies have shown that women have a more highly differentiated body image and are more negative in their appraisal of personal physical characteristics (Calden *et al.*, 1959; Kurtz, 1969). Body image is, moreover, related to general self-image (Rosen and Ross, 1968; Zion, 1965). It might be predicted on this basis alone that mastectomy will, by altering physical appearance and reducing attractiveness, challenge a woman's self acceptance and esteem. It has also been argued that the breast has a profound emotional significance, because of its strong associations with both sexuality and motherhood, and a similar prediction would follow from this analysis: "The breast is the emotional symbol of the woman's pride in her sexuality and in her motherliness. To threaten the breast is to shake the very core of her feminine orientation" (Renneker and Cutler, 1952, p. 834). On the other hand, several writers have pointed out that the breast does not have any functional significance, at the stage when most women would have a mastectomy, and have suggested that its loss should therefore be easier to bear than that of body parts which do have such a physical function. This claim receives some support from studies which have asked women the value they place on different body parts and which they would be most concerned to lose. From this perspective, the breast would seem to be less important than many other parts including the tongue, nose, leg, eye, arm, foot, hand, and ear (Weinstein *et al.*, 1964).

Should it be assumed that the greater the importance of a body part, whether symbolic or functional, the greater will be the difficulty of adjusting to its loss? The possibility of a non-linear relationship between adjustment and the apparent significance of mutilation or handicap might also be considered, with least successful adjustment in intermediate or ambivalent cases. One study found that people with marginal physical disabilities were more maladjusted than those with severe disability, supporting a hypothesis that particular difficulties are engendered by an ambiguity of status (Colman, 1971). The woman who is disfigured by her mastectomy does, in many respects, have such a status, and adjustment to her loss may not be possible until this ambiguity is resolved. The disfigurement is a "stigma", but one which the individual may choose either to disclose or to conceal (Goffman, 1963). If the former strategy is adopted, then this may produce social awkwardness and tension; if, alternatively, the woman seeks concealment, she is making herself vulnerable to possible future disclosure beyond her control. Most women will, in fact, disclose in some contexts, but not in others. Another source of ambiguity is the woman's evaluation of the implications of her disfigurement for her social roles and relationships. She may, for example, worry that others are embarrassed by the fact of her mastectomy, even if they do not reveal such a reaction; that she attracts a pity which she does not seek; or that it is felt that she is "no longer a woman". Similarly, she may wonder about the legitimacy of seeking to establish a relationship with a man, or even of behaving in a lightheartedly flirtatious way in everday encounters. Her reactions will thus comprise not only regret and perhaps resentment at the fact of her disfigurement, but also anxiety elicited by the ambiguity of its implications and the social ambivalence and personal dilemmas which this generates.

The Diagnosis of Cancer

An awareness of cancer has been termed an "informational crisis" in that it challenges the individual's identity and requires a restructuring of expectations for the future (Shands, 1966). Surgeons and psychiatrists have described the anxiety, depression, and anger experienced by many cancer patients (Craig and Abeloff, 1974; Crary and Crary, 1974; Peck, 1972; Stehlin and Beach 1966; Vujan, 1956), together with defensive reactions such as denial, suppression, and avoidance (Feder, 1966; Hinton, 1973; Peck, 1972). Such responses are not, of course, specific to the cancer situation, but are common sequelae of many different kinds of threat and crisis.

Cancer is second only to cardiovascular disease as a cause of death; and public opinion acknowledges and may even exaggerate its potency. It is seen as more painful, more threatening, and more alarming than other diseases; and most people believe that it is responsible for more deaths than any other disease (Briggs and Wakefield, 1967; Jenkins and Zyzanski, 1968; Williams *et al.*, 1972). There is a tendency to view cancer as a single disease entity, rather than as a family of conditions with differing onset, activity, and prognosis; and people's perceptions and expectations may be distorted because of this (Wakefield, 1969). Even cancers which share a common site do not conform to any regular pattern in terms of these dimensions. Much of the literature concerned with psychological reactions to cancer has concentrated on patients whose illness is progressive and who face the prospect of an unpleasant disease process and early death. The plight of the patient with a primary cancer which may be successfully treated is rather different. In such cases, it will generally not be possible to predict whether or not the disease will recur and the timing of a recurrence if this were to happen. The "informational crisis" here has a particular character. In one sense, it is more acute for the individuals in this situation than for patients with progressive disease, because of the conflicting expectations and perspectives that may be entertained. They cannot, realistically, be confident that they are cured and healthy; nor can they identify themselves as future cancer victims. They can neither project confidently into the future nor prepare for future illness and a shortened life. The possibility of recurrence, as opposed to an awareness of illness, creates a degree of uncertainty which can, in its own right, be aversive (Averill, 1973).

3. PSYCHOLOGICAL IMPACT OF MASTECTOMY

Reactions before Surgery

It seems that as many as 80 per cent of the public are familiar with the symptoms of breast cancer, that nearly the same percentage know personally of someone who has had the disease, and that there is a general tendency to over- rather than to under-estimate the likelihood of a breast lump being malignant (American Cancer Society, 1973; Knopf, 1974). Given these facts, it is probable that most women will consider the possibility of cancer, however fleetingly, when they first become aware of the symptom. Many, nevertheless, delay before consulting their general practitioner; the reasons for their behaviour have been extensively debated and will be discussed in a later section. Where there is doubt or suspicion about the nature of the symptom, the G.P. will usually refer the patient to the hospital for a further examination. The outcome of this visit may be crucial, whether positive or negative in its implications; and women with breast symptoms attending outpatients' clinic for the first time have been shown to be more anxious than those attending other clinics (Hardesty *et al.*, 1973). Where the possibility of cancer cannot be dismissed on the basis of the outpatient examination, the woman will be asked to come into hospital for surgery. The admission procedure is generally swift; and this in itself may be interpreted as a confirmation of her fears and thus increase anxiety. Maguire (1976) noted that by the time of admission many women with breast symptoms will be anxious or depressed, with most thinking that they have cancer, especially when they have had some direct experience of this among family or friends. Similarly, Polivy (1977) found higher levels of anxiety among breast patients than among those undergoing general surgical procedures and noted that the former were more likely to express spontaneously a fear of disfigurement or death.

Reactions after Surgery

Studies of psychological reactions to mastectomy have considered several inter-related issues: the incidence and duration of emotional disturbance in patients; factors influencing the degree of distress experienced; and sources of concern. They have varied widely in methodology and design. Methods of assessment have included unstructured and structured inverviews, questionnaires and self-rating scales administered within an interview context, and questionnaires distributed by post. In some studies, patients are randomly or exhaustively selected and high rates of cooperation obtained; in others, the initial selection of subjects is non-random, or the response rate is low, with the possibility that this self-selection will involve a systematic bias. Relatively few studies have employed a control group for the purpose of comparison; and where control groups are incorporated in the design their nature has differed from one investigation to another. They may be patients with benign breast disease (Maguire et al., 1978; Morris et al., 1977), patients with cancer at other sites (Polivy, 1977; Worden and Weisman, 1977), general surgical patients (Polivy, 1977), or a specific surgical group, such as cholecystectomy patients (Ray, 1977). In several studies, the breast cancer group has acted as its own control, these being longitudinal studies in which patients were interviewed on several occasions (Maguire et al., 1978; Morris et al., 1977; Polivy, 1977; Worden and Weisman, 1977). It is obviously desirable to match the breast cancer and other groups on dimensions relevant to the assessment, but this will be difficult where the study is prospective; a post hoc method of control may, however, prove suitable (Morris et al., 1977). In spite of considerable differences in the method, design, and conduct of these investigations, a general picture has emerged of both the extent and nature of the distress experienced by patients after mastectomy, together with some indication of its course over time.

One of the most consistent observations is that of marked individual differences in reaction, with the latter ranging from an apparent absence of concern to extreme distress. For some patients, the predominant feeling after surgery is one of relief that the operation is over, the ambiguity resolved, and the cancer "taken away". Others are concerned and upset, but are able to view the future constructively and attempt to resign themselves to what has happened. Yet others experience a period of intense grief or depression, which may find expression in hostility against the staff in general, and against the surgeon in particular. A fourth group can also be identified; these are women whose immediate reaction following surgery is one of acceptance and even elation, but where this is quickly followed by a period of depression. The mood change usually occurs on returning home, when the woman has left the now relatively secure environment of the ward and must face her family, her friends, and the everyday routine. Some difficulty in obtaining reliable estimates of the incidence of negative reactions might be anticipated, because of differences between studies in methods of assessment and in the judgemental criteria employed in categorizing reactions. There is, nevertheless, some degree of consistency in the figures that have been presented. Estimates of the incidence of moderate or severe states of anxiety or depression range from 20 to 25 per cent (Maguire *et al.*, 1978; Morris *et al.*, 1977; Worden and Weisman, 1977).[1] Estimates of the proportion admitting to distress consequent upon the mastectomy are, however, more variable, ranging from 45 to 85 per cent (Morris *et al.*, 1977; Roberts *et al.*, 1972; Torrie, 1970). These findings are not incompatible with the earlier conclusion of Renneker and Cutler that "anxiety, insomnia, depressive attitudes, occasional ideas of suicide, and feelings of shame and worthlessness" are quite common sequelae of mastectomy (Renneker and Cutler, 1952, p. 834).

Several investigators have studied the same group of patients at intervals after treatment, enabling them to chart the course of psychological recovery. Morris and her colleagues (1977) found that, while at three months after surgery nearly half of the group reported stress associated with the mastectomy, at 12 months this number had declined to less than 30 per cent. A similar figure was obtained at an interval of 24 months, suggesting that attitudes had stabilized by this time. If, however, a general rating of depression is taken as the criterion of adjustment a rather different trend is apparent. While the number of high scorers on this measure was consistently greater in the cancer group from the preoperative assessment through to the interview at 24 months, the difference increased with time; indeed, it was only at the stage of the final assessment that the difference was statistically significant. The findings of Maguire and his colleagues suggest a similar pattern (1978), with little, if any, decline in emotional disturbance during the first year. At both 4 months and 1 year, there were significant differences between the mastectomy and benign breast groups in the number of patients with moderate or severe anxiety; but a relatively consistent pattern within groups over this period. Polivy (1977) looked at the influence of mastectomy on body- and self-image rather than emotional state. In her benign group, these became more negative immediately after surgery and then remained constant, suggesting that the more positive image noted before surgery may have been defensive in nature. In the breast cancer group, body- and total self-image did not change from before to after surgery, but had become more negative by the time of the follow-up interview, which took place between 6 and 11 months later. Finally, Eisenberg and Goldenberg (1966), in a questionnaire-based investigation of quality of survival, found that this had deteriorated in the 18 months interval since an initial assessment, in spite of an increase in patients' general activity over this period. The conclusion one would draw about the course of adjustment in the first year after mastectomy will thus depend on the index of adjustment employed. While there is some evidence that overt concern decreases over the first year, the patient's emotional state, self-image and quality of life remain constant or become more negative. This apparent stability or deterioration in adjustment perhaps reflects an interval of shock, detachment, and denial, which cushions reactions in the first months after surgery, followed by an increasing realization of the fact and implications of disfigurement and cancer, and a fragmentation of vulnerable defences. The discrepant pattern evident in direct self-reports of concern may reflect a parallel development of the process of coping, with patients expressing more positive attitudes as they seek to bolster viable defences and establish a positive and constructive appraisal of their situation.

---

[1] These percentages must be compared with those obtained from similar assessments of a control group in order to determine the *net* impact of cancer and mastectomy.

There is relatively little evidence concerning adjustment at intervals of more than 2 years after surgery. No significant psychosocial differences were found in one questionnaire study which compared mastectomy patients with a control group, and where the former were patients who had had the operation from 9 months to 5 years previously (Craig *et al.*, 1974). Conflicting results were obtained by Ray (1977). In this study, women who had had a mastectomy from 18 months to 5 years before the interview were found to be significantly more depressed, anxious, and socially withdrawn than a matched group of cholecystectomy patients. There were no significant differences within the mastectomy group dependent upon the time which had elapsed since surgery, suggesting that adjustment on these dimensions had stabilized within the first 18 months.

Sources of Concern

Renneker and Cutler argued that the primary source of concern for the mastectomy patient is the disfigurement suffered, and that concern about health arises only at a later date: "The original trauma ... most often occurs on the level of the woman's realisation that her femininity is endangered. It is, of course, immediately mixed with the concept of cancer, and its potential threat to life, but this does not emerge as the central problem of adjustment until later, after she has become accustomed to the inevitability of mutilation and managed to attain some sort of psychological adjustment to her new physical self" (1952, p. 834). This view was not shared by Bard and Sutherland (1955), who maintained that the relative impact of disfigurement and death will depend upon their emotional significance for the individual, and that it is not appropriate to seek any general statement about which will be the primary source of concern. While recognizing the importance of such individual differences, it should still be possible to describe their distribution and perhaps identify a majority response. However, recent investigations have produced conflicting results. Katz concluded that it is the loss of the breast which most concerns women anticipating surgery, at least at a conscious level (Katz *et al.*, 1970); and, with regard to post-operative concern, Morris found a higher incidence of stress associated with disfigurement than with the diagnosis of cancer, both at 3 months and at 12 months after surgery (Morris *et al.*, 1977). These findings support Renneker and Cutler's claim (1952). Maguire's observations, in contrast, indicated that patients were more likely to attribute their distress to cancer than to the cosmetic effects of the operation; this was the case, both before and after surgery (Maguire, 1976).

It is possible that such inconsistencies are due to variation in the openness with which the surgeon and others have discussed the diagnosis of cancer with the patient, and in the frankness with which the issue is approached within the specific context of the interview. The former will influence the patient's awareness of the diagnosis and the possibility of recurrence, and the latter her readiness to acknowledge any fears to the interviewer. Ray (1978) found apparently equivalent incidences of concern about disfigurement and cancer in her sample of mastectomy patients. Just over half expressed concern about the loss of the breast; when these women were compared with those expressing no, or minimal, concern, they were found to be significantly more depressed and socially withdrawn, and they tended to be more anxious and to have lower self-esteem. A similar number of women expressed concern about cancer, but, when a comparison was made between those who did and did not admit to concern, there were no significant differences on measures of adjustment between the two groups and there was a tendency for those who disclaimed concern to be the more anxious. This finding was contrary to prediction and was attributed to a defensive denial of the cancer and its implications on the part of some patients, together with a possible reluctance to admit to a concern which was privately acknowledged. This conclusion was compatible with the fact that the diagnosis of malignancy had not been explicitly discussed with some of the patients in this sample, thus permitting the existence of denial as a defence—and with the constraints which this placed upon the conduct of the interviews. Thus, observations based on self-report may not adequately reflect the incidence and degree of concern elicited by cancer; and it is indeed difficult to see how one can be confident of estimates obtained without challenging patients' defences and risking the creation of doubt and concern where previously none was felt. For this reason, it is particularly interesting to see what predictions women in the general population make about their responses, were they to have a mastectomy. In the Gallup Poll referred to earlier, similar numbers claimed that their first thoughts after surgery would centre on the fact of cancer and the loss of the breast respectively. However, when asked which would be the greatest *worry*, only 23 per cent indicated that this would be the loss of the breast, while 59 per cent said that cancer would for them be the greater cause for concern.

Sexual Adjustment

The woman who is concerned about the loss of the breast feels distress at the sight of the scar and tries to avoid seeing herself when undressed. Moreover, the disfigurement is regarded by her as a threat to her femininity, making her less of a woman. Given such a reaction in herself, she may anticipate that her partner's feelings will be similar and have difficulties in adjusting sexually because of doubts about her attractiveness and acceptability. A number of variables will have a potential influence on sexual adjustment, including the contribution of the breast to the individual's sexual identity and femininity; her preoperative body-image and the size of the breast; her perception of her partner's reaction; the role of breast stimulation in her sexual response; the quality of the preoperative sexual relationship; the degree of scarring; and residual pain or tenderness (Woods, 1975). The loss of the breast not only takes away a source of erotic pleasure, but may be a cause of inhibition and distraction. Anxiety may be created by the woman's inability to forget about the scar and its associations; love-making may become self-conscious and lack spontaneity because she feels that she has to compensate for the disfigurement; and she may be too concerned with her partner's thoughts and feelings to focus upon her own experience (Wabrek and Wabrek, 1976). Most studies which have looked at sexual adjustment have found a decrease in interest, enjoyment, and frequency of activity after mastectomy (Maguire *et al.*, 1978; Morris *et al.*, 1977). On the other hand, many women appear to adjust without difficulty. In Jamison's questionnaire study (1978), 76 per cent of patients in the sample claimed not to have been adversely affected, while 81 per cent of another sample indicated no change in frequency of sexual activity (Woods and Earp, 1978). Furthermore, while differences between mastectomy and control patients exist in the shorter term, there is evidence from one study that such differences might not exist at longer intervals after mastectomy (Morris et al., 1977); breast cancer patients were more likely to report a deterioration in sexual adjustment after surgery, but the difference between the groups at two years was not statistically significant. This change over time may indicate a process of adjustment within the mastectomy group; it might, on the other hand, be interpreted as an indication that mastectomy is merely a precipitating factor, hastening an imminent deterioration in the sexual relationship. Further studies are required of the sexual problems experienced after mastectomy, and of their resolution. The reports currently available tend to be either clinical investigations, which deal in some depth with the kinds of problems experienced but do not permit conclusions about the general impact of mastectomy, or more extensive investigations, which elicit global reports on rather limited dimensions.

4. DOCTOR-PATIENT COMMUNICATION

The question of what to tell the patient with cancer has been the subject of debate for decades. Many physicians withhold information about the diagnosis and prognosis, or talk in vague and euphemistic terms about the patient's condition; some are willing to give specific information, but only when this is directly requested; others will, as a general policy, be frank and open with every patient. Each individual bases his or her policy upon personal judgement and clinical experience. Several explanations have been offered for the reluctance of some phys- icians to communicate with their patients on the subject of cancer. The most common reason given is that of protecting the latter from anguish which, though perhaps appropriate to the situation, can achieve nothing. Those who do not sup- port this position have suggested alternative or supplementary explanations, claim- ing that keeping the patient uninformed serves to maintain the power relationship between the physican and the patient, to avoid admission of the physician's relative impotence, and to protect the physician's own emotional equilibrium as much as that of the patient (see McIntosh, 1974). It is sometimes argued that if an individual wishes to know, then he or she will ask for information, but this fails to recognize the natural diffidence of most patients. Respect for the surgeon and unfamiliarity with the situation will cause most to look for and follow prompting and directions and to avoid taking the initiative themselves.

Patients, in many contexts, have been found to be dissatisfied with the informa- tion made available to them (Cartwright, 1964; Ley, 1972). It might be argued that cancer patients are a special case, because of the threatening nature of the informa- tion they would receive; but it seems that frank and open communications about diagnosis and treatment are valued in this situation also (Aitken-Swan and Easson, 1959; Feifel, 1963; Gilbertson and Wangensteen, 1962; Kelly and Friesen, 1950). The majority of informed cancer patients claim that they are glad they were so informed and, when healthy individuals are asked whether they would like to be informed if they were in this situation, the majority say that they would. Most of the samples referred to in the literature are restricted to informed cancer patients and people asked to speculate about a hypothetical situation. One study has, in contrast, employed as subjects cancer patients who had not been explicitly informed about their condition, but were instead given a euphemistic account which avoided reference to malignancy (McIntosh, 1976). It seemed that many of these patients knew or suspected that they had cancer (this was especially true of the breast patients), and that many of those who suspected did not want their suspicion to be confirmed. Only a few wished for further information about the diagnosis or prognosis, preferring not to jeopardize their optimism about the illness outcome. McIntosh argued that the surgeon's policy in this situation allowed the patients themselves to regulate their degree of awareness of cancer; those who wished to avoid certainty were able to do so, while those who wished to be informed could draw obvious inferences from the extent of the surgery, the use of adjuvant therapies, the avoidance of an explicit diagnosis and the use of euphemisms, and could seek confirmation of their conclusions from the surgeon.

None of the studies reported can claim to be conclusive, since they share the untested assumption that patients will favour that option which will be of greater benefit to them. In fact, the strategy which they prefer in principle may be maladaptive in practice. In the absence of studies in which the information divulged is systematically controlled, the question of whether to tell or not to tell will remain unresolved. Such studies would involve obvious practical and ethical difficulties; and it is not certain that they would generate recommendations which could easily be put into practice. The outcome of a given policy will doubtless depend upon the personality and coping style of the individual patient. It will probably depend also upon the clinical outcome for that individual. Patients who have been told about the malignant nature of their growth may be less distressed in the event of a recurrence than those who have not been told; in the absence of a recurrence, however, less distress will perhaps be experienced by those who are uninformed. In theory, therefore, the surgeon might be advised to adjust his strategy according to the personality and needs of each patient, an assessment which will be difficult to make within the context of the normal doctor–patient interaction, and according to the likelihood of recurrence and progression of the disease, a factor which may not be open to prediction.

The merits of disclosure or non-disclosure are usually discussed only with respect to the specific impact on the patient of an awareness of cancer. The implications of a particular policy may, however, be farther-reaching; and the surgeon might legitimately take these into consideration when deciding which policy to adopt. One potential disadvantage of withholding information can be identified, and that is its effect on the surgeon's general relationship with the patient. To avoid disclosure, the former might limit personal contact, and be inhibited and evasive while interacting with the patient, and such behaviour is likely to discourage the latter from asking questions or expressing fears about either the condition or the treatment prescribed. As a consequence, the patient may be deprived of a valuable source of support in contexts where the surgeon can be reassuring; entertain false perceptions and expectations which are not discredited; hesitate to seek advice and guidance where these are required; and fail to comply with recommendations whose force is not recognized.

5. INFLUENCES ON ADJUSTMENT

Investigators' primary focus has generally been on an assessment of the over-all impact of mastectomy, in terms of the incidence, duration, and sources of the distress which it elicits. One finding implicit in all studies, however, is the wide variation between women in their reactions. It would indeed be surprising if this were not the case, since reactions to most life crises, and even to stressors applied within the laboratory, are varied. The differences which are observed may be attributed to two main sources: firstly, the patient's appraisal of the threat implied by the situation; and secondly, the coping resources available to her for averting or minimizing the impact of this threat. Appraisal of threat refers to the individual's subjective evaluation of the situation, conscious or otherwise, in terms of its personal significance. This concept has a central role within the model of stress proposed by Lazarus (1966), in which objective features of the situation are seen as factors determining stress only to the extent that they are reflected in the individual's own primary appraisal of threat. Bard and Sutherland (1955) were making a similar point, when they argued that a woman's response to mastectomy will depend upon the particular significance of death and disfigurement within her own emotional life, rather than upon their general symbolic representation within the culture. Given that the situation does have implications which are personally threatening, the process of adjustment will be governed by the effectiveness of the coping strategies that may be adopted. The range and availability of these will depend upon the patient's personal resources and attributes, together with the existence of external constraints and supports.

Coping Strategies

Katz and colleagues (1970) interviewed a group of women prior to biopsy and identified a number of defences they appeared to employ in talking about the breast symptom. These comprised displacement of concern, projection of hostility, denial with rationalization, stoicism or fatalism, and prayer and faith. The authors suggested that it was the effectiveness of such defences which resulted in the absence of any major psychoendocrine disturbance in this sample. Todd and Margarey (1978) have carried out a similar analysis of defences in breast cancer patients. Their study was more detailed and the descriptions presented are therefore more specific. The list is, nevertheless, quite similar to the one above, and comprised a denial of related emotional distress, suppression or avoidance of an awareness of cancer, intellectualization with or without isolation, rationalization of inappropriate or maladaptive behaviour, reaction formation through ideas or affect (that is, by emphasizing the positive aspects of the experience or appearing to be exhilarated by this), displacement of concern (possibly to the husband) projection of hostility, and stoicism or fatalism. The first and last of these were noted as particularly common responses.

With regard to coping styles apparent postoperatively, Morris and her colleagues (1977) identified five types of general attitude towards the diagnosis: denial; a hopeful attitude and search for information; stoic acceptance; an active seeking for information, but a pessimistic interpretation of this; and, finally, an attitude of helplessness and hopelessness. A similar analysis of reactions to the loss of the breast was not attempted. At a more specific level of coping, there are a number of strategies that individuals quite consciously use in the social management of their breast loss (Ray, 1978). Some of the women interviewed in this study took the decision to conceal their operation from all but those closest to them, while others adopted the very different course of disclosing their mastectomy freely and refusing to treat, or let it be treated, as a source of embarrassment. Some of the latter would joke about their lack of a breast, thereby signalling a personal absence of concern and a desire that others should feel similarly at ease; some tried to dress more attractively and with greater boldness, demonstrating to themselves and to others that there was no cause for sympathy or concern. The open and carefree attitude adopted by these women should not be taken as a faithful reflection of their inward response, but rather as a form of "impression management" prompted by underlying feelings of insecurity and inadequacy (Goffman, 1959).

The coping strategies employed by breast cancer patients may be defensive or non-defensive in nature and take the form of changes in either appraisals or behaviour. The range of strategies appropriate, factors determining their employment, and their relationship to general adjustment and well-being merit more detailed investigation. In this and in other areas, research should be concerned not only with the difficulties experienced by those who fare badly but also with the successes of those who fare well, since, without this, our understanding of reactions to crisis and stress will be incomplete and unbalanced. Moreover, a study of how successful copers manage the problems with which they are confronted will assist in the guidance of those who adjust less well.

While non-defensive forms of coping are relatively open to investigation, the study of defensive coping presents some difficulties. One is that of distinguishing cases in which an individual adjusts well because the situation is not problematic for him or her, from cases in which adjustment is achieved through the employment of defences. For example, if a patient claims that she is not distressed by the loss of the breast and is able to account for and justify this position, are we to interpret this as a valid indication of a low emotional investment in the breast or as a denial of concern accompanied by rationalization? As has been pointed out elsewhere, distress in reaction to any given stressor will depend upon how the latter is perceived, interpreted *and* defended against (Katz *et al.*, 1970). It is only by relatively subtle, and perhaps less reliable, techniques of observation, that realistic appraisals and defensive reactions may be effectively distinguished. The second problem concerns the adaptiveness of defensive reactions. There have been attempts to determine this empirically, by correlating the employment of specific defences with degree of maladjustment, but any causal interpretation of such a correlation is highly suspect. The *a priori* criteria according to which adaptiveness might be judged have been widely discussed. There is some consensus that defences are, in principle, undesirable, because any distortion of reality may have adverse implications for future coping, but that this does not mean that defences are in all circumstances maladaptive. Some have argued that they may be adaptive to the extent that they do not prevent an eventual confrontation with the problem (Haan, 1977; Weisman and Worden, 1976). Defences which are limited in time or strength may meet this criterion; thus Weisman and Worden (1976) point to the difference between an attempted wiping out of reality which will prevent a realistic adjustment, and a minimization or redefining of the situation in such a way that it modulates distress without avoiding the problem entirely. Others have argued that any absolute judgement about the adaptiveness of defences must be value-laden, and that their advantages and disadvantages should not be judged without considering the individual, the situation, and the exact nature of the defence employed. In the final analysis, the adaptiveness of defensive reactions may be an issue for clinical judgement in the individual case, rather than a subject for either philosophical discussion or empirical investigation at a more general level.

The complexities involved are well-illustrated by the different aspects of the breast cancer situation. Considering the response to the initial discovery of the symptom, a defensive reaction to this which prevents the individual from seeking medical advice would generally be seen as maladaptive. Other defences which reduce distress without this consequence, or which facilitate consultation by neutralizing an interfering emotional response, would probably be viewed as benign. With respect to the loss of the breast, a degree of defensiveness may here be quite generally accepted as adaptive, since it is more likely to assist than to impede a return to normal social and physical activities. With a full return to her normal overt functioning, the individual will then be better able to make a personal and more realistic adjustment to the breast loss. Another criterion according to which the adaptiveness of a defence may be judged is its vulnerability to challenge; and this is particularly apparent in the context of reactions to the diagnosis of malignancy. A woman who denies the fact of her breast cancer may experience less distress than one who confronts her disease, provided that she does not have a recurrence. If she does not, then the defence might possibly be regarded as having been adaptive *in this case*. If, on the other hand, the same woman is unfortunate enough to suffer a recurrence, then she will be psychologically unprepared for this outcome; and the denial may, in retrospect, be regarded as maladaptive. As a final consideration, it should perhaps be recognized that some individuals will lack the resources to resolve a problem, even where this is openly confronted. In circumstances where the alternative is fragmentation and disintegration, defences which prevent this will be a lesser evil, whatever their negative implications (Haan, 1977).

Social Support

There is now a relatively extensive literature on the role of social support as a protection or "buffer" against stress (Dean and Lin, 1977). Reactions to natural disasters, imprisonment, military involvement, bombardment, and bereavement have been shown to be less acute, where they occur within the context of a close community, or where the individual has strong links with family and friends; and the impact of stressful life events on physical illness is also reduced in these circumstances (see Cobb, 1976). The existence of a supportive social network can increase the effectiveness of the individual's coping both by generally enhancing feelings of self-worth and security and by providing specific emotional and practical support at the time of crisis. There are a number of ways in which social support might be defined and investigated. Woods and Earp (1978) have studied its influence on the depression experienced after mastectomy, taking as an index the patient's ratings of the help that she might expect to receive from others and the preparedness of these others to listen. A relationship between social support and depression was found, but only where few physical symptoms were experienced as a result of surgery. It appeared that, at a certain threshold where symptoms were relatively severe, support no longer ameliorated the depressive impact of the mastectomy. Different indices of support, might, however, be investigated with different results. Its effectiveness is likely to depend upon the source and specific nature of the support in relation to the crisis under consideration.

One important source of potential support for those women who are married will be the husband. He will have a dual significance; it is to him that the patient may most naturally look to for comfort, while at the same time his reaction may be one of the principal causes for her concern. If he did react adversely, then his role might be an undermining rather than a supportive one. Few studies have systematically investigated the influence of mastectomy on the marital relationship. The evidence which does exist suggests that the operation does not detract significantly from the quality of the relationship, and that the husband's contribution to his wife's adjustment is generally positive. Morris and colleagues (1977) looked at ratings of the marital relationship, including feelings toward the spouse, and found no difference between the mastectomy group and patients who had had benign breast disease; any deterioration in the status of the relationship from before to two years after surgery in the former group were matched by equivalent changes in the latter. In some cases the crisis of mastectomy may even bring a couple closer together: Maguire found this to be the case in 18 per cent of couples (Maguire, 1976). These findings bear out the predictions made by women in the general population (American Cancer Society, 1973) that an existing happy marriage will not be endangered by this operation.

While it seems that few marriages are endangered by the woman's mastectomy, many writers have pointed to the difficulties that the husband will experience as an individual. He has not only to come to terms himself with his wife's disfigurement and the fact of her illness, but will at the same time be confronted with his own worries and problems of adjustment. Each of the partners will in fact have to cope simultaneously with their personal feelings and with their partner's real or projected feelings. Most husbands will find themselves involved in events from the time when the woman first discovers the breast symptom. They will be involved emotionally, but some may also take an active part in decision making and act as confidant and counsellor both before and after surgery. Patients' perception of the importance of their husband's role was apparent in the interviews carried out within the author's own study (Ray, 1977). It was possible to distinguish, on the basis of the woman's own accounts at least, a number of strategies which couples employed for coping with the wife's disfigurement within the context of the marriage.

At one extreme, there were husbands who seemed to their wives to be essentially non-reactive in terms of their overt responses. Here, there was little change in the man's behaviour, little conversation about the mastectomy, and little direct expression of sympathy. Such an attitude was not generally seen as inadequate by the wives involved, since it often reflected a typical style of communication and interaction within that couple; the husband's underlying sympathy and concern were either assumed or inferred from subtle cues. In only a few cases was there an acknowledged asymmetry of needs, with the woman wishing to talk about her mastectomy and its implications but the husband avoiding this issue; such avoidance was attributed to a fear of cancer and a distaste for illness. At the other extreme, there were husbands who were active to the point of assertion, refusing to tolerate in their wives attitudes or behaviour which they saw as maladaptive. They would express anger when the woman voiced feelings of inadequacy or concern about the possible loss of her husband's love, ask to see the scar, and insist that she abandon her modesty about this. The patients interviewed did not seem to resent such behaviour. Some found it distressing in the short term, but in retrospect all claimed that it had made a decisive and positive contribution to their adjustment. Renneker and Cutler (1952) have pointed out that it is possible for a husband in this situation to be too concerned for his wife's feelings; too solicitous an attitude may lead her to believe that he feels as sensitive about the scar as she does, and reinforce her "anxious concealment". Other strategies adopted by husbands for dealing with the woman's distress were supportive rather than assertive. One was to attempt to reason this away, pointing out the futility of grieving for something that cannot be changed and arguing that she should feel relief that the cancer had been detected and controlled. Many realized that their wife needed reassurance that she would still have their love, and that the mastectomy could not change their relationship in any fundamental way. However, the strategy that was most evidently appreciated was that of humour. Where the husband was able to joke about the mastectomy in a loving way which stressed the bond between the couple, this appeared to convey with greatest conviction the message that all was well. Treating the mastectomy in this "irreverent" manner also created an atmosphere in which the couple could talk openly and with less embarrassment about the problems which they each faced.

6. PATIENT DELAY

Past Research

In spite of continuing controversy about the nature and course of breast cancer, there is general agreement that early treatment will enhance the disease's prognosis. Women are thus encouraged to check their breasts for lumps and other symptoms and to avoid delay in seeking medical advice. However, only a few women do examine their breasts regularly (George *et al.*, 1976; Holleb, 1974; Phillips and Brennan, 1976; Richards, 1977), and as many as 20 per cent or more delay for at least three months before consulting their doctor (Cameron and Hinton 1968; Williams *et al.*, 1976). The psychological aspects of patient delay have been quite extensively researched (there has until recently been less emphasis on the issue of breast self-examination). Interest was stimulated by an early recognition that ignorance could account only in part for the delay observed. Even in the mid-fifties, it was possible to write: "One could almost say axiomatically that every adult woman knows what a *lump* in the breast *may* mean. Ignorance is rare..." (Paterson, 1955). Many studies have looked at patients with cancer in miscellaneous sites, in an attempt to determine generally applicable explanations of delay behaviour. This approach may cloud the picture, since symptoms of cancer will vary in their salience and ambiguity according to site. There are, however, several studies which have separated patients according to the site of their symptom, or which have focused exclusively upon breast conditions.

Investigators have related a number of diverse variables to delay behaviour in breast patients. These include:

(a) *Demographic characteristics.* Delayers tend to be of lower social class and education level (Cameron and Hinton, 1968; Greer, 1974; Williams *et al.*, 1976) and to be from older age groups (Greer, 1974; Williams *et al.*, 1976).

(b) *Personality characteristics.* Studies have failed to find evidence of a relationship between delay and either neuroticism (Cameron and Hinton, 1968; Greer, 1974) or extraversion (Greer, 1974). Two studies have noted a correlation with body barrier scores (Fisher, 1967; Hammerschlag *et al.*, 1964). This finding was interpreted as suggesting that delayers are more independent, self-steering and goal-oriented, since these are characteristics associated with a body image of this kind. Greer (1974) found that patients who delay tend habitually to deny when faced with crisis; Hammerschlag and colleagues (1974), however, found no relationship between delay and repression scores on the MMPI.

(c) *Symptom characteristics and prior experience of cancer.* Contact with mastectomy or other cancer patients appears to have no influence on delay behaviour (Cameron and Hinton, 1968; Greer, 1974). A personal history of breast lumps, does, however, seem to encourage early presentation (Greer, 1974). Intriguingly, patients who are found to have cancer, rather than benign breast conditions, are more likely to have delayed (Cameron and Hinton, 1968; Greer, 1974; Worden and Weisman, 1975). Pain or discomfort associated with the symptom does not seem to bear any simple relationship with delay, but may act as a trigger for presentation (Eardley, 1974; Williams *et al.*, 1976).

(d) *Emotional state and defensiveness at time of interview.* Patients who have delayed appear more depressed and express feelings of helplessness and hopelessness (Margarey *et al.*, 1977; Sugar and Watkins, 1961). They tend to be more anxious (Cameron and Hinton, 1968; Margarey *et al.*, 1977); and other states that have been noted include anger, confusion, and fatigue (Worden and Weisman, 1975). Defences such as denial of cancer or associated affect, suppression, and avoidance are positively associated with delay, while intellectualization and isolation are negatively correlated (Margarey *et al.*, 1977; Worden and Weisman, 1975).

(e) *Barriers to action.* One such barrier is fear. Margarey and colleagues (1977) concluded that delay is unrelated to conscious fears and Cameron and Hinton (1968) similarly concluded that these play a minor role. On the other hand, fear of mastectomy (Gold, 1964; Greer, 1974), fear of malignancy (Buls *et al.*, 1976; Gold, 1964; Greer, 1974; Williams *et al.*, 1976), and general fear of hospitalization or surgery (Gold, 1964), are given as explanations for delay by some patients. Another potential barrier is a lack of awareness of the implications of a breast abnormality. Delayers, according to their self-reports, are less likely to have thought of the possibility of cancer and to have seen the symptom as a cause for concern (Cameron and Hinton, 1968; Eardley, 1974; Williams *et al.*, 1976). Finally, a failure to recognize the importance of early treatment may also contribute to delay (Eardley, 1974).

(f) *Other influences.* These include a reluctance to be examined (Gold, 1964; Greer, 1974; Williams *et al.*, 1976) and domestic difficulties or commitments which prevent early consultation or encourage procrastination (Cameron and Hinton 1968; Greer, 1974).

There are inconsistencies between studies which are not apparent in the brief review above. Some failures to replicate are not surprising in view of considerable differences in methodology. These not only comprise variations in the tools of the investigation, whether these are essentially interview procedures, self-rating scales, questionnaires, or personality inventories. There are also basic differences in design, the most important of which is the stage at which the patients are investigated. In some studies interviews have taken place prior to diagnosis, while in others patients were seen after diagnosis or treatment, and a differential awareness of the diagnosis and its implications could well influence both patients' self-reports and behaviour in interview. Variables such as emotional state, defensiveness, and attitudes towards cancer and its treatment will be responsive to the situation as perceived by the individual, and even personality scores will be affected by the context in which the assessment is made. Such influences might, indeed, be a general source of contamination in studies of patient delay, since they are all essentially retrospective in nature. The topic cannot be experimentally investigated and non-experimental prospective studies would be costly in terms of both time and resources; patients are thus assessed *after* the discovery of the breast symptom and *after* they have presented with this symptom. This might affect the individual's actual status on any given dimension, and the way in which she presents this to herself and to the investigator. Distortions which operate differentially in the case of delayers and non-delayers respectively would be of particular concern, and it is not difficult to suggest ways in which these might arise. Mood disturbances in patients who have delayed could be an outcome of, rather than an explanation for, the behaviour under investigation, since the woman who delays and who is aware of recommendations for prompt consultation may be worried about the implications of delay for the illness outcome, given a diagnosis of malignancy. Similarly, a defensive orientation toward cancer might in some cases be interpreted as a rationalization of delay, since a denial of previous awareness of the need for action will avoid implications of cowardice or guilt. It should also be remembered that subjects in interview will be less committed to providing a frank and open account of their behaviour than the interviewer will be to elicit this. If embarrassed by her delay, a patient may, therefore, attempt to present herself in a favourable light by providing what she would consider to be a socially acceptable account of her behaviour.

Data from studies of patient delay should then be interpreted with caution. One general strategy which can be recommended is to draw together evidence for any given explanation from studies which have looked at different kinds of variable or which have looked at the same variable but in different ways. There is, in fact, some cross-validating evidence for each of the principal explanations of delay. Taking these in turn, the first points to a lack of awareness of the implications of the breast symptom. Evidence for this comes from both interview material and from correlations between delay and demographic characteristics. Thus some patients who delay claim that they were unfamiliar with the symptoms of breast cancer and were not concerned about their own breast abnormality, and it might be argued that the tendency for delayers to have a lower level of education offers some support for this account, since on this basis they would be expected to be less well-informed. A second explanation for delay is a defensive denial of the implications of the breast symptom and the need to seek advice. Patients' behaviour in interview suggests that those who delay are more likely to employ defences such as denial when talking about their condition, and an inference of a generally defensive orientation to cancer is supported by the parallel finding that delayers are predisposed to denial and have habitually employed this in situations other than the present. The third explanation attributes delay to a conscious, even if not articulated, fear of a diagnosis of cancer and its treatment consequences. Interview data suggest that fear has some influence in inhibiting prompt consultation and there is other, indirect, evidence for this explanation from a study by Ray and Baum (1979). In this study, delayers were found to have higher scores on a planning and organization dimension of personality, reflecting a disposition to behave in a considered rather than an impulsive fashion. A plausible explanation of this finding is that individuals with such a disposition would be more vulnerable to the inhibiting effect of fear on action. Eardley (1974) noted also that many of those women who consulted promptly did so automatically, without considering what the implications of either consultation or a failure to consult might be.

Future Directions

A broad consideration of the evidence suggests that there is no single explanation for delay behaviour and that several factors play a role. Future research might profitably focus upon the manner in which a given factor influences the decision-making process, rather than further charting the relationships between delay and other variables. This strategy may not only be theoretically fruitful but be more effective in practical terms, that is, in indicating ways in which delay may be discouraged. For example, it may be easier to neutralize the role of conscious or unconscious fears in inhibiting action than to eliminate these fears. A second, but related, reorientation would be to distinguish different stages in the decision-making process. It is not appropriate to treat the discovery of the breast symptom and the seeking of medical advice as two events in direct sequential relationship. They are linked by a chain of intermediate events. Thus, the woman has first to interpret the breast symptom as a cause for concern, then to take the decision to seek advice, and only then will she arrange a consultation. Each stage in the sequence may be subject to delay, and the factors influencing delay may be different at each stage. Finally, most studies of delay behaviour have asked the question, "Why do some patients delay?" rather than "why do some patients consult promptly?", and there is a need to redress the imbalance by placing greater emphasis on triggers to action (Eardley, 1974). This approach permits the investigator to question the patient directly about her behaviour with less risk of causing distress by implying that this behaviour was inappropriate. With regard to its theoretical advantages, a focus on inducements to action brings to attention the fact that some variables which account for delay will also account for an absence of delay; a fear of cancer can be an incentive as well as a disincentive for early presentation (Cameron and Hinton, 1968; Eardley, 1974). Influences not covered by hypotheses framed as explanations for delay also become evident. Thus Eardley and Wakefield (1976) noted that circumstantial factors play a part in triggering consultation, and that many women are influenced in their decision to go to the doctor by family and friends whom they have consulted informally about their breast symptom. There is a common and implicit assumption in most research that early consultation is in some way the norm and does not require explanation. This assumption is untenable and a model of patient delay cannot claim to be complete unless it takes as its starting point, or at least encompasses, an account of why women who seek advice promptly do so.

The problem of delay in breast patients has been considered independently of other issues which are in some respects similar; studies have tended not to adopt any general model of health behaviour as a framework for their investigation. One such model, which has been applied in many different contexts, is the health-belief model (Rosenstock, 1974). Here, behaviour is seen as the outcome of beliefs about the severity of the condition, the individual's personal vulnerability to the condition, the benefits of the recommended action, and potential barriers to this, whether psychological, physical or, financial. One distinctive feature of the model is that it is the individual's appraisal of the costs and benefits of action which are seen as primarily important, with fear and other emotions being viewed as responses to this appraisal, rather than as drives or motivators (Lazarus, 1966; Leventhal, 1970). It was initially intended for application to preventive health behaviour and the avoidance of the threat of disease, but it can be applied to health motivation in general, including symptomatic health behaviour (Leavitt, 1979). The model has intuitive appeal, but evidence relating to its empirical validity is mixed. It has one apparent deficiency which may account in part for this inconsistency: while it takes a subjective perspective which focuses upon the individual's appraisals of the factors described above, it does not allow for the defensive adjustment of these appraisals as a response to fear. It addresses itself to danger rather than to fear-control processes (Leventhal, 1970); yet, where there is a barrier to coping with a perceived danger, the individual may abandon this as an objective and seek instead to cope with the anxiety elicited by the perception of danger. Thus health beliefs may indeed generate independently coping behaviour and emotional responses (Lazarus, 1966; Leventhal, 1970; Rogers, 1975), but these emotional responses will in turn generate coping behaviour in the form of a defensive modification of the initial health beliefs. In consequence, the health beliefs elicited from subjects may be consistent with the behaviour observed, but might not correspond with those beliefs to which the individual would have ascribed prior to an awareness of personal threat. The model therefore lacks a dynamic component, and is likely to be most appropriate as it stands in areas of investigation where the relevant threat is a minor one or where action to avoid threat is easily undertaken.

7. IMPLICATIONS FOR PATIENT CARE

The picture which emerges from investigations of reactions to early breast cancer and its treatment is that, while many women adjust quickly and successfully, a proportion do experience considerable distress. Concern about the diagnosis of cancer and loss of the breast, and the psychological impact in terms of emotional disturbance, self-image, and general well-being, will in some cases be apparent several years after the operation. Such a response may be totally appropriate, given the personal significance of the mastectomy for that individual, and does not necessarily indicate any inadequacy on her part. She can nevertheless be helped toward a better adjustment by encouraging a reinterpretation of this significance and the avoidance of coping strategies which are obviously maladaptive. In this way, it will be possible to preempt adverse reactions, or to hasten psychological recovery and prevent long-term maladjustment. Similar kinds of protective and therapeutic interventions have been recommended, put into practice, and evaluated in other stressful contexts (Auerbach and Kilmann, 1977). The reduction of psychological distress does not require extrinsic justification; but in achieving this goal there might be some parallel benefits to patients' physical recovery. There is now good evidence of a correlational relationship between psychological stress and coping resources on the one hand, and the onset or the recovery from physical illness on the other (Dohrenwend and Dohrenwend, 1974; Rahe, 1978); and the hypothesis that stress will affect the function of the immunologic system and lower body resistance to disease has been quite widely considered (Cassel, 1974; Holmes and Masuda, 1974). Psychological reactions to the loss of the breast and diagnosis of cancer might therefore not only influence recovery from surgery, but could conceivably have some effect on resistance to recurrence. A few studies have examined the relationship between psychological variables and the recurrence or progression of malignant disease (e.g. Blumberg et al., 1954; Shrifte, 1962; Stavraky et al., 1968). The many difficulties of interpreting relationships between psychological factors and cancer have been detailed by Fox (1978), and the results of these studies are inconclusive. Nevertheless, a model of the role of stress in both the initiation and promotion of malignant transformation has recently been proposed (Wayner et al., 1979), and the possibility of the host–tumour relationship being influenced by psychological stress factors cannot yet be dismissed.

There are several organisations which exist to provide help for the breast cancer patient, most notably the Reach to Recovery Program in the U.S.A. and the Mastectomy Association in the U.K. Both employ volunteers who have themselves had mastectomies, and these volunteers are able to offer practical advice and emotional support, together with encouragement by example. An alternative approach, which has been adopted by some centres in the U.S.A., is the establishment of a multidisciplinary rehabilitation team within the hospital. Patients will typically meet several times as a group, under the supervision of the surgeon, a nurse, a physical therapist, a social worker, and a Reach to Recovery volunteer, the aim being to help the group members achieve a functional and cosmetic rehabilitation, and to encourage discussion of social and emotional problems. A third intervention strategy is to provide counselling on an individual basis, in order to give support and establish healthy coping patterns in the critical period after surgery (Klein, 1971). Such counselling may be undertaken before, as well as after surgery; there is some evidence that this is the time of greatest distress, and one in which the patient communicates least with those close to her (Jamison et al., 1978). In these sessions, patients can both be given the opportunity to express their fears to a sympathetic listener and be encouraged to prepare for the outcome of their surgery. Just as maladaptive coping strategies adopted post-operatively may prejudice later adjustment, so inadequate anticipatory coping may be reflected in adverse reactions immediately after mastectomy. Such surgical interviews also serve to identify those patients who are most at risk; for example, a previous psychiatric history or general emotional instability suggests the likelihood of a poor adjustment (Jamison *et al.*, 1978; Morris *et al.*, 1977; Renneker and Cutler, 1952), as does preoperative depression, irrespective of psychiatric history (Morris *et al.*, 1977). Whatever the nature of the programme, there is no reason why patients should be pressured to take part against their will. Some individuals will resist intervention by others at time of personal crisis—in one study, 56 per cent of respondents indicated that they would prefer not to have a counselling service after mastectomy (Downie, 1976)—and an optimal outcome will probably be achieved by permitting and even encouraging self-selection.

Where explicit rehabilitation or counselling programmes are not a possibility, then the psychological support that the patient receives must be given in the course of routine procedures and interactions directed toward her physical care. Nursing staff can and do contribute here (Anstice, 1970; Hobbs, 1975), and many surgeons also treat this as an essential aspect of their role, without which the practice of medicine is reduced "from a professional art to a technical skill" (Lewison, 1956 p. 99). In spite of this, patients still seem to be dissatisfied with the information that they are given, and claim that they do not have the opportunity to discuss their problems in full. Two factors perhaps contribute to the reluctance of physicans and nursing staff to provide opportunities for such communication. Firstly, they may fail to recognize the existence of the need for further information and support and, secondly, they may anticipate and wish to avoid the distress which they themselves might experience in interacting with the patient at this level. In one study, it was noted that surgeons at an outpatients' clinic did not respond to nonverbal cues of anxiety, nor did patients verbally express the degree of their concern (Lee and Maguire, 1975). The latters' diffidence as outpatients can be attributed to an awareness of the pressure of time, to timidity, or to a definition of the situation as one in which physical and not emotional problems are relevant. Similar influences will again be present after surgery, inhibiting the expression of concern. In addition, the patient at this stage will be aware that it is the wish of all that she should adjust quickly and easily, and she may refrain from asking inconvenient questions, attempt to give an impression of adjustment, and inwardly deny her negative feelings in order to justify this expectation (Wabrek and Wabrek, 1976). At the same time, staff may reinforce her concealment by actively discouraging the expression of negative attitudes, and by adopting a cheerful and optimistic manner in an effort to provide reassurance and raise morale. In order to overcome this reluctance to disclose concern, it might therefore be necessary to initiate discussion with the patient, rather than wait for her to take the initiative. It is sometimes claimed that such probing could exacerbate or create emotional difficulties, but there is little justification for this position; attempts to foster a positive and constructive attitude to the mastectomy are more likely to be successful where existing problems are acknowledged rather than denied. Interactions with patients which confront their distress may, however, create additional stresses for staff. Writers who have offered guidelines for the emotional management of the cancer patient have generally pointed out that such interactions will be stressful for the physician and warn that this can act as an incentive to avoid a supportive role (Crary and Crary, 1974; Stehlin and Beach, 1966; Vujan, 1956). Nursing staff will be similarly affected and might be even more vulnerable because of their closer contact with the patient (Quint, 1963).

8. CONCLUDING COMMENTS

It is only recently that the psychological aspects of breast cancer and its treatment have been systematically investigated; a number of methodological difficulties have yet to be overcome, although the existence of these is not always acknowledged. One of the most important is that of determining the extent to which self-reports and behaviour are biased by social influences. Patients will be motivated to present themselves in a relatively desirable light, and will be reluctant to admit to feelings, or give explanations for their behaviour, which would prompt the attribution of undesirable characteristics such as cowardice, neuroticism, or vanity. Those who delay seeking medical advice because of fear may prefer not to admit to this; and those who cannot adjust to the loss of the breast may view their negative feelings as unworthy and feel obliged to express gratitude at the success of their treatment rather than bitterness at the form of this treatment. Patients' accounts of their behaviour and experiences will also be influenced by intra-personal defensive needs: protestations of a lack of awareness of the significance of the breast symptom, and of lack of concern at the loss of the breast or possibility of recurrence, may in some cases constitute the patient's attempts to deny or suppress a more threatening view of her situation.

A further influence on patients' self reports and behaviour is their perception of the aims of the investigation in which they are involved. Very few studies give an account of the way in which the project was presented to patients: if patients are aware that certain emotional states and attitudes are anticipated, then these could become more salient and be more freely expressed than under other circumstances. Researchers too can be influenced by an awareness of the aims of the investigation. Their behaviour in interview may be affected by their expectations of the study's outcome, producing responses which conform with these expectations, and ratings of the patient's behaviour may be similarly subject to unconscious bias, particularly where these involve a strong element of subjective judgement. While it might be possible to conceal the aims of a research project from the subjects involved, it is difficult to see how individuals called upon to interview or to rate the content of interviews could do this blindly, without being aware of the nature of the study or the group to which the subject belongs. These comments are generally relevant to research in this area, but specific types of designs and individual studies will incorporate additional factors which can influence the data and cloud their interpretation. Taking as an example those studies in which the same patients are seen repeatedly at intervals after surgery, these regular assessments will not only monitor reactions over time, but may have some independent influence on these. It could in principle be argued either that patients would benefit from the opportunity to express their feelings or, alternatively, that a focus on their concerns would make these more salient in the future. Methodological problems of the kinds described above are not, of course, limited to this area of study, and are common in laboratory-experimental contexts as well as in investigations of naturally occurring events (Adair, 1973). The acknowledgement of sources of possible bias should not discourage researchers from pursuing their investigations, but provide the stimulus for the development of techniques and methodologies that will minimize their impact.

Work in this field not only has implications for the specific issue of breast cancer and mastectomy, since an understanding of stress and coping within this context should generalize to that of other naturally occurring events. It is from this point of view, a particularly rich and complex situation. Firstly, the patient is simultaneously presented, on the one hand, with the threat of cancer and the possibility of recurrence and, on the other hand, with the loss of the breast and the consequences of this for her self image, marital relationship, and social role. This dual theme permits an exploration of the relationship between stress and coping within different areas of threat, so that independent and interactive influences of the individual and the specific nature of the threat might be identified. Secondly, the relevant threats and stressors continue to develop from the discovery of the breast symptom until, and into, the post-surgical period. This provides the opportunity to observe changes and consistencies in coping over time and to develop a dynamic, transactional model of stress and adjustment. There has, as yet, been less research emphasis on the coping strategies adopted by women with mastectomy than on the extent and nature of the problems which they face and their emotional reaction to these. In any sample, there are a significant proportion of women who either appear to have few difficulties or who manage to adjust quite swiftly to their illness and disfigurement. Future work might explore in greater depth the characteristics of these women and the strategies they pursue. The outcome of such research will have intrinsic theoretical interest, in highlighting the nature of the resources which people bring to such challenges and the way in which the effects of these are mediated. Moreover, a greater awareness of what constitutes effective coping within the context of breast cancer may be used to encourage similar strategies in those who lack these resources.

REFERENCES

Adair, H. S. (1973) *The Human Subject: The Social Psychology of the Psychological Experiment*, Little, Brown and Co.

Aitken-Swan, J. and Easson, E. C. (1959) Reactions of cancer patients on being told their diagnosis, *British Medical Journal*, **1**, 779–783.

American Cancer Society (1973) *Women's attitudes regarding breast cancer*, The Gallup Organisation, Princeton, N.J.

Anstice, E. (1970) Coping after a mastectomy, *Nursing Times*, **66**, 882–883.

Auerbach, S. M. and Kilmann P. R. (1977) Crisis intervention: A review of outcome research, *Psychological Bulletin*, **84**, 1189–1217.

Averill, J. R. (1973) Personal control over aversive stimuli and its relationship to stress, *Psychological Bulletin*, **80**, 286–303.

Bard, M. and Sutherland, A. M. (1955) Psychological impact of cancer and its treatment: IV. Adaptation to radical mastectomy, *Cancer*, **8**, 656–672.

Blumberg, E. M., West, P. M. and Ellis, P. W. (1954) A possible relationship between psychological factors and human cancer, *Psychosomatic Medicine*, **16**, 277–286.

Briggs, J. E. and Wakefield, J. (1967) *Public opinion on cancer: a survey of knowledge and attitudes among women in Lancaster*, A report for the Manchester Regional Committee on Cancer.

Buls, J. G., Jones, I. H., Bennett, R. C. and Chan, D. P. S. (1976) Women's attitudes to mastectomy for breast cancer, *The Medical Journal of Australia*, **2**, 336–338.

Calden G., Lundy, R. M. and Schlafer, R. J. (1959) Sex differences in body concepts, *Journal of Consulting Psychology*, **23**, 378.

Cameron, A. and Hinton, J. (1968) Delay in seeking treatment for mammary tumours, *Cancer*, **21**, 1121–1126.

Cartwright, A. (1964) *Human relations and hospital care*, Routledge and Kegan Paul, London.

Cassel, J. (1974) Psychosocial processes and "stress": theoretical formulation, *International Journal of Health Sciences*, **4**, 471–482.

Cobb, S. (1976) Social support as a moderator of life stress, *Psychosomatic Medicine*, **38**, 300–314.

Colman, A. M. (1971) Social rejection, role conflict and adjustment: psychological consequences of orthopaedic disability, *Perception and Motor Skills*, **33**, 907–910.

Craig, T. M. and Abeloff, M. D. (1974) Psychiatric symptomatology among hospitalised cancer patients, *American Journal of Psychiatry*, **131**, 1323–1327.

Craig, T. J., Comstock, G. W. and Geiser, P. B. (1974) The quality of survival in breast cancer: a case-control comparison, *Cancer*, **33**, 1451–1457.

Crary, W. G. and Crary, G. C. (1974) Emotional crises and cancer, *Cancer Journal for Clinicians*, **24**, 36–39.

Dean, A. and Lin, N. (1977) The stress-buffering role of social support, *Journal of Nervous and Mental Disease*, **165**, 403–417.

Dohrenwend, B. S. and Dohrenwend, B. P. (1974) (Eds.) *Stressful Life Events: their nature and effects*, Wiley, New York.

Downie, P. A. (1976) Post-mastectomy survey, *Nursing Mirror*, March 25th, 65–66.

Eardley, A. (1974) Triggers to action: a study of what makes women seek advice for breast conditions, *International Journal of Health Education*, **27**, 3–12.

Eardley, A. and Wakefield, J. (1976) Lay consultation by women with a lump in the breast, *Clinical Oncology*, **2**, 33–39.

Eisenberg, H. S. and Goldenberg, I. S. (1966) Measurement of quality of survival of breast cancer patients, in J. L. Hayward and R. D. Bulbrook (eds.) *Clinical Evaluation in Breast Cancer*, Academic Press, London.

Feder, S. L. (1966) Psychological considerations in the care of patients with cancer, *Annals of the New York Academy of Science*, **125**, 1020–1027.

Feifel, H. (1963) Death, in N. Farberow (Ed.) *Taboo Topics*, Prentice Hall, London.

Fisher, S. (1967) Motivation for patient delay, *Archives of General Psychiatry*, **16**, 676–678.

Fox, B. H. (1978) Premorbid psychological factors as related to cancer incidence, *Journal of Behavioral Medicine*, **1**, 45–133.

Friedman, S. B., Chodoff, P., Mason, J. W. and Hamburg, D. (1963) Behavioural observations on parents anticipating the death of a child, *Paediatrics*, **32**, 610–625.

George, W. O., Gleave, E. N., England, P. C., Wilson, M. C., Wellwood, R. A., Asbury, D., Hartley, G., Barker, P. G., Hobbs, P. and Wakefield, J. (1976) Screening for breast cancer, *British Medical Journal*, **2**, 856–860.

Gilbertson, V. A. and Wangensteen, O. H. (1962) Should the doctor tell the patient that the disease is cancer? *Cancer*, **12**, 82–86.

Goffman, E. (1959) *Presentation of Self in Everyday Life*, Anchor, New York.

Goffman, E. (1963) *Stigma*, Prentice-Hall, New Jersey.

Gold, M. A. (1964) Causes of patient delay in diseases of the breast, *Cancer*, **17**, 564–577.

Greer, S. (1974) Psychological aspects: delay in the treatment of breast cancer, *Proceedings of the Royal Society of Medicine*, **67**, 470–473.

Haan, N. (1977) *Coping and Defending: processes of self-environment organisation*, Academic Press, New York.

Hamburg, D., Hamburg, B. and Degoza, S. (1953) Adaptive problems and mechanisms in severely burned patients, *Psychiatry*, **16**, 1–20.

Hammerschlag, C. A., Fisher, S., De Cosse, J. and Kaplan, E. (1964) Breast symptoms and patient delay: Psychological variables involved, *Cancer*, **17**, 1480–1485.

Hardesty, A. S., Burdock, E. I., Lenn, E. A. and Trachtman (1973) Profile of psychological distress in physical illness, in *The proceedings of the Annual Convention of American Psychology Association*, Montreal, **8**, 369–370.

Hinton, J. (1973) Bearing cancer, *British Journal of Medical Psychology*, **46**, 105–113.

Hobbs, P. (1975) Community aspects of breast cancer, *Nursing Mirror*, April 3rd, 52–54.

Holleb, A. I. (1974) Women's attitudes regarding breast cancer: The Gallup Poll, *Journal of the Cancer Association*, **24**, 117–118.

Holmes, T. H. and Masuda, M. (1974) Life change and illness susceptibility, in B. S. Dohrenwend and B. P. Dohrenwend (Eds.) *Life Events: their nature and effects*, Wiley, New York.

Imboden, J. B., Canter, A. and Cluff, L. E. (1961) Convalescence from influenza, *Archives of International Medicine*, **108**, 393.

Jamison, K. R., Wellisch, D. K. and Pasnau, R. O. (1978) Psychological aspects of mastectomy: I. The woman's perspective, *American Journal of Psychiatry*, **135**, 432–436.

Janis, I. L. (1958) *Psychological Stress*, Wiley, New York.

Jenkins, C. D. and Zyzanski, S. J. (1968) Dimensions of belief and feeling concerning three diseases: poliomyelitis, cancer and mental illness: a factor analytic study. *Behavioural Science*, **13**, 372–381.

Katz, J. L., Weiner, H., Gallagher, T. F. and Hellman, L. (1970) Stress, distress and ego defences, *Archives of general psychiatry*, **23**, 131–142.

Kelly, W. O. and Friesen, S. R. (1950) Do cancer patients want to be told? *Surgery*, **27**, 822–826.

Klein, R. (1971) A crisis to grow on, *Cancer*, **28**, 1660–1665.

Knopf, A. (1974) *Cancer: changes in opinion after 7 years of public education in Lancaster*, Manchester Regional Committee on Cancer.

Krasnoff, A. (1959) Psychological variables and human cancer. *Psychosomatic Medicine*, 291–295.

Kurtz, R. M. (1969) Sex differences and variations in body attitudes, *Journal of Consulting and Clinical Psychology*, **33**, 625–629.

Lazarus, R. S. (1966) *Psychological stress and the coping process*, McGraw-Hill, New York.

Leavitt, F. (1979) The health-belief model and utilization of ambulatory care services, *Social Science and Medicine*, **13**, 105–112.

Lee, E. C. G. and Maguire, G. P. (1975). Emotional distress in patients attending a breast clinic, *British Journal of Surgery*, **62**, 162.

Letang, G. B. W. (1977) Coordinated supportive services benefit the breast cancer patient, *Delaware Medical Journal*, **11**, 623–624.

Leventhal, H. (1970) Findings and theory in the study of fear communications, in L. Berkowitz (Ed.) *Advances in Experimental Social Psychology*, Vol. 5, Academic Press, New York.

Lewis, F. M. and Bloom, J. R. (1978) Psychosocial adjustment to breast cancer, *International Journal of Psychiatry in Medicine*, **9**, 1–17.

Lewison, E. F. (1956) The psychologic aspects of breast cancer, *General Practitioner*, **13**, 99–105.

Ley, P. (1972) Complaints made by hospital staff and patients: a review of the literature, *Bulletin of the British Psychological Society*, **25**, 115–120.

Maguire, P. (1976) The psychological and social sequelae of mastectomy, in J. G. Howells (Ed.) *Modern Perspectives in the Psychiatric Aspects of Surgery*, Brunner/Mazel, New York.

Maguire, G. P., Lee, E. G., Bevington, D. J., Kuchemann, C. J., Crabtree, R. J., and Cornell, C. E. (1978) Psychiatric problems in the first year after mastectomy, *British Medical Journal*, 963–965.

Margarey, C. J., Todd, P. B. and Blizard, P. J. (1977) Psycho-social factors influencing delay and breast self-examination in women with symptoms of breast cancer, *Social Science and Medicine*, 229–232.

McIntosh, J. (1974) Processes of communication, information seeking and control associated with cancer: a selective review of the literature, *Social Science and Medicine*, **8**, 167–187.

McIntosh, J. (1976) Patients' awareness and desire for information about diagnosed but undisclosed malignant disease, *The Lancet*, August 7th, 300–303.

Morris, T., Greer, H. S. and White, P. (1977) Psychological and social adjustment to mastectomy, *Cancer*, **40**, 2381–2387.

Paterson, R. (1955) Why do cancer patients delay? *The Canadian Medical Association Journal*, **73**, 931–939.

Peck, A. (1972) Emotional reactions to having cancer, *Cancer*, **22**, 284–291.

Phillips, A. J. and Brennan, M. (1976) The reaction of Canadian Women to the Pap test and breast self examination, in J. Wakefield (Ed.) *Public Education about Cancer*, Technical Report Series Vol. **24**, UICC, Geneva.

Polivy, J. (1977) Psychological effects of mastectomy on a woman's feminine self-concept, *The Journal of Nervous and Mental Disease*, **164**, 77–87.

Quint, J. C. (1963) The impact of mastectomy, *The American Journal of Nursing*, **63**, 88–92.

Rahe, R. H. (1978) Life change and illness: past history and future directions, *Journal of Human Stress*, **3**, 3–15.

Ramsay, M. A. E. (1972) A survey of preoperative fear, *Anaesthesia*, **27**, 396–402.

Ray, C. (1977) Psychological implications of mastectomy, *British Journal of Social and Clinical Psychology*, **16**, 373–377.

Ray, C. (1978) Adjustment to mastectomy: the psychological impact of disfigurement, in P. C. Brand and P. A. Van Keep (Eds.) *Breast Cancer.· psycho-social aspects of early detection and treatment*, MTP Press, Lancaster.

Ray, C. and Baum, M. (1979) The relationship between personality and delay in the presentation of breast lumps, *Clinical Oncology*, **5**, 194.

Renneker, R. and Cutler, M. (1952) Psychological problems of adjustment to cancer of the breast, *Journal of the American Medical Association*, **148**, 833–838.

Richards, J. G. (1977) An experiment in public health education about cancer, in J. Wakefield (Ed.) *Public Education about Cancer*, Technical Report Series Vol. 26, UICC, Geneva.

Roberts, M. M., Furnival, I. G. and Forrest, A. P. M. (1972) The morbidity of mastectomy, *British Journal of Surgery*, **59**, 301–302.

Rogers, R. W. (1975) A protection motivation theory of fear appeals and attitude change, *Journal of Psychology*, **91**, 93–114.

Rosen, G. M. and Ross, A. O. (1968) Relationship of body image to self concept, *Journal of Consulting and Clinical Psychology*, **32**, 100.

Rosenstock, I. (1974) Historical origins of the health belief model, *Health Education Monographs*, **2**, 328–335.

Ryan, D. W. (1975) A questionnaire survey of preoperative fears, *British Journal of Clinical Practitioners*, **29**, 3ff.

Schmid, W. L., Kiss, M. and Hibert, L. (1974) The team approach to rehabilitation after mastectomy. *AORN Journal*, **19**, 821–836.

Schottenfield, D. and Robbins, G. F. (1970) Quality of survival among patients who have had radical mastectomy, *Cancer*, **26**, 650–654.

Shands, H. C. (1966) The informational impact of cancer on the structure of the human personality, *Annals of the New York Academy of Science*, **125**, 883–889.

Shrifte, M. L. (1962) Toward identification of a psychological variable in host resistance to cancer, *Psychosomatic Medicine*, **24**, 390–397.

Silberfarb, P. M. (1978) Psychiatric themes in the rehabilitation of mastectomy patients, *International Journal of Psychiatry in Medicine*, **8**, 159–167.

Solomon, G. F., Amkraut, A. A. and Kasper, P. (1974) Immunity, emotions and stress, *Psychotherapy and Psychosomatics*, **23**, 209–217.

Spielberger, C. D., Auerbach, S. M., Wadsworth, A. P., Dunn, T. M. and Taulbee, E. S. (1973) Emotional reactions to surgery, *Journal of Consulting and Clinical Psychology*, **40**, 133–138.

Stavraky, K. M., Buck, C. W., Lott, S. S. and Wanklin, J. M. (1968) Psychological factors in the outcome of human cancer, *Journal of Psychosomatic Research*, **12**, 251–259.

Stehlin, J. S. and Beach, K. H. (1966) Psychological aspects of cancer therapy, *Journal of the American Medical Association*, **197**, 140–144.

Sugar, M. and Watkins, C. (1961) Some observations about patients with a breast mass, *Cancer*, **14**, 979–988.

Todd, P. B. and Margarey, C. J. (1978) Ego defences and affects in women with breast symptoms: a preliminary measurement paradigm, *British Journal of Medical Psychology*, **51**, 177–189.

Torrie, A. (1970) Like a bird with broken wings, *World Medicine*, April 7th, 36–47.

Visotsky, H. M., Hamburg, D. A., Goss, M. E. and Lebovitz, O. Z. (1961) Coping behaviour under extreme stress, *Archives of General Psychiatry*, **5**, 423–443.

Volicer, B. J. and Bohannon, M. W. (1975) A hospital rating scale, *Nursing Research*, **24**, 352–359.

Vujan, A. S. (1956) The emotional aspects of malignancy, *The Pennsylvania Medical Journal*, **59**, 479–483.

Wabrek, A. J. and Wabrek, C. J. (1976) Mastectomy: sexual implications, *Primary Care*, **3**, 803–810.

Wakefield, J. (1969) Social and educational factors affecting the early diagnosis of cancer, *Schweizerische Medizinische Wochenschrift*, **99**, 833–839.

Wayner, L., Cox, T. and Mackay, C. (1979) Stress, immunity and cancer, in D. J. Oborne, M. M. Gruneberg and J. R. Eiser (Eds.) *Research in Psychology and Medicine*, Academic Press, London.

Weinstein, S., Sersen, E. A., Fisher, L. and Vetter, R. J. (1964) Preferences for body parts as a function of sex, age, and socio-economic status, *American Journal of Psychology*, **77**, 291–294.

Weisman, A. D. and Worden, J. W. (1976) The existential plight in cancer: significance of the first 100 days, *International Journal of Psychiatry in Medicine*, **7**, 1–15.

Wellisch, D. K., Jamison, K. R. and Pasnau, R. O. (1978) Psychosocial aspects of mastectomy: II. The man's perspective. *American Journal of Psychiatry*, **135**, 543–546.

Williams, E. M., Baum, M. and Hughes, L. E. (1976) Delay in presentation of women with breast disease, *Clinical Oncology*, **2**, 327–331.

Williams, E. M., Cruickshank, A. and Walker, W. M. (1972) *Public opinion on cancer: a survey of knowledge and attitudes in S.E. Wales*, Tenovus.

Wilson-Barnett, J. (1978) In hospital: patients' feelings and opinions, *Nursing Times*, **74**, 29–32.

Witkin, M. H. (1978) Psycho sexual counselling of the mastectomy patient, *Journal of Sex and Marital Therapy*, **4**, 20–28.

Woods, N. F. (1975) Influences on sexual adaptations to mastectomy, *Journal of General Nursing*, **4**, 33–47.

Woods, N. F. and Earp, J. A. L. (1978) Women with cured breast cancer, *Nursing Research*, **27**, 279–285.

Worden, J. W. and Weisman, A. D. (1975) Psychosocial components of lagtime in cancer diagnosis, *Journal of Psychosomatic Research*, **19**, 69–79.

Worden, J. W. and Weisman, A. D. (1977) The fallacy in postmastectomy depression, *The American Journal of the Medical Sciences*, **273**, 169–175.

Zion, L. C. (1965) Body concept as it relates to self concept, *Research Quarterly*, **36**, 490–495.

8

THE PSYCHOLOGY OF OBESITY: ITS CAUSES, CONSEQUENCES, AND CONTROL

PHILIP LEY

Plymouth Polytechnic

CONTENTS

1. INTRODUCTION

Obesity, its causes, and its treatment have become the focus of increasing experimental and theoretical interest. Inevitably, this has led to a mushrooming of reviews of research in this area. Therefore, the only justification for another one is either that the previous reviews are deficient, which is not true, or that it is still possible to say new things about obesity, which, it is hoped, is true.

This review, as well as examining the claim that behaviour modification is the treatment *par excellence* for obesity, also discusses the social psychology of this condition. In many ways, the obese would seem to be a victimized group, who are subject to anxiety-inducing social pressures, and prejudice on account of their fatness. In so far as current treatments have yet to prove their long-term success in even a majority of cases of obesity, it might well be that therapeutic effort should be devoted, at least in part, to the alleviation of the psychological consequences of being obese.

It certainly seems to be true that cultural pressures, as much as the hypothetical medical risks, are what drive the obese to seek help in losing weight. Because of this, it might be worth pointing out that several human societies have had fatting sheds instead of slimming clinics. Indeed, in the pre-industrial societies surveyed by

Ford and Beach (1965) fatness was more often considered beautiful than either thin or average build. Thirteen societies considered that fat physique was ideal, five that average build was ideal, and five that thinness was best. Despite these cultural differences in attitudes, it appears that absolute prevalence rates for obesity in women do not vary very much from culture to culture (Ley, 1980). Perhaps, women have a higher set-point for fatness than men. Perhaps, they are more likely to be biologically programmed to be fat. Considerations such as these, added to the low long-term success rates of current treatments, suggest that in the absence of significant medical risk, careful thought should be given before trying to produce weight loss.

However, the study of obesity is a very active field, and there are enough promising leads to encourage the hope that successful long-term treatments might not be far off. Even if these do not emerge in the near future, the obese can take some comfort from the fact that, although they seem to suffer more in adolescence and early adulthood, the obese in middle age are probably less anxious and depressed than their leaner colleagues.

2. DEFINITION AND MEASUREMENT OF OBESITY

James (1976) defines obesity as "a condition in which there is an excessive amount of body fat". Methods for assessing obesity are dealt with below. The definition of "excessive" is usually based on the probably established relationship between obesity and excess mortality and various diseases such as ischaemic heart disease, diabetes, hypertension, and osteoarthritis. While there are some who doubt the contribution of milder degrees of obesity to the development of these illnesses e.g. Keys (1975), Fullarton (1978), received opinion is that obesity is an undesirable characteristic. Further there is, in western cultures, strong social pressure in favour of slimness, and a great deal of prejudice against the obese (Ley, 1980). Because of this many people will seek help in becoming thinner for cosmetic reasons.

The main methods used in the assessment of obesity are:

(1) relative weight
(2) skinfold thickness
(3) weight/height ratios
(4) densitometry

Relative weight is the commonest of these. The subject's weight is compared with a standard weight and usually expressed as a percentage of the standard weight: i.e.

$$\text{relative weight} = \frac{\text{actual weight}}{\text{standard weight}} \times 100$$

The standard weights used are either average weights based on samples drawn from applicants for jobs or workers in an organization e.g. Montegriffo (1968); applicants for insurance policies e.g. Society of Actuaries (1959); or state and national samples e.g. Bray (1975). Many of these average weight tables are based on American samples, and it is known that there are differences in weight between British and American groups (Montegriffo, 1968). However, average weights for

British samples are available from a number of studies, Montegriffo, (1968); Khosla and Lowe (1967); Silverstone et al. (1969); Baird et al. (1974). Problems with the average weight data are the obvious ones of the deficiencies of the sample, and the fact that average weights will be influenced by the existence of obesity in the sample being assessed.

The second type of standard is ideal weight. This means in practice the ideal weights established by the Metropolitan Life Insurance Company, and published in 1959. The ideal weights were presumably chosen, because they were the weights associated with greatest survival. The weights are based on ideal weights of people in their early twenties and are given for small, medium, and large framed men and women. No way of assessing frame is presented, and it is possible that higher weights in older people might be quite compatible with survival. A general problem with relative weight methods is the relatively low correlations with more accurate measures of body fat (Grande, 1975; James, 1976).

Skinfold thickness can be measured either at one or at a number of sites. Normative data are available for skinfolds. Seltzer and Mayer (1965) provide them for triceps skinfold thickness, and Durnin and Womersley (1974) for the *sum* of four skinfolds (biceps, triceps, subscapular, and suprailiac). Skinfold thickness has the advantage of being a more direct measure of body fat. It can be carried out fairly easily, and is in many ways preferable to relative weight as a measure. Correlations with body density are usually in the range 0.7–0.9 (James, 1976).

Weight/height indices have no real advantages over relative weights. If they are to be used the preferred formula is

$$\text{Index} = W/H^2$$

$$W = \text{weight in kg}$$

$$H = \text{height in metres}$$

Cut-off values for obesity have to be chosen, and this is usually done by relating the index to the Metropolitan desirable weight tables e.g. 120 per cent of desirable weight for a medium framed woman is equal to an index value of 27.

Densitometry involves assessing the density of the body by measuring its displacement of water or gas (Archimedes' principle). It is most unlikely that psychologists will be using this method, but the interested reader can find a full account in Grande (1975).

The moral of this survey of methods of measuring obesity is that if relative weight is used as the sole criterion of obesity, then it is probable that several non-obese individuals will be accepted and that several obese ones will be rejected. The first danger can be guarded against by taking a very high cut-off for obesity e.g. 15–20 lbs over average weight for age and height or by using skinfold thickness as well. Use of skinfold thickness should also reduce the risk of missing obese individuals not detected by the relative weight method.

In the case of measuring the success of treatments for obesity, some authors have argued—so far largely in vain—that more sophistication should be shown in the choice of a measure of weight loss (Feinstein, 1959) and indeed in the choice of dependent variables generally (Bellack and Rozensky, 1975). Despite these pleas the usual measures used are either absolute weight lost, or percentage of overweight

TABLE 1.
Prevalence of Obesity in UK and USA Studies

Investigation	Age	Country	% Obese Female	Males
Metropolitan Life Insurance Company (1960)[1]	20–29	USA	12	12
	30–39		25	25
	40–49		40	32
	50–59		46	34
	60–69		45	29
Moore et al. (1962)[2]		USA	42	58
National Health Survey (1964)[1]		USA	29	30
Montegriffo (1968)[3]	20–29	UK	21	33
	30–39		33	47
	40–49		53	60
	50–59		64	50
	60–69		60	51
Silverstone et al. (1969)[1]		UK	49	37
Baird et al. (1974)[1]	15–29	UK	24	31
	30–49		50	53
	50–65		82	61

Definition of obesity: 1 = 20% above ideal weight; 2 = 15% above ideal weight; 3 = above mid-point ideal weight for large frame.

lost, or percentage change in weight. It is hard to see this situation changing, despite the arguments for changes.

3. THE PREVALENCE OF OBESITY

The prevalence of obesity has been investigated by the Metropolitan Life Insurance Company (1960), Moore et al. (1962), National Health Survey (1964), Montegriffo (1968), Silverstone et al. (1969) and Baird et al. (1974). The results of these surveys are summarized in Table 1. Socio-demographic variables associated with obesity rates include age and socio-economic status. Men seem to reach their peak

TABLE 2.
Prevalence of Obesity in Children

Sample	Age	% Obese Girls	Boys
Northampton children[1]	2	18	7
	3	26	10
	4	17	8
Aylesbury children[1]	6–8	2	1
	9–11	15	6
	12–14	32	9
Edinburgh children[2]	13	7	4
Exeter children[3]	13–14	16	12

After James, 1976.
Definition of obesity: 1 = skinfold (triceps + subscapular) > 20 mm; 2 = > 125% average weight for height; 3 = > 120% average weight for height.

weight earlier than women (Montegriffo, 1968; Silverstone et al., 1969; Baird et al., 1974). In childhood and after age 50, women have higher obesity rates than men, in groups drawn from western cultures, but not in West Indian and Polynesian groups where women have higher rates of obesity than men at all ages (Ley, 1980). Social class seems to be associated with rates of obesity in both the UK and USA, particularly so in women, lower class women being more obese (Dwyer et al., 1970; Silverstone 1974; Ashwell and Etchell, 1974).

It is also true that obesity is not uncommon amongst children. The data shown in Table 2 are taken from James (1976) who also provides other results not shown in the table. (Perhaps it should be stated here, that obesity in childhood has been relatively neglected by psychologists, especially from the point of view of treatment. For a review of what has been done see Lebow, 1977).

From the results of these surveys it can be confidently concluded that obesity is common, and that, in so far as it is a health hazard, psychologists should be interested in its prevention and treatment.

4. ATTITUDES TOWARDS THE OBESE AND THEIR CONSEQUENCES

There is a considerable amount of evidence to show that the obese are a negatively evaluated group. Investigations of stereotypes associated with fat and endomorphic physiques have shown that these physiques evoke general unfavourable stereotypes. (Fat and endomorphic physiques have been lumped together because of the high empirical correlations between them (Rees, 1973). For example, Lindegard (1956), found a correlation of +0.96 between his fatness factor and measures of endomorphy). Fat males and females are seen as less masculine and less feminine respectively (Dwyer et al., 1969). Even amongst 6-year-olds, fat outlines evoke the description: "cheats, forgets, lazy, sloppy, naughty, dirty, stupid" (Staffieri, 1967). Fat people are also usually ranked as less likeable than people with deformities and handicaps (Richardson et al., 1961; Goodman et al., 1963; Maddox et al., 1968). Better educated groups also view the obese unfavourably. Doctors were found to do so by Maddox et al. (1966), and university students by Chetwynd et al. (1975). In this last study, the obese were considered to be "like a mother" and "kind", but also "unattractive, weak, unsuccessful, not like a wife, old, not like a sister, a follower, and uninfluential". These attitudes seem to be shared by the obese themselves (Dwyer et al., 1970). Because physical appearances appears to be the strongest basis of perceived attractiveness (Berscheid and Walster, 1969) the obese can also be expected to show the disadvantages of the physically unattractive generally.

These negative stereotypes are likely to lead to discrimination against the obese, and there is some evidence that this might happen. For example, Canning and Mayer (1966) reported various findings suggesting that the obese are less likely than their lean counterparts to obtain university places. This was especially true of obese women. It was also shown by Canning and Mayer (1967) that this discrimination occurred despite the fact that the obese did not differ from the non-obese in IQ, scores on tests of verbal and quantitative aptitude, school attainment, health record, participation in school activities, and vocational aspirations.

These pressures against obesity affect females more than males. Dwyer *et al.*
(1970) report that surveys show that more women than men want to lose weight,
and Dwyer *et al.* (1969) that while 80 per cent of adolescent girls wished they were
thinner this was true of only 20 per cent of boys. Even amongst thin girls (mean
height—5 feet 5 inches, mean weight—110 lbs), 59 per cent wished to lose some
weight and three per cent worked to lose 9 lbs or more. Girls also appear to
overestimate their fatness more than boys. Hueneman *et al.* (1966) found that twice
as many girls thought they were fat as were judged to be so by objective criteria.
Guggenheim *et al.* (1977) report similar findings. This tendency becomes less pronounced with age, but women of normal weight were still found to overestimate
their weight more than men (Ashwell and Etchell, 1975). These investigators also
found that women are more likely to have tried to lose weight, a finding echoing
that of other investigators (Dwyer *et al.*, 1970). The finding of a sex difference in
overestimation of weight is not however universal (Gray, 1977).

Taken over all these investigations lead to the expectation that there will be a
great deal of anxiety about weight amongst women. In cases of mild obesity, given
the fairly low long-term success rates, it might be desirable to consider treating this
anxiety, rather than embarking on reducing programmes.

It is also worth noting, as mentioned in the Introduction, that although these
cultural pressures produce concern and anxiety in the obese, there is little evidence
that they actually lead to lower weights. For example, comparisons of western
societies, which by and large have slimness as an ideal, with Polynesian and black
societies which are much more tolerant of fatness, and indeed sometimes value it,
shows that absolute obesity rates for women do not differ significantly. The relevant
data are summarized in Table 3.

TABLE 3.
Percentages of Men and Women 20% or more above Ideal Weight in
Western and Developing Societies

Investigation	% 20 per cent over ideal weight	
	Male	Female
(a) Western cultures		
National Health Examination		
Survey (1964) USA	30	29
Silverstone *et al.* (1969) UK	37	49
Baird *et al.* (1974) UK	16	21
Osancova (1975) Czechoslovakia	9	34
Strata *et al.* (1977) Italy	15	24
(b) Developing societies		
Prior & Davidson (1966) Fiji	29	41
Johnson (1970) Africa	5	28
Hawley and Jansen (1971) NZ Maoris	15	38
Richards and De Casseres (1974)		
Jamaica	5	24
Barbados	7	31
Guyana	13	39
Trinidad	13	28
Barbados	3	41
Jamaica	10	63

Obviously no firm conclusions can be drawn from these data, but their implications are worth considering.

5. PSYCHOLOGICAL THEORIES CONCERNING THE ORIGINS OF OBESITY

Because it has been widely assumed that the obese are that way merely because they eat too much, psychological theories have, by and large, tried to explain why the obese eat more than they should. Theoretical explanations have tended to fall into two main camps. One camp suggests that the obese eat more, because they have personality problems which are reduced by eating. The other camp suggests that the obese respond differently from the non-obese to stimuli which control eating. Specifically, it has been suggested that either or both of the following propositions is true. Eating in the obese is less controlled by internal stimuli than in the non-obese. Eating in the obese is more controlled by external stimuli than in the non-obese. Another stimulus-based hypothesis is that the obese are unable to distinguish and correctly label different arousal states. They mistake any internal arousal state for hunger and this serves as a cue for eating. Finally Nisbett (1972) has provided a theory about why the obese should be externally controlled. These theories will now be reviewed.

Personality and Obesity

The theory that the obese have personality problems alleviated by eating has been investigated in the straightforward way by measuring such variables as anxiety, depression, and neuroticism in the obese. It has also been investigated more indirectly, by looking for evidence of deleterious personality or mood changes following weight loss. The argument being that if eating too much is a defence against unpleasant affective states, then a reduction in such eating should unleash the unpleasant affects.

Investigations into the personality characteristics of the obese have often been characterized by (1) a concentration on clinic populations, (2) small samples, and (3) a lack of control groups. There is also the further problem of whether any personality difficulties discovered are causal or reactive.

Levitt and Fellner (1963) investigated twenty-eight obese female in-patients who were divided into three groups; those with no physiological cause for their obesity (simple obesity), those with a definite physiological cause, and a mixed group. On ten of the thirteen MMPI scales, the simple group obtained significantly higher scores. A group of twenty-one very obese adults was investigated by Atkinson and Ringuette (1967). No control group was used, but the subjects were judged to have significant problems as assessed by the MMPI. Other authors, who have used control groups, have also reported more problems in obese adolescent girls (Werkman and Greenberg, 1967; Held and Snow, 1972; Karpowitz and Zeiss, 1975). However, all of these investigations were conducted in a medical or quasi-medical setting, with the exception of that of Karpowitz and Zeiss. Their finding was that obese school children who refused to participate in a weight reduction programme

had more problems than normal, but the obese children who did agree to participate had *fewer* problems.

Investigations carried out with community samples reveal a different picture.
Although Moore *et al.* (1962) found that the obese were less mature and more
suspicious, Simon (1963) found them to be less depressed; Silverstone (1968) found
them no more neurotic; and Crisp and McGuiness (1976) found overweight men'
and women to be significantly lower in anxiety, and men in depression as well.

These findings of good or better adjustment amongst the obese, suggest that the
findings of greater pathology amongst clinic populations are due to self-selection.
Perhaps, only the more neurotic, anxious, and depressed go to hospital for treatment.

However, it is possible to argue, as indeed Simon (1963) does, that the obese
obtain lower depression scores *because* obesity is a defence against depression and
other maladjustment. Certainly the belief that losing weight will lead to depression,
anxiety, or even psychosis has been put forward by many authorities (Stunkard,
1957; Bruch, 1973; Stunkard and Rush, 1974). There are, of course, a number of
methodological problems involved in demonstrating that this hypothesis is correct.
Firstly, weight loss is usually brought about by severely restricted calorie intake. It
is, therefore, necessary to differentiate between the effects of low calorie intake,
which has been shown to produce a variety of "symptoms" in normals (Keys *et al.*,
1952; Kollar *et al.*, 1964), and the specific effects of weight loss on the obese. Many
patients are hospitalized, e.g. for semi-starvation regimes. This means that the
effects of hospitalization must be controlled for. In so far as the treatment is
successful, the patient will leave with a different looking body. Again the effects of
this must be controlled for. If the patient is required to keep to a diet, a whole class
of reinforcers is no longer available. This too must be controlled for, as the reduction of availability of reinforcers might in itself be expected to lead to depression
(Lewinsohn, 1975). Finally, in the case of surgery, the effects of this, including the
frequent diarrhoea, must be controlled for. All of these factors argue for the need
for carefully selected controls. To date, no investigation has controlled for these
variables.

Because of the lack of methodologically adequate studies, it is impossible to draw
any firm conclusions. Stunkard (1957) found (probably) fewer psychopathological
reactions in a nutrition clinic population, than were found in normals undergoing
semi-starvation, but, in a special group of twenty-five severely obese patients who
had presented managment problems to other clinics, nine showed severe emotional
reactions to dieting. Glucksman and Hirsch (1966) report on the reactions of four
obese patients who were kept in hospital on a 600 calorie per day diet. Kollar and
Atkinson (1966) put seven severely obese patients in a psychiatric ward for 4–17
months. Swanson and Dinello (1970) followed up twenty-five patients for one to 50
months, and Robinson and Winnick (1973) report a study of ten patients admitted
to a general psychiatric hospital after displaying severe psychological disturbances
coincident with dieting. It is hard to comment on these reports, which clearly leave
all the methodological problems unresolved. They have been described to give the
flavour of the evidence on which the debate is based.

Slightly more satisfactory is the study reported by Ley (1978), which looked at
changes in anxiety and depression as measured by standardized techniques in re-

lation to weight loss. Patients were obese women volunteers exposed to information, group support, and a low carbohydrate diet. It was found that: (1) degree of overweight was positively correlated with depression and anxiety; the more overweight the women the greater the anxiety and depression; (2) that weight loss since the previous visit was negatively correlated with anxiety and depression; women who had lost more weight were less anxious and depressed; (3) that women whose weight loss over the whole programme was above median showed greater drops in depression and anxiety by the end of the programme than those who had lost less weight. This investigation would seem to rule out the possibility that losing weight will inevitably lead to increases in depression and anxiety. However, it cannot be taken as showing that weight loss leads to decreases in these variables, as it was in essence a correlational study, and leaves open the possibility that it was the existence of anxiety and depression that prevented some of the subjects from losing weight.

The matter is clearly unresolved with regard to semi-starvation and diet, but there seems to be no convincing evidence that adverse psychological reactions are to be generally expected when the obese lose weight. It is also of interest that in cases of by-pass operation, long-term follow-up reveals adequate adjustment (Crisp, 1978; Solow et al., 1978).

Emotional Arousal and Eating

Bruch (1974) and Schachter (1971) considered it possible that the obese often confused their various arousal states with hunger and, therefore, ate when aroused. However, the clinical observations which led to this suggestion were not that the obese label grief, anxiety, and the like as hunger, but that the obese seem to eat, when emotionally aroused, more often than leaner people. Indeed, there appears to be no evidence that the obese cannot label their arousal states correctly (Coddington and Bruch, 1970). The hypothesis, therefore, needs to be restated—that the obese have learned to eat in response to a wide range of arousal stimuli. It has also been suggested that this might be because eating reduces arousal.

The evidence in favour of these two hypotheses is mixed. Leon and Chamberlain (1973) found that weight regainers reported that they ate in response to a variety of emotional stimuli, more often than the subjects who successfully kept off the weight they had lost. Lipinski (1975) using the Holmes and Rahe Life Events Scale found an association between weight gain and stressful life events in the obese, but not in those of normal weight. Laboratory experiments have produced mixed results. Schachter et al. (1968) found that the obese did not eat more when anxious, but McKenna (1972) found that they did eat more good tasting food when anxious, but that eating did not reduce anxiety. Herman and Polivy (1975) found that restrained eaters (the latent obese) ate more when anxious, but that eating did not reduce anxiety, and Abramson and Stinson (1977), conceptualizing boredom as an unpleasant arousal state, found the obese no more likely to eat more in this state than normals. However, to complicate matters, Slochower (1976) reported that the obese ate more when their arousal state was unlabelled and showed significant reduction in affect after they had eaten.

Externality and Obesity—Stimulus-bound Behaviour on the Obese

Schachter (1968; 1971a; 1971b) proposed the theory that eating behaviour in the obese was under the control of external stimuli, while, in the non-obese, it was under the control of internal stimuli. The lean eat because they are hungry, the fat eat because the environment presents them with food-related cues.
The experimental observations on which this theory relied were:

(1) While there is a correlation between hunger sensations and stomach contractions in the lean, there is no such correlation in the obese (Stunkard and Koch, 1964; Schachter et al., 1968).
(2) Preloading (i.e. filling subjects with food before the experimental observations) reduces probability of eating in the lean, but not in the obese (Schachter et al., 1968; Nisbett, 1968).
(3) Palatability of food has much more effect on the eating of the obese than of the lean (Hashim and Van Itallie, 1965; Nisbett, 1968; Goldman et al., 1968; Decke, 1971).
(4) In the absence of food related cues, the obese are less affected by hours of food deprivation than the lean (Goldman et al., 1968; Ross, 1974; Johnson, 1974; Nisbett, 1968).
(5) Eating in the obese is triggered by apparent time (even when clocks are deliberately altered), while in the lean it is triggered by real time (Schachter and Gross, 1968; Goldman et al., 1968).

These experiments and observations were designed with great ingenuity and conducted in both laboratory and naturalistic settings.
Schachter was also impressed by the similarity of the behaviour of his obese subjects and the behaviour of rats with lessons in the ventro-medial hypothalamus (Schachter, 1971b; Schachter and Rodin, 1974). Amongst the similarities seen were that both the obese humans and the VMH lesioned rats:

(1) were strongly affected by the taste of food—eating relatively more of good tasting foods and less of bad tasting ones;
(2) ate fewer meals per day, but ate more each meal, and ate their food faster;
(3) showed more response to emotional stimuli;
(4) were less prepared to expend effort to obtain food.

These and the other analogies between the obese humans and rats led Schachter to wonder whether there was some hypothalamic dysfunction in the obese.
Having shown that the obese were more responsive to external stimuli related to food, the theory was put forward that the obese were generally stimulus-bound—that they would be reactive to all salient external stimuli not merely food-related ones. Rodin (1975a; 1975b; 1976a; 1977) has investigated this hypothesis and in a series of studies has shown that the obese:

(1) are more reactive to electric shock (Rodin, 1974a);
(2) are more reactive to emotional stimuli (Rodin et al., 1974a);
(3) show better recall of what they see (Rodin et al., 1974b);
(4) are faster at recognizing visual stimuli (Rodin et al., 1974b);
(5) show better incidental learning (Rodin and Slochower, 1973);

(6) are more affected by distracting stimuli (Rodin, 1974b);

(7) are more influenced in their estimations of the passage of time, by the extent to which boring or interesting events are occurring (Rodin, 1975a); and that

(8) measures of externality predict weight change (Rodin 1975b; 1976a).

The theory that the obese are externally controlled has come under attack on a number of grounds. Firstly critics have pointed out that the subject samples in the early research were largely highly selected American male under-graduate students, most of whom were only mildly obese (Milich, 1975; Rodin, 1975a; Leon and Roth, 1977). The fact that the theory was based on experiments done with highly selected subjects does not, of course, mean that it is wrong. Unfortunately, a mass of empirical evidence has accumulated which makes it now untenable in its strong original form.

Stunkard and Fox (1971) in a review of the evidence concerning gastric motility and hunger concluded that there was no strong correlation between these two variables in either the normal or the obese. Preloads seem to affect the lean no more than they affect the obese (Price and Grinker, 1973; Jordan, 1974; Wooley and Wooley, 1974). Further, the non-obese seen to be just as susceptible to many external cues as the obese (Grinker, 1975; Price et al., 1975; Pudel, 1975; 1976; 1978). The obese, as a whole, are not more generally external than the lean. Indeed, on many measures, the severely obese are closer to normals and it is only the mildly obese who show exaggerated external responsivity (Rodin, 1975a; Leon and Roth, 1977; Rodin, 1978). Finally, measures of externality are not consistently associated with weight change (Vincent et al., 1976). However, the idea that at least in some of the obese eating is strongly affected by external controls still has some mileage in it. Rodin (1978), for example, has shown that insulin release to the sight of food varies with degree of overweight, palatability of the food, and the extent to which subjects are externally controlled. The concept of external control is also a lively part of the research on restrained eaters (Herman and Polivy, 1975; Herman et al., 1978).

Set-point Theory

Nisbett (1972) has proposed the theory that individuals defend a given body weight and composition. People are biologically programmed to be of a certain degree of fatness. There is an in-built set-point for body mass. Amongst the chief determinants of this will be the number of adipocytes (fat cells) possessed by an individual. This number will be determined either genetically or as the result of very early feeding experience. By late childhood and in adulthood, it is not possible to alter the number of adipocytes, although their size can vary. (For reviews of the adipocyte and factors affecting it see, for humans: Bjorntorp, 1978; and Brook, 1978; and for rodents: Greenwood et al., 1978; and for possible differences between humans and rats: Smith, 1978).

Because it could be supposed that obese persons had a higher set point, Nisbett proposed that, therefore, the obese were more likely to be in a deprived state than the non-obese. Further, like all deprived organisms, they would therefore be more responsive to external stimuli. This explains their performance in Schachter's experiments.

Various pieces of evidence can be adduced to support the notions that individuals defend a set body weight. Firstly, it was found in the semi-starvation experiments reported by Keys *et al.* (1950) that although subjects lost about 25 per cent of their body weight while on the starvation regime, when they returned to *normal* diet, they rapidly regained their former weights. It should be emphasized that this was return to *normal* diet. They did *not* need to consume more than normal.

Secondly, there is the research of Sims and his associates (Sims and Horton, 1968; Sims *et al.*, 1973; Horton *et al.*, 1974; Goldman *et al.*, 1975) and that of Miller and his co-workers (Miller, 1975). These investigators have been concerned with experimental overfeeding. Once more, subjects have regained their normal weights on return to normal diets.

Further it is extremely difficult in many cases to obtain weight gain. Miller (1975) states: "It is quite remarkable how some individuals can consume 10,000 excess calories a week and show a weight loss". Similarly, Sims and his associates expected 20–25 per cent weight gain in subjects given approximately double their usual calorie intake for 200 days or so. This expectation was *not* achieved in all cases, and in some it was achieved only with great difficulty.

Investigations of overfeeding in the obese are relatively rare, but Bray (1972) reported that obese subjects near their maximum weight gained weight more slowly when overfed, than those who had reduced their weight. It is also probably true that many of the obese can maintain their overweight on a fairly low calorie intake. Sims *et al.* (1973), estimated that to maintain their weight many of the spontaneously obese required only about half the calories which would be required to keep a normally thin person about 20 per cent overweight.

Findings such as these should provoke a possibly less sceptical glance at the many reports in the literature which purport to show that the obese actually eat *less* than leaner people. (This point will be taken up later in a later section of this paper).

The animal literature also provides parallels. Thus, in addition to the well-known capacity of rats to regulate their intake in response to differences in calorie density, it appears that the VMH lessioned rat also maintains its new increased weight (Hoebel and Teitelbaum, 1966; Hamilton, 1969). In addition, the rat with a lateral hypothalmic lesion (which usually results in cessation of eating and starvation) appears to defend its new post-operative set-point (Powley and Keesey, 1970; Keesey *et al.*, 1976). Stunkard (1977) provides a fuller review of these investigations.

However, Nisbett's theory implies that some people at all weight levels will be below their set-point. Some slim people will really be fat people who are keeping their weight down by restrained eating, as will some moderately obese people. Amongst the grossly obese, however, the proportions of these below their set-point should be lower. This leads to the prediction that they should not be over-sensitive to external stimuli and indeed this appears to be so (Rodin, 1975, 1978). Conversely, those amongst the lean who are restraining their eating should be relatively deprived and, therefore, behave more like the obese. This appears to be the case (Herman and Polivy, 1975; Herman *et al.*, 1978; Polivy *et al.*, 1978).

Obviously people can lose weight by dieting, but often not as much as might be expected, and there is a strong probability that they will regain their pre-dieting weights. Nisbett's theory gives an explanation of why this might be so. (For mechanisms likely to be involved in the defence of body weight see the reviews in Bray, 1975; and that of Garrow, 1978).

6. THE EFFECTIVENESS OF TREATMENT FOR OBESITY

General

For present purposes, the main interest in treatment is in the comparative effectiveness of psychological treatments. Unfortunately, there is the usual lack of randomized comparative controlled trials of treatments, so it is very difficult to produce good scientific evidence concerning the relative effectiveness of psychological as opposed to other treatments. For this reason, an attempt has been made to work out a variety of measures, including average total weight loss, the average number of pounds lost per week by obese persons exposed to different procedures, and the percentage of subjects losing various amounts of weight. For comparative data about medical and surgical treatments, there has been heavy reliance on other reviewers especially Stunkard and McLaren-Hume (1959); Asher and Dietz (1973); Chlouverakis, (1975); Scoville (1975); James (1976); and Bray (1978). These treatments include diet, medication, starvation, and surgery. In the case of behaviour modification procedures, the sample of papers used consisted mainly of those collected by Foreyt (1977) for which it was possible to work out the required statistics, but other available studies have also been included. This is obviously not a complete and exhaustive survey of all possible papers, but it is unlikely to be significantly biased.

The use of pounds lost per week is open to two main objections. The first is that, if, as is sometimes supposed, weight loss follows a negatively accelerating curve, then shorter-term studies should be more likely to report higher weight loss. The second objection is that the longer the follow-up, the more likely it is that the obese will have become less compliant, or that treatment effects will have worn off. This objection also leads to the prediction that the shorter-term studies should report higher success rates, as judged by this criterion. The opposite is, of course, true of total or percentage weight losses. Because of these objections, the durations of treatment and follow-up periods are given. As it is notorious that many behaviour modification studies are conducted with student populations who might behave very differently from non-student groups, information on this is also provided.

Quality of experimental design in these investigations is patchy. Simple procedures, such as random assignment to treatment and control groups, are not always used. Further, control groups do not always control for possibly significant variables. Thus, sometimes, behaviour modification *plus* diet is compared with no treatment of any sort. In such a case, it is obviously impossible to conclude, in the presence of a significant difference, whether it was the behaviour modification or the diet which achieved the result.

Placebo treatments are also often omitted. Even where they are included, they are sometimes not very effective. It has been argued elsewhere (Ley, 1978) that placebos should be convincing to the subjects, and that where possible they should be theoretically strong, i.e. they should be of such a nature as to embarrass the theory behind the treatment, if it does no better than the placebo. Examples of this are the use by Foreyt and Hagen (1973) of a pleasant UCS in an aversive conditioning paradigm, and the use by Ley *et al.* (1974) of a willpower control for self-control procedures. In this last, subjects were instructed to do the opposite of what was recommended by the usual self-control procedures. Thus, they were told to shop only when they were hungry, to leave tempting foods around etc. The rationale given was that by frequent exposure to temptation they could learn to build up their ability to resist temptation. It is encouraging to see that some investigators are now making attempts to assess the credibility of the placebo used e.g. Kingsley and Wilson (1977).

It should also be recalled that it is not logically necessary that procedures which are useful in the instigation of weight loss will also be useful in the maintenance of weight loss. There do not seem to be any investigations which experimentally analyse the relative contributions of, say, aversive conditioning and self-control, in relation to instigation and maintenance.

It would also be useful to have more parametric studies of the techniques used. This would be useful in relation to several treatments. For example, the number of CS–UCS pairings in the various aversive conditioning treatments ranges from 40 to 300+ and their density varies from about 10 a week to 300 a day. Presumably, most psychologists would be prepared to entertain the notion that the effectiveness of aversive techniques might well be affected by such variables as frequency and density of shock administration.

Finally, attention should be drawn to the large number of excellent recent reviews of behaviour modification in the control of obesity. These all provide to some extent different interpretations of the data from the views put forward here and include: Stuart (1975); Yates (1975); Stunkard and Mahoney (1976); Abramson, (1977); Bellack, (1977); Foreyt (1977). This last work contains reprints of several earlier important reviews.

The behaviour modification procedures to be reviewed are:

(1) aversive conditioning, including covert sensitization,
(2) coverant control and reinforcement,
(3) self-control packages.

This list is a brief one and leaves out contract procedures, and more esoteric approaches, such as induced anxiety (Bornstein and Siprelle, 1973) and sensory deprivation (Suedfeld, 1977). These techniques have been reviewed in the sources cited above.

Aversive Procedures

The use of aversive procedures, either alone or as components of packages, has been frequent. Usually, the paradigm has been a classical conditioning one, with attempts being made to put the subject off a limited range of fattening foods. Aversive stimuli used include:

(a) electric shock,
(b) foul-smelling substances, e.g. butyric acid, acetimide, pure skunk oil,

(c) cigarette smoke,

(d) pictures of the subject in scanty underwear or swim-wear,

(e) imaginal stimuli (used in covert sensitization procedures).

Perhaps, surprisingly, in view of the research into conditioned food aversion in the rat, and notions of biological preparedness in learning (Seligman and Hager, 1972), there seem to have been no attempts to use chemically induced vomitting and nausea as UCR, although, of course, suggestions of nausea and vomitting have been used in covert sensitization procedures. Nor have there been comparative trials of the effectiveness of biologically related aversive stimuli, such as foul smells and tastes, and non-biologically related ones, such as electric shock and photographs. Table 4 summarizes investigations of the effectiveness of aversive procedures.

TABLE 4.
The Effectiveness of Aversive Procedures in Producing Weight Loss

Investigation	Subjects	Number of trials		Duration in weeks	Mean weight loss total	per week
Stollak[1]	A	80	T	8	4	0.48
(1967)			FU	8–10	3	0.36
Foreyt and Kennedy[2]	A	330	T	91	13	1.48
(1971)			FU	48	9	0.19
Ley et al[2]	A	96	T	3	2	0.60
(1974)			FU	5	1	0.18
Maher[2]	A	40	T + FU	8	13	1.68
(1974)						
Janda and Rimm[3]	S	60	T	6	10	1.58
(1972)			FU	6	12	0.75
Manno and Marston[3]	A;S		T	4	4	1.03
(1972)			FU	13	9	0.56
Murray[3] and Harrington	A		T	10	6	0.59
(1972)			FU	26	1	0.02
Foreyt and Hagen[3]	S	270	T	9	4	0.46
(1973)			FU	9	1	0.07
Ley et al.[3]	A	96	T	3	2	0.43
(1974)			FU	5	2	0.26
Elliot and Denney[3]	S	300	T	4	4	0.98
(1975)			FU	4	4	0.55

A = adults; S = students; T = length of treatment period; FU = length of follow-up period; 1 = electrical aversion; 2 = olfactory aversion; 3 = covert sensitization.

In six of these investigations, the aversive technique produced significantly more weight loss than the control treatments (Foreyt and Kennedy, 1971; Janda and Rimm, 1972; Manno and Marston, 1972; Ley et al., 1974; Maher, 1974), while in three no significant effect was obtained (Stollak, 1967; Foreyt and Hagen, 1973; Elliot and Denney, 1975). The medians of the mean reported weight losses were: (a) at the end of treatment: 4.1 lbs, range 1.7–13.4 lbs; (b) at follow-up: 2.9 lbs, range 0.4–11.7 lbs. These compare with median losses in the no-treatment control groups of: (a) at the end of the treatment period: 1 lb, range 0–7.5 lbs; (b) at follow-up: 0.7 lbs, range 0–9.8 lbs. The placebo results reported by Janda and Rimm, Foreyt and Hagen, and Elliot and Denney were respectively: at end of treatment, 0.7, 8.5, and 5 lbs; and at follow-up 2.3, 15.6, and 6.8 lbs.

Mean weekly weight losses in treated groups ranged from 0.43 to 1.68 lbs, with a median of 0.8 lbs. However, it is worth noting that this median figure was exceeded by the control groups in three studies (Foreyt and Hagen, 1973; Maher, 1974; Elliot and Denney, 1975). This suggests that Jeffrey's (1974) argument that, because weight loss in control groups is negligible, they are no longer necessary in behaviour modification research, is suspect on empirical as well as logical grounds.

Coverant Control and Reinforcement Techniques

Coverant (covert operant) control techniques are based on Homme's (1965) suggestions that cognitive behaviours obey the same laws as overt behaviour, and that, therefore, their frequency can be increased by the application of reinforcement. The usual reinforcer used is a high probability behaviour, following Premack's principle which states that high probability behaviour can be used to reinforce behaviours with lower probabilities of occurrence (Premack, 1965). The cognitive behaviour to be reinforced will consist of aversive thoughts about being fat, and pleasant thoughts about being slim. The client will be asked to think one of these first before high probability behaviour occurs, e.g. answering a knock on the door, or opening a favourite magazine. Investigations of coverant control of obesity have been reported by Tyler and Straughan (1970)—possibly a very strict test, as the Christmas period occurred during treatment, Horan and Johnson (1971) and Horan et al. (1975).

Reinforcement of weight loss has been investigated by (amongst others) Hall (1972), Mahoney et al. (1973) and Jeffrey (1974). In these studies, the reinforcer has been money either provided by the experimenter, or by the subject at the beginning of the programme.

The results of these investigations are summarized in Table 5 which also includes the results obtained by Manno and Marston (1972) with a technique which required the client to imagine obesity-incompatible behaviour and imagine being reinforced for it.

Taken over all, these studies show at the end of the treatment period a median mean weight loss of 5.4 lbs, range 0.8–10.98 lbs, and at follow-up, for the operant reinforcement studies, a median of 10 lbs, range 7.3–12 lbs. There were no follow up data reported in the coverant control studies. The differences in mean total weight loss between coverant and operant groups are not significant when assessed by the Mann Whitney "U" test.

Median mean weekly weight loss during treatment was 0.92 lbs, range 0.11–1.60; and over the whole of the treatment and follow-up period; 0.59 lbs, range 0.37–0.74. Control group weight losses ranged from a mean loss of 3.1 lbs to a gain of 0.5 lbs.

Self-Control Packages

Self-control packages are based on the principles outlined by Ferster et al. (1962); Stuart (1967, 1971); and Stuart and Davis (1972). Recently, some investigators e.g. Paulsen et al. (1976) have tried to incorporate into these procedures a stronger

TABLE 5.
Coverant and Operant Control and Weight Loss

Investigation	Subjects	Duration in weeks	Mean weight loss	
			Total	Per week
Tyler and Straughan[1] (1970)	A	T = 7	1	0.11
Horan and Johnson[1] (1971)	S	T = 8	(a) 6	0.71
			(b) 3	0.34
Horan et al.[1] (1975)	A	T = 8	(a) 8	1.00
			(b) 11	1.37
			(c) 5	0.66
			(d) 5	0.67
Manno and Marston[2] (1972)	A; S	T = 4	5	1.28
		FU = 12	9	0.74
Hall[3] (1972)	A	T = 5	6	1.17
Mahoney et al.[3] (1973)	A	T = 4	(a) 6	1.60
			(b) 4	0.93
			(c) 5	1.30
		FU = 16	(a) 12	0.58
			(b) 7	0.37
			(c) 12	0.60
Jeffrey, D. B.[3] (1974)	A	T = 8	(a) 6	0.70
			(b) 7	0.90

A = adults; S = students; T = treatment length; FU = length of follow-up; 1 = coverant control; 2 = imagined positive reinforcement; 3 = material reinforcement and/or punishment.

emphasis on stimulus control techniques, based on the experiments of Schachter and his associates (Schachter, 1971; Schachter and Rodin, 1974), but this seems more a matter of degree than a qualitative change. In brief, the elements of self-control packages have included: modification of eating style e.g. by pausing between bites, chewing food a set number of times; stimulus control e.g. avoiding exposure to unsuitable tempting foods, eating meals in specific stimulus situations; reducing the probability of buying inappropriate foods by shopping when full; self-reinforcement; covert sensitization and self-monitoring of food intake and weight. They are the most successful of the currently available behaviour modification techniques for the treatment of obesity. They have a good record in controlled trials; and mean absolute weight losses are often high. Significantly greater weight loss than control treatments has been reported by Harris (1969); Wollersheim (1970), Harris and Hallbauer (1973), Balch and Ross (1974), Hagen (1974), Ost and Gotestam (1976), Paulsen et al. (1976), Kingsley and Wilson (1977), and Heckerman and Prochaska (1977). Negative results have been reported by Penick et al. (1971) who found that a self-control package was no better than psychotherapy; by Ley et al. (1974) who found no significant difference between written self-control instructions and a will-power placebo treatment; and by Weisenberg and Fray (1974) who found that their self-control clients lost less weight than those exposed to group procedures. It will be shown below that the addition of self-control procedures to other treatments is also valuable.

The results of the use of self-control procedures are summarized in Table 6. (In

TABLE 6.
Self-control Packages and Weight Loss

Investigation	Subjects	Duration study in weeks	Mean weight loss Total	Per week
Stuart (1967)	A	52	38	0.73
Harris (1969)	S	17	10	0.58
Wollersheim (1970)	S	20	9	0.43
Stuart (1971)	A	40	35	0.88
Penick et al. (1971)	A	12	(a) 24	2.00
			(b) 13	1.08
Hall (1972)	A	10	6	0.64
Harris and Hallbauer (1973)	S	28	6	0.23
			11	0.31
Balch and Ross (1974)	A	9	11	1.18
Hagen (1974)	S	15	(a) 12	0.81
			(b) 14	0.93
			(c) 11	0.70
Ley et al. (1974)	A	8	10	1.24
Weisenberg and Fray (1974)	A	16	6	0.40
Ost and Gotestam (1976)	A	52	10	0.19
Paulsen et al. (1976)	S	12	(a) 7	0.55
	A	15	(b) 19	1.24
	A	15	(c) 16	1.07
Heckerman and Prochaska (1977)	A	52	(a) 10	0.19
			(b) 13	0.26
			(c) 12	0.23
Kingsley and Wilson (1977)	A	60	(a) 14	(a) 0.23
			(b) 12	(b) 0.20
			(c) 0	(c) 0
			(d) 9	(d) 0.15

A = adults; S = students.

view of the nature of these methods, weight loss at the end of the study is given, as it does not seem sensible to refer to a "treatment" period).

The median of the mean weight losses reported is 11 pounds range 0–38 lbs, and median weekly loss is 0.61 lbs, range 0–2.00 lbs.

Psychotherapy and Social Psychological Techniques

It is very difficult to find evidence on the effectiveness of psychotherapy in the treatment of obesity. Rand and Stunkard (1977) reported on sixty-seven cases treated by psychoanalysis, some 28 per cent of whom lost more than 20 lbs, but in most of these obesity was not either the main or the presenting problem. Investigations of behaviour modification techniques have sometimes used a psychotherapy group as one of the controls (Wollersheim, 1970; Penick et al. 1971); and Stunkard (1978) reports an impressive mean weight loss of 30 lbs for a group treated by medication plus Rogerian psychotherapy.

Groups exposed to social pressures have been used as controls in a number of behaviour modification investigations, e.g. Wollersheim (1970), but the effects of group membership have been most extensively studied by Ley and his co-workers (Ley et al., 1974; Ley, 1978). In these investigations, all subjects were exposed, in

TABLE 7.
Effectiveness of Psychotherapy, Group Membership and Commercial/
Self-help Slimming Groups

Investigation	Subjects	Duration in weeks	Mean weight loss Total	Per week
Wollersheim (1970)[1]	S	T = 12	7	0.58
		FU = 8	7	0.33
Penick et al. (1971)[1]	A	T = 12	(a) 18	1.50
			(b) 11	0.92
Wollersheim (1970)[1]	S	T = 12	5	0.45
		FU = 8	4	0.17
Ley et al. (1974)[2]	A	T = 8	9	1.14
Weisenberg and Fray (1974)[2]	A	T = 16	16	1.00
Kingsley and Wilson (1977)[2]	A	T = 8	(a) 7	0.88
			(b) 7	0.88
		FU = 52	(a) 7	0.12
			(b) 11	0.18
Ley (1978)[2]	A	T = 8	(a) 13	1.58
			(b) 12	1.55
			(c) 12	1.45
Garb and Stunkard (1974)[3]	A	T $\bar{X}$ = 67	(a) 14	0.21
		$\bar{X}$ = 84	(b) 15	0.18
Williams and Duncan (1976)[3]	A	T $\bar{X}$ = 16	(a) 23	1.43
		$\bar{X}$	(b) 18	1.06
Ashwell (1978)[3]	A	T $\bar{X}$ = 29	(a) 26	0.88
		24	(b) 19	0.79
		24	(c) 16	0.68

A = adults; S = students; T = treatment length; FU = length of follow-up;
1 = psychotherapy; 2 = group effect; 3 = membership of commercial or self-help
group.

addition to group effects, to information about the causes of overweight, and its treatment, and were all put on a low carbohydrate diet. Group pressure and the effects of group membership are also an important element in commercial and self-help group treatments. The studies of commercial and self-help groups reviewed include those of Garb and Stunkard (1974) on TOPS (Take Off Pounds Sensibly) members in the USA; Williams and Duncan (1976) on members of Weight Watchers Australia; and Ashwell (1978) on three UK groups: Weight Watchers, Slimming Magazine Clubs, and Silhouette Slimming Clubs.

The results of these investigations are shown in Table 7.

The median mean weight loss in these different investigations was 14.5 lbs range 5–26 lbs; and median mean weekly weight loss was 0.90 lbs, range 0.12–1.58 lbs. Commercial weight loss groups seem to do particularly well, with a median mean weight loss of 18 pounds. These figures are impressive in relation to others and suggest that the effects of group membership should be used more frequently and systematically.

Combinations of Treatment

With the exception of the study reported by Stunkard (1978) which compared a combination of psychotherapy and fenfluramine with other treatments, most

studies seem to be of combinations of self-control programmes and other procedures.

In view of the success of commercial and self-help groups, it is interesting to note
that Jordan and Levitz (1973), and Levitz and Stunkard (1974) working with TOPS
groups, and Stuart (1977) working with Weight Watchers all found that the addition of behaviour modification, or its replacement of the usual routine led to
significant increases in weight loss. Lindner and Blackburn (1976) and Musante
(1976) report on combinations of behaviour modification and fasting. These results
are summarized in Table 8 and the last of these in Table 10. While the gains from
adding behaviour modification to group effects show quite a range, they seem to be
sustained over a long period. The combination of behaviour modification and
fasting seems to be particularly potent with about two thirds of those treated
showing weight losses of 20 lbs or more.

TABLE 8.
Effects of Combinations of Treatments on Weight Loss

Investigation	Duration in weeks	Mean total weight loss (lbs)	
Stunkard (1978)	26	(a) fenfluramine	14
		(b) group BM	24
		(c) (a) + PT	30
		(d) (a) + (b)	32
Jordan and Levitz (1973)	24	(a) TOPS group	3
		(b) (a) + BM	13
Levitz and Stunkard (1974)	12	(a) TOPS group	−1
		(b) Nutrition education	0
		(c) (a) + amateur BM	2
		(d) (a) + professional BM	4
	52	(a) as above	−4
		(b) as above	−3
		(c) as above	0
		(d) as above	6
Stuart (1977)	12	(a) WW group	14
		(b) (a) + BM	16
Lindner and Blackburn (1976)	52	(a) Fast	11
		(b) BM + fast	42
		(c) BM + fast	52
		(d) BM + fast	45

BM = behaviour modification; PT = psychotherapy; TOPS = Take Off Pounds Sensibly; WW = Weight Watchers.

Medical Treatment of Obesity

It is obviously desirable for comparative purposes to provide some data on the
effectiveness of medical treatments. Those to be considered are:

(1) severe fasts,
(2) intestinal by-pass surgery,
(3) medication.

James (1976) has provided a review of the effectiveness of starvation in the treatment of obesity. The eighty-seven cases he reviewed lost an average of 59 lbs.

Comparable figures are reported by Drenick (1975) for a series of 137 patients. Their average weight loss was 65 pounds. The treatment has its dangers and is obviously applied only in cases of severe obesity. Unfortunately, despite its impressive immediate results, relapse is common (Campbell *et al.*, 1974; Drenick, 1975; Genuth *et al.*, 1978).

Intestinal by-pass surgery also produces dramatic results. Quaade (1974) reports mean weight losses of 80 pounds in one group of patients, and 135 pounds in a group who had a slightly different operation. Moreover weight loss continued for 18 months and more after the operation. The various operations are, of course, dangerous, and often lead to unpleasant after-effects (Salmon, 1975; Sandstead, 1975; Solow *et al.*, 1978). It is, therefore, only the very obese who are likely to be considered for this type of treatment.

Medication is, however, a treatment which could be used in much milder cases. Probably the commonest types of treatment have been amphetamine-like drugs. Scoville (1975) summarizes the evidence collected on these by the US Food and Drug Administration; and, while on them, 44 per cent of patients lost a pound or more a week. Burland (1975) reviewed the literature on the effectiveness of fenfluramine. Mean weight loss was more pounds in six of the twenty groups studied, and median weekly weight loss was 0.96 lbs range 0.58–1.83 lbs. Longest treatment length in these trials was 12 weeks, but a 36 week trial by Steel *et al.* (1973) showed that both fenfluramine and phentermine produced mean weight losses of more than 20 lbs.

A salutary warning for all types of treatment is sounded by Scoville's (1975) report that 26 per cent of patients on placebos lost a pound or more a week. Scoville further reported that only in 40 per cent of the controlled studies did patients on the active drug lose more than those on the placebo.

Further evidence on the efficacy of medication is provided by Asher and Dietz (1973), whose results are summarized in Table 10. These investigators report most of their results in terms of percentage losing more than 20 lbs and 40 lbs, but, for a smaller sample, report a mean loss of 22 lbs, in both active medication and placebo groups. For further discussion of the effectiveness of medical treatments, see the reviews cited above.

Comparison of Effectiveness of Different Treatments

The only safe way to compare the effectiveness of the various treatments for obesity is to conduct properly designed controlled trials. These are unfortunately lacking. Two inferior methods will therefore be used. The first is a comparison of the number of studies of different treatments which yielded a mean weight loss of ten pounds or more. This comparison is open to at least the following objections:

(1) the sample of studies reviewed is not exhaustive
(2) lengths of treatment vary, this is probably especially unfavourable to medication results as many are based on investigations of less than 12 weeks.

The results of the comparison can therefore be no more than suggestive. They are shown in Table 9. (The investigations summarized are those reviewed above). On this comparison the treatments fall into two groups in terms of effectiveness. Aver-

TABLE 9.

Numbers of Investigations of Various Treatments of Obesity Resulting in a Mean Weight
Loss of 10 lbs or more

Treatment	Number of studies showing 9 lbs or less	Mean weight loss of 10 lbs or more
A. Aversive conditioning	6	3
B. Reinforcement (Coverant and operant)	11	3
C. Self-control	7	19
D. Psychological (psychotherapy and group effects)	4	14
E. Medication (Fenfluramine)	14	11
F. Mixed treatments including a BM component	1	6
Significance	0.10 = A vs. D; A vs. C. 0.05 = A vs. C; A vs. D; A vs. F; C vs. E; D vs. E; E vs. F. 0.01 = B vs. C; B vs. D.	

sive conditioning, reinforcement techniques and medication do not differ significantly, and tend to be significantly inferior to self-control and psychological techniques, which, in turn, do not differ in effectiveness. It should be emphasized again that the medication studies were short term, and indeed that this also applies to many of the aversive conditioning and reinforcement studies. However, five out of the ten short-term psychological treatments, and four out of the five self-control investigations using short-term treatment produced mean weight losses of ten pounds or more, so it is not self-evident that differences are attributable to differences in length of treatment. In any case, for practical clinical purposes, it is the demonstration that a given treatment has actually achieved worthwhile results that is important.

Passing the 10, 20 and 40 lb Barriers

The second way of assessing treatment effectiveness is in terms of the criteria used by Stunkard and McLaren-Hume (1959), and repeated by Stunkard (1972). These investigators reported the percentage of clients losing more than 20 lbs and the number losing more than 40 lbs. Obviously, in cases of mild obesity, such as that suffered by many subjects in behaviour modification experiments, it is likely that many will not be 20 lbs or more overweight. Nevertheless, in clinical practice weight losses of less than 20 lbs will be of little interest to either the severely obese patient or the clinician. Data are available in suitable form for this type of assessment for a number of treatments including psycho-analysis (Rand and Stunkard, 1977); medical treatments (Stunkard and McLaren-Hume, 1959; Asher and Dietz, 1973; Craddock, 1977); TOPS (Garb and Stunkard, 1974); Weight Watchers—Australia, (Williams and Duncan, 1976); Weight Watchers—UK, Slimming Magazine Clubs, and Silhouette Slimming Clubs (Ashwell and Garrow, 1975; Ashwell, 1978); behaviour modification (Stuart, 1967; Harris, 1969; Penick et al., 1971; Jordan and Levitz, 1973; Balch and Ross, 1974; Weisenberg and Fray, 1974; Ost and Gotestam, 1976; Paulsen et al., 1976; Currey et al., 1977; Heckerman and

Prochaska, 1977); behaviour modification plus protein—sparing fast (Lindner and Blackburn, 1976); behaviour modification plus supervised low calorie diet (Musante, 1976).

The results of this comparison are shown in Table 10.

Long-term Results, and Drop-out Rates

The long-term effects of treatments for obesity have been assessed with some pessimism by Stunkard and McLaren-Hume (1959); Hall (1973); Hall et al. (1974); Abramson (1976); Brightwell and Sloan (1977); Stunkard (1977). It is clear that relapse is common. It is not, however, universal. Thus, Craddock (1977) reported that 28 per cent of a group of 150 patients lost 20 lbs or more at some stage of treatment and that 19 per cent maintained a loss of 20 lbs or more, for at least ten years. In behaviour modification studies reported by Foreyt and Kennedy (1971), Ost and Gotestam (1976), Heckerman and Prochaska (1977), and Stunkard (1977), 20 out of the 59 patients involved showed a loss of 20 lbs or more at the end of treatment and 16 (27 per cent) showed such a loss a year after treatment. Paulsen et al. (1976), Currey et al. (1977) and Kingsley and Wilson (1979) also provide evidence of sustained weight loss in behaviour modification programmes. Although the relapse rate after treatment by starvation can be high e.g. Swanson and Dinello (1970), more successful results have been reported by Genuth et al. (1978), and in a sample of seventy-five patients Campbell et al. (1974) found that 21 per cent were successful in maintaining adequate weight loss for at least 12 months. On these figures, taken across treatments, about one patient in five will maintain a substantial weight loss for a year or more after treatment. Successful maintenance of weight loss amongst the clients of commercial groups has also been reported by Stuart and Guire (1978) and Ashwell (1978). However, it is clear from this evidence that while the induction of weight loss can be achieved by several methods of treatment, the problem of maintaining clients at their reduced weights is not yet resolved. Perhaps, it will yield to a combination of behaviour modification, medication, and fasting. Such combinations of treatments seem to be very powerful (Lindner and Blackburn, 1976; Musante, 1976; Stunkard, 1978).

A further possible basis for comparison of treatments is that of drop-out rates. Hall and Hall (1974) reviewed the effectiveness of behavioural treatments and include in their review data on drop-out rates. These ranged from 0–83 per cent, with a median of 12 per cent, and a mode of zero. These data contrast dramatically with those for compliance with other types of health advice. Ley (1977) reviewing survey of patients' adherence to a variety of medical regimens reported a median of 44 per cent non-compliance, range 8–92 per cent. In the case of medication treatments of obesity, Scoville (1975) reported that in controlled trials involving 8,000+ patients the mean placebo drop-out rate was 49 per cent, while for the active medication it was 48 per cent. Ley (1978) provided further data on drop-out rates in fourteen experiments involving obese women. Median drop-out was 48 per cent, range 23–74 per cent. While it is possible that behaviour modification leads because of its intrinsic characteristics to lower drop-out than some other treatments (Penick et al., 1971), it is also possible that the effect is due to the extensive use of (a)

TABLE 10.
Effects of Different Treatments on Absolute Weight Loss

Investigation		Number of patients	% losing 10–19 lbs	20–39 lbs	40+ lbs
Psychoanalysis					
Rand and Stunkard (1977)		67	9	19	9
Mixed Medical I—Diet + Support					
Fellows (1931)		294	27	21	5
Evans (1938)		130	19	17	5
Munves (1953)		48	27	8	4
Harvey and Simmons (1954)		290	30	17	6
Young *et al.* (1955)		131	32	25	3
Feinstein *et al.* (1958)		106	24	28	31
Stunkard and McLaren-Hume (1959)		100	?	11	1
Asher and Dietz (1973)		50	?	28	16
(Placebo group)					
Mixed Medical II—Diet + Drugs + Support					
Gray and Kallenbach (1939)		314	20	20	8
Osserman and Dolger (1951)		55	36	27	2
(Amphetamine)					
Asher and Dietz (1973)	(a)	1409	?	28	10
	(b)	39	?	33	13
Craddock (1977)		150	?	29	?
Self-Help and Commercial Groups					
Garb and Stunkard (1974)	(a)	485	?	29	6
	(b)	560	?	29	8
Williams and Duncan (1976)	(a)	112	?	35	11
	(b)	5446	?	26	7
Ashwell (1978) WW	(a)	119	19	52	14
SM	(b)	107	28	38	4
SL	(c)	115	25	33	1
Behaviour Modification					
Stuart (1967)		8	—	5*	3*
Harris (1969)		14	3*	3*	—
Penick *et al.* (1971)		15	?	3*	2*
Jordan and Levitz (1973)		11	7*	3*	—
Balch and Ross (1974)		19	6*	2*	—
Weisenberg and Fray (1974)		8	3*	—	—
Ost and Gotestam (1976)		11	5*	5*	—
Paulsen *et al.* (1976)		41	?	15*	?
Currey *et al.* (1977)		144	28	23	8
Heckerman and Prochaska (1977)		27	10*	7*	—
Behaviour Modification Plus Fasting					
Lindner and Blackburn (1976)	(a)	67	?	36	45
	(b)	100	?	38	50
Musante (1976)		229	?	30	24
Summary					
Psychoanalysis		—	9	19	9
Diet–Plus–Support		—	27	20	7
Diet–Plus–Drugs–Plus–Support		—	22	27	9
Self-Help		—	24	27	7
Behaviour Modification		—	31	26	7
Behaviour Modification–Plus–Fasting		—	?	33	34

* These figures are not percents as the total number is so small.

students as subjects, and (b) deposits to ensure compliance. Drop-out rates in more naturalistic settings reported by Stuart (1967), Ost and Gotestam, (1976) Paulsen *et al.* (1976), and Currey *et al.* (1977) do not however support this hypothesis. In these studies, 20, 27, 21, 13, 27 per cent, respectively, failed to complete treatment. These are low rates and might reflect an unexpected benefit from the use of behaviour modification techniques.

Future Directions

At present, it would seem from the evidence reviewed above that mixed treatments might well offer powerful methods for helping the obese. No doubt, there will be a proliferation of studies of these.

Behaviour modification procedures might possibly be improved in two main ways. The first of these is to make more use of modern theories of eating and satiety, many of which include conditioned responses amongst their constructs (Booth 1976, 1978; Booth *et al.*, 1976; Stunkard, 1975). The second source of improvement might lie in more careful observations of those obesity-inducing behaviour shown by the individual client. Many of the beliefs about the obese are dubious in the light of currently available evidence. Thus many investigators have found that the obese eat no more, or even less than the lean, and there is no convincing evidence concerning an eating style which is generally characteristic of the obese (Thompson *et al.*, 1961; Garrow, 1974; Schachter and Rodin, 1974; Mahoney, 1975; Stunkard and Kaplan, 1977; Guggenheim *et al.*, 1977; Adams *et al.*, 1978).

The problem of maintenance of weight loss is also deserving of attention. Further research is needed on the effectiveness of booster treatments, (Kingsley and Wilson, 1977); and frequency of therapist contact (Jeffrey and Wing, 1979; Ley, 1979). It would also be of interest to tackle the problems of how best to recruit subjects for obesity programmes. If obesity is seen as a public health problem, then psychologists should be interested not only in the instigation and maintenance of weight loss, but also in recruiting subjects for slimming programmes (Ley *et al.*, 1977). Also in terms of public health some effort should go into the evaluation of possible preventive techniques.

Research is also needed into the causes of variation in the effectiveness of a given treatment. This variation can be seen in many of the summary tables presented above, and is emphasized by a number of investigators. Garb and Stunkard (1974) and Williams and Duncan (1976) reported great variations in the success rates for self-help and commercial weight loss groups; and Atkinson *et al.* (1977) and Ley (1978) reported similar variations in the case of medication and social psychological techniques respectively. The extent to which these differences in outcome are due to therapist or subject characteristics is not known. However, one subject characteristic which does affect outcome is gender. Men lose more weight than women, e.g. Williams and Duncan (1976); Craddock (1977); Stuart (1977); Genuth *et al.* (1978). This is a finding consistent across treatments and if it is not an artefact—men more often slimming for health, and women for cosmetic reasons—deserves further investigation.

REFERENCES

Abramson, E. E. (1977) Behavioural approaches to weight control: an up-dated review, *Behaviour Research and Therapy*, **15**, 355–363.

Abramson, E. E. and Stinson, S. G. (1977) Boredom and eating in obese and non-obese individuals, *Addictive Behaviours*, **2**, 181–185.

Adams, N., Ferguson, J., Stunkard, A. J. and Agras, S. (1978) The eating behaviour of obese and non-obese women, *Behaviour Research and Therapy*, **16**, 225–232.

Asher, W. L. and Dietz, R. E. (1973) Effectiveness of weight reduction involving weight reduction pills, *Current Therapeutics Research*, **14**, 510–524.

Ashwell, M. (1978) Commercial weight loss groups, in G. A. Bray (Ed.), *Recent advances in obesity research*, II. Newman Publishing, London.

Ashwell, M. and Etchell, L. (1974) Attitude of the individual towards his own body weight. *British Journal of Social and Preventive Medicine*, **28**, 127–132.

Ashwell, M. and Garrow, J. S. (1975) A survey of three slimming and weight control organizations in the UK, *Nutrition, London*, **29**, 347–356.

Atkinson, R. L., Greenway, F. L., Bray, G. A., Dahms, W. T., Molitch, M. E., Hamilton, K. and Rodin, J. (1977) Treatment of obesity, *International Journal of Obesity*, **1**, 113–120.

Atkinson, R. M. and Ringuette, E. L. (1967) A survey of biographical and psychological features in extraordinary fatness, *Psychosomatic Medicine*, **29**, 121–133.

Baird, I. M., Silverstone, J. T., Grimshaw, J. J. and Ashwell, M. (1974) Prevalence of obesity in a London borough, *Practitioner*, **212**, 706–714.

Balch, P. and Ross, A. W. (1974) A behaviourally oriented didactic group treatment of obesity: an exploratory study, *Journal of Behaviour Therapy and Experimental Psychiatry*, **5**, 239–243.

Bellack, A. S. (1977) Behavioural treatment for obesity: appraisal and recommendations, in M. Hersen, R. M. Eisler, and P. M. Miller (eds.), *Progress in behaviour modification*, Volume 4, Academic Press, New York.

Bellack, A. S. and Rozensky, R. H. The selection of dependent variables for weight reduction studies, *Journal of Behaviour Therapy and Experimental Psychiatry*, **6**, 83–84.

Berscheid, E. and Walster, H. (1969) *Interpersonal attraction*, Addison-Wesley, Reading, Mass.

Bjorntorp, P. (1978) The fat cell: a clinical view, in G. A. Bray (ed.) *Recent advances in obesity research 2*, Newman Publishing, London.

Booth, D. A. (1976) Approaches to feeding control, in J. T. Silverstone (ed.), *Appetites and food intake*, Abakon, for Dahlem Konferenzen. Berlin.

Booth, D. A. (1978) Acquired behaviour controlling energy intake and output, *Psychiatric Clinics of North America*, **1**, 545–579.

Booth, D. A., Toates, F. M. and Platt, S. V. (1976) Control system for hunger and its implications in animals and man, in D. Novin, W. Wyrwicka, and G. A. Bray, (eds.) *Hunger: basic mechanisms and clinical implications*, Raven Press, New York.

Bornstein, P. M. and Siprelle, C. N. (1978) Group treatment of obesity by induced anxiety, *Behaviour Research and Therapy*, **11**, 339–341.

Bray, G. A. (1972) Lipogenesis in human adipose tissue: some effects of nibbling and gorging *Journal of Clinical Investigations*, **51**, 537–541.

Bray, G. A. (ed). (1975) *Obesity in perspective*, Department of Health, Education and Welfare, (NIH) 75–708, Washington, D. C.

Bray, G. A. (1978) To treat or not to treat? in G. A. Bray (ed.) *Recent advances in obesity research*, 2, Newman Publishing, London.

Brightwell, D. R. and Sloan, C. L. (1977) Long-term results of behaviour therapy for obesity, *Behaviour Therapy*, **8**, 898–905.

Brook, C. G. D. (1978) Fat cells and infant feeding, in G. A. Bray (ed.) *Recent advances in obesity research 2*, Newman Publishing, London.

Bruch, H. (1973) *Eating disorders*, Basic Books, New York.

Burland W. L. (1975) A review of experience with fenfluramine, in G. A. Bray (ed.) *Obesity in perspective*, Department of Health Education and Welfare. (NIH) 75–708, Washington DC.

Campbell, C. J., Campbell, I. W., Innes, J. A., Munro, J. F. and Needle, A. L. (1974) Further follow-up experience after prolonged therapeutic starvation, in W. Burland, P. D. Samuel and J. Yudkin (eds.) *Obesity*, Churchill–Livingstone, London.

Canning, H. and Mayer, J. (1966) Obesity: its possible effect on college acceptance, *New England Journal of Medicine*, **275**, 1172–1174.

Canning, H. and Mayer, J. (1967) Obesity: an influence on high school performance, *American Journal of Clinical Nutrition*, **20**, 352–354.

Chetwynd, S. J., Stewart, R. A. and Powell G. E. (1975) Social attitudes towards the obese physique, in A. Howard (ed.) *Recent advances in obesity research*, 1, Newman Publishing, London.

Chlouverakis, C. (1975) Dietary and medical treatments for obesity: an evaluative review, *Addictive Behaviours*, **1**, 3–21.

Coddington, R. D. and Bruch, H. (1970) Gastric perceptivity in normal obese and schizophrenic subject, *Psychosomatics*, **11**, 571–579,

Craddock, D. (1977) The free diet: 150 cases personally followed-up after 10 to 18 years, *International Journal of Obesity*, **2**, 127–136.

Crisp, A. H. (1978) Some psychiatric aspects of obesity in G. A. Bray (ed). *Recent advances in obesity research*, 2, Newman Publishing, London.

Crisp, A. H. and McGuiness, B. (1976) Jolly fat: relation between obesity and psychoneurosis in a general population, *British medical Journal*, **1**, 7–10.

Currey, H., Malcolm, R., Riddle, E. and Schachte, M. (1977) Behavioural treatment of obesity, *Journal of the American medical Association*, **237**, 2829–2831.

Decke, E. (1971) Effects of taste on the eating behaviour of obese and normal persons. Cited in S. Schachter, *Emotion Obesity and Crime*, Academic Press, New York.

Dole, V. P., Schwartz, I. L., Thaysen, J. H., Thorne, N. A. & Silver, L. (1954) Treatment of obesity with a low protein calorically unrestricted diet, *American Journal of clinical Nutrition*, **2**, 381–390.

Drenick, E. J. (1975) Weight reduction by prolonged fasting, in G. A. Bray (ed) *Obesity in perspective*, Department of Health Education and Welfare, (NIH) 75–708, Washington D.C.

Durnin, J. V. G. A. and Womersley, J. (1974) Body fat assessed from total body density and its estimations from skinfold thickness, *British Journal of Nutrition*, **32**, 77–97.

Dwyer, J. T., Feldman, J. J., Seltzer, C. C. and Mayer, J. (1969) Body image in adolescents: attitudes towards weight and perception of appearance, *Journal of Nutrition Education*, **1**, 14–19.

Dwyer, J. T., Feldman, J. J. and Mayer, J. (1970) The social psychology of dieting, *Journal of Health and Social Behaviour*, **11**, 269–287.

Elliot, C. H. and Denney, D. R. (1975) Weight control through covert sensitization and false feedback, *Journal of consulting and clinical Psychology*, **43**, 842–850.

Evans, F. A. (1938) Treatment of obesity with low calorie diets, *International Clinics*, **3**, 19–23.

Feinstein, A. R. (1959) The measurement of success in weight reduction, *Journal of Chronic Diseases*, **10**, 439–456.

Feinstein, R., Dole V. P. and Schwartz, I. L. (1958) The use of a formula diet for weight reduction of obese out-patients, *Annals of internal Medicine*, **48**, 330–343.

Fellows, H. H. (1931) Studies of relatively normal obese individuals during and after dietary restriction, *American Journal of medical Sciences*, **181**, 301–312.

Ferster, C. B., Nurnberger, J. I. and Levitt, E. E. (1962) The control of eating, *Journal of Mathetics*, **1**, 87–109.

Ford, C. S. and Beach, F. A. (1965) *Patterns of sexual behaviour*, Methuen, London.

Foreyt, J. P. (1977) *Behavioural treatments of obesity*, Pergamon Press, Oxford.

Foreyt, J. P. and Hagen, R. L. (1973) Covert sensitization: conditioning or suggestion, *Journal of abnormal Psychology*, **82**, 17–23.

Foreyt, J. P. and Kennedy, W. A. (1971) Treatment of overweight by aversion therapy, *Behaviour Research and Therapy*, **9**, 29–34.

Fullarton, J. E. (1978) Obesity: a new social perspective, *International Journal of Obesity*, **2**, 267–285.

Garb, J. R. and Stunkard, A. J. (1974) Effectiveness of a self-help group in obesity control, *Archives of internal Medicine*, **134**, 716–720.

Garrow, J. S. (1978) Energy expenditure in man, in: G. A. Bray (ed) *Recent advances in obesity research*, 2, Newman Publishing, London.

Genuth, S. M., Vertes, V. and Hazleton, I. (1978) Supplemented fasting in the treatment of obesity, in G. A. Bray (ed.) *Recent advances in obesity research*, 2, Newman Publishing, London.

Glucksman, M. L. and Hirsch, J. (1968) Response of obese patients to weight reduction: a clinical evaluation of behaviour, *Psychosomatic Medicine*, **30**, 1–11.

Goldman, R., Jaffa, M. and Schachter, S. (1968) Yom Kippur, Air France, dormitory food, and the eating behaviour of obese and normal persons, *Journal of Personality and Social Psychology*, **10**, 117–123.

Goldman, R. F., Haisman, M. F., Bynum, G., Horton, E. S. and Sims, E. A. H. (1975) Experimental obesity in man: metabolic rate in relation to dietary intake, in G. A. Bray (ed.) *Obesity in perspective*, Department of Health Education and Welfare (NIH) 75–708, Washington, DC.

Goodman, N., Richardson, S., Dornbusch, S. and Hastorf, A. (1963) Variant reactions to physical disability *American sociological Review*, **28**, 429–435.

Grande, F. (1965) Assessment of body fat in man, in G. A. Bray (ed) *Obesity in perspective*, Department of Health, Education and Welfare, (NIH) 75–708, Washington, D.C.

Gray, S. H. (1977) Social aspects of body image: perception of normality of weight and effect of college undergraduates, *Perceptual and Motor Skills*, **45**, 1035–1040.

Gray, H. and Kallenbach, D. C. (1939) Obesity treatment: results on 212 out-patients, *Journal of the American dietetic Association*, **15**, 239–245.

Greenwood, M. R. C., Gruen, R. and Cleary, M. P. (1978) Adipose tissue growth and the development of fat cells, in G. A. Bray (ed.) *Recent advances in obesity research*, 2, Newman Publishing, London.

Grinker, J. A. (1975) Obesity and taste, in G. A. Bray (ed.) *Obesity in perspective*, Department of Health Education and Welfare, (NIH), 75–708, Washington, D.C.

Guggenheim, K., Poznanski, R. and Kaufman, N. A. (1977) Attitudes of adolescents to their body build and the problem of juvenile obesity, *International Journal of Obesity*, **1**, 135–149.

Hagen, R. L. (1974) Group therapy vs. bibliotherapy in weight reduction, *Behaviour Therapy*, **5**, 222–234.

Hall, S. M. (1972) Self-control and therapist control in the behaviour treatment of overweight women, *Behaviour Research and Therapy*, **10**, 59–68.

Hall, S. M. (1973) Behavioural treatment of obesity: a two year follow-up, *Behaviour Research and Therapy*, **11**, 647–648.

Hall, S. M. and Hall, R. G. (1974) Outcome and methodological considerations in behavioural treatments of obesity, *Behaviour Therapy*, **5**, 352–364.

Hall, S. M., Hall, R. G., Hanson, R. W. and Borden, B. L. (1974) Performance of two self-managed treatments of overweight in university and community populations, *Journal of consulting and Clinical Psychology*, **42**, 781–786.

Hamilton, C. L. (1969) Problems of refeeding after starvation in the rat, *Annals of the New York Academy of Sciences*, **157**, 1004–1017.

Harris, M. B. (1969) Self-directed program for weight control, *Journal of abnormal Psychology*, **74**, 263–270.

Harris, M. B. and Hallbauer, E. S. (1973) Self-directed weight control through eating and exercise, *Behaviour Research and Therapy*, **11**, 523–529.

Harvey, H. L. and Simmons, W. D. (1954) Weight reduction: a study of the group method, *American Journal of medical Sciences*, **227**, 521–525.

Hashim, S. A. and Van Itallie, T. B. (1965) Studies in normal and obese subjects with a monitored food dispensing device, *Annals of the New York Academy of Sciences*, **131**, 654–661.

Hawley, T. G. and Jansen, A. A. J. (1971) Weight, height, body surface, and overweight of Fijian adults from coastal areas, *New Zealand Medical Journal*, **74**, 18–23.

Heckerman, C. L. and Prochaska, J. O. (1977) Development and evaluation of weight reduction procedures in a health maintenance organization, in R. B. Stuart (ed.) *Behavioural self-management*, Brunner Mazel, New York.

Held, M. L. and Snow, D. L. (1972) MMPI, internal-external control, and problem check list scores of obese adolescent females, *Journal of clinical Psychology*, **28**, 523–525.

Herman, C. P. and Polivy, J. (1975) Anxiety restraint and eating behaviour, *Journal of abnormal Psychology*, **84**, 666–672.

Herman, C. P., Polivy, J., Pliner, P., Threlkeld, J. and Munic, D. (1978) Distractibility in dieters and non-dieters: an alternative view of externality, *Journal of Personality and social Psychology*, **36**, 536–548.

Hoebel, R. G. and Teitelbaum, P. (1966) Weight regulation in normal and hypothalamic rats, *Journal of comparative and physiological Psychology*, **61**, 189–193.

Homme, L. E. (1965) Control of coverants, the operants of the mind, *Psychological Record*, **15**, 501–511.

Horan, J. J. and Johnson, J. G. (1971) Coverant conditioning through a self-management application of Premack's Principle *Journal of Behaviour Therapy and Experimental Psychiatry*, **2**, 243–249.

Horan, J. H., Baker, S. B., Hoffman, A. M. and Shute, R. E. (1975) Weight loss through variations in the coverant control paradigm, *Journal of consulting and clinical Psychology*, **43**, 68–72.

Horton, E. S., Danforth, E., Sims, E. A. H. and Salans, L. B. (1974) Endocrine and metabolic alterations associated with overfeeding in man, in W. L. Burland, P. D. Samuel, and J. Yudkin (eds.) *Obesity*, Churchill–Livingstone, London.

Hueneman, R. L., Shapiro, L. R., Hampton, M. C., Mitchell, B. W. and Behnke, A. R. (1966) A longitudinal study of gross body composition and body conformation, *American Journal of Clinical Nutrition*, **18**, 325–338.

James, W. P. T. (1976) *Research on obesity: a report of a joint DHSS/MRC Group*, HMSO, London.

Janda, L. H. and Rimm, D. C. (1972) Covert sensitization in the treatment of obesity, *Journal of abnormal Psychology*, **80**, 37–42.

Jeffrey, D. B. (1974) A comparison of the effects of external control and self-control on the modification and maintenance of weight, *Journal of Abnormal Psychology*, **83**, 404, 410.

Jeffrey, D. B. (1974) Some methodological issues in research on obesity, *Psychological Reports*, **35**, 623, 626.

Jeffrey, R. W. and Wing, R. R. (1979) Frequency of therapist contact in the treatment of obesity, *Behaviour Therapy*, **10**, 186–192.

Johnson, T. O. (1970) Prevalence of overweight and obesity among adult subjects of an urban African population, *British Journal of preventive and social Medicine*, **24**, 105–109.

Johnson, W. G. (1974) The effects of cue prominence and obesity on effort to attain food, in S. Schachter and J. Rodin, (eds.), *Obese humans and rats*, Erlbaum–Wiley, Washington, D.C.

Jordan, H. A. (1975) Physiological control of food intake in man, in G. A. Bray (ed.), *Obesity in perspective*, Department of Health, Education and Welfare, (NIH) 75–708, Washington, D.C.

Jordan, H. A. and Levitz, L. S. (1973) Behaviour modification in a self-help group, *Journal of the American dietetic Association*, **67**, 27–29.

Karpowitz, D. H. and Zeis, F. R. (1975) Personality and behavioural differences among obese and non-obese adolescents, in A. Howard (ed.) *Recent advances in obesity research* I, Newman Publishing, London.

Keesey, R. E., Boyle, P. C., Kemnitz, J. W. and Mitchell, J. S. (1976) The role of the lateral hypothalamus in determining the body weight set point, in D. Novin, W. Wyrwicka and G. A. Bray (eds.). *Hunger: basic mechanisms and clinical implications*, Raven Press, New York.

Keys, A. (1975) Overweight and the risk of heart attack and sudden death, in G. A. Bray (ed.) *Obesity in perspective*, Department of Health, Education and Welfare, (NIH) 75–708, Washington, D.C.

Keys, A., Brozek, J., Henschel, A., Mickelsen, O. and Taylor, H. L. (1950) *The biology of human starvation*, University of Minnesota Press, Minneapolis.

Kingsley, R. G. and Wilson G. T. (1977) Behaviour therapy for obesity: a comparative investigation of long-term efficacy, *Journal of consulting and clinical Psychology*, **45**, 288–298.

Kohsea, and Lowe, C. R. (1968) Height and weight of British men. *Lancet*, **1**, 742–745.

Kollar, E. J. and Atkinson, R. M. (1966) Responses of extremely obese patients to starvation, *Psychosomatic Medicine*, **28**, 227–246.

Kollar, E. J., Slater, G. R., Palmer, J. O., Docter, R. F. and Mandell, A. J. (1964) Measurement of stress in fasting man, *Archives of general Psychiatry*, **11**, 113–120.

Lebow, M. D. (1977) The fat child, *Canadian Psychological Review*, **18**, 322–331.

Leon, G. R. and Chamberlain, K. (1973) Comparison of daily eating habits and emotional states of overweight persons successful or unsuccessful in maintaining a weight loss, *Journal of consulting and clinical Psychology*, **41**, 108–115.

Leon, G. R. and Roth, L. (1977) Obesity: psychological causes and correlates, *Psychological Bulletin*, **84**, 117–139.

Levitt, H. and Fellner, C. (1965) MMPI profiles of three obesity subgroups, *Journal of consulting Psychology*, **29**, 91.

Levitz, L. S. and Stunkard, A. J. (1974) A therapeutic coalition for obesity: behaviour modification and self help, *American Journal of Psychiatry*, **131**, 423–427.

Lewinsohn, P. M. (1975) The behavioural study and treatment of depression, in M. Hersen, R. M. Eister, and P. M. Miller (eds.) *Progress in behaviour modification*, Volume 1, Academic Press, New York.

Ley, P. (1977) Psychological studies of doctor–patient communication, in: S. Rachman (ed.) *Contributions to medical psychology* 1, Pergamon Press, Oxford.

Ley, P. (1978) Psychological and behavioural factors in weight loss, in G. A. Bray (ed.) *Recent advances in obesity research* 2, Newman Publishing, London.

Ley, P. (1980) Cultural, social and psychological determinants of acceptable fatness, in M. R. Turner (ed.) *Lifestyles and nutrition*, Applied Science Publishers, London.

Ley, P. (1979) The psychology of compliance, in: D. J. Oborne, M. M. Gruneberg and J. R. Eiser (eds) *Research in psychology and medicine*, Academic Press, London.

Ley, P., Bradshaw, P. W., Kincey, J. A., Couper-Smartt, J. and Wilson, M. (1974) Psychological variables in weight control, in W. L. Burland, P. D. Samuel and J. Yudkin (eds) *Obesity*, Churchill-Livingstone, London.

Ley, P., Whitworth, M. A., Woodward, R. and Yorke, R. (1977) Effects of sidedness and fear arousal on willingness to volunteer for an obesity programme, *Health Education Journal*, **36**, 67–69.

Lindegard, B. (1956) *Body build, body function and personality*, Gleerup, Lund.

Lindner, P. G. and Blackburn, G. L. (1976) Multi-disciplinary approach to obesity, utilizing fasting modified by protein sparing therapy, *Obesity/Bariatric Medicine*, **5**, 198–216.

Lipinski, B. G. (1975) Life change events as correlates of weight gain, in A. Howard (ed.) *Recent advances in obesity research* I, Newman Publishing, London.

McCann, M., and Trulson, M. F. (1955) Long term effects of weight reducing programs, *Journal of the American dietetic Association*, **31**, 1108–1110.

McKenna, R. J. (1972) Some effects of anxiety level and food cues on the eating behaviour of obese and normal subjects, *Journal of Personality and Social Psychology*, **22**, 311–319.

Maddox, G. L., Anderson, C. F. and Bogdonoff, M. (1966) Overweight as a problem of medical management in a public out-patient clinic, *American Journal of medical Sciences*, **252**, 394–402.

Maddox, G. L., Back, K. and Liederman, V. (1968) Overweight as social deviance and disability, *Journal of Health and Social Behaviour*, **9**, 287–298.

Maher, J. (1974) Aversive conditioning and respiratory relief in the treatment of obesity. Unpublished M. Psychol. Dissertation, University of Liverpool.

Mahoney, M. J. (1974) Self-reward and self-monitoring techniques for weight control *Behaviour Therapy*.

Mahoney, M. J. (1975) The obese eating style: bites, beliefs and behaviour modification, *Addictive Behaviours*, **1**, 47–53.

Mahoney, M. H., Moura, N. G. M. and Wade, T. C. (1973) Relative efficacy of self-reward, self-punishment and self-monitoring techniques for weight loss, *Journal of counsulting and clinical Psychology*, **40**, 404–407.

Mann, R. A. (1972) Behaviour therapeutic use of contingency contracting to control an adult behaviour problem. *Journal of applied Behaviour Analysis*, **5**, 99–109.

Manno, B. & Marston, A. R. (1972) Weight reduction as a function of negative covert reinforcement (sensitization) vs. positive covert reinforcement, *Behaviour Research and Therapy*, **10**, 201–207.

Metropolitan Life Assurance Co. (New York) (1959) New weight standards for men and women *Statistical Bulletin*, **40**, Nov–Dec.

Metropolitan Life Assurance Company (New York) (1960) Frequency of overweight and underweight, *Statistical Bulletin*, **41**, 4th June.

Milich, R. S. (1975) A critical analysis of Schachter's externality theory of obesity, *Journal of abnormal Psychology*, **84**, 586–588.

Miller, D. S. (1975) Overfeeding in man, in G. A. Bray (ed.) *Obesity in perspective*, Department of Health, Education and Welfare, (NIH) 75–708, Washington, D.C.

Montegriffo, V. M. E. (1968) Height and weight of a United Kingdom population, with a review of the anthropometric literature, *Annals of human Genetics*, **31**, 389–399.

Moore, M. E., Stunkard, A. J. and Sroles, L. (1962) Obesity, social class and mental illness, *Journal of the American medical Association*, **181**, 962–966.

Munves, E. D. (1953) Dietetic interview or group discussion–decision in reducing, *Journal of the American Dietetic Association*, **29**, 1197–1203.

Murray, D. C. and Harrington, L. G. (1972) Covert aversive sensitization in the treatment of obesity, *Psychological Reports*, **30**, 560.

Musante, G. J. (1976) The dietary rehabilitation clinic: evaluation report of a behavioural and dietetic treatment of obesity, *Behaviour Therapy*, **7**, 198–204.

National Health Examination Survey (1964) *Blood pressure, height, and selected body dimensions, United States, 1960–1962*, PHS, No. 1000, Series 11, No. 8.

Nisbett, R. E. (1968) Taste, deprivation, and weight as determinants of eating behaviour, *Journal of Personality and Social Psychology*, **10**, 107–116.

Nisbett, R. E. (1972) Hunger, obesity and the hypothalamus, *Psychological Review*, **79**, 433–453.

Osancova, K. (1975) Trends of dietary intake and prevalance of obesity in Czechoslavakia, in A. Howard (ed.) *Recent advances in obesity research* I, Newman Publishing, London.

Osserman, K. E., and Dolger H. O. (1951) Obesity in diabetics: a study of therapy with anorexigenic drugs, *Annals of internal Medicine*, **34**, 72–79.

Ost, L. G. and Gotestam, K. G. (1976) Behavioural and pharmacological treatments for obesity: an experimental comparison, *Addictive Behaviours*, **1**, 331–338.

Paulsen, B. K., Lutz, R. S., McReynolds, W. T. and Kohrs, M. B. (1976) Behaviour therapy for weight control: long term results of two programs with nutritionists as therapists, *American Journal of Clinical Nutrition*, **29**, 880–888.

Peck, J. W. (1976) Situational determinants of the body weights defended by normal rats and rats with hypothalamic lesions, in D. Novin, W. Wyrwicka and G. A. Bray, (eds) *Hunger: basic mechanisms and clinical implications.* New York: Raven Press.

Penick, S. B., Filion, R., Fox, S. and Stunkard, A. J. (1971) Behaviour modification in the treatment of obesity, *Psychosomatic Medicine*, **33**, 49–55.

Polivy, J., Herman, C. P. and Warsh, S. (1978) Internal and external components of emotionality in restrained and unrestrained eaters, *Journal of abnormal Psychology*, **87**, 497–504.

Powley, T. L. and Keesey, R. E. (1970) Relationship of body weight to the lateral hypothalamic feeding syndrome, *Journal of comparative and physiological Psychology*, **70**, 25–36.

Premack D. (1965) Reinforcement theory, in D. Levine (ed.) *Nebraska Symposium on motivation*, University of Nebraska Press, Lincoln, Nebraska.

Price, J. M. and Grinker, J. (1973) The effects of degree of obesity, food deprivation, and palatability on eating behaviour in humans, *Journal of comparative and physiological Psychology*, **85**, 265–271.

Price, J. M., Sheposh, J. P. and Tiano, F. E. (1975) A direct test of Schachter's internal–external theory of obesity in a natural setting, in A. Howard (ed.) *Recent advances in obesity research* I, Newman Publishing, London.

Prior, I. A. M. and Davidson, F. (1966) The epidemiology of diabetes in Polynesians and Europeans in New Zealand and the Pacific, *New Zealand Medical Journal*, **65**, 375–385.

Pudel, V. (1975) Psychological observations on experimental feeding in the obese, in A. Howard (ed.) *Recent advances in obesity research* I. Newman Publishing, London.

Pudel, V. (1976) Experimental feeding in man, in J. T. Silverstone (ed.) *Appetite and food intake*, Abakon, for Dahlem Konferenzen, Berlin.

Pudel, V. (1978) Human feeding in the laboratory, in G. A. Bray (ed.) *Recent advances in obesity research*, 2, Newman Publishing, London.

Quaade, F. (1974) Untraditional treatment of obesity, in W. Burland, P. D. Samuel and J. Yudkin (eds.), *Obesity*, Churchill–Livingston, London.

Rand, C. S. and Stunkard, A. J. (1977) Psychoanalysis and obesity, *Journal of the American Academy of Psychoanalysis*, **5**, 459–497.

Rees, L. (1973) Constitutional factors and abnormal behaviour, in H. J. Eysenck (ed.) *Handbook of abnormal psychology*, Pitman Medical, London.

Richards, R. and de Casseres, M. (1974) The problem of obesity in developing countries: its prevalence and morbidity, in W. L. Burland, P. D. Samuel and J. Yudkin (eds.) *Obesity*, Churchill–Livingstone, London.

Richardson, S., Goodman, N., Hastorf, A. and Dornbusch, S. (1961) Cultural uniformity and reaction to physical disability, *American sociological Review*, **26**, 241–247.

Robinson, S. and Winnick, H. (1973) Severe psychotic disturbances following crash diet weight loss, *Archives of general Psychiatry*, **29**, 559–562.

Rodin, J. (1974a) Shock avoidance behaviour in obese humans and normal subjects, in S. Schachter and J. Rodin (eds.) *Obese humans and rats*, Erlbaum–Wiley, Washington, D.C.

Rodin, J. (1974b) Effects of distraction on the performance of obese and normal subjects, in S. Schachter and J. Rodin. (eds.) *Obese humans and rats*, Erlbaum–Wiley, Washington, D.C.

Rodin, J. (1975a) Responsiveness of the obese to external stimuli, in G. A. Bray, (ed.) *Obesity in perspective*, Department of Health, Education and Welfare, (NIH) 75–708, Washington, D.C.

Rodin, J. (1975b) Obesity and external responsiveness, in A. Howard (ed.) *Recent advances in obesity research* I, Newman Publishing, London.

Rodin, J. (1976a) The role of perception of internal and external signals on the regulations of feeding in overweight and non-obese individuals, in J. T. Silverstone (ed.) *Appetite and food intake*, Abakon, for Dahlem Konferenzen, Berlin.

Rodin, J. (1976b) The relationship between external responsiveness and the development and maintenance of obesity, in D. Novin, W. Wyrwicka, and G. A. Bray (eds.), *Hunger: basic mechanisms and implications*, Raven Press, New York.

Rodin, J. (1977) Bidirectional influences of emotionality, stimulus responsivity, and metabolic events in obesity in J. D. Maser and M. E. P. Seligman (eds.) *Psychopathology: experimental models*, W. H. Freeman, San Francisco.

Rodin, J. (1978) Has the distinction between internal versus external control of feeding outlived its usefulness? in G. A. Bray (ed.) *Recent advances in obesity research* 2, Newman Publishing, London.

Rodin, J. and Slochower, J. (1974) Fat chance for a favour: obese–normal differences in compliance and incidental learning, *Journal of Personality and Social Psychology*, **29**, 557–565.

Rodin, J., Elman, D. and Schachter, S. (1974a) Emotionality and obesity, in S. Schachter and J. Rodin (eds.) *Obese humans and rats*, Erlbaum/Wiley, Washington, D.C.

Rodin, J., Herman, C. P. and Schachter, S. (1974b) Obesity and various tests of external sensitivity, in S. Schachter and J. Rodin (eds.) *Obese humans and rats*, Erlbaum/Wiley Washington, D.C.

Romanczyk, R. G., Tracy, D. A., Wilson, T. and Thorpe, G. L. (1973) Behavioural techniques on the treatment of obesity: a comparative analysis, *Behaviour Research and Therapy*, **11**, 629–640.

Ross, L. (1964) Effects of manipulating salience of food on consumption by obese and normal eaters, in S. Schachter and J. Rodin (eds.) *Obese humans and rats*, Erlbaum/Wiley, Washington, D.C.

Salmon, P. A. (1975) Intestinal by-pass: clinical experience and experimental results, in G. A. Bray (ed.) *Obesity in perspective*. Department of Health, Education and Welfare, (NIH) 75–708, Washington, D.C.

Sandstead, H. H. (1975) Jejunoileal shunt in morbid obesity, in G. A. Bray (ed.) *Obesity in perspective*, Department of Health, Education and Welfare, (NIH) 75–708, Washington, D.C.

Schachter, S. (1964) The interaction of cogntive and physiological determinants of emotional state, in L. Berkowitz. (ed.) *Advances in experimental social psychology*, I, Academic Press, New York.

Schachter, S. (1968) Obesity and eating, *Science*, **161**, 751–756.

Schachter, S. (1971a) *Emotion, obesity and crime*, Academic Press, New York.

Schachter, S. (1971b) Some extraordinary facts about obese humans and rats, *American Psychologist*, **26**, 129–144.

Schachter, S. and Rodin J. (Eds.) (1974) *Obese humans and rats*, Erlbaum–Wiley, Washington, D.C.

Schachter, S. and Gross, L. (1968) Manipulated time and eating behaviour, *Journal of Personality and social Psychology*, **10**, 98–106.

Schachter, S., Goldman, R. and Gordon, A. (1968) Effects of fear, food deprivation and obesity on eating, *Journal of Personality and Social Psychology*, **10**, 91–97.

Scoville, B. A. (1975) Review of amphetamine-like drugs by the Food and Drug Administration, in G. A. Bray (ed.) *Obesity in perspective*, Department of Health Education and Welfare, (NIH: 75–708), Washington, D.C.

Seligman, M. E. P. & Hager, J. L. (1972) *Biological boundaries of learning*, Appleton Century Crofts, New York.

Seltzer, C. C. and Mayer, J. (1965) A simple criterion of obesity, *Postgraduate Medicine*, **38**, 101–107.

Silverstone, J. T. (1968) Psychosocial aspects of obesity, *Proceedings of the Royal Society of Medicine*, **61**, 371–372.

Silverstone, J. T., Stunkard, A. J. and Gordon, R. P. (1969) Social factors in obesity in London, *Practitioner*, **202**, 682–689.

Simon, R. I. (1963) Obesity as a depressive equivalent, *Journal of the American Medical Association*, **183**, 134–136.

Sims, E. A. H. and Horton, E. S. (1968) Endocrine and metabolic adaptation to obesity and starvation, *American Journal of Clinical Nutrition*, **21**, 1455–1470.

Sims, E. A. H., Danforth, E. Horton, E. S., Bray, G. A., Glennon, J. A. and Salans, L. B. (1973) Endocrine and metabolic effects of experimental obesity in man, *Recent Progress in Hormone Research*, **29**, 457–496.

Slochower, J. (1976) Emotional labelling and overeating in obese and normal weight individuals, *Psychosomatic Medicine*, **38**, 131–139.

Smith, U. (1978) Human fat cell metabolism, in G. A. Bray (ed.) *Recent advances in obesity research 2*, Newman Publishing, London.

Society of Actuaries (1959) *Build and blood pressure study*, Society of Actuaries, Chicago.

Solow, C., Silberfarb and Swift, K. (1978) Psychological and behavioural consequences of intestinal bypass, in G. A. Bray (ed.) *Recent advances in obesity research 2*, Newman Publishing, London.

Staffieri, J. R. (1967) A study of social stereotype of body image in children, *Journal of Personality and social Psychology*, **7**, 101–104.

Steel, J. M., Munro, J. F. and Duncan, L. J. P. (1973) A comparative trial of different regimens of fenfluramine and phentermine in obesity, *Practitioner*, **211**, 232–236.

Stollak, G. E. (1967) Weight loss obtained under different experimental procedures, *Psychotherapy: Theory, Research and Practice*, **4**, 61–64.

Strata, A., Zuliani, U., Caronna, S., Magnati. G. and Pugnoli. C. (1977) Epidemiological aspects and social importance of obesity, *International Journal of Obesity*, **1**, 191–206.

Stuart, R. B. (1967) Behavioural control of overeating, *Behaviour Research and Therapy*, **5**, 357–365.

Stuart, R. B. (1971) A three dimensional programme for the treatment of obesity, *Behaviour Research and Therapy*, **9**, 177–186.

Stuart, R. B. (1975) Behavioural control of overeating: a status report, in G. A. Bray (ed.) *Obesity in perspective*, Department of Health Education and Welfare, (NIH) 75–708, Washington D.C.

Stuart, R. B. (1977) A self-help group approach to self-management, in R. B. Stuart (ed.) *Behavioural self management*, Brunner-Mazel, New York.

Stuart, R. B. and Davis, B. (1972) *Slim chance in a fat world*, Research Press, Champaign, Illinois.

Stuart, R. B. and Guire, K. (1978) Some correlates of the maintenance of weight loss through behaviour modification, *International Journal of Obesity*, **2**, 225–235.

Stunkard, A. J. (1957) The dieting depression, *American Journal of Medicine*, **23**, 77–86.

Stunkard, A. J. (1972) New therapies for the eating disorders, behaviour modification of obesity and anorexia nervosa, *Archives of general Psychiatry*, **26**, 391–398.

Stunkard, A. J. (1975) Satiety is a conditioned reflex, *Psychosomatic Medicine*, **37**, 383–387.

Stunkard, A. J. (1977) Behavioural treatments for obesity: failure to maintain weight loss, in R. B. Stuart (ed.) *Behavioural self management*, Brunner-Mazel, New York.

Stunkard, A. J. (1978) Behavioural treatment of obesity: the first ten years, in G. A. Bray (ed.) *Recent advances in obesity research 2*, Newman Publishing, London.

Stunkard, A. J. and Fox, S. (1971) The relationship of gastric mobility and hunger: A summary of the evidence, *Psychosomatic Medicine*, **33**, 123–134.

Stunkard, A. and Kaplan, D. (1977) Eating in public places: a review of reports of the direct observation of eating behaviour, *International Journal of Obesity*, **1**, 89–101.

Stunkard, A. J. and Koch, C. (1964) The interpretation of gastric mobility: I Apparent bias in the reports of hunger by obese persons, *Archives of general Psychiatry*, **11**, 74–82.

Stunkard, A. J. and McLaren-Hume, M. (1959) The results of treatment for obesity, *Archives of internal Medicine*, **103**, 79–85.

Stunkard, A. J. and Mahoney, M. J. (1976) Behavioural treatment of eating disorders, in H. Leitenberg (ed.) *Handbook of behaviour modification and behaviour therapy*, Prentice Hall, Englewood Cliffs, N.J.

Stunkard, A. H. & Rush, J. (1974) Dieting and depression re-examined, *Annals of internal Medicine*, **81**, 526–533.

Suedfeld, P. (1977) Using environmental restriction to initiate long term behaviour change, in R. B. Stuart (ed.) *Behavioural self-management*, Brunner-Mazel, New York.

Swanson, D. W. and Dinello, F. A. (1970) Follow-up of patients starved for obesity, *Psychosomatic Medicine*, **32**, 209–214.

Thomson, A. M., Billewicz, W. Z. & Passmore, R. (1961) The relation between calorie intake and body weight in man, *Lancet*, **1**, 1027–1028.

Tyler, V. O. and Straughan J. H. (1970) Coverant control and breath holding as techniques for the treatment of obesity, *Psychological Record*, **20**, 473–478.

Vincent, J. P., Schiavo, L., and Nathan, R. (1976) Effect of deposit contracts and distractibility on weight loss and maintenance, in J. B. Williams, S. Martin, and J. P. Foreyt (eds.) *Obesity: behavioural approaches in dietary management*, Brunner-Mazel, New York.

Weisenberg, M. and Fray, E. (1974) What's missing in the treatment of obesity by behaviour modification? *Journal of the American dietetic Association*, **65**, 410–414.

Werkman, S. L. and Greenberg, E. S. (1967) Personality and interest patterns in obese adolescent girls, *Psychosomatic Medicine*, **29**, 72–80.

Williams, A. F. and Duncan, B. (1976) A commercial weight-reducing organization, *Medical Journal of Australia*, **1**, 781–785.

Wollersheim, J. P. (1970) Effectiveness of group therapy based upon learning principles in the treatment of overweight women, *Journal of Abnormal Psychology*, **76**, 462–474.

Wooley, O. W. and Wooley, S. C. (1975) Short term control of food intake, in G. A. Bray (ed.) *Obesity in perspective*, Department of Health, Education and Welfare, (NIH), 75–708, Washington, D.C.

Yates, A. J. (1975) *Theory and practice in behaviour therapy*, Wiley, New York.

Young, C. M., Moore, N. S., Berresford, K., Einset, B. M. and Waldner, B. G. (1955) The problem of the obese out-patient, *Journal of the American dietetic Association*, **31**, 1111–1115.

9

MEDICAL APPLICATIONS OF BIOFEEDBACK TRAINING: A SELECTIVE REVIEW

LARRY D. YOUNG[1] and EDWARD B. BLANCHARD[2]

[1]*University of Mississippi*
[2]*State University of New York at Albany*

CONTENTS

1. INTRODUCTION

Although only slightly more than a decade has passed since the coining of the term *biofeedback*, the concept, the field, and its devotees have grown rapidly. This fact is attested to by a rapidly growing society, a journal, several books, and a recent bibliography (Butler, 1978) containing over 2,000 citations. With the demonstration that individuals could learn to control various aspects of their own physiology, the idea naturally arose that this ability might be employed as adjunctive or alternative treatment for a variety of medical conditions. These legitimate speculative hypotheses soon became speculative claims. These, in turn, became less cautious and biofeedback was hailed as "the new panacea" (Brown, 1974), as the ultimate treatment for everything, from cancer to "the heartbreak of psoriasis." The present chapter will critically survey the literature on the medical applications of biofeedback training.

The Biofeedback Society of America has suggested that the clinical efficacy of biofeedback in the treatment of several medical conditions (tension headaches, migraine headaches, neuromuscular reeducation, Raynaud's disease, and fecal incontinence) is sufficiently established to warrant removal of the "experimental" label. In addition to evaluating the available data supporting this conclusion, we will also review data relating to other disorders.

As in previous reviews of this topic (Blanchard and Young, 1974a; Blanchard and Epstein, 1977), our basic position is that the efficacy of clinical applications to any new form of therapy regardless of whether it is psychological, pharmacological or surgical. Several issues and criteria need to be considered in this evaluation and are discussed in the subsequent section. In general, however, we have taken the position that the effects of biofeedback need to be ascertained alone or, at worst, in addition to one other component. For example, demonstration of a clinical effect with a treatment package containing three types of biofeedback (Sedlacek and Heczey, 1977) cannot be meaningfully evaluated. This is especially true when the additional components in the treatment package have demonstrated independent efficacy in the treatment of the problem (e.g., biofeedback and systematic desensitization or Progressive Relaxation). In the absence of data for the independent, or incremental, efficacy of biofeedback procedures, then confidence in its therapeutic contribution is markedly reduced.

2. EVALUATION ISSUES

Ultimately, decisions about the efficacy and utility of biofeedback training for the treatment of medical disorders must be based upon the results of clinical research. The evaluation of these data should be based upon criteria similar to those employed in the evaluation of any therapeutic venture. In our original review of clinical biofeedback (Blanchard and Young, 1974a), we based our evaluation exclusively upon the criterion of experimental design. In the interim, however, the inadequacy of any single criterion for evaluating the therapeutic potential of biofeedback has become apparent to us. In fact, seven separate dimensions have been suggested (Blanchard, 1979) as important for consideration in this regard. These are:

(1) the degree of clinical meaningfulness of the changes obtained;
(2) the experimental design used in gathering or reporting the data;
(3) the extent of follow-up obtained or reported;
(4) the fraction of the treated patient sample which improved significantly;
(5) the degree to which changes obtained in the laboratory transfer to the patient's natural environment;
(6) the degree of replicability of the results;
(7) the degree of change in the biological response for which feedback training was supplied.

Each of these points is worthy of brief explanation, before being employed in an evaluative overview of the clinical biofeedback literature.

Clinical Effects

In the final analysis, the extent to which clinically meaningful effects are obtained through biofeedback training is the most important criterion for evaluating the therapeutic adequacy of the procedures. In an earlier review of basic research in cardiovascular biofeedback (Blanchard and Young, 1973), we arbitrarily defined an effect as *clinically* significant dependent upon its magnitude. In essence, we confounded the issue of clinical significance with that of magnitude of change (which will be discussed later). Engel (1974) very appropriately criticized us on this issue and made the point that a change can be clinically significant only if it is obtained with a clinical problem. We later (Blanchard and Young, 1974b) acknowledged the wisdom of Engel's comment.

Ultimately, therefore, unless the research focuses on a clinical problem, changes cannot constitute clinically meaningful results. Analogue studies may provide some information about relevant parameters or mechanism of effect with normals (typically college students), but the lack of population comparability may bring such information into serious question as was demonstrated by the difference in degree of heart-rate control of college students and patients with ischemic heart disease (Lang, Troyer, Twentyman, and Gatchel, 1975). The distinction between clinically significant and statistically significant results had been discussed elsewhere (Hersen and Barlow, 1976), but the point is often overlooked that statistical significance may be achieved with clinically trivial changes. For example, the 2–6 mm Hg changes in blood pressure typically encountered in basic biofeedback research (Blanchard and Young, 1973), even if they were obtained in a group of hypertensive patients, would not be clinically meaningful effects, even if they did attain conventional levels of statistical significance. To reiterate, unless a clinically meaningful change is obtained, all the other features of the research, no matter how elegantly designed and executed, are trivial.

Although each of the seven evaluation criteria previously listed are concerned with the question, "Does the treatment (biofeedback) work?", they each focus on slightly differing issues. The issues highlighted by an emphasis on *clinical* effects are those of *efficacy* (are meaningful effects obtained?) and *relative efficacy* (are these effects better than those obtainable by other treatment procedures?). That efficacy is important is succinctly illustrated by a comment made by Neal Miller, "It is a waste of time to design difficult control experiments only to find that there is no effect to control" (1978, p. 396). Only after an effect, a clinically meaningful effect, is obtained, is it worthwhile to consider whether it is superior (on a variety of dimensions) to those produced by other therapeutic interventions. Inasmuch as many of the conditions for which biofeedback has been suggested are considered stress related, a logical treatment comparison would be between biofeedback and standard relaxation induction procedures (Tarler-Benlolo, 1978). Equally desirable would be the comparison of biofeedback with the standard medical treatment for a particular disorder. Unfortunately, in only an instance or two has this even been attempted.

Experimental Design

We have previously described (Blanchard and Young, 1974a) five general categories of experimental designs which have been used in biofeedback research. These categories provide some ordering of the degree of confidence one can have that the treatment procedures are responsible for the results obtained. Thus, the credibility of the conclusions increases as more rigorous designs are used.

These experimental designs are ordered in terms of the number of factors that various designs control, so that these potentially confounding factors are eliminated as explanations for the observed changes. In ascending order of rigor, these five general categories of experimental designs are: anecdotal case reports; systematic case studies and multiple systematic case studies; single-group outcome studies; single-subject experiments and replicated single-subject experiments; and controlled group outcome studies.

In the anecdotal case report, little, if anything, is controlled. A general clinical description of the patient's condition prior and subsequent to treatment, as well as some description of the treatment itself are usually included. However, aspects of the treatment that are not mentioned in the description cannot be ruled out as potentially responsible for the observed effects, nor can extraneous events in the life of the patient during the course of therapy.

The systematic case study provides regularly collected data from both pretreatment baselines and during treatment itself. It is possible to observe the time course of change in the response of interest, if these data are provided. There still are no controls for concurrent events in the patient's life, nor for unspecified aspects of the treatment situation. However, a long baseline and change in the target response coincident with the introduction of treatment can provide slightly stronger evidence, particularly if this pattern is repeated with several patients.

The results of a single group outcome study are presented on a group, rather than individual, basis which makes it possible to ascertain the proportion of patients for whom a treatment is effective. Frequently, this design includes only pre- and post-treatment measurement of the target behavior. The quality of the data can be improved, if observations are made systematically during treatment, as well as before and after. It is difficult on logical grounds to ascribe any observed effects solely to treatment, as this design includes no controls for either the nonspecific effects of being in treatment or other life events. A controlled single group outcome study is possible by the introduction of another form of treatment following baseline and before the treatment of interest. Although within group comparisons are possible, conclusions are less reliable than with a controlled group outcome study. As was previously mentioned, there remains a point of controversy as to whether placebo effects are actually controlled in this design.

Single subject experiments, as opposed to case studies, are designed to elucidate functional relationships between treatments and outcome variables. The design is potentially capable of providing information regarding factors that exert a controlling function on the response of interest. Although still misunderstood (cf., Fotopoulos and Sunderland, 1978), single subject experimental designs are capable of controlling for several alternative hypotheses, including the presence of other events in the life of the patient. Replication is necessary to demonstrate that the obtained results are not idiosyncratic to the particular patient. Although certain nonspecific treatment effects are potentially controllable in single subject designs, a simple withdrawal design (A–B–A) probably does not adequately control placebo or expectancy effects (Miller, 1978). While this conclusion is accurate, it fails to consider that different factors may be important in the acquisition and subsequent utilization of a response. In particular, if a patient has learned a behavior (perhaps through biofeedback) that either alleviates or ameliorates an aversive state of affairs, then it is naive to assume that they will not perform this behavior subsequently, regardless of whether or not the "treatment" is still being given. Theoretically, the effect of this self-control response should be in opposition to demand characteristics and expectancy effects when the treatment is withdrawn, but its demonstration remains an empirical matter.

In a controlled group outcome design, the addition of a control group makes it possible to eliminate regression to the mean, spontaneous improvement, or extratherapeutic events in the patient's life as causal explanations for the change observed in the experimental group. A placebo control group allows greater confidence that the obtained effects are due to the experimental treatment itself, rather than to therapeutic expectancy or other "placebo" effects. However, as was noted earlier, the issue of effective controls for placebo effects in biofeedback research is far from simple.

Treatment Durability

Obtaining clinically meaningful changes by the conclusion of treatment is a necessary, but not sufficient, condition to justify that an intervention has utility. Treatment effects that are durable, that is, that are sustained over time are not simply a treatment bonus. Placebo effects, regression to the mean, and a naturally fluctuating time course can each produce transient effects. If therapeutic change occurs and is maintained for a sufficiently long period of time, the likelihood of its being a genuine treatment effect is enhanced. Even when follow-up data indicate that the effects are not sustained to the degree anticipated, this data provides the basis for treatment to improve the longevity of the treatment effects. We would suggest that assessment be continued for six months post-treatment as the bare minimum, with at least 12 months being a desirable minimum for follow-up duration.

Treatment Generality

A further point of distinction between clinical and statistical significance is illustrated in group research designs for which statistically significant results are reported. In these changes, it is possible that large and clinically meaningful changes were obtained from only a small proportion of patients, with the majority showing little, if any, clinical benefit. It is, therefore, important to know the percentage of patients with a particular disorder who are likely to benefit from a particular treatment. The greater the proportion of patients who benefit significantly from a particular treatment, the greater this treatment's utility. However, if the fraction of patients with a particular condition who are most likely to benefit from a particular treatment is small, but still can be reliably identified prior to treatment, then a step toward rational selection of treatments will have been made.

Transfer to the Natural Environment

Almost all the clinical biofeedback data have been of changes in physiological responses obtained in the laboratory or clinic setting. This demonstration is a necessary first step toward establishing the utility of an intervention. The ultimate benefit, however, of a procedure that is capable of effecting changes only in the laboratory or training environment is quite limited. Regardless of whether the desired physiological change is phasic and involves altering a pattern of physiological responses to a particular stimulus context in a manner analogous to a physiological coping skill (as might be required to abort a migraine headache) or is more tonic and involves altering systemic responding on a chronic, perhaps permanent, basis (as in the control of hypertension), the measure of therapeutic benefit will depend on changes that take place outside of the laboratory or clinic. It is desirable, therefore, to be able to document that the desired changes occurred outside the laboratory, as well as inside. Independent evaluation by the patient's physician would be desirable. With elevated blood pressure, for example, family members or colleagues at work could take periodic readings of the patient's blood pressure with minimal cost or inconvenience. Telemetry (Blanchard, Haynes, Young, and Scott, 1977) or portable recorders are additional technological advances that could be employed in clinical biofeedback research, to document that the desired changes are actually occurring in the patient's natural environment.

Replicability

The ability of independent investigators working in different laboratories to obtain results comparable to those reported by the original investigator is an important facet in the complete evaluation of a treatment. The degree of confidence that can be placed in a set of data is greatly diminished, if similar results cannot be attained by other investigators or by the original researcher in subsequent attempts. Systematic replication (Hersen and Barlow, 1976; Sidman, 1960) improved both reliability and generality of the results of a particular treatment. Miller (1978) has described three phases of clinical investigation. The first two phases correspond to the five classes of experimental design previously mentioned. The third phase he describes is relevant to the discussion of replicability. This last stage in clinical evaluation requires widespread clinical trials under real life, as opposed to research laboratory, conditions. In spite of the current widespread application of biofeedback techniques, Miller is of the opinion, and we concur, that our present data base is insufficient at the present time and that it is still premature to begin broad clinical trials.

Mechanism of Effect

Although we have emphasized the importance of clinically meaningful effects of biofeedback in preceding sections, the mechanism by which these effects are achieved is also worthy of consideration in evaluating clinical biofeedback research. Before this discussion can occur, the concept of mechanism must be clarified and two separate aspects of the term differentiated.

One aspect of the concept of mechanism focuses on the physiological or psychophysiological foundation of the observed changes. Only occasionally have clinical reports of biofeedback concerned themselves with this type of mechanism. In addition to broad theoretical consequences, knowledge of the physiological mechanism or substrate could make a valuable contribution by providing a more rational basis on which to develop treatment. This issue is typically investigated in one of two ways, even though other strategies are occasionally employed. The first involves the recording of multiple psychophysiological measures during the biofeedback training, with subsequent analysis of the change in the response pattern providing information from which to infer potential mechanisms. Secondly, pharmacological manipulations are utilized to block certain physiological affector systems to pinpoint more precisely the neural and endocrinological substrate for the observed changes. Engel's research (Bleecker and Engel, 1973a and b; Weiss and Engel, 1971), which permitted rather precise dissection of the physiological mechanisms used by patients with cardiac rhythms or cardiac conduction pathways, is an excellent example of this method. The understanding of mechanism in this sense, though important, is not essential in the evaluation of clinical applications of biofeedback.

The second aspect of the concept of mechanism is more frequently encountered, but less frequently acknowledged. It pertains to the theoretical framework whereby an operation is presumed to affect a theoretical construct in either the biological or psychological realms which, in turn, is presumed responsible for the observed effects in the domain of interest. This might be thought of as an indirect effect of biofeedback. Direct effects refer to those situations for which the biofeedback information is provided for the biological response that constitutes the clinical problem. Examples of direct application of biofeedback include hypertension, cardiac arrhythmias, and fecal incontinence. Indirect effects, by contrast, represent conditions for which biofeedback is not given for the clinical problem, but rather for a biological response that ostensibly alters an important mediating factor which can be either biological or psychological. An example of both types of presumed mediators involves providing digital temperature biofeedback as treatment for migraine headache. Cerebral arterial vasodilation, not cold hands, is presumed to be responsible for the pain of migraine, and, therefore, digital temperature biofeedback is presumed to operate by altering cerebral blood flow patterns in a beneficial manner. Secondly, the response of clinical importance is neither hand temperature nor cerebral blood flow; rather it is the self-report of the patient of a diminuation in headache pain.

Therefore, when evaluating these indirect effects of clinical biofeedback, this aspect of mechanism has both theoretical and practical significance. First, if improvement in the target behavior occurs without concomitant change in the physiological response for which biofeedback was provided, then the likelihood is increased that the changes were due to placebo factors, rather than to the biofeedback itself. In light of this possibility, a "manipulation check", or demonstration that changes actually occurred in the response for which feedback was given, aids in the evaluation of clinical biofeedback.

A related issue pertains to the magnitude of the physiological change affected by biofeedback and the assumptions underlying the choice of biofeedback as a treatment for a particular disorder. When physiological changes in the range of $1–5\,\mu V$ (frontalis EMG) or $0.2°–2°F$ (digital temperature) are reported, even if they are associated with clinical improvement, the magnitude of the physiological change seems insufficient to be directly responsible for the effect. Alternative explanations include the possibility of placebo factors, an indirect alteration of central effector mechanisms (admittedly speculative and difficult to demonstrate), or the possibility that the therapeutic results were effected by processes other than those theorized to be responsible for the disorder or theorized to be the active components of the biofeedback treatment. Such data certainly question many of the assumptions that originally provided the rationale and justification for employing biofeedback clinically.

Contraindications and Side Effects

Few treatments, either medical or behavioral, are so discrete in their action that they produce no effects concomitant to those desired therapeutically. In fact, many of the more potent pharmacological preparations are responsible for a broad spectrum of effects. Knowledge of the prevalence and magnitude of these concomitant effects is necessary for making a responsible choice of treatment technique. Equally important to responsible treatment planning is knowledge regarding whether conditions or circumstances exist which would render an otherwise acceptable procedure not merely ineffective but actually dangerous to a particular class of patients. Neither of these factors are of importance in evaluating the results of a single study, although both are very important in the overall evaluation of the therapeutic utility of a particular procedure such as biofeedback.

In the spirit of Miller's comment, that "There is much more need for the mundane task of rigorously evaluating the most promising of the current therapeutic applications than for the exciting adventure of trying to devise ingenious new ones," (1978, p. 374), we will next briefly evaluate the evidence for the clinical applications of biofeedback with medical disorders.

3. THE CARDIOVASCULAR SYSTEM

A. Hypertension

The role of psychological factors in the genesis of hypertension (Pickering, 1968), in combination with magnitude of the public health problem in the U.S. represented by hypertension (Stambler, Stambler, Riedlinger, Algera, and Roberts, 1976), has rendered this condition the focus of a number of studies using biofeedback technology. Several of these investigations are presented in Tables 1 and 2. Table 1 outlines those studies in which direct biofeedback for blood pressure was presented, while Table 2 contains a summary of hypertension treatment studies which presented biofeedback for some other physiological response. Anecdotal reports and systematic case studies have been omitted from these tables.

The methodological sophistication in research design is attested to by the presence of five controlled group outcome studies using direct biofeedback for blood pressure. Almost all of the studies have reported a change in blood pressure, although some report only within-session changes (Surwit, Shapiro, and Good, 1978). Although mean blood pressure reductions of 16–25 mm Hg have been obtained, the majority of studies report more modest effects in the range of 4–8 mm Hg. In light of the criteria previously outlined, it is clear that clinically significant reductions have seldom been achieved on a majority of the treated sample. However, even for those investigations which demonstrated somewhat larger effects, two difficulties seemed to be especially common.

First, baselines were either abbreviated (1–4 sessions) or nonexistent. The establishment of a stable baseline is especially crucial, to demonstrate clearly that effects during the treatment phase do not represent a continued habituation to the treatment setting. This point is substantiated by Benson et al.'s (1971) report in which an average of eleven baseline sessions were required to establish stability. Additionally, the origin of the baseline blood pressure values (which typically are among criteria in patient selection) has been demonstrated to be important by Surwit et al. (1978b). The average blood pressure of their patients dropped from 165/103 to 144/89 from the initial physician's screening exam and the initial blood pressure value in baseline session 1.

Of equal importance clinically, is the general absence of good follow-up data. That is, the data either were not collected or indicated that the level of blood pressure reduction that had been achieved was returning toward baseline values within one or two months. The only study that has reported a potentially meaningful blood pressure reduction, adequate baseline, and systematic follow-up (although it was for three months) was that of Kristt and Engel (1975). It is of interest that they had instructed the patients in certain self-management skills, including regular blood pressure monitoring and regular practice of the blood pressure lowering response learned with biofeedback. It seems reasonable that regular practice of these self-management responses may have played a major role in maintaining effects at follow-up.

In terms of the generality of effects, for all studies combined in which the fraction of patients who were able to lower their blood pressure successfully was mentioned, it appears that approximately 50 percent of the patients were capable of effecting some decrease in their blood pressure. Only the Kristt and Engel study provided adequate documentation of the transfer of the biofeedback effect into the patient's natural environment. The replicability of clinical effects with direct biofeedback of blood pressure has been poor. An attempt by the Harvard investigators to replicate their earlier success (Schwartz and Shapiro, 1973) failed. Two other research teams using similar constant-cuff biofeedback procedures were somewhat more successful. The true extent of both success and replication must be regarded with caution, inasmuch as Goldman et al. (1975) did not employ even a single baseline assessment and the Kristt and Engel treatment paradigm was radically different from that of the Harvard group in spite of using constant cuff blood pressure biofeedback.

Miller (1975) has reported that his initial success has been followed by over twenty successive failures to obtain clinically meaningful changes in the blood pressure of hypertensives. Neither the magnitude of effect nor the proportion of patients who benefitted, reported by Elder et al. (1973), was subsequently replicated (Elder and Eustis, 1975). Finally, our own initial success (Blanchard et al., 1975) in providing direct feedback of blood pressure was not replicated in a controlled group outcome study using an identical procedure (Blanchard et al., 1979).

It appears, at the present time, that direct biofeedback of blood pressure offers little in the way of applicability in the treatment of hypertension. The studies suffer from several methodological weaknesses, but more than that they suffer from a lack of replicable and clinically meaningful results. Also, for those patients capable of

TABLE 1.
Direct Biofeedback of Blood Pressure in the Treatment of Hypertension

Study	Experimental design	Number of patients	Type of treatment	Results	Follow-up
Benson, Shapiro, Tursky, and Schwartz (1971)	Single group outcome	7	Biofeedback of systolic BP	5/7 patients showed decreases; av. decrease in systolic BP = 16.5 mm Hg	None
Schwartz and Shapiro (1973)	Single group outcome	7	Relaxation instruction plus biofeedback of diastolic BP	No overall change in diastolic BP; 1/7 patients showed decrease of 14 mm Hg	None
Goldman, Kleinman, Snow, Bidus and Korol (1975)	Single group outcome	7	Biofeedback of systolic BP	Av. decrease in systolic BP = 6 mm Hg; av. decrease in diastolic BP = 15 mm Hg	None
Kristt and Engel (1975)	Single group outcome	5 (baseline data on 4)	Biofeedback of BP plus home monitoring of BP plus home practice	Av. decrease in systolic BP = 18 mm; av. decrease in diastolic BP = 7.5 mm; all 4 patients were able to lower systolic or diastolic BP; all 5 patients could lower BP at home	2 or 3 months, all 4 patients maintained gains with regular practice of BP lowering
Elder and Eustis (1975)	Single group outcome	22	Biofeedback of systolic BP	Av. decrease in systolic BP = 7.8 mm; av. decrease in diastolic BP = 6.5 mm; 9/22 patients showed significant decrease	2 months on 4 patients; no maintenance of gains
Blanchard, Young and Haynes (1975)	Replicated single subject experiments	4	Biofeedback of systolic BP	All 4 patients showed BP decreases during biofeedback training; av. decrease in systolic BP = 26 mm (range 9–51 mm)	1–4 weeks, 3/4 patients maintained 65 + % of gains

Study	Design	N	Conditions	Results	Follow-up
Elder, Ruiz, Deabler, and Dillenkoffer (1973)	Controlled group outcome	18	(1) Biofeedback of BP plus social reinforcement (2) Biofeedback of BP (3) Monitoring of BP	(1) 4/6 showed BP decreases; diastolic BP = 80% of baseline (2) Diastolic BP = 93% of baseline (3) No change in BP. Overall: no between group difference in systolic BP; for diastolic BP, biofeedback plus social reinforcement superior to biofeedback alone, which was superior to monitoring	1 week; differential drop out precludes analysis
Shoemaker and Tasto (1975)	Controlled group outcome	15	(1) Biofeedback of BP (2) Progressive relaxation (3) Monitoring of BP	No improvement for either biofeedback or monitoring groups; 4/5 relaxation patients improved; av. reduction = 8 mm	None
Frankel, Patel, Horowitz, Friedewald, and Gaarder (1978)	Controlled group outcome with partial crossover	22	(1) Biofeedback of diastolic BP plus EMG biofeedback plus autogenic and relaxation training and home practice (2) Sham biofeedback of BP (3) No treatment control	Overall, outside of lab changes in BP for treated patients were minimal (0/−1) and +1/0 mm Hg, supine and standing respectively). In the lab setting, av. BP reduction for (1) was −3/−2 mm while that for (2) was −5/−2 mm	None
Surwit, Shapiro and Good (1978b)	Controlled group outcome	24	(1) Biofeedback for systolic BP and heart rate (2) EMG biofeedback (3) Benson's relaxation—meditation; all patients were to practice at home	No between group differences; greater within session BP reduction during baseline than during training	6 weeks and 1 year; no between group differences; overall, BP was unchanged relative to pretreatment
Blanchard, Miller, Abel, Haynes and Wicker (1979)	Controlled group outcome	33	(1) Biofeedback for systolic BP (2) EMG biofeedback (3) Relaxation	For (1) av. BP reductions were −8.1/−1.9; for (2), +1.4/+1.2; and for (3) −9.5/−2.8	4 months; Reductions were maintained for (1), but returned to baseline values for (3)

TABLE 2.
Biofeedback of Other Responses in the Treatment of Hypertension

Study	Experimental design	Number of patients	Type of treatment	Results	Follow-up
Moeller and Love, 1974	Single group outcome	6	Frontalis EMG biofeedback plus autogenic training	5/6 showed significant BP reductions; av. decrease in systolic BP = 18 mm; av. decrease in diastolic BP = 12 mm	None
Love, Montgomery and Moeller, 1974	Single group outcome	40 (27 completed treatment)	Frontalis EMG biofeedback plus relaxation training	Av. decrease in systolic BP = 15 mm; av. decrease in diastolic BP = 13 mm	8 months, N = 23; further decrease in BP: systolic = 6.5 mm; diastolic = 4 mm
Patel, 1973	Single group outcome	20	GSR biofeedback plus passive relaxation training plus meditation	16/20 showed significant response; 12/20 reduced medication; av. decrease in systolic BP = 25 mm; av. decrease in diastolic BP = 14 mm	None
Patel, 1975	Controlled group outcome	40	(1) Same as Patel, 1973 (2) Resting quietly for 30 min	(1) 12/20 reduced medication; av. BP reduction = 20 mm systolic and 14 mm diastolic (2) Av. BP reduction = 1 mm systolic and 2 mm diastolic	12 months; 5 mm av. rise in systolic BP for treatment group, control group unchanged
Patel and North, 1975	Controlled group outcome with partial crossover (controls treated at end of experiment)	34	(1) Same as Patel, 1975 (2) Same as Patel, 1975	(1) Av. decrease in BP = 26 mm systolic and 15 mm diastolic (2) Av. decrease in BP = 9 mm systolic and 4 mm diastolic; after treatment BP decreases were 28 mm systolic and 16 mm diastolic	After 7 months initial treatment group showed an av. increase in systolic BP of 4 mm

producing reasonable blood pressure reductions during treatment, the effects were generally not maintained for more than a few weeks. The sole exception to these difficulties (Kristt and Engel, 1975) is a single group study with a small patient sample. However, it does appear that the patients learned to control reliably their blood pressure, so that the effects are probably not due to placebo effects. It has been speculated elsewhere (Blanchard, 1979) that this self-control and self-management aspect of the training procedure may be largely contributory to the therapeutic effects. However, even this lone success for direct blood pressure biofeedback has not yet been replicated.

Indirect Biofeedback Treatment for Hypertension

The widely held view that psychologic stress contributes to the genesis of hypertension has probably been responsible for the application of several general relaxation strategies, including frontal EMG biofeedback, to the treatment of hypertension.

Frontalis EMG biofeedback plus a relaxation training technique were employed in two separate investigations from the same laboratory (Moeller and Love, 1974; Love, Montgomery, and Moeller, 1974). The reported blood pressure reductions were respectable (18/12 mm and 15/13 mm, respectively) and the second study (Love et al., 1974) even reported a continuation of blood pressure reduction at follow-up eight months post-treatment. Unfortunately, the one or two session baseline conditions were inadequate and data were not available on the degree of learned reduction of frontalis EMG levels. More problematic, however, have been the issues of replicability and relative contribution of EMG biofeedback to the total treatment effect.

Regarding replicability, two independent evaluations of the efficacy of EMG biofeedback in the treatment of hypertension (Blanchard et al., 1979; Surwit et al., 1978b; see Table 1) have failed to document effects comparable to those obtained by Love and Moeller. The patients in the EMG biofeedback condition in the Surwit et al. investigation were able to produce only modest within-session changes in blood pressure and their level of hypertension at the conclusion of treatment and at follow-up was unchanged, relative to pre-treatment baselines. Those hypertensive patients in the Blanchard et al. (1979) study who were treated with EMG biofeedback actually showed concomitant *increases*, not decreases, in their blood pressure readings. The failure of two independent investigators to substantiate blood pressure reductions with frontalis EMG biofeedback raises serious questions about the therapeutic efficacy of this procedure by itself in the treatment of hypertension.

This conclusion questioning the degree of the therapeutic contribution provided by the EMG biofeedback procedures themselves is strengthened by data from two separate comparative studies demonstrating moderate effects in blood pressure reduction with relaxation procedures. Of the three studies comparing a biofeedback treatment with a verbal general relaxation procedure (Blanchard et al., 1979; Shoemaker and Tasto, 1975; Surwit et al., 1978b), none have found the biofeedback procedure superior to general relaxation strategies. Although Surwit et al. did not obtain blood pressure reductions with Benson's mediation–relaxation technique, this procedure has been reported (Benson, Rosner, Marzetta, and Klemchuk, 1974a and 1974b) to effect modest blood pressure reductions. Specifically, the meditation–relaxation procedures were associated with 8/4 mm Hg reduction with untreated borderline hypertensive patients and 11/5 mm decreases in hypertensives who were receiving medications. These reductions are comparable to the 8 mm decreases reported by Shoemaker and Tasto and the 9.5/2.8 mm reductions obtained by Blanchard *et al.* using self-administered relaxation procedures.

Perhaps, the most impressive biofeedback treatment "package" for hypertension has been developed by Patel and her colleagues (Patel, 1973, 1975; Patel and North, 1975). This composite treatment includes biofeedback of galvanic skin response (GSR) and the yogic exercise "shavasan", which involves elements of passive relaxation training and meditation. The Patel and North (1975) study had shortened the treatment to 12 sessions over a six-week interval and, although transfer to the natural environment was not assessed, a "blind examiner" was used to obtain all blood pressure measurements. In addition to employing in all the studies a patient population which was clearly hypertensive and many of which were on anti-hypertensive medication, Patel and North utilized a partial crossover research design, such that patients in the control condition were given the treatment package providing within-subject data, as well as additional replication.

To data, 74 hypertensives have received the GSR biofeedback plus Shavasan treatment package with remarkable results. The average blood pressure decrease for the treatment group from the original study and the two replications combined is approximately 25 mm Hg for systolic blood pressure and 15 mm Hg for diastolic blood pressure. The magnitude of this effect is undoubtedly large enough to be regarded as clinically meaningful. In addition, data from the two initial studies indicated that 24/40 (60 percent) of those pharmacologically treated hypertensives who received the treatment were able to effect some reduction in their medication regimen. Follow-up results suggest only a slight loss of durability. In the cross-over study, systolic blood pressure for the treated group had risen approximately 4 mm Hg by 7-month follow-up, which is comparable to the 5 mm Hg increase in systolic blood pressure noted at 12-month follow-up in the treated group of the other controlled group study.

The series of three investigations elegantly documents the attainment of clinically meaningful effects that are replicable, possess reasonable generality, and are maintained at a respectable follow-up interval. It would be desirable to have independent verification that the effects do generalize to the natural environment. More serious, from the point of view of an evaluation of the clinical efficacy of biofeedback, is the lack of information regarding the relative contribution of the biofeedback component to the overall therapeutic efficacy of the treatment package. A related point is that data indicating that patients actually were able to control their electrodermal activity might help to broaden our understanding of the mechanism employed in achieving these results. Finally, Miller (1978), after speaking of the studies (particularly Patel and North) in quite positive terms, suggests that their greatest weakness was the failure to include sufficient procedures to control for placebo effects. The durability of the effects at follow-up is certainly encouraging. Even if the modest reversals toward baseline levels are reliable, periodic booster sessions might be sufficient to restore initial levels of therapeutic effect. One would also hope to see independent replication of the treatment effects by investigators in another laboratory.

In summary, broadly based psychological treatment which includes biofeedback appears to have merit in the treatment of hypertension, at least as adjunctive to standard pharmacological treatments. There is no data to support its use as alternative therapy. However, since 60 percent of Patel's (1973, 1975) treated patients were able to reduce their medication, the possibility exists that, for less extreme hypertensives, drugs could possibly be gradually reduced and ultimately eliminated, as the patient's requirement for them decreased.

B. Cardiac Arrhythmias and Rate

The literature of basic research in biofeedback contains a large number of investigations for which feedback was provided for heart rate changes; yet, paradoxically, the clinical biofeedback literature contains few reports of the application of heart rate biofeedback to clinical problems. Clinical applications of heart rate biofeedback have been concentrated in two areas: treatment of irregular or abnormal cardiac rhythms and the treatment of sinus tachycardia, an elevated heart rate without other irregularities in cardiac functioning. Sinus tachycardia is a relatively benign condition from a medical perspective, although its psychological and psychophysiological concomitants are occasionally unpleasant. In fact, sinus tachycardia may be present in a reasonable proportion of patients with anxiety-based complaints and may be alleviated by the pharmacological or relaxation therapies prescribed as treatment for the "anxiety." By contrast, the other arrhythmias are viewed as more serious medical problems and consequently are more likely to be treated strictly with drugs. Finally, this is an area for which few recent investigations have been reported.

The most important problem clinically in this area is that of premature ventricular contractions (PCVs) and the best data of heart rate biofeedback application is the series of eight systematic case studies reported by Weiss and Engel (1971). Each of these patients was given heart rate biofeedback training while they were hospitalized. The standard treatment sequence involved training to increase heart rate, then to decrease heart rate, followed by training to alternate increases and decreases of heart rate for 1–3 minute intervals. Next, patients were instructed and given feedback to keep their heart rate within a particular range. In addition to providing practice at heart rate stabilization, this phase was designed such that feedback was also provided for each PVC. The final phase in the treatment sequence involved the gradual "fading" of the biofeedback information, while the patient continued his attempts to maintain heart rate within the restricted range.

Five of the eight patients were successful in reducing their PVC rate to less than 1/minute while in the lab. Additionally, follow-up data obtained 3–21 months after training indicated that four of five were maintaining the therapeutic effects. So, in terms of efficacy, durability, and generality, the study is excellent. Similarly, transfer to the natural environment was elegantly documented by outside-the-laboratory telemetry assessment, while patients were still in the hospital, as well as by independent assessment after discharge. Engel and Bleecker (1974) successfully replicated these results with another patient, in a somewhat strengthened experimental design that included assessment of baseline frequency of PVCs in the laboratory, rather than only by history. Independent replication of the efficacious application of heart rate biofeedback in the treatment of PVCs has been provided with three patients by Pickering and Gorham (1975) and Pickering and Miller (1977).

Two problematic aspects of the Weiss and Engel series deserve comment. First, the data are at the level of systematic case studies. The base rate of PVCs was not documented in the laboratory, although it was established by case history. As previously noted, the subsequent replication by Engel and Bleecker remedied this shortcoming. The second troublesome issue relates to mechanism. The rationale for the biofeedback training sequence appeared to be to teach patients to control heart rate with the hope that ability to control heart rate would enable patients to exercise similar control of PVCs. Only three out of eight patients completed only a portion of the fading phase. Unfortunately, those patients who improved did not do so in the same training phase. Since the data fail to indicate a consistent relationship between clinical improvement and phase of training, the relative contributions of each of the training phases is uncertain. Also treatment outcome is positively related to length of treatment. If the patient sample is divided into those receiving 47 or more training sessions and those receiving fewer than 47 sessions, those patients receiving more treatment demonstrated greater improvement ($p < 0.05$, Fisher's Exact Probability Test). Although the obtained data do not address the assumption contained in the apparent rationale for the treatment sequence (it is not known, for example, whether heart rate stabilization which provides direct feedback of PVC occurrence would be sufficient), the training and demonstration in instructed heart rate control probably serves several ends. First, bidirectional instructional control of heart rate makes placebo or expectancy explanations less likely. Secondly, patients were taught a self-control or self-management strategy which they could later employ without biofeedback. Finally, the perception that one can successfully control one's own physiology, regardless of whether or not this perception is veridical, has been demonstrated to exert some beneficial elements (cf. Gatchel, 1978).

In addition to being used in the treatment for PVCs, heart rate biofeedback has also been reported in the treatment of paroxysmal atrial tachycardia (PAT) and episodic sinus tachycardia (one case, anecdotal data), PAT plus supraventricular tachycardia (one case, systemic case study) (Engel and Bleecker, 1974). Improvement, noted for both patients, was maintained through five- and six-month follow-ups.

For cases of abnormally high heart rate in which cardiac rhythm is still controlled by the sinoatrial node, a condition known as sinus tachycardia, the use of heart rate biofeedback to enable patients to learn to reduce their heart rate seems made to order. In each of the four cases where this has been attempted, clinically meaningful changes have been obtained. Patients' resting heart rates were lowered generally into the normal range with 18–30 rpm changes in cardiac rate being reported. Each of the three cases reported by Blanchard and his colleagues (Scott, Blanchard, Edmundson, and Young, 1973; Blanchard and Abel, 1976) represented single subject experiments Engel and Bleecker's (1974) case was at the level of a systematic case study. Unfortunately, the superior experimental designs highlighted problems in the data. For none of the patients reported by Blanchard did withdrawal of the biofeedback treatment lead to a complete reversal of the target behavior (increase in heart rate). The clinical desirability of such robust changes is unarguable, but, experimentally, this failure calls into question the degree to which the biofeedback treatment is the variable responsible for the changes. The fact that all three patients reported by Blanchard showed positive effects coincident with treatment, coupled with Engel and Bleecker's independent replication provides some strengthening of the data. Formal follow-up at four months with one patient and informal follow-ups at 12 and 18 months with two others indicate that heart rates maintained at lowered levels. Follow-up data is not provided for Engel and Bleecker's patient, but independent evaluation by the patient's personal physician confirmed that the effects were not confined to the laboratory setting. Concomitant effects were reported for both of Scott *et al.*'s patients. Both reported subjective improvement and increased activity, with one who had previously received disability compensation due to the arrhythmia decreasing his medication and obtaining employment.

In sum, heart rate biofeedback as a treatment of two cardiac arrhythmias, PVCs, and sinus tachycardia, seems promising. Successful results with both conditions have been replicated and there has been good follow-up data. That all the data are from systematic case studies or single subject experiments, coupled with the small overall number of patients treated with heart rate biofeedback, indicate the need for further work before much generalization is claimed. Heart rate biofeedback singly or in combination with pharmacological treatments needs to be compared with standard drug therapies alone in a controlled group outcome format.

C. Peripheral Vascular Disorders

Raynaud's disease is a condition of the peripheral vasculature in which episodic vasospastic attacks of the hands, and occasionally of the feet, occur. These attacks are characterized by pronounced initial vasoconstriction, such that the skin blanches, even appears bluish, and is cold to the touch. This phase is followed by reflex dilation, during which the skin is red and pain is experienced. Although the attacks are frequently precipitated by exposure to cold objects or a cold environment, emotional upsets have also been reliably implicated as triggers of vasospastic episodes. In addition to pain, the condition can result in retarded healing of cuts and even gangrene in the affected tissues. Medical treatments for the disorder have been noted neither for their innocuousness (surgically severing the sympathetic neural connections to the peripheral blood vessels being done when drugs have proved ineffective) nor for their success. In a context of therapies that were often unpleasant, radical, and/or minimally effective, the possibility that patients could learn to control their peripheral vascular physiology had considerable appeal. In spite of the fact that the relevant underlying physiological response appears to be vasoconstriction, only two anecdotal cases are reported in the literature (Schwartz, 1972) for which biofeedback was given of blood flow or pulse volume directly. (Complete relief was obtained for one case and no improvement in the other.) All subsequent biofeedback has utilized digital temperature as the relevant response.

As the summary in Table 3 indicates, all of the investigations with systematically collected data have demonstrated clinically meaningful improvement. This ranged

TABLE 3.
Biofeedback Treatment of Raynaud's Disease

Study	Experimental design	Number of patients	Type of treatment	Results	Follow-up
Jacobson, Hackett, Surman and Silverberg, 1973	Systematic case study	1	Hypnosis plus biofeedback of skin temperature	No improvement with hypnosis; with biofeedback, hand temperature increases were from 3.9–4.6°C; much symptomatic improvement	7½ months, improvement maintained
May and Weber, 1976	Multiple systematic case studies	8	Biofeedback of skin temperature	All patients showed a least 2°C increase in temperature; all reported some transfer and some clinical improvement; for severe cases, vasospastic episodes reduced from 5 to 1/week	
Stephenson, 1976	Systematic case studies	2	Relaxation training, autogenic training, digital temperature biofeedback, and EMG biofeedback	Both patients could raise hand temperature to least 10°F with final temperature of 94°F; complete remission of symptoms	2 and 16 months; improvement maintained
Blanchard and Haynes, 1975	Single subject experiment	1	Biofeedback of skin temperature	Overall hand temperature increased 12°F (a 5°F increase of biofeedback over effects of instructions alone); symptomatic improvement	7 months with improvement maintained
Surwit, Pilon and Fenton, 1978	Controlled group outcome	30	(1) Skin temperature biofeedback plus autogenic training in laboratory (2) Autogenic training in laboratory (3) Autogenic training at home (4) Same as (1) but conducted at home	All patients showed increased skin temperature over treatment; all patients showed clinical improvement; no differences between treatment groups were evident	None

from total symptomatic remission (Stephenson, 1976) to a reduction in the frequency of vasospastic attacks (May and Weber, 1976). Until recently, the literature of biofeedback treatment of Raynaud's phenomenon was made up of predominantly anecdotal data and systematic case studies with the exception of a lone single subject experiment reported by Blanchard and Haynes (1975). The quality of data in this area of clinical research was substantially advanced by the recent completion of a controlled group outcome study (Surwit, Pilon, and Fenton, 1978a). In this investigation thirty patients with diagnosed idiopathic Raynaud's disease were each given Schultz–Luthe Autogenic Training to assist in relaxation and hand warming. Half of the patients who received each type of treatment were given their training in the laboratory, while the remainder had three group meetings before completing their training at home. Half of each of these two groups were given digital temperature biofeedback training, either in the laboratory or at home.

The results are indicative of clinical improvement. All treated groups were superior to untreated controls in their ability to warm their hands during a cold challenge period at the end of treatment. Likewise, the treated groups overall experienced declines in frequency of vasospastic attacks form a baseline frequency of $2\frac{1}{2}$ per day to approximately 1 per day post-treatment. When control patients were given treatment at the end of the first phase, their results replicated those from the other patients. Additionally, no differences obtained between those patients who completed their training in the laboratory versus those who trained at home. More importantly, the addition of digital temperature biofeedback conferred no extra advantage in therapeutic gains to those who received autogenic training alone.

Follow-up data for this application of biofeedback are woefully inadequate, in terms of percentage of patients followed up. Moreover, the data are insufficient to address adequately the issue of treatment generality. All the patients whose data are reported in anecdotal, case study, or single subject format (total $N = 18$) are described as demonstrating clinical improvement with the exception of one of two patients reported by Schwartz. This sample is obviously, and unfortunately, biased, since an unsuccessful case study is not likely to be published. Since Surwit et al. indicate that all of their patients showed clinical improvement, this remarkable proportion of patients experiencing benefit of their Raynaud's symptoms from autogenic training and/or digital temperature biofeedback may not be overinflated, however.

The final issue for discussion in evaluating biofeedback of Raynaud's disease is that of mechanism. Although all studies reported that their patients increased their temperature over the course of treatment, the ability of patients to control their own temperature was not as universally reported. The use of a cold challenge to assess patient's ability to demonstrate meaningful digital temperature increases under adverse circumstances was an ingenious addition to Surwit et al.'s assessment procedure. The magnitude of temperature increase was somewhat variable, ranging from 2°C to 12°F.

Thus, biofeedback of digital temperature seems to be a fairly efficacious and noninvasive treatment procedure for Raynaud's disease. Its comparative efficacy has been evaluated only once and there it clearly added no therapeutic benefit to a simple home-based treatment utilizing autogenic training. Although placebo responses could not be totally discounted, their effects are minimized by the demonstration of temperature control during the cold challenge assessment procedure. Taub and Stroebel (1978) however, do criticize the Surwit et al. investigation in that it failed to provide independent evidence that the patients had developed the ability to increase their hand temperature on the basis of the feedback, as opposed to adaptation and general relaxation.

D. Migraine Headache

Headaches, both migraine and muscle tension, are both disorders for which the Biofeedback Society of America claims efficacy of treatment. Migraine headaches are a type of vascular headache characterized by: painful episodes recurring periodically, variations in frequency, duration, and intensity, often preceded with an aura, and accompanied by nausea and/or photosensitivity; and usually unilateral in onset. Two broad pathophysiologic processes are generally regarded as operative in the occurrence of migraines. After initial vasoconstriction of the cerebral and cranial arteries, a reflex vasodilation of these vessels takes place, particularly in the extra-cranial arteries. The resulting inflammation of the arterial wall and vascular edema are responsible for the pulsatile pain.

In contrast with the linkage between pathophysiological mechanism presumed responsible for muscle-contraction headaches and the type of biofeedback most often applied, the most prevalent biofeedback treatment for migraines had its origins in serendipity. While conducting basic research in digital temperature control, a group of investigators at the Menninger Clinic noted with interest the information volunteered by one of their subjects that her migraine headaches were less severe coincident with her handwarming via biofeedback. Following up on this, the Menninger group developed a treatment "package" comprised of autogenic training, relaxation training, and biofeedback of the difference in temperature between hand and forehead. Results from 75 patients were included in the initial report from the Menninger group (Sargent, Green, and Walters, 1972). In spite of the size of the sample, the quality of the data is essentially at the level of a case report.

In the past several years, several controlled group outcome evaluations of the efficacy and relative efficacy of biofeedback of digital temperature in the treatment of migraines have been performed. In all of these studies, diminuation in headache frequency, duration and/or intensity was noted and was reported to result from biofeedback of digital temperature. Relative efficacy of this biofeedback treatment was evaluated in comparison with groups receiving EEG alpha biofeedback (Andreychuck and Skriver, 1975; Cohen, Levee, McArthur and Rickles, 1976), self-hypnosis (Andreychuck and Skriver, 1975), EMG biofeedback (Cohen et al., 1976; Lake, Rainey and Papsdorf, 1979), false biofeedback of digital temperature (Mullinix, Norton, Hack and Fishman, 1978) and progressive relaxation plus home practice (Blanchard, Theobold, Williamson, Silver and Brown, 1978). The Blanchard et al. and the Lake et al. investigations included waiting list controls. These latter two studies combined digital temperature biofeedback with other procedures in a treatment package. The treatment package used in the Blanchard et al. study also included autogenic training and home practice in relaxation while Lake et al.

compared hand temperature biofeedback alone with biofeedback plus Rational Emotive Therapy.

The data on relative efficacy of digital temperature as a treatment for migraine headache support a more cautious conclusion than some apparently believe (cf. Shealy, 1972). Although the biofeedback procedures were more effective than being placed on a waiting list for treatment, only one of the comparisons, that with biofeedback of EEG alpha supported the superiority of hand temperature biofeedback (Cohen et al., 1976). The "standard" digital temperature biofeedback intervention did not demonstrate superior clinical effects, when compared to self-hypnosis, biofeedback of frontalis EMG, a false feedback condition, the combination of biofeedback plus RET, or progressive relaxation plus home practice. In fact, Blanchard et al. found a slight statistical advantage favoring progressive relaxation over biofeedback of skin temperature in frequency, duration, and peak intensity of headaches, and on reduction in medication usage. This failure to obtain differential effectiveness, especially when compared with self-hypnosis or nonveridical feedback, raises the serious question of whether or not the effects are attributable to placebo factors or not. Thus, although the efficacy of digital temperature biofeedback training for migraine headaches seems established, its differential efficacy in comparison to relaxation or non-specific treatments remains to be demonstrated.

For the three studies which report follow-up assessment (only three months in each case), it appears that symptomatic improvements are maintained. Perhaps the most important observation to emerge at follow-up was noted by Blanchard et al., although their high dropout rate (50 percent) precludes definitive statements. They noted that it was those patients who continued regular practice of the relaxation or hand warming exercises who experienced the maintenance of symptomatic relief. Other sets of data on treatment durability have been obtained retrospectively at intervals up to five years after completion of biofeedback training. These data will be more fully described in the discussion of treatment generality.

The percentage of patients suffering from migraine who derive benefit from the biofeedback treatment is typically estimated to be between 50–70 percent (Diamond, Diamond–Falk, and DeVeno, 1978). This range is not disproportionate compared to the controlled group outcome data from Table 4. Reliable predictive criteria for identifying those who will respond favorably to biofeedback are currently unknown.

In view of the relatively positive response to frontalis EMG biofeedback, and because a number of patients present with both migraine and muscle-tension headache or with headaches that appear to contain both muscle tension and migraine elements, several groups have begun to treat headache patients with a combination of frontalis EMG plus skin temperature biofeedback package. Most of these patients have been treated clinically and the data obtained retrospectively.

Adler and Adler (1975) treated 19 muscle contraction, 22 migraine, 12 mixed, and 5 cluster headache patients with a combination of skin temperature biofeedback and EMG biofeedback plus psychotherapy. Assessment of continued symptomatic relief was made $3\frac{1}{2}$ to 5 years after discontinuation of treatment. The reported success rates are 81 percent for migraine, 88 percent for tension headache, and 60 percent for both mixed and cluster headache.

Diamond, Medina, and Franklin (1975) treated 83 migraine and 254 mixed head-

TABLE 4.
Biofeedback Treatment of Migraine Headaches

Study	Experimental design	Number of patients	Type of treatment	Results	Follow-up
Feuerstein and Adams, 1977	Single subject experiment	4 (2 migraine; 2 muscle contraction)	Sequential presentation of biofeedback for cephalic vasomotor activity and EMG biofeedback	All patients could control both responses; clinical improvement was associated with biofeedback for response in "relevant" physiological system	None
Sturgis, Tollison, and Adams, 1978	Single subject experiment	2 mixed headache patients	Sequential presentation of biofeedback for cephalic vasomotor activity and EMG biofeedback	Both could control both responses; migraine headache improvement associated with vasomotor biofeedback; muscle contraction headache associated with EMG biofeedback	20 weeks; symptomatic improvement maintained
Friar and Beatty, 1976	Controlled group outcome	19	(1) biofeedback of temperal artery vasoconstriction (2) biofeedback of hand vasoconstriction	Significant reduction in the number of severe headaches for (1)	None
Sargent, Green and Walters, 1972	Anecdotal case reports	75	Biofeedback of digital temperature plus autogenic training	29–30% of patients were "improved"	Unspecified
Sargent, Green and Walters, 1973	Single group outcome	22	Biofeedback of digital temperature plus autogenic training	63% of migraine patients "improved"	Variable

Study	Type	N	Treatment	Results	Follow-up
Turin and Johnson, 1976	Single group outcome	7	Biofeedback of digital temperature	4/7 definitely improved; reductions in headache frequency and duration; reduction in medication use	
Andreychuck and Skriver, 1974	Controlled group outcome	33	(1) Biofeedback of digital temp. (2) Biofeedback for EMG (3) Self-hypnosis	All groups showed symptomatic improvement; no differences between groups	None
Cohen, Levee, McArthur and Rickles, 1976	Controlled group outcome	45	(1) Biofeedback for digital temp. (2) EMG biofeedback (3) EEG alpha biofeedback	(1) and (2) were superior to (3) in producing therapeutic effects	None
Mullinix, Norton, Hack and Fishman, 1978	Controlled group outcome	11	(1) Biofeedback of digital temp. (2) False temperature biofeedback	Both groups improved; no differences between groups were obtained	3 months
Blanchard, Theobold, Williamson, Silver, and Brown, 1978	Controlled group outcome	30	(1) Biofeedback of digital temp. plus autogenic training and home practice (2) Progressive relaxation plus home practice (3) Waiting list control	Significant improvement for both (1) and (2) in headache frequency, duration, and intensity; 50% of patients in both groups significantly improved; 25% somewhat improved; relaxation more effective than biofeedback at conclusion of treatment	3 months; improvement maintained *with* continued practice; differences between 2 treatment groups disappeared
Lake, Rainey and Papsdorf, 1979	Controlled group outcome	24	(1) EMG biofeedback (2) Biofeedback for digital temp. (3) Biofeedback for digital temp. plus RET (4) Waiting list control	No difference between treatment groups at end of treatment	3 months; at the 3-month assessment, 6/6 in (1), 4/6 in (2), and 2/6 in (3) had reduced headache activity at least 33% from baseline levels

ache patients with either frontalis EMG biofeedback, biofeedback of digital temperature, or a combination of the two types of biofeedback. Of those with migraines who were given EMG biofeedback, eight showed a negative response and only two showed a good response. Response to hand temperature biofeedback was seventeen good and three negative. The combination treatment resulted in thirty-eight good, four fair, and eleven negative responses.

In addition to digital temperature biofeedback, two other physiological responses have been used in biofeedback treatment of migraines. Both of these responses, cephalic vasomotor activity and frontalis EMG, have plausible rationales to support their application in the treatment of migraine headache: cephalic vasomotor activity because the extracranial vascular system is the locus of headache pain, and frontalis EMG because the muscles of the head are equally tense for migraine as for muscle-contraction headache.

In spite of the theoretically advantageous position of peripheral vasculature in the development of migraine headaches, few patients have been treated with biofeedback for temporal artery vasoconstriction. Adams and his associates (Feuerstein and Adams, 1977; Sturgis, Tollison, and Adams, 1978) have reported on the use of this procedure with six patients, two each with migraine, muscle contraction, or mixed headache symptoms. Single subject experimental methodology was employed in each case and all were presented both biofeedback of frontalis EMG and of cephalic vasomotor activity in sequential fashion. In both reports, all patients learned to control both physiological responses. Likewise, all patients showed clinical improvement. Importantly and interestingly, the authors report that improvement in migraine headaches was associated with the cephalic vasomotor biofeedback phase, while the EMG biofeedback component was associated with improvement of muscle-contraction headaches. Follow-up data are available only for the two mixed headache patients (Sturgis et al., 1978), for whom maintenance of symptomatic improvement twenty weeks post-treatment is reported.

Friar and Beatty (1976) compared biofeedback for temporal artery vasoconstriction with biofeedback for constriction of the vasculature of the hand, in a controlled group outcome study. A significant reduction in the number of migraine attacks was effected for patients in the experimental group. Inasmuch as biofeedback for vasodilation of the hand is rather commonly used in the treatment of migraines, this involved the comparison of the therapeutic efficacy of the experimental treatment with an intervention that could have been (theoretically at least) actively antitherapeutic. In light of this, the value of the between group clinical difference which obtained is considerably reduced.

The issue of mechanism in the biofeedback digital temperature treatment of vascular headache is currently a matter of speculation. The favorable results obtained with biofeedback of pulse volume amplitude of the temporal artery suggests that patients learned to control their cephalic vasomotor activity prior to or during their headache. This notion is certainly face valid, but nonetheless requires documentation. Regional differences in cerebral blood flow were not obtained between eight subjects who were raising and those who were lowering the temperature of their hands (Mathews, Claghorn, Meyer, Largen, and Dobbins, 1978). Additionally, the hypothesis that increased digital blood flow would lead to diminuation of cephalic blood flow has not been supported (Price and Tursky, 1976).

Jointly, these two sets of data are quite damaging for the informal speculative mechanism that had been postulated to account for the observed improvement. That the effects might be an indirect result of general relaxation has been suggested by Price and Tursky (1976), who found no significant differences in digital vasodilation between groups presented feedback and a general relaxation strategy. The opposing view, that the mechanism for effecting hand temperature changes may be different between biofeedback and a general relaxation procedure (Taub, 1977), is still speculative. Although Taub (1977) reports that the biofeedback trainer can alter the physiological data (an impersonal investigator was able to train two of twenty-two subjects to control temperature, while a warm, friendly experimenter was successful with nineteen of twenty-two), it is not known how this would affect clinical outcome. The data certainly make it mandatory to require the demonstration that learned temperature control actually occurred, rather than reporting simply that patients were exposed to the biofeedback procedures.

In summary, Price and Tursky's data suggesting that the physiological changes from biofeedback or general relaxation strategies are not significantly different is consistent with the idea that the clinical effectiveness of biofeedback may be due to general relaxation effects. The slight clinical superiority of the traditional relaxation procedures may be due to their greater effectiveness in producing whole body relaxation or their superiority as a general coping skill. This does not deny the efficacy of biofeedback, but merely acknowledges the data indicating the slight relative inferiority of biofeedback when compared with standard relaxation techniques.

4. MUSCULO-SKELETAL SYSTEM

A. Muscle-Contraction Headaches

According to the Biofeedback Society of America, tension, or muscle-contraction, headaches are one of the five conditions for which demonstrated efficacy of biofeedback therapy has obtained. The proximal etiology of this disorder is thought to consist of sustained contraction of the skeletal muscles in the head, face, neck, and shoulders. The pain, generally described as a dull pressure or tightness that encircles the head like a band or clamp, often arises from the neck or occipital region and rotates around the head. Biofeedback treatment of muscle-contraction headaches is focused on reducing the level of tension in the affected muscles. This is typically accomplished by providing feedback for electromyographic activity of the forehead. Although the electrodes are generally placed over frontalis muscles, the feedback signal usually reflects activity of other facial muscles and the muscles of the neck and possibly the shoulders as well (Basmajian, 1976). This research is summarized in Table 5.

From the initial systematic case studies reporting the efficacy of EMG biofeedback in alleviating tension headaches (Budzynski, Stoyva, and Adler, 1970), this form of treatment has been subjected to repeated evaluation, much of it of considerable sophistication. Much of this research has employed a treatment package consisting of frontalis EMG biofeedback plus home relaxation practice. The specific

TABLE 5.
Biofeedback Treatment of Tension Headache

Study	Experimental design	Number of patients	Type of treatment	Results	Follow-up
Epstein, Hersen and Hemphill, 1974	Single subject experiment	1	EMG biofeedback plus relaxation training	Headaches reduced with biofeedback but eliminated only with addition of relaxation training	7 months; no return of headaches with continued relaxation
Epstein and Abel, 1977	Single subject experiment	6	EMG biofeedback *alone*	3/6 patients were much improved	Up to 18 months; treatment effects maintained
Wickramasekera, 1973	Single group outcome	5	EMG biofeedback	No data analysis; group data show decrease in headache	None
Budzynski, Stoyva, Adler and Mullaney, 1973	Controlled group outcome	18	(1) EMG biofeedback plus relaxation practice (2) False EMG biofeedback (3) Weekly monitoring	(1) 4/6 patients headache free (2) 1/6 patients was much improved	3 months; gains of patients in (1) were maintained
Cox, Freundlich and Meyer, 1975	Controlled group outcome	27	(1) EMG biofeedback plus home practice in relaxation (2) Relaxation training plus home practice (3) Placebo medication plus weekly monitoring	(1) and (2) showed marked reduction in headache activity with no difference between (1) and (2); (3) showed slight improvement	4 months; gains were maintained with slight further improvement
Chesney and Shelton, 1976	Controlled group outcome	24	(1) EMG biofeedback plus relaxation training plus home practice (2) EMG biofeedback (3) Relaxation training plus home practice (4) Monitoring only	(1) and (3) showed significant improvement in headache activity; (2) and (4) were essentially unchanged	None
Haynes, Griffin, Mooney and Parise, 1975	Controlled group outcome	21	(1) Relaxation training (2) EMG biofeedback (3) Monitoring	(1) and (2) showed marked reduction in headache activity; (3) remained unchanged	5–7 months by telephone; gains were maintained with further improvement for relaxation group
Hutchings and Reinking, 1976	Controlled group outcome	18	(1) Relaxation training (2) EMG biofeedback (3) Combination of (1) and (2)	(2) and (3) decreased headache by 66%; (1) decreased headache activity by 20%	4 weeks; both therapeutic gains and between group differences were maintained
Kondo and Canter, 1977	Controlled group outcome	20	(1) EMG biofeedback (2) Noncontingent EMG biofeedback	(1) reduced headache activity by approximately 80%; (2) reduced headache activity by approximately 30%	12 months; half of each group was located; 4/5 in (1) and 2/5 in (2) had maintained symptomatic improvement

contribution of the biofeedback component to this treatment combination is generally not directly evaluated.

In spite of relatively small patient samples in individual studies, the presence of several informative single subject experiments and six controlled group outcome studies provided a reasonable foundation on which to base conclusions. Epstein and his colleagues (Epstein and Abel, 1977; Epstein, Hersen and Hemphill, 1974) have reported positive therapeutic effects with 4/7 tension headache patients, which have been maintained for up to a year and a half past treatment. The patient in the earlier report achieved a reduction in headache activity with biofeedback alone, but did not totally eliminate them until relaxation training was added.

The efficacy of Budzynski *et al.*'s (1970) combined frontalis EMG feedback plus relaxation procedure in enabling patients to achieve reduction or elimination of muscle-contraction headache symptoms has been repeatedly documented including a controlled prospective study by Budzynski, Stoyva, Adler and Mullaney, 1973. As Epstein's and Philips's data suggest, however, a growing issue in this area of clinical research pertains to the degree to which biofeedback makes a unique contribution to the Budzynski *et al.* procedure. A related issue concerns the question of whether or not frontalis EMG biofeedback alone is significantly different in effectiveness from a standard relaxation procedure.

Certainly, when frontalis EMG biofeedback is presented as the only treatment for muscle contraction headaches (with no instructions for regular relaxation practice at home), its results have not been as uniformly effective as those of the combination. Hahnes, Griffin, Mooney and Parise (1975) found biofeedback effective on a group basis, but details of instructions for home practice were absent from the report. Only 50 percent of Epstein and Abel's (1977) patients responded positively to biofeedback alone. Finally, Chesney and Shelton (1976) found it ineffective on a group basis with a rather intensive training schedule. Indirect evidence from Budzynski's laboratory also points to a decrement in effectiveness, when regular practice of relaxation is not included in the treatment regimen. Two of the five cases in the initial report (Budzynski *et al.*, 1970) reported a return of their headache, associated with failure to continue regular practice in home relaxation. Additionally, the two patients in the veridical feedback condition of the controlled group study (Budzynski *et al.*, 1973) who were unsuccessful in achieving clinically meaningful reductions in their headaches were those who failed to practice relaxation at home regularly. In contrast, the only improved patient in the false feedback control group had practiced relaxation regularly. The results of Epstein *et al.*'s (1974) patient, who was previously mentioned, likewise substitute the importance of regular practice of relaxation, outside the biofeedback training sessions.

Philips (1977), in a small-scale refinement of the study by Budzynski *et al.* (1973), compared true and false EMG biofeedback, without regular relaxation practice, in six patients. At the conclusion of treatment, the two groups did not differ in their reported headache activity, although those in the veridical feedback condition significantly decreased EMG, while those receiving false feedback did not. However, at a follow-up 6–8 weeks after treatment, the true feedback patients reported headache improvement.

Given the success of frontalis EMG biofeedback and relaxation training in combination in reducing report of headache activity, it is not surprising that the two components should be compared with one another. To date, at least four controlled group outcome comparisons have been published.

The first, and in many ways the best, study was a comparison by Cox, Freundlich and Geyer (1975) which compared frontalis EMG biofeedback and progressive relaxation to a glucose placebo capsule given the strong therapeutic suggestion. The two behavioral treatment conditions both included instructions to practice relaxation at home regularly. Both behavioral treatment groups significantly reduced frontal EMG levels and headache activity more than the placebo group. At follow up, the improvement was still evident for 7/8 available patients in each group. No differences between groups were obtained.

Haynes *et al.* (1975) compared biofeedback of frontalis EMG, relaxation training, and a control condition consisting of instructions to "try to relax", with continued monitoring. Again, both treatment procedures led to significant reduction in headache activity, as compared with the control condition, but were not significantly different from one another. The effects lasted until a 1-week follow-up. The 5–7 month follow-up suggested maintenance of therapeutic effects, but subject loss makes these data only suggestive.

The three active treatment conditions in Chesney and Shelton's (1976) study are particularly interesting, in spite of the relatively small sample size. They compared frontalis EMG biofeedback, relaxation training, and home practice, the combination of the two to a no-treatment control. Results indicated that both treatment conditions which included relaxation training and home practice produced significant improvements. The biofeedback alone group improved no more than the control condition.

Finally, EMG biofeedback was compared with a relaxation condition, described as a combination of Jacobson–Wolpe procedures with Autogenic Training procedures, and a combination of the two approaches (Hutchings and Reinking, 1976). All patients were instructed to practice regularly at home. Patients in both conditions receiving biofeedback experienced a 66 percent reduction in headache activity, in comparison with those in the relaxation-only treatment who reported only a modest 20 percent reduction. Both therapeutic improvement and between-group differences were maintained. Three months post-treatment data were unchanged, but at both the 6 month and the one year follow-up assessments differential treatment effects had disappeared and continued improvement was apparently related only to continued regular practice in relaxation (Reinking, 1976).

In summary, the efficacy of the combined frontalis EMG biofeedback plus regular relaxation practice at home has repeatedly demonstrated efficacy in reducing report of tension headache activity. Relative efficacy over alternative interventions has not yielded such positive results. Miller (1978) has suggested that a pill placebo is probably an ineffective method of producing positive therapeutic expectancies in a group of patients who had been moderately refractive to traditional medical procedures, especially when compared to the placebo value of biofeedback. If this is so, then effective placebo controls are missing from this area of research also. In three quarters of the direct comparisons with relaxation training, biofeedback of frontal EMG produced equivalent reductions in headache measures, when both conditions practice relaxation regularly. When the regular practice component was removed from the biofeedback treatment procedure, its effectiveness was inferior to relaxation training. In the one study which found an advantage for EMG biofeedback training over relaxation training, follow-up revealed that the advantage was one of efficiency rather than efficacy.

In addition to the clinical improvement resulting from the combination treatment, a result that continually reappears in the data is the importance of maintaining a regular schedule of relaxation practice after the conclusion of treatment. Those who continued to practice maintained their improvement and those who discontinued practice either failed to derive benefit at all or else they relapsed after treatment.

The replicability of these results and the fact that several small controlled group outcome studies have been performed have both been noted previously. Although all reports did not contain follow-up data, those that did uniformly reported the maintenance of clinical effects. The interval since treatment was generally 3–7 months, although occasionally 12 month durations were noted with consistent effects. To reiterate, continued improvement was significantly associated with continued relaxation practice, with relapse occurring frequently when regular relaxation was discontinued.

Approximately 65–85 percent of the muscle-contraction headache patients who were treated with the combination treatment package reported clinical improvement. Although transfer to the patient's natural environment is typically assessed only by self-report, the addition of relaxation outside the laboratory in the patient's home or occupational setting would be expected to maximize the likelihood of transfer.

Finally, the question of mechanism of response has not been satisfactorily answered. Although resting EMG levels are higher for headache than non-headache patients (Vaughn, Pall and Haynes, 1977) and higher during headache than non-headache periods for headache periods for headache reporters (Haynes, *et al.* 1975), these data do not justify the conclusion that the increased EMG levels are responsible for the reports of headache pain. Recent data (Epstein, Abel, Collins, Parker and Cinciripini, 1978) subject this assumption to further doubt. They report that fluctuations in EMG activity and self-reports of pain were relatively independent. Furthermore, when EMG changes were directly altered with biofeedback in headache clients, correspondence of the two response classes was noted for only one of two subjects. Philips (1977) has noted and replicated many of these points in her own independent work on tension headaches.

Environmental factors seemed to make a reasonable contribution to changes in self-reports of pain. These results call into question the theoretical rationale supporting the application of EMG biofeedback technology to tension headache. In spite of the theoretical doubt regarding the physiological mechanism of the therapeutic efficacy of EMG biofeedback treatment of tension headache, the empirical results indicate first, that the combination treatment is clinically effective; and secondly, that EMG biofeedback results are generally indistinguishable from standard relaxation therapies. This does not mean that the mechanism of EMG biofeedback is relaxation. It does, however, place the burden of demonstrating a difference squarely on those who believe the two procedures operate via separate mechanisms.

B. Neuromuscular Rehabilitation

Our earlier review of clinical applications of biofeedback concluded that, "the work on the application of EMG feedback training to clinical problems is the oldest and the soundest work in the biofeedback area" (Blanchard and Young, 1974a). The basis for this evaluation was the clinical research done in the general area of rehabilitative medicine. The use of EMG feedback in neuromuscular rehabilitation began in the late 1950s and continued with little significant contribution from psychology until the advent of "biofeedback". This relationship changed only slightly after neuromuscular reeducation was recognized as part of the biofeedback movement. In spite of more psychologists engaged in research and service delivery in this area, neuromuscular reeducation continues to be dominated primarily by rehabilitation specialists.

In general, two factors were responsible for our conclusion of efficacy in the previous review. The patients almost invariably had suffered significant functional impairment several *years* before the rehabilitative attempts with feedback and this impairment had either failed to respond to traditional rehabilitative therapy attempts or else the initial positive response had plateaued with substantial impairment remaining. Secondly, a reasonable proportion of patients responded favorably to the addition of biofeedback to therapy and, more importantly, this improvement represented significant functional gains.

Given the status of biofeedback at the time of the earlier review, these two factors probably justified the favorable conclusions in spite of the fact that all of the evidence for biofeedback's efficacy was at the level of anecdotal or systematic case reports or single group outcome studies. However, the intervening years have witnessed an increase in the sophistication of biofeedback research in many areas that has not been matched in the area of neuromuscular reeducation. The majority of the research reports continue to be systematic case studies and single group outcome studies. In fact, only two controlled group outcome studies have been reported.

However, these were both performed in the same laboratory and utilized essentially the same design, so the second is basically only a replication of the first. Basmajian and his colleagues (Basmajian, Kukulka, Narayan and Takebe, 1975; Takebe and Basmajian, 1976) compared 40 minutes of conventional exercises to 20 minutes of exercises plus 20 minutes of biofeedback in 52 patients with residual foot dorsiflexion paresis following stroke. Both groups of patients made improvement in range of motion and ankle strength with the biofeedback group's progress almost double that of those given only traditional therapy. The biofeedback group also showed greater improvement in gait. These gains were maintained in follow-up evaluations 1–4 months post treatment.

Although the evidence clearly documents the clinical efficacy of the combination procedure and its relative efficacy over traditional procedures alone given for the same amount of time, a couple of issues remain. First, the independent contribution of EMG biofeedback was not assessed, so that conclusions must refer to the adjunctive use of biofeedback with traditional rehabilitation exercises. Secondly, Miller (1978) has noted that the control group which received only traditional therapy made substantial progress and raised the possibility that traditional approaches to treatment might be more, perhaps equally, effective, if they were successful in motivating patients to reach their full potential.

Both of these concerns are relevant to the issue of mechanism. Discussion in previous sections has focused on general relaxation and therapeutic expectancy as two of the more potent factors in competition with learned control of physiology via biofeedback as the mechanism underlying the observed effects. That biofeedback in neuromuscular rehabilitation might function to increase the patient's involvement in treatment more than standard procedures is a real possibility. There is some agreement on this point, as the following quotation from the Biofeedback Society Task Force Report Indicates:

> The uses of EMG feedback as an attention-getter, as a general motivator, as an added evaluation tool for the therapist, and as a generator of new approaches to old problems is important. These uses in themselves probably warrant the widespread use of EMG device in the PM and R clinic. It is important, however, to differentiate between contributions to treatment outcome due to these and other nonspecific factors and contributions that may or may not be made by the EMG feedback *per se*.... There is, however, no direct and final evidence that these gains are due to the specific effects of EMG feedback. (Fernando and Basmajian, 1978, p. 440).

Reports of the efficacy of EMG biofeedback in rehabilitation have appeared for assisting patients in gaining some functional control of paralyzed muscles, as well as in relaxing spastic muscles. Clinical improvement has been reported for a number of conditions, even if for only one or two cases. These include hemiplegia of both upper and lower extremities, incomplete lesions of the spinal cord, blepharospasm, spasmodic torticollis, chronic pain due to muscle spasm, temporomandibular joint pain and bruxism, poliomyletis, reduction of subvocalization while reading, teaching appropriate facial expression to the blind, reduction of stuttering, Parkinson's disease, and cerebral palsy. For a more complete report of EMG biofeedback application to these conditions the reader is referred to several recent reviews of the area (Basmajian and Hatch, 1979; Fernando and Basmajian, 1978; Keefe and Surwit, 1978).

5. ELECTROENCEPHALOGRAM

A. Alpha Training

Although biofeedback training to produce relatively high levels of alpha in the EEG was one of the initial areas of biofeedback to receive extensive popular attention (Kamiya, 1968; Brown, 1974) because of its purported ability to produce a drug-free "high", such training has proved to have little clinical utility. A major clinical trial of alpha biofeedback with a general psychiatric population (Glueck and Stroebel, 1975) failed to find any clinical utility for it. Other attempts at using it to treat alcoholism, drug abuse, and headaches have been reported (Kurtz, 1974; Lamontagne *et al.*, 1975; McKenzie, 1974). However, these studies seem so poorly controlled as to yield few interpretable data.

Chronic pain. Another application of biofeedback of EEG alpha has been in the treatment of chronic pain. The hypothesis for this approach originated in the observation that some experienced mediators and yogis had very high levels of alpha in their EEGs and were also able to tolerate experiences that would normally be considered painful.

Gannon and Sternbach (1971) described a systematic case study of one patient with chronic head pain. Over the course of 70 training sessions, he learned to produce fairly high levels of alpha, even without the assistance of feedback. However, there was no noticeable reduction in his pain.

In a very ambitious study, Melzack and Perry (1975) treated three groups of patients suffering from chronic, continuous, unremitting pain which was not completely relieved by analgesics or narcotics. One group received alpha biofeedback training, the second hypnotic training, and the third a combination of biofeedback and hypnotic training. Only the group receiving the combination treatment reported significant reductions of pain on a self-report measure during the treatment. Unfortunately, this potentially valuable study contains a major confusion. The group receiving the combination treatment also had 50 percent more treatment sessions than the other groups. Furthermore, there were no tests of differences in pain reduction between groups, so it is not known if the obtained change was reliably different from that of the other groups.

Once again, the clinical utility of biofeedback training of EEG alpha is unsupported. Since the original rationale was based on correlation evidence and since the production of occipital alpha with biofeedback training appears to involve primarily an oculomotor strategy of "not looking" (Plotkin, 1976), there appears to be no basis to expect occipital alpha biofeedback training to have any clinical value.

B. Epilepsy

Although the responsivity of seizure activity to emotional and placebo factors has been recognized and the utility of behavioral techniques in its treatment documented (Mostofsky and Balaschak, 1977), the original notion that biofeedback might be of clinical value with these disorders came from the basic research laboratory. Sterman and his associates (Sterman, 1973; Sterman and Friar, 1972) adopted the techniques which has resulted in an increased seizure threshold in their laboratory cats to work with humans. These procedures involved providing feedback for the production of 12–14 hr EEG activity recorded over the sensorimotor cortex and called the sensorimotor rhythm (SMR).

Sterman's initial reports were systematic case studies and informal single subject experiments with four patients whose frequent seizures were poorly controlled with medication. As treatment continued, both the frequency and intensity of seizure activity diminished. Discontinuation of treatment was acccompanied by a return of seizure activity. These results were replicated by Lubar and Bahler (1976) with eight patients and by Kuhlman (1976) with five. However, Kaplan (1975) was unsuccessful in her attempt at replication.

Other investigators have reported clinical success when feedback was given for the occurrence of EEG frequencies other than those of the SMR (Kaplan, 1975; Finley, Smith and Etherton, 1975; Wyler, Lockard, Ward and Finch, 1976; Quy,

1976; Sterman and Macdonald, 1978). The level of sophistication of this research has not progressed beyond the stage of controlled single-subject experiments, regrettably.

In their review of EEG biofeedback for epilepsy Kuhlman and Kaplan (1979) indicate that 27 of 38 patients with poorly controlled seizure activity showed clinical improvement following biofeedback. For those states reporting the degree of effect, seizure activity was reduced an average of approximately 65 percent. That this improvement occurred outside the laboratory is probably begging the question, since the seizures were episodic and typically occurred outside of the laboratory setting. A more pertinent question relates to persistence of effects, after discontinuance of training; and this will be discussed subsequently.

The issue of mechanism in biofeedback treatment of seizure activity is intriguing. Given the small number of patients and the current sophistication of the literature, all answers to this question must be quite tentative. Previously, we (Blanchard and Young, 1974) had pointed out that the interruption or discontinuation of biofeedback training for Sterman's patients constituted an informal withdrawal phase and that the concomitant increase in seizure frequency, coupled with a subsequent reduction with resumption of training, provided good evidence that the training procedure was responsible for the change in epileptic activity. These results were replicated by Lubar and Bahler (1976).

The attribution of this therapeutic change to increased SMR, however, is far from clear cut. First, several investigators (Sterman, Macdonald and Stone, 1974; Finley et al., 1975; Lubar and Bahler, 1976; Wyler et al., 1976; Quy, 1976; Sterman and Macdonald, 1978) positively reinforced suppression of various categories of high-voltage slow-frequency activity, in addition to enhancement of SMR or activity in other frequency bands. Second, clinical improvement was generally *not* related to feedback for a particular EEG frequency. Even Sterman and Macdonald (1978), who reported that three patients improved specific to the "enhance 12–15 Hz" condition, noted that the other three patients improved steadily across time. In fact, positive clinical results have been obtained with feedback of EEG frequencies ranging from 7–30 Hz. Generally, when the biofeedback treatment procedures are discontinued, a reversal in seizure activity occurs. Significantly, however, when training sessions continue but feedback is noncontingent (Finley, et al., 1975; Kuhlman, 1976) or the contingency is reversed (Sterman and Macdonald, 1978), clinical improvement is generally maintained.

Finally, data from concomitant change in the EEG has failed to show a consistent increase within frequency bands patients were attempting to increase. As we mentioned earlier, failure to obtain SMR enhancement seriously undermines the case for SMR increases being the causal factor in observed clinical changes. More importantly, however, investigators have repeatedly observed that the resting EEGs of their patients appear to "normalize." That is, the patients' EEGs contain less epileptiform activity, less high-amplitude slow-wave activity and more low-voltage fast activity typical of normal, alert EEGs. Perhaps, the inclusion of contingencies to suppress certain abnormal EEG frequencies has been the most important aspect of the training procedures. One thing is certain, however, and that is that the time has arrived for better controlled investigations with a larger patient sample. The clinical improvement appears to be real, but adequate controls and follow-ups are going to have to be included to allow informed evaluation of the clinical utility of biofeedback in the treatment of epilepsy.

6. CONCLUSIONS

In 1974, we (Blanchard and Young, 1974a) published a fairly comprehensive review of the published research on clinical applications of biofeedback. That review was compiled during 1973, approximately six years ago. In that review, we drew our conclusions as to the state of development and knowledge of the field. As a conclusion for this current review, it is our intention to contrast the present state of the field of clinical biofeedback with our view of it six years ago. (Of course, our current review has been limited to medical problems for which some body of literature exists.)

(1) *Blood pressure.* In 1974, we concluded, "... it does appear that biofeedback procedures can have beneficial effects on elevated BP. However, definitive conclusions must await a controlled outcome study..." As noted in the first section of this chapter, much further research has been completed in the area of hypertension, including several controlled group outcome studies. Our conclusion at this point must be that direct biofeedback of BP has not stood the test of rigorous experimental testing. Initial promising results fail to hold up on replication (Blanchard et al., 1979); there is a lack of consistent, clinically-meaningful decreases in BP across a randomly selected group of hypertensive patients given BP biofeedback. Despite this overall negative evaluation, the fact remains that some individuals show very good responses to BP biofeedback. It may be that a promising avenue for research would be to try to capitalize on these individual differences, by determining if we can select patients on psychological or physiological parameters, who have a high probability of responding favorably to this treatment.

Other forms of biofeedback training, such as frontal EMG for relaxation, have also failed to live up to initial promise. The one exception, of course, is Patel's work which has shown repeatedly that the combination of passive relaxation training, yoga, and GSR biofeedback is a consistently powerful treatment package with hypertensive patients.

(2) *Cardiac arrhythmias.* We concluded in 1974, "... these results are very interesting and highly suggestive, but they do not represent strong *scientific* evidence for the efficacy of biofeedback procedures because of the lack of adequate controls." Six years later, almost the same conclusions can be drawn. There has been some replication of the beneficial effects on PVCs and also on episodic sinus tachycardia of heart rate biofeedback. However, the lack of much recent research in this area leaves us in the same place we were six years ago: the work is interesting and provocative, but has not been subjected to rigorous controlled evaluation.

(3) *Peripheral vascular disorders* (*Raynaud's disease*). In 1974, there were three reported cases of the treatment of Raynaud's disease with biofeedback. We concluded, "... the results are suggestive but certainly not conclusive; ..." As noted in the appropriate section of the chapter, there is much stronger evidence now. At a recent meeting of the Biofeedback Society of America (San Diego, 1979), investigators from four separate laboratories presented results of groups of patients from 10 to 50, all showing definite widespread therapeutic effects from digital temperature

training. We conclude that temperature biofeedback training does seem an effective treatment for idiopathic Raynaud's disease. However, we must also conclude, based on Surwit et al.'s (1978a) study, that autogenic training is equally as effective as digital temperature biofeedback.

(4) *Migraine headaches.* In 1974, we wrote, "The Menninger group may have discovered an important treatment for migraine headaches.... it is difficult to assess the role biofeedback of skin temperature plays. The suggestive results warrant further investigation but not the wholesale adoption of this technique." As the section of this chapter notes, digital temperature biofeedback, either alone or in combination with autogenic training, has been shown in controlled group outcome studies to be more effective than no treatment or mere monitoring of headache activity. However, it has not been shown to be more effective than various forms of relaxation training. We concluded that there was reason to conclude that the major active components were either a placebo (like expectancy effect) or a relaxation effect, or some combination of these two. Digital temperature biofeedback has certainly not been shown to be more effective than control conditions utilizing these two factors.

(5) *Tension headaches.* For this problem, we concluded in 1974, "It is also fairly well established that a combination of EMG feedback training and home practice in relaxation is very effective in the treatment of tension headaches.... However, the question remains as to the therapeutic contribution of EMG feedback." Six years later, a very similar conclusion obtains: it has now been demonstrated at least four more times in controlled outcome studies that the combination of frontal EMG biofeedback and regular practice of relaxation is very helpful in the initial treatment of tension headaches. It has also been demonstrated that relaxation training alone is almost equally effective as the combination. Moreover, frontal EMG biofeedback training in the absence of instruction in relaxation is *not* consistently effective. In fact, serious question has been raised about the role of muscle contraction in tension headaches (Epstein et al., 1978; Philips, 1977; 1979). Thus, although we now know several ways to help the patient with chronic tension headaches, we are not sure what causes the headache or exactly how our techniques help. Our best guess is that it is a combination of relaxation training and learning to apply this training as a stress coping strategy.

(6) *Neuromuscular re-education.* We optimistically concluded in 1974, "In such areas as ... the retraining of paralyzed muscles in hemiplegics, the evidence is quite sound that EMG feedback training has marked therapeutic effects." Re-examining the data presented in that article, we note our own caveat, "Although there are no controlled group outcome studies in the literature, ...", which we went on to ignore because of "the prolonged baseline periods ... and the failures of previous attempts at traditional rehabilitation procedures ..." Thus, failing to heed our own standards, we enthusiastically endorsed this work. Six years later, our enthusiasm is somewhat dampened. There is one controlled group outcome study (Basmajian et al., 1976), which ostensibly shows an advantage in adding EMG biofeedback to standard rehabilitation training. However, as noted in a critique of that study, that conclusion should be tempered because of potential confusions.

We are thus left with a field in which much clinical work has taken place and some additional systematic case reports and series have been reported, but for which the clearcut scientific demonstration of additional benefits from adding EMG biofeedback to good, standard physical therapy are lacking.

(7) *Alpha training.* In 1974, we concluded, "the evidence for clinical efficacy of training to produce alpha is very poor." In light of the research since then, we see no reason to change that conclusion.

(8) *Epilepsy.* Again examining our 1974 paper, we concluded, "the work on bio-feedback training to produce a high incidence of sensorimotor rhythm seems quite promising... this training does seem to lead to a suppression of a variety of types of seizure disorders." The same general conclusion seems true, but in slightly altered form. There is now evidence, from four separate laboratories, that training to produce or suppress certain aspects of the EEG has beneficial effects on seizure disorders. There are several series of single case experiments which confirm this. The major change seems to be that the most efficacious training approach is one in which there are efforts to "normalize" the EEG; that is, to suppress excessive slow activity in some patients or to increase faster activity in other patients. This normalization makes much use of power spectral analyses. Thus, it is not training in producing sensorimotor rhythm, *per se*, that has emerged as beneficial, but rather it is training to alter the power spectral analysis of the EEG in direction of appearing more "normal" which is beneficial to epileptics with motor seizures.

Biofeedback training as a clinical enterprise is now about a dozen years old. As the conclusions listed above enumerate, its early promise as a major new thera-peutic modality has yet to be realized, except in a few limited instances, such as with Raynaud's disease and chronic fecal incontinence. As noted in this review and in other places (Silver and Blanchard, 1978), non-machine based techniques, such as varieties of relaxation training, seem equally efficacious with most of the medical disorders treated by biofeedback.

The primary long-range legacy of biofeedback as an area of study may not be its clinical efficacy; instead, that legacy may be that it led to a major interest in, and research in, the psychological treatment of traditionally medical disorders. As such, it was certainly one of the chief forbears of the new "behavioral medicine" move-ment in the American and of the new medical psychology described in this volume. Another legacy of biofeedback will certainly be a better, and empirically based, understanding of many medical disorders. Philips' (1977) work on tension head-aches is an example of this. The new interest in medical problems by behavioral scientists, chiefly psychologists, has uncovered new insights into these disorders.

Finally, we would like to call for more research in one particular area of research pertaining to biofeedback, the role of individual differences. There is ample evi-dence that some individuals are helped by a biofeedback-based treatment; more-over, in many disorders 50 percent or better of a randomly selected population of victims of a disorder are helped. What is needed now is a study of individual differences to enable us to predict ahead of time who is a good candidate and who is not, so that patient and treatment strategy can be better matched.

ACKNOWLEDGEMENT

Preparation of this manuscript was supported in part by a grant from the National Institute of Neurological and Communicative Disorders and Stroke, NS-15235.

REFERENCES

Adler, C. S. and Adler, S. M. (1975) Biofeedback-psychotherapy for the treatment of headache: A five-year follow-up. Paper presented at the joint meeting of the American Association for the Study of Headache and the Scandinavian Migraine Society, Bergen, Norway, June, 1975.

Andreychuk, T. and Skriver, C. (1975) Hypnosis and biofeedback in the treatment of migraine headache, *International Journal of Clinical and Experimental Hypnosis*, **23**, 172–183.

Basmajian, J. V. (1976) Facts vs. myths in EMG biofeedback, *Biofeedback and Self-Regulation*, **1**, 369–371.

Basmajian, J. V. and Hatch, J. P. (1979) Biofeedback and the modification of skeletal muscular dysfunctions, in R. J. Gatchel and K. P. Price (Eds.) *Clinical Applications of Biofeedback: Appraisal and Status*, Pergamon Press, New York.

Basmajian, J. V., Kukulka, C. G., Narayan, M. G. and Takebe, K. (1975) Biofeedback treatment of foot-drop compared with standard rehabilitation technique: Effects on voluntary control and strength, *Archives of Physical Medicine and Rehabilitation*, **56**, 231–236.

Benson, H., Shapiro, D., Tursky, B. and Schwartz, G. E. (1971) Decreased systolic blood pressure through operant conditioning techniques in patients with essential hypertension, *Science*, **173**, 740–742.

Benson, H., Rosner, B. A., Marzetta, B. R. and Klemchuk, H. M. (1974a) Decreased blood pressure in pharmacologically treated hypertensive patients who regularly elicited the relaxation response, *Lancet*, **I**, 289–291.

Benson, H., Rosner, B. A., Marzetta, B. R. and Klemchuk, H. P. (1974b) Decreased blood pressure in borderline hypertensive subjects who practiced meditation, *Journal of Chronic Diseases*, **27**, 163–169.

Blanchard, E. B. (1979) Biofeedback and the modification of cardiovascular dysfunctions, in R. J. Gatchel, and K. P. Price (Eds.) *Clinical Applications of Biofeedback: Appraisal and Status*, Pergamon Press, New York.

Blanchard, E. B. and Young, L. D. (1973) Self-control of cardiac functioning: A promise as yet unfulfilled, *Psychological Bulletin*, **79**, 145–163.

Blanchard, E. B. and Young, L. D. (1974a) Clinical applications of biofeedback training: A review of evidence, *Archives of General Psychiatry*, **30**, 573–589.

Blanchard, E. B. and Young, L. D. (1974b) Of promises and evidence: A reply to Engel. *Psychological Bulletin*, **81**, 44–46.

Blanchard, E. B. and Haynes, M. R. (1975) Biofeedback treatment of a case of Raynaud's Disease, *Journal of Behavior Therapy and Experimental Psychiatry*, **6**, 230–234.

Blanchard, E. B. and Abel, G. G. (1976) An experimental case study of the biofeedback treatment of a rape-induced psychophysiological cardiovascular disorder, *Behavior Therapy*, **7**, 113–119.

Blanchard, E. B. and Epstein, L. H. (1977) Clinical applications of biofeedback, in M. Hersen, R. M. Eisler and P. M. Miller (Eds.), *Progress in Behavior Modification*, Vol. IV, Academic Press, New York.

Blanchard, E. B., Young, L. D. and Haynes, M. R. (1975) A simple feedback system for the treatment of elevated blood pressure, *Behavior Therapy*, **6**, 241–245.

Blanchard, E. B., Haynes, M. R., Young, L. D. and Scott, R. W. (1977) The use of feedback training and a stimulus control procedure to obtain large magnitude increases in heart rate outside of the laboratory, *Biofeedback and Self-Regulation*, **2**, 81–91.

Blanchard, E. B., Theobald, D. E., Williamson, D. A., Silver, B. V. and Brown, D. A. (1978) Temperature biofeedback in the treatment of migraine headaches, *Archives of General Psychiatry*, **35**, 581–588.

Blanchard, E. B., Miller, S. T., Abel, G. G., Haynes, M. R. and Wicker, R. (1979) Evaluation of biofeedback in the treatment of borderline essential hypertension, *Journal of Applied Behavior Analysis*, **12**, 99–109.

Bleecker, E. R. and Engel, B. T. (1973a) Learned control of ventricular rate in patients with atrial fibrillation, *Psychosomatic Medicine*, **35**, 161–175.

Bleecker, E. R. and Engel, B. T. (1973b) Learned control of cardiac rate and cardiac conduction in the Wolff–Parkinson–White Syndrome, *New England Journal of Medicine*, **288**, 560–562.

Brown, B. B. (1974) *New Mind, New Body*, Harper & Row, New York.

Budzynski, T., Stoyva, J. and Adler, C. (1970) Feedback-induced muscle relaxation: Application to tension headache, *Journal of Behavior Therapy and Experimental Psychiatry*, **1**, 205–211.

Budzynski, T. H., Stoyva, J. M., Adler, C. S. and Mullaney, D. J. (1973) EMG biofeedback and tension headache: A controlled outcome study, *Psychosomatic Medicine*, **6**, 509–514.

Butler, F. (1978) *Biofeedback: A Survey of the Literature*, Plenum, New York.

Chesney, M. A. and Shelton, J. L. (1976) A comparision of muscle relaxation and electromyogram biofeedback treatments for muscle contraction headache, *Journal of Behavior Therapy and Experimental Psychiatry*, **7**, 221–225.

Cohen, M. J., Levee, J. R., McArthur, D. L. and Rickles, W. H. (1976) Physiological and psychological
    dimensions of migraine headache and biofeedback training, *Biofeedback and Self-Regulation*, **1**, 348
    (abstract).
Cox, D. J., Freundlich, A. and Meyer, R. G. (1975) Differential effectiveness of electromyograph feed-
    back, verbal relaxation instructions, and medication placebo with tension headaches, *Journal of
    Consulting and Clinical Psychology*, **43**, 892–899.
Diamond, S., Diamond–Falk, J. and DeVeno, T. (1978) The value of biofeedback in the treatment of
    chronic headache: A five year retrospective study, *Proceedings of the Biofeedback Society of America
    Ninth Annual Meeting*, pp. 30–31, Biofeedback Society of America, Denver.
Diamond, S., Medina, J. L. and Franklin, M. (1975) The treatment of headache with different modalities
    of biofeedback therapy. Unpublished manuscript. Diamond Headache Clinic, Chicago.
Elder, S. T. and Eustis, N. K. (1975) Instrumental blood pressure conditioning in out-patient hyperten-
    sives, *Behaviour Research & Therapy*, **13**, 185–188.
Elder, S. T., Ruiz, Z. B., Deabler, H. L. and Dillenkoffer, R. L. (1973) Instrumental conditioning of
    diastolic blood pressure in essential hypertensive patients, *Journal of Applied Behavior Analysis*, **6**,
    377–382.
Engel, B. T. (1974) Comment on self-control of cardiac functioning: A promise as yet unfulfilled,
    Psychological Bulletin, **84**, 43.
Engel, B. T. and Bleecker, E. R. (1974) Application of operant conditioning techniques to the control of
    cardiac arrhythmias, in P. A. Obrist, A. H. Black, J. Brener, and L. V. DiCara (Eds.) *Cardiovascular
    Psychophysiology*, Aldine, Chicago.
Epstein, L. H. and Abel, G. G. (1977) An analysis of biofeedback training effects for tension headache
    patients, *Behavior Therapy*, **8**, 37–47.
Epstein, L. H., Abel, G. G., Collins, F., Parker, L. and Cinciripini, P. M. (1978) The relationship between
    frontalis muscle activity and self-reports of headache pain, *Behaviour Research and Therapy*, **16**,
    153–160.
Epstein, L. H., Hersen, M. and Hemphill, D. P. (1974) Contingent music and anti-tension exercises in the
    treatment of a chronic tension headache patient, *Journal of Behavior Therapy and Experimental
    Psychiatry*, **5**, 59–63.
Fernando, C. K. and Basmajian, J. V. (1978) Biofeedback in physical medicine and rehabilitation,
    Biofeedback and Self-Regulation, **3**, 435–455.
Feuerstein, M., and Adams, H. E. (1977) Cephalic vasomotor feedback in the modification of migraine
    headache, *Biofeedback and Self-Regulation*, **2**, 241–254.
Finley, W. W., Smith, H. A. and Etherton, M. D. (1975) Reduction of seizures and normalization of the
    EEG in a severe epileptic following sensorimotor biofeedback training, *Biological Psychology*, **2**,
    195–209.
Fotopoulos, S. S., and Sunderland, W. P. (1978) Biofeedback in the treatment of psychophysiologic
    disorders, *Biofeedback and Self-Regulation*, **3**, 331–361.
Frankel, B. L., Patel, D. J., Horwitz, D., Friedewald, W. T. and Gaarder, K. R. (1978) Treatment of
    hypertension with biofeedback and relaxation techniques, *Psychosomatic Medicine*, **40**, 276–293.
Friar, L. R. and Beatty, J. (1976) Migraine: Management by a trained control of vasoconstriction,
    Journal of Consulting and Clinical Psychology, **44**, 46–53.
Gannon, L. and Sternbach, R. A. (1971) Alpha enhancement as a treatment for pain: A case study,
    Journal of Behavior Therapy and Experimental Psychiatry, **2**, 209–213.
Gleuck, B. C. and Stroebel, C. F. (1975) Biofeedback and meditation in the treatment of psychiatric
    illnesses, *Comprehensive Psychiatry*, **16**, 303–321.
Goldman, H., Kleinman, K. M., Snow, M. Y., Bidus, D. R. and Korol, B. (1975) Relationship between
    essential hypertension and cognitive functioning: Effects of biofeedback, *Psychophysiology*, **12**,
    569–573.
Haynes, S. N., Griffin, P., Mooney, D. and Parise, M. (1975) Electromyographic biofeedback and
    relaxation instructions in the treatment of muscle contraction headaches, *Behavior Therapy*, **6**,
    672–678.
Hersen, M. and Barlow, D. H. (1976) *Single Case Experimental Designs: Strategies for Studying Behavior
    Change*, Pergamon Press, New York.
Hutchings, D. F. and Reinking, R. H. (1976) Tension headaches: What form of therapy is most effective?
    Biofeedback and Self-Regulation, **1**, 183–190.
Jacobson, A. M., Hackett, T. P., Surman, O. S., and Silverberg, E. L. (1973) Raynaud phenomenon:
    Treatment with hypnotic and operant technique, *Journal of American Medical Association*, **225**,
    739–740.
Kamiya, J. (1968) Conscious control of brain waves, *Psychology Today*, **1**(1), 57–60.
Kaplan, B. J. (1975) Biofeedback in epileptics: Equivocal relationship of reinforced EEG frequency to
    seizure reduction, *Epilepsia*, **16**, 477–485.

Keefe, F. J. and Surwit, R. S. (1978) Electromyographic biofeedback: Behavioral treatment of neuro-muscular disorders, *Journal of Behavioral Medicine*, **1**, 13–24.

Kondo, C. and Canter, A. (1977) True and false electromyographic feedback: Effect on tension headache, *Journal of Abnormal Psychology*, **86**, 93–95.

Kristt, D. A. and Engel, B. T. (1975) Learned control of blood pressure in patients with high blood pressure, *Circulation*, **51**, 370–378.

Kuhlman, W. N. (1976) EEG feedback training of epileptic patients: Clinical and electroencephalo-graphic analysis. Unpublished doctoral dissertation, Yale University.

Kuhlman, W. N. and Kaplan, B. J. (1979) Clinical applications of EEG biofeedback training, in *Clinical Applications of Biofeedback*, Gatchel, R. and Price, K. (Eds.), Pergamon Press, New York.

Kurtz, P. S. (1974) Treating chemical dependency through biofeedback, *Hospital Progress*, **55**, 68–69.

Lamontagne, Y., Hand, I., Annable, L. and Gagnon, M. (1975) Physiological and psychological effects of alpha and EMG feedback training with college drug users: A pilot study, *Canadian Psychiatric Association Journal*, **20**, 337–349.

Lang, P. J., Troyer, W. G., Twentyman, C. T. and Gatchel, R. J. (1975) Differential effects of heart rate modification training on college students, older males, and patients with ischemic heart disease, *Psychosomatic Medicine*, **37**, 429–446.

Love, W. A., Montgomery, D. D. and Moeller, T. A. (1974) Working paper number 1. Unpublished manuscript. Nova University, Ft. Lauderdale, Fla.

Lubar, J. F. and Bahler, W. W. (1976) Behavioral management of epileptic seizures following EEG biofeedback training of the sensorimotor rhythm, *Biofeedback and Self-Regulation*, **1**, 77–104.

Mathews, R. J., Claghorn, J. L., Meyer, J. S., Largen, J. and Dobbins, K. (1978) Relationship between volitional alteration in skin temperature and regional cerebral blood flow in normal subjects, *Proceedings of the Biofeedback Society of America Ninth Annual Meeting*, Biofeedback Society of America, Denver.

May, D. S. and Weber, C. A. (1976) Temperature feedback training with a symptom reduction in Raynaud's Disease: A controlled study. Paper presented to 7th Annual Meeting of Biofeedback Research Society, Colorado Springs.

Melzack, R. and Perry, C. (1975) Self-regulation of pain: The use of alpha-feedback and hypnotic training for the control of chronic pain, *Experimental Neurology*, **46**, 452–469.

Miller, N. E. (1975) Clinical applications of biofeedback: Voluntary control of heart rate, rhythm, and blood pressure, in H. I. Russek (Ed.) *New Horizons in Cardiovascular Practice*, p. 245–246, University Park Press, Baltimore.

Miller, N. E. (1978) Biofeedback and Visceral Learning, in *Annual Review of Psychology*, Vol. 29, Annual Reviews Inc., Palo Alto, Cal.

Moeller, T. A. and Love, W. A. (1974) A method to reduce arterial hypertension through muscular relaxation. Unpublished manuscript. Nova University, Ft. Lauderdale, Fla.

Mostofsky, D. I. and Balaschak, B. A. (1977) Psychological control of seizures, *Psychological Bulletin*, **84**, 723–750.

Mullinix, J., Norton, B., Hack, S. and Fishman, M. (1978) Skin temperature biofeedback and migraine, *Headache*, **17**, 242–244.

Patel, C. H. (1973) Yoga and biofeedback in the management of hypertension, *Lancet*, **II**, 1053–1055.

Patel, C. H. (1975) 12-Month follow-up of yoga and biofeedback in the management of hypertension, *Lancet*, **I**, 62–67.

Patel, C. H. and North, W. R. S. (1975) Randomized controlled trial of yoga and biofeedback in management of hypertension, *Lancet*, **II**, 93–99.

Philips, C. (1977) The modification of tension headache pain using EMG biofeedback, *Behaviour Research and Therapy*, **15**, 119–129.

Philips, C. (1978) Tension headache: Theoretical problems, *Behaviour Research and Therapy*, **16**, 249–261.

Pickering, G. W. (1968) *High blood pressure*, 2nd Ed., Grune & Stratton, New York.

Pickering, T. and Gorham, G. (1975) Learned heart-rate controlled by a patient with a ventricular parasystolic rhythm, *Lancet*, **II**, 252–253.

Pickering, T. G. and Miller, N. E. (1977) Learned voluntary control of heart rate and rhythm in two subjects with premature ventricular contractions, *British Heart Journal*, **39**, 152–159.

Plotkin, W. B. (1976) On the self-regulation of the occipital alpha rhythm: Control strategies, states of consciousness, and the role of physiological feedback, *Journal of Experimental Psychology: General*, **105**, 66–99.

Price, K. P. and Tursky, B. (1976) Vascular reactivity of migraineurs and non-migraineurs: A compari-son of responses to self-control procedures, *Headache*, **16**, 210–217.

Quy, R. J. (1976) Biofeedback training in the treatment of epilepsy. Paper presented at Psychophysiology Group, London, December, 1976.

Reinking, R. (1976) Follow-up and extension of "Tension headaches: What method is most effective?". Paper presented at the meeting of the Biofeedback Research Society, Colorado Springs, Colorado, Feb., 1976.

Sargent, J. D., Green, E. E. and Walters, E. D. (1972) The use of autogenic feedback training in a pilot study of migraine and tension headaches, *Headache*, **12**, 120–125.

Schwartz, G. E. (1972) Clinical applications of biofeedback: Some theoretical issues, in D. Upper and D. S. Goodenough (Eds.) *Behavior Modification with the Individual Patient: Proceedings of Third Annual Brockton Symposium on Behavior Therapy*, Roche, Nutley, N.J.

Schwartz, G. E. and Shapiro, D. (1973) Biofeedback and essential hypertension: Current findings and theoretical concerns, in L. Birk (ed.), *Biofeedback: Behavioral Medicine*, Grune & Stratton, New York.

Scott, R. W., Blanchard, E. B., Edmundson, E. D. and Young, L. D. (1973) A shaping procedure for heart-rate control in chronic tachycardia, *Perceptual and Motor Skills*, **37**, 327–338.

Sedlacek, K. and Heczey, M. (1977) A specific biofeedback treatment for dysmenorrhea, in *Proceedings of the Biofeedback Society of America*, p. 26, 8th Annual Meeting, March, 1977, Orlando, Florida.

Shoemaker, J. E. and Tasto, D. L. (1975) The effects of muscle relaxation on blood pressure in essential hypertensives, *Behavior Research and Therapy*, **13**, 29–43.

Sidman, M. (1960) *Tactics of Scientific Research*, Basic Books, New York.

Silver, B. V. and Blanchard, E. B. (1978) Biofeedback and relaxation training in the treatment of psychophysiological disorders: Or, are the machines really necessary? *Journal of Behavioral Medicine*, **1**, 217–239.

Stambler, J., Stambler, R., Riedlinger, W. F., Algera, G. and Roberts, R. H. (1976) Hypertension screening of 1 million Americans, *JAMA* **235**, 2299–2306.

Stephenson, N. L. (1976) Two cases of successful treatment of Raynaud's Disease with relaxation in biofeedback training supportive psychotherapy. Paper presented to 7th Annual Meeting of Biofeedback Research Society, Colorado Springs, February 1976.

Sterman, M. B. (1973) Neurophysiological and clinical studies of sensorimotor EEG biofeedback training: Some effects on epilepsy, in L. Birk (Ed.), *Biofeedback: Behavioral Medicine*, Grune & Stratton, New York.

Sterman, M. B. and Friar, L. (1972) Suppression of seizures in an epileptic following sensorimotor EEG feedback training, *EEG and Clinical Neurophysiology*, **33**, 89–95.

Sterman, M. B. and Macdonald, L. R. (1978) Effects of central cortical EEG feedback training on seizure incidence in poorly controlled epileptics, *Epilepsia*, **19**, 207–222.

Sturgis, E. T., Tollison, C. D. and Adams, H. G. (1978) Modification of combined migraine–muscle contraction headaches using BVP and EMG biofeedback, *Journal of Applied Behavior Analysis*, **11**, 215–223.

Surwit, R. S., Pilon, R. N. and Fenton, C. H. (1978a) Behavioral treatment of Raynaud's disease, *Journal of Behavioral Medicine*, **1**, 323–336.

Surwit, R. S., Shapiro, D. and Good, I. M. (1978b) Comparison of cardiovascular biofeedback, neuromuscular biofeedback, and meditation in the treatment of borderline essential hypertension, *Journal of Consulting and Clinical Psychology*, **46**, 252–263.

Takebe, K. and Basmajian, J. V. (1976) Gait analysis in stroke patients to assess treatments of foot-drop, *Archives of Physical Medicine and Rehabilitation*, **57**, 305–310.

Tarler-Benlolo, L. (1978) The role of relaxation in biofeedback training: A critical review of the literature, *Psychological Bulletin*, **85**, 727–755.

Taub, E. (1977) Self-regulation of human tissue temperature, in G. E. Schwartz and J. Beatty (eds.) *Biofeedback: Theory and Research*, pp. 265–300, Academic Press, New York.

Taub, E. and Stroebel, C. F. (1978) Biofeedback in the treatment of vasoconstrictive syndromes, *Biofeedback and Self-Regulation*, **3**, 363–373.

Turin, A. and Johnson, W. G. (1976) Biofeedback therapy for migraine headaches, *Archives of General Psychiatry*, **33**, 517–519.

Vaughn, R., Poll, M. L. and Haynes, S. N. (1977) Frontalis response to stress in subjects with frequent muscle-contraction headaches, *Headache*, **16**, 313–317.

Weiss, T. and Engel, B. T. (1971) Operant conditioning of heart rate in patients with premature ventricular contractions, *Psychosomatic Medicine*, **33**, 301–321.

Wickramaskera, I. (1973) The application of verbal instructions and EMG feedback training to the management of tension headache—preliminary observations, *Headache*, **13**, 74–76.

Wyler, A. R., Lockard, J. S., Ward, A. A. and Finch, C. A. (1976) Conditioned EEG desynchronization and seizure occurrence in patients, *EEG and Clinical Neurophysiology*, **41**, 501–512.

10

BEHAVIORAL PSYCHOLOGY IN PEDIATRICS

BARBARA G. MELAMED

University of Florida

CONTENTS

1. A RATIONALE FOR COLLABORATION BETWEEN PSYCHOLOGY AND PEDIATRICS

Behavioral pediatrics recognizes that environmental and social factors influence the course of growth and development of the child, both in times of sickness and in the maintenance of good health. There is now a research and clinical data foundation to establish the validity of a collaboration between pediatricians and psychologists, particularly those with behavioral expertise (Christophersen and Rapoff, 1979; Melamed and Siegel, 1980; Schaefer, Millman and Levine, 1979).

The nature of the bond was set down over fifty years ago, in Anderson's (1930) plea to the American Medical Association for a greater emphasis in pediatrics on methods of child training and problems of adjustment. The knowledge contributed by developmental psychologists on socialization of the child (Mussen, 1970) has shifted our thinking from the view of a child as a passive recipient of environmental stimulation and parental influence, to that of an active, complex human being with the potential for influencing his/her own state of being (Berger, 1977). In this regard, the influence that children exert on their caretakers has received recognition (Lewis and Rosenblum, 1974). Social learning theory (Bandura, 1977) emphasizes the child's competence in approaching novel and stressful experiences. Thus, the problems brought into the pediatrician's office reflect the preventive and rehabilitative needs of the individuals at varying points of development, within the framework of their individual differences, as well as in their relationships with family, peers, and the social institutions of society.

The medical practitioner needs to pay attention to psychological factors as it has become evident that physical disorders are often precipitated, developed, and maintained within the context of multiple, complex factors including physical, environmental, genetic, and social influences (Kimball, 1970; Lipton, Sternschneider and Richmond, 1966; Schwab, McGinnis, Morris and Schwab, 1970). The emotional state of the patient is now recognized as playing an important role in the precipitation or exacerbation of many childhood illnesses, including seizure disorders, enuresis, asthma, and juvenile diabetes (Melamed and Siegel, 1980).

The application of behavioral principles and procedures of behavior therapy has contributed greatly over the past two decades to the practice of pediatrics (Stedman, 1970). The goal of this chapter is to present the rationale for behavioral intervention as an adjunctive to medical treatment. This will be supplemented through examples of progress made in three areas: problems during developmental stages; special considerations due to chronic illness; and prevention of more serious illness through dealing with fears, improving compliance with medical, dietary, and exercise regimens, and preparation for medical intervention.

Learning or conditioning mechanisms have been found to be a significant factor in a variety of somatic disorders, regardless of the specific etiology of bodily dysfunction. Although conditioning may not play a causative role in psychophysiological disorders, it modifies or exacerbates an already existing illness (Davison and Neale, 1974). There are several ways in which behavioral principles may function.

A. Maintenance of Symptomatic Behavior

Respondent and operant conditioning may serve to maintain symptomatic behavior, even in the absence of the organic problem. For instance, an eight-year-old child had experienced abdominal cramps for several days, as a result of gastrointestinal symptoms developed during a viral infection. The child's drinking of milk during the illness worsened his stomach pains. As a result of the learned association between the abdominal pains and the milk, the act of drinking milk alone was sufficient to elicit the stomach pains after the virus was no longer present. This illustrates the process of classical conditioning, in which a previously neutral stimulus (milk) can acquire the ability to elicit the physiological response (stomachache). In addition, the stomach complaints resulted in a number of positive consequences during the illness and after, which served to maintain the reports of pain. The child received considerable adult attention and comfort for these reports. When he later complained of stomachache, he may have been allowed to stay home from school, or to avoid unpleasant tasks such as completing household chores or homework. As a result, these positive consequences serve as reinforcers that maintain the symptomatic behavior, despite the fact that the illness, which may have initially precipitated the abdominal pain, no longer exists. Secondary gain contributes to sick role behavior in association with many health problems. The fact that most patients give up their illness behavior attests to the operation of other factors in the individual and the family, which serve to maintain healthy, more adaptive behavior.

There is evidence that some families with children who have psychosomatic disorders tend to avoid conflict resolution by focusing on the illness (Minuchin, Rosman and Baker, 1978). The special psychological problems that confront these families, who must learn to manage complex medical regimens over a long period of time, adjusting their priorities and finding compensatory activities for the restricted patient, require careful behavioral analysis. It has been stated (Creer and Christian, 1976; Mattson, 1972) that parents of chronically ill children tend to be overprotective, use less consistent discipline, and provide reinforcement for dependency behavior. These factors contribute to the development of behavioral management problems, including a whiny, demanding child who may express exaggerated symptoms in order to command attention. The physician is forced to intervene in order to assure that proper management of the illness is maintained.

B. Modification of Somatic Component

Behavioral approaches have been used successfully in the modification of seizure activity (Mostofsky and Balaschak, 1977), asthma (Miklich, Renne, Creer, Alexander, Chai, Davis, Hoffman and Danker-Brown, 1977), and the insulin requirements of a juvenile diabetic (Fowler, Budzynski and Vandenbergh, 1976). The efficacy of these treatments does not provide information about the etiology of a given disorder, but does emphasize that events in the patients' environment can maintain symptomatic behavior.

C. Biofeedback

As an outgrowth of Miller's (1969) findings on the conditionability of visceral responses, several applications of biofeedback to medical conditions have been reported. There is evidence with asthmatic children that operant feedback about the nature of airway resistance through either electromyographic (EMG) or pulmonary flow rate can be used to reduce the frequency and intensity of wheezing episodes (Kotses, Glaus, Bricel, Edwards and Crawford, 1978). Electroencephalogram (EEG) patterns have also been modified through sensorimotor rhythm biofeedback procedures, resulting in the reduction or short-circuiting of seizures (Sterman, Macdonald and Stone, 1974). The clinical utility of biofeedback procedures for the management of chronic illness and psychophysiological disorders has been challenged (Blanchard and Young, 1974; Miklich et al., 1977). However, the continued use of psychophysiological monitoring devices may yield information regarding the mechanisms that mediate physiology and behavior. The deliniation of emotional triggers of psychophysiological disturbances, which can thus be assessed, can provide information pertinent to therapeutic intervention (i.e. systematic desensitization).

D. Modification of Maladaptive Behavior Secondarily Resulting from Illness

Behavioral approaches can be applied to problems which develop as a result of the medical condition. Wright (1977) argues that dysfunctional behavior which outlasts the medical treatment, such as tracheostomy addiction (Wright *et al.*, 1968), nebulizer dependency (Sirota and Mahoney, 1974), or addiction to medications, should be considered in the definition of psychosomatic disorders. This provides a rationale for the application of behavioral methods to eliminate such problems.

E. Prevention

Health care professionals are focusing more on preventive examination and inoculation in the well-baby care clinics. The emphasis on the education of parents and patients in the management of health-related behavior will lead to early recognition of potentially troublesome symptoms and hopefully increase adherence to medical regimens.

The role of behavioral specialists in the preparation of children and families for medical procedures and surgery (Melamed, Meyer, Gee and Soule, 1976; Melamed and Siegel, 1975; Vernon and Bailey, 1974), as well as for routine dental care (Melamed, Hawes, Heiby and Glick, 1975; Melamed, Weinstein, Hawes and Katin-Berland, 1975; Melamed, Yurcheson, Fleece, Hutcherson and Hawes, 1978), has already affected routine hospital practices (Peterson and Ridley-Johnson, 1980). The importance of alleviating injection phobias in patients in need of diagnostic procedures (Nimmer and Kapp, 1974; Taylor, Ferguson and Wermuth, 1977) or in need of hemodialysis treatment (Katz, 1974), and other life-threatening circumstances is obvious. However, equally important is the education of patients and their families in the routine management of juvenile diabetes, hemophilia, asthma, and other conditions in which anxiety about symptoms may lead to under or overmedication, and may often precipitate attacks.

F. Adherence to Medical Regimens

The factors that affect adherence to medical regimens are in need of clarification. Knowledge about the illness does not by itself guarantee compliance (Etzwiler and Robb, 1972; Kasl, 1975; Marston, 1970; Sackett, Haynes, Gibson, Hackett, Taylor, Roberts and Johnson, 1975). The behavioral framework postulates the need to consider such factors as: the complexity of the program; the ease with which it fits into the daily life pattern; saliency of cues; and the speed with which it alleviates discomfort (Kirscht and Rosenstock, 1979). If the drug has aversive consequences, or if there is no clear relationship between the symptoms and their treatment, desirable health-related behavior will not be maintained. When viewed within the operant conditioning paradigm this avoidance behavior is understandable. Motivational incentives for maintaining behavior in the absence of immediate relief need to be explored. In a study of mothers instructed to administer a ten day course of antibiotics (penicillin being provided free), it was found that over 50 percent of them had stopped giving the medication by the fifth day. Mothers cited remission of symptoms as their reason (Becker, Drachman and Kirscht, 1972). The use of response-cost programs and the inclusion of social allies in monitoring treatment adherence have been promoted by behavioral specialists in attempts to enhance compliance (Epstein and Masek, 1978; Zeisat, 1978).

The advent of certain behavioral engineering devices has assisted in compliance with pill-taking (Azrin and Powell, 1969). The use of negative reinforcement procedures has assisted in prevention of bedsores, by encouraging patients who are bedridden or confined to wheelchairs to change their body positions (Malament, Dunn and Davis, 1975). Cerebral palsied children have improved their muscular control with similar procedures (Halperin and Kottke, 1968). Dworkin and his colleagues (1980) have been exploring a biofeedback device with adolescents suffering from scoliosis, to decrease the tendency to increased curvature of the spine, by signalling incorrect posture. A noxious sound is terminated or avoided, if they assume better posture. These procedures have value in medical care in preventing more serious problems.

The innovation of behavioral pediatrics is not meant as a replacement for medical care. It should be emphasized that somatic disorders result in tissue damage and physical changes in the body's organ systems. A thorough medical examination should always be completed prior to behavioral intervention to determine if concurrent medical intervention is required. Particularly, in the event that behavioral technology proves strong enough to alter metabolic states such as insulin requirements, or pulmonary functioning, the medically trained practitioner must be an integrated team member. Epstein, Katz and Zlutnick (1979) outline several reasons why behavioral treatment should be available for the treatment of medical problems. First, behavioral treatments may produce better outcomes than the nonbehavioral, including pharmacologic procedures. Second, a behavioral treatment may be preferred to a pharmacologic approach, as the behavioral treatments may have fewer negative effects compared to the side effects of the drug. Third, behavioral procedures may be more cost effective than long-term, expensive pharmacologic procedures. Fourth, many medical problems may be a function of social or behavioral factors, and a behavioral approach may be the best way to modify these factors directly. Finally, some patients, because of religious or financial factors, may prefer a nonmedical alternative.

The studies reviewed here represent a sample of the behavioral management of problems seen in pediatric outpatient clinics. The unique feature of behavioral medicine is its ability to document the efficacy of prevention and treatment programs, a task which requires an interdisciplinary alliance between the physician and the behavioral scientist (Christophersen and Rapoff, 1979). These studies were selected as being well-controlled single-case designs, or between-group designs that have already advanced the state of health care in pediatrics. The problem-oriented approach depicted in these studies is compatible with the physician's goal in the treatment of the medical condition. The target behavior must be clearly specified, so that it can be monitored during treatment, in order to evaluate the effectiveness of the procedure. The behavioral specialist, like the physician, attempts to clarify antecedents which may have prompted the occurrence of the symptom. The consequences of the symptom are elaborated in terms of its effects not only on the physical condition of the child, but on the psychological well-being, and the social environment, including family and friends of the patient.

2. DEVELOPMENTAL PROBLEMS

A. Nocturnal Enuresis

Because of its widespread prevalence, enuresis has received considerable attention from behavioral therapists. Predominant behavioral methods for treating enuresis include urine detection devices, retention control training, contingency management approaches, and combinations of these procedures. Reviews by Doleys (1977) and Christophersen and Rapoff (1978) present the comparative effectiveness of these approaches. The need for long-term follow-up data is suggested by the fact that, although remission is achieved in about 75 percent of the cases treated by urine detection devices, the relapse rate within six months averages about 41 percent. Often, a simple booster treatment restores control.

Bed-wetting can be caused by physical defects in the urinary–genital tract, by neurological disorders, or by urinary–tract infections. While less than 10 percent of enuresis in children can be attributed to these organic factors, they need to be ruled out or, if indicated, medication assisted (Siegel and Richards, 1977). Otherwise, behavioral treatment will not be as effective. In order to decide if the child should be treated, two criteria must be met: (1) involuntary discharge of urine during sleep must be seen beyond the normal age of 3–4 years when children usually gain bladder control and (2) there must be an absence of organic causes for this behavior, or these should be under medical control.

Yates (1970) suggested that a distinction between primary enuresis (control has never been achieved) and secondary enuresis (toileting accidents, after a period of sustained dryness) is useful in the selection of appropriate treatment. Secondary enuresis may be due to infection, or, more commonly, it can accompany periods of emotional stress. Primary enuresis involves a more elaborate form of treatment, since it implies the learning of new behaviors. If this is the case, then the treatment approach should assume a skill deficit and use positively-oriented approaches, perhaps with the aid of a commercially available bell-and-pad device, or toilet-training book (Azrin and Foxx, 1974). The parents of the enuretic child have a most crucial role in the treatment process. The enuretic child may not have learned to exercise adequate control of the bladder's sphincter muscles and, therefore, fails to inhibit the bladder reflex controlling urination under conditions of bladder extension. Sometimes, this occurs because the child is a heavy sleeper. In the bell-and-pad method, the child sleeps on a specially constructed pad. As soon as he begins to urinate, the circuit activates a bell (or buzzer). This serves to inhibit further urination by causing the bladder muscles to contract reflexly. The parent can assist by accompanying the child to the bathroom immediately, as he/she is still likely to have a full bladder. The parent should encourage the drinking of fluids before bedtime, to insure that sufficient pairings of the bell and the act of urination occur. This differs considerably from advice that parents are typically given, which is to limit the child's fluid intake and to wake the child up for "potty" when they prepare to go to bed. If used as instructed, the use of the device is considered by many to be an example of respondent conditioning (Mowrer and Mowrer, 1938).

The child will learn in a few short trials to wake up to the cues for bladder fullness and the need to urinate. The older child can be taught to shut off the bell immediately and go to urinate. The device should be reset and a dry sheet placed on the bed. The parents can usually handle the treatment on their own, with therapist consultation, encouragement, and the instructions which come with the device. To evaluate its effectiveness and maintain parental cooperation, a daily record of clean sheets should be reported. The child should also be praised and reinforced for each dry night. The use of the device is discontinued after fourteen consecutive dry nights. Any relapses that exceed two or more wet nights a week should prompt reinstatement of the device. Many children require four to eight weeks before the bed-wetting is completely controlled. This procedure has been found superior to traditional psychotherapy (DeLeon and Mandell, 1966; Werry and Cohressen (1965) and drug therapy (Forrester, Stein and Susser, 1964; Young and Turner, 1965). Detailed descriptions are presented in Lovibond and Coote (1970) and Werry (1967). The success rate is over 80 percent; and the 20 percent relapse rate following termination of treatment (O'Leary and Wilson, 1975) is probably due to lack of reintroducing the bell and pad when warranted.

Enuretic children tend to urinate a smaller volume at more frequent intervals than normal children (Muellner, 1960). Therefore, a treatment program focused at increasing bladder control has been used. The child is encouraged to drink frequently. When the child feels the need to urinate, he/she is asked to "hold it in" for five minutes and then to use the bathroom. This withholding period is gradually increased several minutes each day, until the child can delay 30–45 minutes (Kimmel and Kimmel, 1970). The child is reinforced with praise and tokens (later exchangeable for TV shows, favorite food, and toys). Although the training is carried out during the daytime, Paschalis, Kimmel and Kimmel (1972) found significant reductions in nighttime wetting in 23 out of 31 children following 2–3 weeks of retention-control exercises.

The same retention-control procedures work for the child who has previously been trained and has a relapse. Miller (1973) was able to eliminate bed-wetting in two adolescents who had become enuretic several years prior to treatment. They kept three-week baseline records of the number of times they wet their beds each week and the frequency of daytime urinations. They delayed urination an additional ten minutes each week. At the end of treatment, they had achieved three consecutive weeks of dry nights, and no relapse was reported after seven months.

These retention-control procedures assume that the children learned to increase their bladder capacities. However, in a well-controlled study, Harris and Purohit (1977) failed to demonstrate a relationship between increased bladder capacity and decreased frequency of enuresis. A 35-day bladder-training program resulted in a significant mean increase in bladder capacity for experimental subjects over controls, but there was no significant difference in frequency of enuresis.

A combination of bell-and-pad and retention-control training procedures has also been used effectively (Azrin, Sneed and Foxx, 1974). This involves operant procedures, such as hourly wakenings, positive practice in going to the toilet, punishment (child changes sheet), and positive reinforcement for going to the bathroom at night. Dry-bed training, in a child of sufficient age to ensure the capability for bladder control, has been found to work in as short a time as one intensive evening of training. It requires more active participation of the parents, but the reinforcement is much quicker. This is the treatment of choice with highly motivated parents and a child old enough to understand the procedures. There has been no substantial relapse reported during six month follow-up evaluations of this procedure.

Two additional investigations (Butler, 1976; Lutzker and Drake, 1976) provided evidence that parents can achieve toilet training in their child using only the book by Azrin and Foxx (1974) describing the steps of the procedure. Bollard and Woodroffe (1977), in a component analysis of the treatment package, found that the urine alarm device greatly facilitated training, probably because the consequences can be immediate, whenever bed-wetting occurs.

B. Encopresis

Encopresis is defined as any voluntary or involuntary passage of feces that results in soiled clothing (Wright, 1973b). It is usually accompanied by chronic constipation. The stool retention for prolonged periods can result in relaxed sphincter muscles and a distended colon. As a result, periodic involuntary passage of fecal matter may occur. A thorough physical examination, to evaluate organic problems, must be carried out prior to any behavioral procedure. Often, mineral oil or suppositories can alleviate the discomfort involved in defecation after severe constipation. However, a careful functional analysis should be obtained to understand each case, so that appropriate treatment can be achieved. Operant techniques (positive reinforcement strategies and changing the focus of parental attention) work best and sometimes necessitate adjunctive medical procedures (enemas to clear the colon, suppository before meals if a spontaneous bowel movement does not occur, or stool softener).

Although the treatment of encopretics often involves a practical set of instructions by the physician regarding the use of medication, the psychologist contributes by enhancing compliance and developing reward systems to encourage cooperation with the treatment.

Wright and Walker (1977) suggest the use of glycerin suppositories in the morning before breakfast, to assure the timing of the bowel movement. Parental attention for reinforcing appropriate bowel movements can then be immediate. This, combined with punishment for accidents by removal of television privileges or outdoor play, has led to bowel training. Christophersen and Rainey (1976) increased compliance by giving the parents a summary of instructions and having them keep daily records on the number and consistency of bowel movements. Unlike Wright, they do not recommend the use of punishment.

One frequently reported difficulty in treating encopretics is their reported inability to tell when they have to defecate. It appears that fecal impaction or megarectum contributes to decreased rectal sensitivity (Meunier, Mollard and Marechal, 1976). In such cases, biofeedback procedures, such as the one employed by Schuster (1974), might be indicated. In a six-year-old with continuous soiling and chronic constipation, a balloon was inserted into the rectum to record internal and external pressure of sphincter muscles. Then, arousal biofeedback and verbal praise were used to obtain sphincter control in four sessions.

C. Eating Disturbances

Evidence suggests that eating difficulties represent a significant clinical problem, with the incidence in young children reported to be as high as 45 percent (Bentovim, 1970). Most eating problems can be treated with little professional assistance. It is only the most serious form of food refusal known as anorexia nervosa, however, that usually requires intensive medical and psychological involvement. The review by Christophersen and Rapoff (1979) stresses a need for systematic data collection on treatment effectiveness. Agras, Barlow, Chapin *et al.* (1974) are cited as having the only experimentally controlled within-subject reversal design. Their failure to obtain follow-up data limits the conclusions about the long-term maintenance of weight by positive reinforcement and feedback about progress.

The problems that more commonly face the pediatrician are those in which children have very limited food preferences or where childhood obesity is recognized by the parent to be a potential problem. Both operant and respondent behavioral treatment programs have modified eating patterns of food refusal in children. Typically, the treatment consists of gradually shaping the range of foods a child will accept, by using preferred foods to reinforce the eating of foods that the child dislikes. Social reinforcement, such as praise and attention, and TV viewing were also used, contingent upon eating small amounts of table food (Bernal, 1972). Siegel and Richards (1977) review treatment programs that have been used to reinstate normal eating patterns in children who may have developed eating disorders as a result of temporary illness or faulty dietary patterns.

D. Obesity

Obesity in children is an important concern for the pediatric practitioner, not only because of its effects on the physical health of the child, but also because of the ensuing psychosocial problems that often result. In addition, data indicate that over 85 percent of the overweight children are likely to become overweight as adults (Abraham and Nordsieck, 1960). The problems of eating have then become so well established that the patients may be more resistant to treatment.

In viewing childhood obesity as primarily a disorder in the regulation of body weight, where the intake of food is greater than the expenditure of energy (once metabolic factors have been explored), the behavioral program focuses on establishing better eating habits and greater exercise involvement. The child's eating patterns are developed within the context of the family and are controlled to a large extent by parental attitudes about food consumption and nutrition. The program most likely to produce permanent change in the development of eating habits most conducive to appropriate body weight is one which involves the parent.

The efficacy of behavioral treatment for producing short-term weight loss has been demonstrated in several investigations. Argona, Cassady and Drabman (1975) found that parent training groups in which the parents were instructed in keeping daily records of the child's caloric intake, weight and kind of food eaten and then instructed in reinforcing the child for exercising, and following self-control procedures were successful in producing weight loss which was maintained at a 7-month follow-up. The use of response cost, having the parent forfeit a deposit which could be earned back through compliance with the program and weight gain, served as additional motivation.

Wheeler and Hess (1976) reported on the results of individualized treatment programs that involved joint participation of the parent and the child. The program emphasized changing the conditions in the environment that maintained overeating (e.g., free access to high caloric snacks) and altering the parent's reinforcement of overeating behaviors. Their results are encouraging. Kingsley and Shapiro (1977) also provided evidence that mothers' involvement in treatment led to significantly better maintenance. It appears that improvement was due to better eating habits rather than dieting. It should be remembered in guiding a weight reduction program over a period of time, that the children are continually developing and some weight increases are expected. Also, as a monitor of the treatment progress, it is important to use a more objective measure than number of pounds, by taking into account the child's height, weight and skin fold thickness. In addition, reinforcing the changes in eating and exercising patterns, which may occur more rapidly than actual weight loss, may be a more effective strategy in maintaining the family's active participation.

E. Phobias

Fear is an emotion produced by present or impending danger. Many fears are experienced in the normal course of development in children. Most of these fears are adaptive and prevent harmful consequences such as fear of hot objects, deep crevices, strangers, falling, etc. Marks (1969) described developmental trends in the acquisition and extinction of fears. The common fears change in children with increasing age. Fears can come and go in children in a very volatile fashion. Fears of animals are more common in children between the ages of 2 and 4 years. By the age of 4–6, fears of the dark and imaginary creatures begin to predominate. After age 6, children become resistant to acquiring new animal fears unless a traumatic incident occurs. The older child fears bodily injury and interpersonal awkwardness (Jersild and Holmes, 1935). Fears and rituals may appear and disappear for no apparent reason. Children may regress during illness, and forgotten fears may reappear, disappearing when the child recovers from the illness. Therefore, the pediatrician when faced with parental concern for a fearful child must decide when fearful behavior should receive treatment. A phobia is a special form of fear which (1) is out of proportion to the demands of the situation, (2) cannot be explained or reasoned away, (3) is beyond voluntary control, and (4) leads to avoidance of the feared situation. Therefore, a debilitating fear interferes with daily functioning or social development. Actually only a small percentage of all referrals to psychiatric clinics involve phobic disorders in children. Agras, Chapin and Oliveau (1972) report that 100 percent of untreated phobic children improved over a five-year period; this did not occur for phobic adults. They also noted that the more specific and focused the fear the better the prognosis for behavior change.

There is an additional problem of defining when a child is excessively fearful. Girls and younger children of both sexes may be more willing to admit their fears due to a variety of social and cultural factors. Fear may be expressed in a variety of ways. These would include what the child says, how he behaves in a fear situation, and what autonomic indices might be present. No one response system necessarily connotes fear. Often there is inconsistency between what one says and what one does.

Thus, in assessing children's fears one must consider their age and whether the fears are typical at that developmental level. Fears that have lasted beyond the age at which they normally disappear would be appropriate for treatment, particularly true if they interfere with the child's normal social development, or are associated with somatic complaints, sleeping difficulties, nightmares, or obsessive ruminations (Johnson and Melamed, 1979).

School phobia remains a prevalent problem that necessitates immediate intervention to reinstate consistent school attendance. Each school year 17 out of 1000 children are estimated to stay out of school due to excessive fears (Kennedy, 1965). Any treatment program that puts the child back in the classroom before failure to attend becomes a chronic pattern, is likely to lead to improvement.

The treatment programs focusing on early intervention emphasized forced school attendance, parental praise for attendance, and systematic extinction of the child's somatic complaints and expressions of fear or anxiety. Medical examinations for complaints of abdominal pains or headaches were dealt with by scheduling medical examinations before or after school hours, and did not serve as a means for the children to avoid going to school. In several cases, the parents were found to be inadvertently reinforcing the child's staying home from school. This was dealt with by instructing them not to attend to the child's complaints, and to reward going to school (Tahmasian and McReynolds, 1971).

A central issue in choosing a treatment for facilitating school attendance is identifying which factors are responsible for the child's avoidance behavior. Occasionally, the child's separation anxiety from mother must be treated concurrently with decreasing the anxiety of the school situation. However, the longer the child stays home, the more isolated he/she becomes from peers and the more difficult it is to catch up on school work missed. The reinforcing consequences children sometimes receive from adults and peers for being school phobic must be identified and eliminated. The child's school phobia can then be treated according to whether anxiety mediates the problem. In this case, systematic desensitization, social skills training, or gradual reexposure would be the treatment of choice. If, however, the child has been reinforced for school avoidance behavior in the absence of emotional responses, then an operant approach to treatment would be appropriate. In this case one alters reinforcers so that school attendance becomes a prerequisite to gaining the attention and approval of individuals important to the child.

F. Shyness or Excessive Dependency

As in the case of childhood fears, a fairly large proportion of individuals who considered themselves as shy in childhood are able to overcome these problems with increasing age (Zimbardo, Pilkonis and Norwood, 1974, 1975). The appropriate treatment approach depends on a careful functional analysis on what relationship anxiety or skill deficit may have to the absence of appropriate interpersonal performance. It is important to consider whether inability to make friends, or express opinions, or enjoy social occasions is a result of a skill deficit. Many anxious and withdrawn children do not possess the social skills necessary to effectively deal with their problems. They must be given the opportunity to observe others behave assertively, and to try out other responses that are comfortable for them. Socially awkward children are likely to have equally socially inept parents (Sherman and Farina, 1974). Therefore, treatment usually requires more than just offering the parent's advice. Teaching the parent to directly reinforce assertive responses led to a lessening of dependency behavior in a child whose frequent crying and lack of appropriate play was maintained by his inability to stand up for his own rights (Patterson, 1972). Interventions which focus on teaching social skills have a better chance of success. Film modeling proved effective (O'Conner, 1969, 1972) in modifying the social withdrawn behavior of preschool children, but not of older children (Walker and Hops, 1973). A current trend is to treat socially isolated children in groups with normally assertive peers (Clement, Roberts and Lantz, 1970). Once the new behavior is learned it must be reinforced in order to be maintained. Teacher attention has been found to act as a powerful reinforcing stimulus for preschool children (Buell, Stoddard, Harris and Baer, 1968). Older children may require tangible as well as social reinforcers (Clement, 1968). If a child is so inhibited that he cannot speak in the classroom, stimulus fading procedures may be used (Jackson and Wallace, 1974) in order to increase social participation in a gradual manner. A five-year-old boy's interaction with his classmates was improved simply by having him pass out candy (Kirby and Toler, 1970).

G. Aggressive Behavior Problems

The whining, crying child is reinforced for his/her tantrums. These aversive responses on the part of the child pay off. The child gets what he/she wants, or avoids an unpleasant situation. The parent receives short-term relief for giving in. The screaming child temporarily stops, thereby reinforcing the parents' use of nagging, leaving the scene, or giving in to the child's demands.

It is necessary to demonstrate to the parents how their reaction influences the child's behavior. A classic illustration of the degree of control the parents really have was demonstrated in a treatment program involving a time-out procedure to reduce tantrums in a two-year-old child (Williams, 1959). Figure 1 illustrates the immediate success the parents had in extinguishing the tyrant-like tantrum behavior of their son by merely staying out of his bedroom once he had been put to bed. It is of interest to note that the child had been seriously ill during the first 18 months of life and had had much special care and attention from his parents and aunt. In the course of treatment it was noted that spontaneous recovery of the tantrums occurred after a week and that this was reinforced by the aunt's attention. A second extinction period was necessary to completely eliminate the tantrum behavior.

A child who appears hyperaggressive may have learned through cumulative experiences that he/she gets his/her way by exhibiting high intensity negative behaviors. Patterson (1976) regards attempts to modify these patterns through treatment by a professional therapist unlikely to produce lasting effects. Instead he recommends retraining parents and teachers to alter the reinforcement schedules they inadvertently provide. In the studies of families with aggressive, out of control boys,

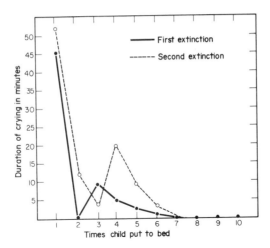

FIG. 1. Length of crying in two extinction series as a function of successive occasions of being put to bed.

Patterson and Reid (1970) found that the deviant child tended to obtain more positive reinforcers in family interaction than other family members and received more aversive consequences. A correlation was found (Reid, 1967) between the amount of aversive stimuli given by family members and the amount received. The need to teach parents to track their own behavior in responding to the demands of the child is an important part of the treatment program. A programmed textbook (Patterson and Gullion, 1968) can help specify the problem behavior. This book reduces the parents' tendency to focus on guilt and blame. The parents of the aggressive child are asked to provide more appropriate ways for the child to gain attention. In 1975, Patterson and his colleagues described their clinical and research procedures for professionals.

Wahler and his colleagues (1977) found that parent training is less effective in low socio–economic families living in overcrowded high-crime rate areas who are poorly educated and often have only one parent. They are insulated from the extra-family network and are difficult to reach by traditional psychotherapy.

H. Hyperactivity

The childhood disorder most typically referred to as "hyperactivity" (also referred to as hyperkinetic behavior syndrome, hyperkinetic reaction of childhood, and minimal brain dysfunction) represents a frequent complaint of parents and teachers which is brought to the attention of pediatricians and mental health professionals who work with children. There are some estimates that as many as 20 percent of elementary school children are affected by this disorder (Lambert, Sandoval and Sassone, 1978; Minskoff, 1973). Thirty to fifty percent of all children seen at child guidance centers have been referred because of hyperactive behaviors, with the majority being boys (Cantwell, 1975; Wender, 1971). While there is considerable lack of agreement as to the nature of this disorder (Werry and Sprague, 1970), hyperactive children are usually characterized by the following problem behaviors:

short attention span, distractability, excessive and purposeless motor activity, impulsivity, overexcitability and aggressiveness (Millichap, 1968; Safer and Allen, 1976). In addition, these children often have learning problems or specific learning disabilities which may result from attentional deficits (Ross, 1976).

The etiology of the syndrome is unknown. The research is complicated by lack of consistent agreement in classification. Children classified as "hyperactive", "hyperkinetic", "minimal brain dysfunction", and "learning disabled" are all found lumped together increasing heterogeneity of the research population. Theories as to possible causes include organic, psychogenic, disordered metabolism and inborn temperament (Satterfield, *et al.*, 1974).

The most frequently used treatment strategy for children diagnosed as hyperactive is pharmacological intervention, primarily with stimulant drugs (Safer and Allen, 1976). Between 60 to 90 per cent of hyperactive children have been found to show some behavioral improvement with stimulant medications (Whalen and Henker, 1976). However, a number of investigators have discussed potential drawbacks in the use of drugs as the treatment of choice with hyperactive children. For example, there is some evidence that in as many as 30 to 50 percent of the cases in which stimulant drugs are used, they are not effective in managing many of the problematic behaviors associated with this disorder (Wender, 1971). In addition, a number of troublesome side effects, such as appetite loss, insomnia, and delayed growth have been reported with the use of stimulants with children (Freedman, 1971). Furthermore, while these drugs have been shown to improve hyperactive children's performance on various measures of activity level and tasks requiring sustained attention, Sroufe (1975) has noted that there is little evidence that stimulant medication alone improves academic performance or problem-solving abilities. Finally, recent concern has been expressed about the long-term consequences of using drugs to manage the behavior problems of hyperactive children not only because of potential physical side effects of the medication, but also in terms of the child's perceived efficacy to control his/her own behavior and to personally affect the outcomes of various events (Whalen and Henker, 1976). The research findings of Bugental, Whalen and Henker (1977) led them to conclude that "many children taking medication are learning to attribute behavioral *improvement* to causes beyond personal control and to devalue their own potential contributions to problem solutions" (p. 882). In this regard, Ross (1976) suggests that:

> Drug treatment of hyperactive children should, when used, be combined with behavior therapy so that the child can come to view his increased ability to sit still and to attend as something *he* is learning to master. It might be that with such a combination of approaches (chemical and psychological), the improvement could be maintained when the drug is withdrawn after a relatively short time (p. 103).

A number of behavioral strategies have been successfully applied to the management of the problem behavior exhibited by children diagnosed as hyperactive. These behavioral techniques have been used alone and in combination with medication. Behavioral approaches have focused primarily on two aspects of the hyperactive disorder: (1) modifying distractability and attentional deficits by training the child to use more appropriate cognitive strategies, and (2) reducing excessive gross motor activity and disruptive behavior through contingency management procedures.

Possibly the most frequent complaint from a parent or teacher about a hyperactive child is that "he/she never sits still and is always disrupting others or destroying things". Safer and Allen (1976) point out that training parents of hyperactive children in behavior management strategies is particularly important since physicians usually recommend that a child take medication only during school hours to reduce the risks of potential side effects. As a result, the therapeutic effects of the medication would not be operating while the child is at home.

Stableford, Butz, Hasazi, Leitenberg and Peyser (1976) describe a home-based treatment program for an 11-year-old male who had been diagnosed as hyperactive at an early age. He was on a very high dosage level of stimulant medication and both his parents and physician felt that the medication should be discontinued since he had been taking it for a long period of time. However, his parents were continuing to complain about high levels of activity and disruptive behavior at home. The child was reinforced with one point for each desirable behavior such as picking up his clothes, going to bed on time, and any positive behavior that indicated that he was "relaxed" or "calm". For each undesirable behavior such as yelling, stealing, and running around the house after he was asked to stop, one point was subtracted. At the end of each day, he could exchange the points he had earned for money (e.g., 6 points = 25¢). During the first 25 days of the program, the child continued to take his usual medication; then the dosage level was gradually reduced until he was eventually taking a placebo.

This program resulted in a considerable reduction of the child's activity level and negative behavior at home. The gradual reduction in medication did not increase the undesirable behavior. While no intervention program was introduced at school, the child's teacher never reported any behavioral or academic problems despite the fact that medication had been withdrawn.

A treatment program for hyperactive children in the classroom that necessitated parent–teacher cooperation is described by O'Leary, Pelham, Rosenbaum and Price (1976). Treatment involved teacher praise for appropriate classroom behavior and home rewards contingent on daily "report cards" that were individually tailored to specific target behaviors for each child. At the end of each school day, the teacher noted on the report card whether the child had successfully performed the desired behavior such as completing assignments, bringing in homework, and co-operating with others. The focus of treatment was, therefore, not on the hyperactive behavior per se, but on academic performance and desirable behavior (i.e., behavior was reinforced if it was incompatible with hyperactive and disruptive behavior).

The children took their report cards home each day, and if they had successfully met their daily goals, they were reinforced with various desired activities or events. Parents were assisted in selecting meaningful reinforcers for their child including special desserts, time with a parent to play a game, money, and additional TV time. In addition, special rewards such as eating dinner at a restaurant with the family or a fishing trip were provided at the end of the week if the child earned four out of five report cards indicating acceptable classroom behavior. Teacher reports and behavioral observations indicated that this treatment program resulted in much improved classroom performance and considerable reduction in hyperactive behaviors such as excessive motor activity (i.e., fidgeting in the chair, walking around the room, and not attending to appropriate tasks).

Ayllon, Layman and Kandel (1975) were able to decrease disruptive classroom behavior in three chronically hyperactive children using behavioral procedures. The problem behavior, including excessive gross motor movement, disruptive noise, and disrupting others, was decreased to a level similar to that achieved by the stimulant drugs which they had previously taken. The intervention strategy involved a token reinforcement program in which each child was reinforced for satisfactory perform- ance on math and reading assignments. Tokens were exchangeable for a variety of special activities at school. This treatment program improved academic perform- ance over the level obtained when the children were on the medication. Thus, while the drug had reduced undesirable behavior, it failed to improve the children's deficient academic performance. Their academic achievement improved only when it was directly reinforced. Kauffman and Hallihan (1979) reviewed other programs for the learning disabled.

Douglas (1974) has noted that in addition to the problems of high levels of activity and disruptive behavior, hyperactive children also have difficulty in sustain- ing attention for extended periods of time and in approaching tasks in an organized and planful manner. As a result, these children are often diagnosed as having problems in "impulse control". From a behavioral perspective, these children lack self-control and therefore, tend to respond quickly without evaluating or monitor- ing their responses. Because of this deficit in self-control, they are apt to make many errors when they do respond.

Several training programs have been developed to help the hyperactive child to improve his/her performance on tasks that require careful planning prior to re- sponding. These training programs have focused on teaching the child self- instructional or self-guidance skills in which the child learns to use self-directed verbal commands when approaching a task. It is assumed that internalized verbal commands mediate the child's control over reflective responding (Kendall, 1977).

Meichenbaum and Goodman (1971) used a self-instructional program to help seven- to nine-year-old "impulsive" children to gain control over their responding through self-verbalizations. The training program was conducted over a two-week period and consisted of four half-hour individual sessions. Each child learned the self-instructional procedures while performing tasks such as copying various pat- terns or designs. The training program involved the following steps: (1) the thera- pist performed the task while verbalizing aloud as the child observed, (2) the child performed the same task as the therapist instructed aloud, (3) the child performed the task while verbalizing the instructions aloud, (4) the child performed the task while whispering the instructions, and finally, (5) the child performed the task while covertly verbalizing the instructions. An example follows of the instructions that the child was taught to verbalize overtly and then covertly during a particular week.

> Okay, what is it that I have to do? You want me to copy the picture with the different lines. I have to go slow and be careful. Okay, draw the line down, down, good; then to the right, that's it; now down some more and to the left. Good, I'm doing fine so far. Now back up again, No, I was supposed to go down. That's okay. Just erase the line carefully...Good.

Even if I make an error I can go on slowly and carefully. Okay, I have to go down now. Finished. I did it. (Meichenbaum and Goodman, 1971, p. 117).

This brief training program resulted in considerable improvement in the children's performance on a number of tasks. Furthermore, these improvements were maintained at a four-week follow-up assessment.

Ross (1976) aptly notes that given the heterogeneous group of children subsumed under the diagnostic label of hyperactivity, it is unlikely that any one treatment strategy will be effective with all the types of problematic behavior that they present. Behavioral procedures provide an alternative approach with hyperactive children or a useful adjunctive strategy where medication is necessary. Furthermore, when behavioral approaches are used concurrently with pharmacological intervention, a reduction in dosage levels of the medication is often possible (Sroufe and Steward, 1973; Wender, 1973). An excellent overview of issues in the treatment of hyperactive children may be found in Safer and Allen (1976).

3. LONG-TERM ADJUSTMENT TO CHRONIC ILLNESS

The child with a serious medical condition poses special problems for treatment. The literature suggests (Mattson, 1972) that these children suffer lengthy hospitalizations, frequent separations from family, school absences with associated isolation from peer group and deterioration in academic performance. In addition, they must adjust to often painful treatments, and an abundance of health-care specialists. Parents tend to be less restrictive in the behavioral management of these children. They also tend to reinforce dependency behavior and overprotect their child from normal stresses. These tendencies combined with the actual fears of the children concerning their illness, and their future vocation and marriage prospects often result in serious behavioral problems. Emotional stresses often precipitate the occurrence of their illness symptoms. Behavioral therapists in collaboration with the pediatric specialist can often bring the psychophysiological disturbance under the patients' own control by analysing the functional relationships concurrent with the occurence of symptoms.

A. Seizures

Behavioral procedures have been used successfully to reduce the frequency and severity of a wide range of seizure disorders (Mostofsky and Balaschak, 1977). It is estimated that seven out of every 100,000 school-age children have seizures (Bakwin and Bakwin, 1972). Despite the significant reduction in seizures often produced by anticonvulsant drugs, as many as 50 percent of the children who take this medication continue to have occasional seizures. In addition, nearly 20 percent of the children who have a seizure disorder have been completely refractory to drug treatment (Carter and Gold, 1968). The child's daily activities can be seriously disrupted and physical injury is always a possibility if seizures cannot be adequately controlled. Learning problems often require special educational attention.

In a behavioral treatment approach use is made of the fact that pre-seizure behavior can usually be identified reliably prior to the actual seizure. Children sometimes report an aura or a parent or teacher may notice behavior such as stereotyped motor activities or a vacant stare. In self-induced seizures, precipitating factors can be identified such as flashing colors, grid patterns, or arm waving (Wright, 1973a). If the seizure is viewed as the terminal link in a chain of behavior, the prevention of their occurrence by interfering with the preseizure behavior is a possibility. Both positive reinforcement for nonseizure activities and punishment of preseizure behavior have reportedly reduced the frequency and severity of seizures (Siegel and Richards, 1977).

Zlutnick, Mayville and Moffat (1975) describe a series of treatment programs using these two operant procedures, contingent punishment and the reinforcement of behavior incompatible with seizures. These cases illustrate the use of parents and teachers as agents of change in the home and school environment. The children in these studies had a formal diagnosis of epilepsy based upon electroencephalogram records (EEG) or an evaluation by a neurologist. The seizure activity occurred at least once a day. The punishment contingency involved recognizing preseizure activity and (1) shouting "No" loudly and sharply; (2) grasping the patient by the shoulders with both hands and shaking him once vigorously. The following figure is representative of the data presented.

Figure 2 illustrates the record of treatment progress of a 14-year-old female with a seizure history dating to the age of 18 months. EEG results were abnormal, confirming a diagnosis of epilepsy; minor motor and facial types. Even with anti-convulsant medication, seizure activity remained relatively high, averaging slightly less than twice a day. Seizures were preceded by arm raising. The girl was treated at home since the severity and regularity of her seizures prohibited her attending school. The girl's mother was used as the therapist and other siblings were frequently employed as data collectors. During baseline recording, seizure occurrences were not found to be dependent upon people, location, time, or activity. Yet, with the introduction of the punishment contingency, the frequency was quickly reduced and eventually stabilized, averaging one every two days. To substantiate the fact

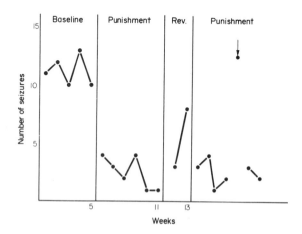

FIG. 2. The number of minor motor seizures per week.

that it was punishment alone that brought about the reduction, this procedure was discontinued during weeks 12 and 13 and a recurrence of seizures was noted. The arrow on the figure indicates another recurrence of seizure coincident with the girls' start of her menstrual cycle, indicating the possible influence of hormonal activity on the behavior. At six month follow up the level of seizure remained far below the initial baseline.

Systematic desensitization of preseizure activity has also been employed successfully (Ince, 1976; Parrino, 1971). In this procedure the self-control of the patient is stressed. A twelve-year-old boy learned how to interrupt the onset of a seizure by calling up the feelings he had learned to associate with the cue work "relax". He had been trained to relax while imagining himself in anxiety-provoking situations related to having a seizure at school. There was a complete cessation of both grand mal and petit mal seizures which persisted at a nine-month follow up.

Biofeedback procedures have also been successful in producing changes in EEG patterns so that seizures do not occur (Finley, Smith and Etheron, 1975; Lubar and Bahler, 1976; Sterman, 1973; Sterman, MacDonald and Stone, 1974). Carefully controlled studies, including placebo or noncontingent feedback (Sterman and MacDonald, 1978; Wyler, Robbins and Dodrill, 1979) revealed the feedback training of reward for central cortical frequencies above 8 Hz but below 25 Hz were most effective in reducing seizures. Patients without abnormal psychopathology (as measured by the Minnesota Multiphasic Personality Inventory) tend to benefit more consistently. It has also been found that patients with seizure activity involving motor functions benefit more from sensorimotor rhythm training than those with psychomotor or hysterical seizures.

The combination of systematic desensitization and biofeedback training has been used in patients with drug-resistant epilepsy associated with anxiety and phobic symptoms (Cabral and Scott, 1976). After three months of EEG training, patients were told to relax or produce the alpha rhythm and then presented with an anxiety provoking stimulus or imagery in a systematic hierarchy. After 15 months there was still a physiological response reduction to anxiety-provoking situations.

These studies do suggest that EEG feedback can serve as an adjunct to assist in seizure control. The issues of how much training is necessary and whether the changes in EEG activity actually decrease seizure frequency need further empirical investigation.

B. Asthma

Asthma has long been recognized as an illness with psychological concomitants. It presents an important problem for the pediatrician since it is estimated that 2–4 percent of the population are affected, with 25 percent of all the school absences due to chronic illness falling in this category.

The research on effectiveness of behavioral treatments is largely based on case studies or between treatment designs on children in residential centers or at summer camp. Lukeman (1975) noted that few of these studies reported follow-up measures. Many of the studies failed to adequately define the characteristics of the population, including somatic predisposition, current drug regimen, or severity of asthma. The lack of appropriate controls for placebo or noncontingent feedback makes it difficult to interpret many of the findings. In fact, Kahn (1977) showed that when the children were classified as reactors versus nonreactors in terms of their suggestibility to a saline vapor inhalation test (described as an allergen), reactive subjects did just as well with supportive therapy as they did with biofeedback and reciprocal inhibition.

The subtyping of asthmatics with regard to somatic predisposition defined in terms of family history of allergy, eosinophile levels, skin test reactivity and ease of diagnosis (Block, 1969; Block et al., 1964) has led to useful predictions regarding which patients will benefit the most from behavioral interventions. It has often been found that those children with less corticosteroid dependent asthma are more reactive to behavioral intervention.

The application of systematic desensitization with asthmatics is based on the assumption and empirical findings that pulmonary functioning can be affected by emotional stimuli (Alexander, 1972; Clarke, 1970; Hahn, 1966; Straker and Tamerin, 1974; Tal and Miklich, 1976). Studies employing relaxation training alone found that children with low somatic predispositions were able to decrease the frequency of episodes and increase peak expiratory flow rates (Alexander, 1972; Alexander, Miklich and Hershkoff, 1972). However, when a controlled study (Moore, 1965) compared relaxation training alone, relaxation plus hypnotic-like suggestions for improvement, and relaxation with reciprocal inhibition, only the reciprocal inhibition group showed actual improvement in maximum peak flow.

In addition to fear, anger has often been associated as a precipitating factor in asthma (Clarke, 1970; Tal and Miklich, 1976). The use of assertiveness training for helping children deal with anger had a paradoxical effect of worsening pulmonary functioning and increasing the number of asthmatic attacks after treatment (Hock, Rodgers, Reddi and Kennard, 1978). However, when assertiveness training was combined with relaxation training there was a significant reduction in the number of attacks and improvement in pulmonary functioning. It is likely that the stress aroused by the assertiveness skills training itself may have interfered with the potential benefits.

Given the fact that pulmonary functioning can be affected by emotional stimuli, it is interesting to view the therapy outcome literature in which biofeedback procedures have been employed in an attempt to regulate specific systems such as airway resistance or muscle tension in an attempt to shortcircuit an attack. It is important to examine the differential effectiveness of these nonpharmacological approaches, in terms of subclassifications based on asthma potential scores, or emotional precipitant indices. Again, it would be predicted that children with less corticosteroid dependent asthma would be more reactive to behavioral intervention. This in fact has often been the case.

The procedures in these biofeedback studies often involve making reward contingent upon improvement, thus motivation effects on the pulmonary effectiveness measures are maximized. Davis, Saunders, Creer and Chai (1973) found that biofeedback of electromyograms (EMG) as an adjunct to Jacobsen's relaxation procedures improved nonsevere asthmatics in terms of increasing their peak respiratory flow, in comparison to severe asthmatics (those receiving steroid drugs). Unfortunately, there was a lack of generalization. The improvement of peak expiratory flow rate did not hold up the week following treatment. The motivational incentives must be considered as they might have been strong enough to produce temporary change, but not maintenance of a new habit.

Given the great difficulty in the reliable assessment of PEFR because of the motivation of the patient, EMG biofeedback might prove more expedient in severe asthmatics. In fact, Kotses, Glaus, Crawford, Edwards and Scherr (1976) demonstrated a relationship between frontalis EMG and peak expiratory flow in asthmatic children. In these children, the use of noncontingent feedback group provided some support that the biofeedback training was indeed facilitating change beyond the possible placebo effect of being hooked up to the apparatus. The children receiving contingent EMG feedback showed greater increase in PEFR from pretraining when the effects were measured inconspicuously throughout the day. Thus, support for the generalization of effects was obtained since training and test sessions were several days apart.

In a subsequent study (Kotses, Glaus, Bricel, Edwards and Crawford, 1978), these investigators replicated their findings with a measure of PEFR immediately prior to and after each frontalis EMG training session thereby providing direct support for the relationship between frontalis relaxation and coincident PEFR changes in asthmatic children. In both these studies there were no systematic effects of medication, with equal numbers of severe and nonsevere asthmatics being assigned to each group.

If the improvement of asthmatics with biofeedback training is due to a reduction of arousal, it would be likely that when combined with other anxiety-reducing procedures such as systematic desensitization (SD), there would be more change than medical or biofeedback treatment alone. This would be particularly true when a low somatic predisposition for asthma existed. The children studied by Miklich, Renne, Creer, Alexander, Chai, Davis, Hoffman and Danker-Brown (1977) were moderate to severe perennial asthmatics, responsive to emotional arousal and thereby likely to improve following change in a stressful environment. In this study EMG frontalis feedback was used to assist relaxation training of some patients. Long term follow-up of patients was reported for many variables, including medication regimens. Support for improved Forced Expiratory Volume and reduced medication was obtained post-treatment and at 6-month follow-up for subjects receiving systematic desensitization. The authors concluded that the data have little clinical utility as all the patients remained chronically ill, moderately severe asthmatics. Thus, the multifaceted nature of asthma suggests other regulating factors, in addition to emotional precipitants or autonomic variables.

Kahn (1977) also combined biofeedback training with systematic desensitization. Therapy consisted of 50 minute sessions for 5–8 weeks. Children were also praised for progressive decreases in airway resistance. An attempt to improve generalization, consisted of giving them the opportunity to use their skill in a situation in which bronchoconstriction was induced by suggestion or inhalation of a bronchoconstrictor. Feedback was provided as to how successful they were. The authors view this as a counterconditioning process in which the child substitutes bronchodilation in situations known to precipitate bronchoconstriction. The control group children were not given any such training. Data were collected over one year on the number of attacks, total length of attacks, number of emergency room visits, number of hospital admissions, amount of medication taken, and severity of asthma. The combined experimental treatment helped reduce the frequency, duration and severity of asthmatic attack in both reactors and non-reactors. However, children classified as reactors in the control group receiving supportive therapy also showed significant improvement.

It seems clear that factors other than physiological arousal contribute to the maintenance of asthmatic episodes. Several therapy studies demonstrate effective control over symptoms associated with asthma by rearranging parental attention or reducing the avoidance of unpleasant activities by playing "sick". "Parentectomies" have even been prescribed, and indeed sometimes the symptoms do decrease rapidly when the parents are removed (Purcell, Brady, Chai, Muser, Molk, Gordon and Means, 1969). This suggests that the increased attention the patient receives from other people may have the paradoxical effect of maintaining the symptoms even in the absence of serious physiological disturbance.

Although the role of the parent in eliciting emotional arousal that might trigger an attack is not clearly understood, evidence does exist that the frequency of asthmatic episodes can be reduced if parental attention is withdrawn contingent upon wheezing (Neisworth and Moore, 1972). Thus, in planning a treatment program where parental attention is going to be used as an operant factor it might be useful to subtype the asthmatic children regarding Asthma Potential Scores and indices of emotional precipitants. The data strongly predicts greater effectiveness of this manipulation in families where low APS scores and high emotional precipitants are obtained.

Miklich (1973) successfully decreased the number of attacks in an asthmatic child when reinforcement was given for increasing periods without attacks. Creer (1970) demonstrated that the residential treatment setting could provide too much support for continued illness. He used time-out from positive reinforcement to decrease both the frequency and duration of hospitalization. In essence, his procedure made continued hospitalization less desirable than a return to the real world. While hospitalized the resident was placed in a room by himself and denied visits from other patients. Only school work was permitted to be in his possession. A reversal procedure clearly demonstrated the importance of social consequences in maintaining the frequency and duration of hospitalization.

Classroom behavior of a child frequently absent because of illness may reflect inattentiveness and hyperactivity that results from being overwhelmed by peer interactions or the inability to catch up on missed work. This may result in a vicious cycle of the child desiring to stay home because of the unpleasant encounters he meets. Creer (1970) found that behavioral disruptions in the classroom could be easily controlled if rewards were given appropriate to task relevant behavior.

Shaping procedures which use operant reinforcers to teach asthmatic children to monitor their symptoms have led to earlier detection of airway obstruction (Renne, Nau, Dretiker and Lyon, 1976). This training may be quite important in view of the data (Dahlem, Kinsman and Horton, 1977) which suggested that if the asthmatic scores at either extreme of a Panic–Fear dimension (implying excessive vigilance or excessive denial), the course of their illness may be unfavorable. If a patient does not respond to the early precipitant wheezing, they usually get admitted to the hospital in a more severe state and often are less responsive to medication.

It would seem from a review of literature (Melamed and Johnson, 1980) that behavioral management with biofeedback, reciprocal inhibition and other conditioning procedures should be considered adjunctive to the medical management of asthma. There is a definite need for more systematic studies to evaluate the components of these different treatments with respect to the type of patient they might best help.

C. Juvenile Diabetes

Behavioral assessment and treatment have not been extensively applied to the problem of juvenile diabetes. Since this is the most common endocrine disorder of childhood, affecting approximately 150,000 American young people it seems appropriate to review the behavioral demands of treatment management and thereby encourage more behavioral specialists to become involved. Many children with juvenile or insulin dependent diabetes have what is termed a "brittle" form of the disease with frequent episodes of ketoacidosis and hypoglycemia, often resulting in hospitalization. This instability is of particular concern to pediatricians as it is associated with greater complications such as retinopathy and kidney failure (Cahill, Etzwiler and Freinkel, 1976). Effective daily management of diabetes can lead to a reasonable life expectancy. It therefore, seems advisable that more emphasis be placed on helping children learn the skills for controlling the illness.

From a behavioral perspective, this involves first, evaluating the set of skills the family must acquire and secondly, investigating the impact of emotional disturbance on the course of the disease process. The patient with diabetes must adopt new health care behaviors and change pre-existing daily routines. Knapp (1977) has aptly described this as essentially a problem in behavior management rather than medical treatment:

> To the patient diabetes is a way of living. It is learning to self-administer insulin of the appropriate type and amount, and within a specified time period each day. It is maintaining a rigid diet, eating exact amounts of food at regular intervals, whether prompted by hunger or not. It is staying on a routine exercise schedule, making adjustments in insulin and meals as exertion varies. It is recording several times each day the level of sugar in one's urine. It is being ever watchful for the altering signs of insulin shock (p. 1).

On top of this formidable management program, there is evidence to suggest that diabetes control is affected by emotional adjustment (Koski, 1969; Loughlin and Mosenthal, 1944; Stersky, 1963). Mothers describe their children with poor diabetes control as having significantly more behavioral and emotional problems (Simonds, 1977). Thus, regardless of whether these disturbances are reactive or causal, the assessment of individual and family factors that increase emotional conflict should be undertaken. Since the quality of mothers interactions may affect the course of the illness and the child's adjustment to diabetes, their behavior needs to be assessed. Steinhauser, Borner and Koepp (1977) noted that well-controlled diabetics described their mothers as being highly supportive at disease onset and less supportive over time, whereas the opposite pattern emerged for children in poor control. Poor control has been related to family disintegration (Simonds, 1977).

Minuchin and his colleagues (Minuchin, Baker, Rosman, Liebman, Milman and Todd, 1975) have developed a model which suggests that psychological factors may influence diabetes in two ways. First, emotional disturbance may result in behavior problems (e.g., refusing to take insulin; eating inappropriately) which can have metabolic consequences. Or emotional disturbance may cause metabolic derangements directly through psycho-physiological mechanisms. These hypotheses regarding family influences are based primarily on subjective report and should be studied directly by behavioral observation.

Behavioral treatments which help the patients modulate their regimen and those which directly attempt to reduce emotional responsivity have begun to appear in the literature. Lowe and Lutzker (1979) provided an example of the application of information and contingency management in improving medical adherence in a nine-year-old child. The mother was used as the therapist. Since the child lacked the basic knowledge regarding dietary requirements, and the proper technique for conducting the glucose and acetone tests, in addition to preventive foot care, the starting point was in providing this information. It has already been established that knowledge does not by itself enhance compliance (Etzwiler and Robb, 1972), and in this case the use of a point-system was instituted to increase the child's motivation.

The multiple baseline design, depicted in Fig. 3, demonstrates that a memo (written instructions regarding allowable diet exchanges) was sufficient by itself in improving adherence to the dietary restrictions. However, it was not until a point system with back-up reinforcers was initiated that any noticeable improvement occurred in her foot care or urine testing behavior. Perhaps the inherently reinforcing properties of eating provided the motivation necessary for diet compliance, whereas, in addition to information about procedures (memo) some tangible incentive had to be added before the other tasks could be reliably performed. Follow up data for ten weeks provided evidence that these habits were still being maintained even though the therapist had withdrawn active participation, and during the period when the mother reduced the frequency of reinforcer exchange. It would have been important to assess whether there was any concomitant improvement in the quality of the mother–daughter interaction.

In a case study, that focused more directly on the problem of emotionality, biofeedback relaxation was used (Fowler, Budzynski and Vandenbergh, 1976). A 20-year-old female, diabetic since age nine, suffered an increase in episodes of ketoacidosis, which is not uncommon in adolescence. During the stress of her first year at college, she was hospitalized eight times for ketoacidosis. Her diabetic instability did seem to be related to shifts in emotionality, pleasure, as well as anxiety. This study was particularly interesting in that the daily dose of insulin required (as determined by results of urine testing) was the primary dependent variable. The treatment followed six weeks of baseline in which the patient kept a daily diary of her diet, exercise, medication, infections, and emotional conflicts. In addition, she gave a quantified subjective estimate of her diabetic state and her emotionality. The treatment consisted of EMG biofeedback of tension from the forehead (frontalis) area. In addition, she listened to cassette tapes containing a

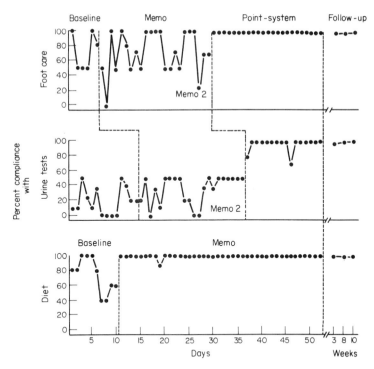

FIG. 3. Percentage compliance to foot care, urine testing, and diet.

progression of relaxation instructions for relaxing major muscle groups, as well as stabilizing and slowing respiration. As she became adept at this she was told to use the relaxation during stressful situations in her everyday situation. An impressive follow-up six months later for a comparable amount of time, revealed the effectiveness of what she had learned.

The results as illustrated in Fig. 4 are particularly impressive in that the level of insulin requirements dropped from a high of 103 units during her baseline (final

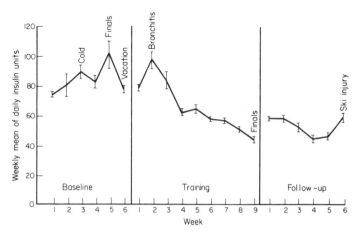

FIG. 4. Weekly mean and standard error of daily insulin.

exam) week, to an average of 44 units during the training period. The fact that self-controlled relaxation was paired with biofeedback training may have assisted the maintenance of this diabetic stability after the program was formally terminated. The patient's reports of diabetic state and emotional stability correlated in the expected direction with the insulin requirements. A word of caution should be noted in that the early stages of training were accompanied by some severe episodes of hypoglycemia, indicating that her need for insulin decreased more rapidly than the rate at which the daily dose was actually adjusted. Therefore, medical supervision is necessary given the potent effects of biofeedback training on metabolic state.

Johnson (1980) discussed the methodological problems that need to be addressed before controlled studies can be undertaken. The problems of defining the population so that relatively homogeneous groups can be studied (instabile versus stable patients), developing appropriate measures for assessing change, and predicting which behavioral programs to use with which patients, are common to a broader range of physical problems than diabetes alone.

Implications are clear for the utility of behavioral intervention with other chronically ill populations (e.g., cystic fibrosis, renal disease, chronic heart condition) in which daily complex regimens must be precisely followed in order for health to be maintained. Behavioral psychologists can take up this challenge within their current base of knowledge if they collaborate with the medical experts who will retain primary responsibility for the medical monitoring of the illness.

4. PREVENTION AND COMPLIANCE

Behavioral psychologists have made contributions to the medical care of children through the application of learning principles in the reduction of medical concerns that may prevent appropriate diagnosis, and by improving treatment adherence.

The fear of injections and painful diagnostic procedures often interferes with good medical treatment by delaying the contact with the professionals or through the child's behavioral disruptions which may interfere with the carrying out of these procedures. Preparation for medical treatment which makes use of filmed modeling procedures have been reviewed (Melamed, 1977). Children having advanced videotaped preparation about what to expect, and instructions on how to cope with these experiences, had decreased anxiety during the procedures and reduced occurrence of lingering behavioral problems (Melamed, Yurcheson, Fleece, Hutcheson and Hawes, 1978; Melamed and Siegel, 1975).

Systematic desensitization has been used to alleviate injection phobias in both adults and children (Katz, 1974; Nimmer and Kapp, 1974; Turnage and Logan, 1974). The treatment involves a hierarchy of injection-related concerns and training in the substitution of relaxation during both imagery and real-life exposure to these anxiety-provoking events. Table 1 presents a sample of a hierarchy used with an adolescent with renal failure who refused hemodialysis because of his injection phobia (Katz, 1974). The treatment was effective with just one ninety-minute session. The patient was then able to receive dialysis from a number of technicians without anxiety.

Participant modeling, which involves actually encouraging the patients to observe others receiving injections, and then handling the apparatus themselves, has increased the desensitization treatment effectiveness (Taylor, Ferguson and Wermuth, 1977).

The use of behavioral treatment in preparation of children for surgery was reviewed by Melamed (1977) and by Melamed and Siegel (1980). The approaches include film modeling, cognitive manipulations, as well as systematic desensitization.

The behavioral psychologist has made an impact on reducing health-risk factors in children through programs to reduce childhood obesity (Wheeler and Hess, 1976) and to reduce cigarette smoking (Bernstein and Glasgow, 1979; Evans, Rozelle, Mittlemark, Hansen, Bane and Havis, 1978).

TABLE 1.
Hierarchy Used in the Treatment of a Hemodialysis Phobia

1. Waking upon the morning of a scheduled dialysis treatment.
2. At the hospital being weighed in and having blood pressure and temperature taken.
3. In bed being prepared for Xylocain injection.
4. Visualizing the dialysis catheter.
5. Having the catheter inserted by a trusted technician.
6. Having the catheter inserted by a new technician.
7. Having the catheter withdrawn immediately after it was inserted.
8. Having the catheter reinserted.

The importance of maintaining adherence to medication regimens in children has also been addressed. The need to include parents in this regard is particularly important since they are the main deliverers of medication. Kirscht and Rosenstock (1979) reviewed the literature on compliance. Becker, Drachman and Kirscht (1972) provided evidence that mothers' prematurely terminated a ten day penicillin treatment regimen for viral infections in their children, because the symptoms remitted. The factors that must be taken into account to optimize adherence to medical regimens are complex and involve both information and motivational considerations. The data currently available suggests that the highest rates of compliance are achieved with the least complicated regimen, that can easily be incorporated into a person's life-style, and that enhances the immediate relief of symptoms and has the fewest aversive side effects.

At present there have appeared only case studies such as, Lowe and Lutzker (1979), which utilize operant principles of learning to increase adherence to complex regimens. The systematic application of learning theory based on the analysis of avoidance learning and reinforcement can lead to programs that have a better chance of being carried out.

Another fertile area for the efforts of the behavioral specialist is the development of carefully specified medical regimens for chronically ill children. These would promote home care of children with such illnesses as cystic fibrosis, hemophilia, and juvenile diabetes, which require constant patient surveillance, and prompt appropriate action.

5. SUMMARY AND CONCLUSIONS

This chapter provided a rationale for the application of learning theory-based treatments to medical disorders in children. The fact that conditioning factors influence the precipitation and the course of a variety of problems including enuresis, encopresis, seizures, hyperkinesis, asthma, and juvenile diabetes was demonstrated through clinical case studies and controlled research. The need to consider family influences both on the emotional behavior of the patient and on the adherence to treatment regimens was emphasized. The successful application of systematic desensitization, operant approaches, and modeling procedures in giving the patient control over the intensity and frequency of illness episodes was described. Biofeedback in the reduction of visceral and central nervous system responses associated with certain somatic problems needs to be further investigated. Although these procedures are often efficacious in the laboratory, their clinical utility and the actual mechanism of the change need to be evaluated. The usefulness of behavioral approaches in reducing medical concerns that might allow better treatment at home and in the clinic was addressed. The need is indicated for more systematic research, predicated on more careful, definition of the clinical population, clearer measurement of symptomatic behavior, and better documented therapeutic procedures.

ACKNOWLEDGMENTS

The author received support from the National Institute of Dental Research Grant No. DE 05305-01 during the preparation of this manuscript. Several portions of the manuscript are revisions from Melamed, B. G. and Siegel, L. J., *Behavioral Medicine: Practical applications in health care.* New York: Springer Publishing, 1980. Also acknowledged is the assistance of Dr. Suzanne Bennett Johnson in the preparation of the juvenile diabetes section and Victoria Casey for the seizure disorders.

REFERENCES

Abraham, S. and Nordseick M. (1960) Relationships of excess weight in children and adults, *Public Health Reports*, **75**, 263–273.

Agras, W. S., Chapin, and Oliveau, D. C. (1972) The natural history of phobia, *Archives of General Psychiatry*, **26**, 315–317.

Agras, S., Barlow, D., Chapin, H., Abel, G. and Leitenberg, H. (1974) Behavior modification of anorexia nervosa, *Archives of General Psychiatry*, **30**, 279–286.

Alexander, A. B. (1972) Systematic relaxation and flow rates in asthmatic children: Relationship to emotional precipitants and anxiety, *Journal of Psychosomatic Research*, **10**, 405–410.

Alexander, A. B., Miklich D. R. and Hershkoff, H. (1972) The immediate effects of systematic relaxation training on peak expiratory flow rates in asthmatic children, *Psychosomatic Medicine*, **34**, 388–394.

Anderson, J. E. (1930) Pediatrics and child psychology, *Journal of the American Medical Association*, **95**, 1015–1020.

Argona, J., Cassady, J. and Drabman, R. S. (1975) Treating overweight children through parental training and contingency contracting, *Journal of Applied Behavior Analysis*, **8**, 269–278.

Ayllon, T., Layman, D. and Kandel, H. S. (1975) A behavioral educational alternative to drug control of hyperkinetic children, *Journal of Applied Behavior Analysis*, **8**, 137–146.

Azrin, N. and Foxx, R. (1974) *Toilet training in less than a day*, Simon and Schuster, New York.

Azrin, N. and Powell, J. (1969) Behavioral engineering: The use of response priming to improve prescribed self-medication, *Journal of Applied Behavior Analysis*, **2**, 39–42.

Azrin, N. H., Sneed, T. J. and Foxx, R. M. (1974) Dry-bed: Rapid elimination of childhood enuresis, *Behavior Research and Therapy*, **12**, 147–156.

Bakwin, H. and Bakwin, R. M. (1972) *Behavior disorders in children*, W. B. Saunders, Philadelphia.

Bandura, A. Self-referent thought: The development of self-efficacy, in J. H. Flavell and L. D. Ross (Eds.), *Development of social cognition*. In press.

Becker, M. H., Drachman, R. H. and Kirscht, D. P. (1972) Predicting mothers' compliance with pediatric medical regimens, *Journal of Pediatrics*, **81**, 843–854.

Bentovim, A. (1970) The clinical approach to feeding disorders of childhood, *Journal of Psychosomatic Research*, **14**, 267–276.

Berger, M. (1977) Psychology in paediatric and child care, in S. Rachman (Ed.), *Contributions to medical psychology*, Vol. 1, Pergamon Press, Oxford.

Bernal, M. E. (1972) Behavioral treatment of a child's eating problem, *Journal of Behavior Therapy and Experimental Psychiatry*, **3**, 43–50.

Bernstein, D. A. and Glasgow, R. E. (1979) The modification of smoking behavior, in O. F. Pomerleau and J. P. Brady (Eds.), *Behavioral medicine: Theory and practice*, Williams & Wilkins, Baltimore.

Birbaumer, N., Dworkin, B. and Miller, N. E. (1979) Biofeedback in scoliosis patients, Paper presented at the European Congress of Behavior Therapy, Paris.

Blanchard, E. B. and Young, L. D. (1974) Clinical applications of biofeedback, *Archives of General Psychiatry*, **30**, 573–589.

Block, J. (1969) Parents of schizophrenic, neurotic, asthmatic, and congenitally ill children: A comparative study, *Archives of General Psychiatry*, **20**, 659–661.

Block, J., Jennings, P. H., Harvey, E. and Simpson E. (1964) Interaction between allergic potential and psychopathology in childhood, *Psychosomatic Medicine*, **26**, 307–320.

Bollard, R. J. and Woodroffe, P. (1977) The effect of parent-administered dry-bed training on nocturnal enuresis in children, *Behavior Research & Therapy*, **15**, 159–165.

Buell, J., Stoddard, P., Harris, F. R. and Baer, D. M. (1968) Collateral social development accompanying reinforcement of outdoor play in a preschool child, *Journal of Applied Analysis of Behavior*, **1**, 167–173.

Bugental, D. B., Whalen, C. K. and Henker, B. (1977) Causal attributions of hyperactive children and motivational assumptions of two behavior-change approaches: Evidence for an interactionist position, *Child Development*, **48**, 874–884.

Butler, J. (1976) The toilet training success of parents after reading *Toilet Training in Less than a Day*, *Behavior Therapy*, **7**, 185–191.

Cabral, R. J. and Scott, D. F. (1976) Effects of two desensitization techniques, biofeedback and relaxation, on intractable epilepsy: Follow-up study, *Journal of Neurology, Neurosurgery and Psychiatry*, **37**, 504–507.

Cahill, G., Etzwiler, D. and Freinkel, N. (1976) "Control" and diabetes, *New England Journal of Medicine*, **294**, 1004.

Cantwell, D. P. (1975) *The hyperactive child*, Spectrum Publications, New York.

Carter, S. and Gold, A. (1968) Convulsions in children, *New England Journal of Medicine*, **278**, 315–317.

Christophersen, E. R. and Rainey, S. (1976) Management of encopresis through a pediatric outpatient clinic, *Journal of Pediatric Psychology*, **1**, 38–41.

Christophersen, E. R. and Rapoff, M. A. (1978) Enuresis treatment, *Issues in Comprehensive Pediatric Nursing*, **2**, 34–52.

Christophersen, E. R. and Rapoff, M. A. (1979) Behavioral pediatrics, in O. F. Pomerleau and J. P. Brady (Eds.), *Behavioral medicine: Theory and practice*, Williams & Wilkins, Baltimore.

Clarke, P. S. (1970) Effects of emotion and cough on airways obstruction in asthma, *Medical Journal of Australia*, **1**, 535.

Clement, P. W. (1968) Operant conditioning in group psychotherapy with children, *Journal of School Health*, **38**, 271–278.

Clement, P. W., Roberts, P. V. and Lantz, C. (1970) Social models and token reinforcement in the treatment of shy, withdrawn boys, *Proceedings of the 78th Annual Convention of the American Psychological Association*, APA, Washington, D.C.

Creer, T. (1970) The use of a time-out from positive reinforcement with asthmatic children, *Journal of Psychosomatic Research*, **14**, 117–120.

Creer, T. L. and Christian, W. P. (1976) *Chronically ill and handicapped children: Their management and rehabilitation*, Research Press, Champaign, Ill.

Dahlem, N. W., Kinsman, R. A. and Horton, D. J. (1977) Requests for as-needed (PRN) medications by asthmatic patients: Relationships to prescribed oral corticosteroid regimens and length of hospitalization, *Journal of Allergy and Clinical Immunology*, **60**, 295–300.

Davis, M. H., Saunders, D. R., Creer, T. L. and Chai, H. (1973) Relaxation training facilitated by biofeedback apparatus as a supplemental treatment in bronchial asthma, *Journal of Psychosomatic Research*, **17**, 121–128.

Davison, G. C. and Neale, J. M. (1974) *Abnormal psychology: An experimental clinical approach*, Wiley, New York.

DeLeon, G. and Mandell, W. A. (1966) A comparison of conditioning and psychotherapy in the treatment of functional enuresis, *Journal of Clinical Psychology*, **22**, 326–330.

Doleys, D. (1977) Behavioral treatments for nocturnal enuresis in children: A review of recent literature, *Psychological Bulletin*, **84**, 30–54.

Douglas, V. I. (1974) Differences between normal and hyperkinetic children, in C. K. Conners (Ed.), *Clinical use of stimulant drugs in children*, Excerpta Medica, Amsterdam.

Dworkin, B. (1980) Biofeedback in the treatment of scoliosis, *Journal of Behavioral Medicine*. In press.

Epstein, L. H., Katz, R. C. and Zlutnick, S. (1979) Behavioral medicine, in M. Hersen, R. M. Eisler and P. M. Miller (Eds.), *Progress in behavior modification*, Vol. 7. Academic Press, New York.

Epstein, L. H. and Masek, N. J. (1978) Behavioral control of medicine compliance, *Journal of Applied Behavior Analysis*, **11**, 1–9.

Etzwiler, D. and Robb, J. (1972) Evaluation of programmed education among juvenile diabetics and their families, *Diabetes*, **21**, 967–971.

Evans, R. I., Rozelle, R. M., Mittlemark, M. B., Hansen, W. B., Bane, A. L. and Havis, J. G. (1978) Deterring the onset of smoking in children: Knowledge of immediate physiological effects and coping with peer pressure, media pressure, and aprent modeling, *Journal of Applied Social Psychology*, **8**, 126–135.

Finley, W. W., Smith, H. A. and Etherton, M. D. (1975) Reduction of seizures and normalization of the EEG in a severe epileptic following sensorimotor biofeedback training: A preliminary study, *Biological Psychology*, **2**, 189–203.

Forrester, R., Stein, Z. and Susser, M. A. (1964) A trial of conditioning therapy in nocturnal enuresis, *Developmental Medicine and Child Neurology*, **6**, 158–166.

Fowler, J., Budzynski, T. and Vandenbergh, R. (1976) Effects of an EMG biofeedback relaxation program on the control of diabetes: A case study, *Biofeedback and Self-Regulation*, **1**, 105–112.

Freedman, D. (1971) Report of the conference on the use of stimulant drugs in the treatment of behaviorally disturbed young school children, *Psychopharmalogical Bulletin*, **7**, 23–29.

Hahn, W. W. (1966) Autonomic responses of asthmatic children, *Psychosomatic Medicine*, **28**, 323–332.

Halperin, D. and Kottke, F. (1968) Training of control of head posture in children with cerebral palsy, *Developmental Medicine and Child Neurology*, **10**, 249.

Harris, L. S. and Purohit, A. P. (1977) Bladder training and enuresis: A controlled trial, *Behavior Research & Therapy*, **15**, 485–490.

Hock, R. A., Rodgers, C. H., Reddi, C. and Kennard, D. W. (1978) Asthmatic children: An evaluation of physiological change, *Psychosomatic Medicine*, **40**, 210–215.

Ince, L. P. (1976) The use of relaxation training and a conditioned stimulus in the elimination of epileptic seizures in a child: A case study, *Journal of Behavior Therapy and Experimental Psychiatry*, **7**, 39–42.

Jackson, D. A. and Wallace, R. F. (1974) The modification and generalization of voice loudness in a fifteen-year-old retarded girl, *Journal of Applied Behavior Analysis*, **7**, 461–471.

Jersild, A. T. and Holmes, F. B. (1935) Children's fears, *Child Development Monographs*, **20**.

Johnson, S. B. Psychosocial factors in juvenile diabetes: A review, *Journal of Behavioral Medicine*. In press.

Johnson, S. B. and Melamed, B. G. (1979) The assessment and treatment of children's fears, in B. Lahey and A. Kazdin (Eds.), *Advances in clinical child psychology*, Vol. 2, Plenum Press, New York.

Kahn, A. U. (1977) Effectiveness of biofeedback and counter-conditioning in the treatment of bronchial asthma, *Journal of Psychosomatic Research*, **21**, 97–104.

Kasl, S. V. (1975) Issues in patient adherence to health care regimens, *Journal of Human Stress*, **1**, 5–17.

Katz, R. C. (1974) Single session recovery from a hemodialysis phobia: A case study, *Journal of Behavior Therapy and Experimental Psychiatry*, **5**, 205–206.

Kauffman, J. M. and Hallahan, D. P. (1979) Learning disability and hyperactivity (with comments on Minimal Brain Dysfunction). In B. Lahey and A. Kazdin (Eds.) *Advances in Clinical Child Psychology* Vol. 2. Plenum Press, New York.

Kendall, P. C. (1977) On the efficacious use of *verbal* self-instructional procedures of children, *Cognitive Therapy and Research*, **1**, 331–341.

Kennedy, W. A. (1965) School phobia: Rapid treatment of fifty cases, *Journal of Abnormal Psychology*, **70**, 285–289.

Kimball, C. P. (1970) Conceptual developments in psychosomatic medicine: 1939–1969, *Annals of Internal Medicine*, **73**, 307–316.

Kimmel, H. D. and Kimmel, E. (1970) An instrumental conditioning method for the treatment of enuresis, *Journal of Behavior Therapy and Experimental Psychiatry*, **1**, 121–123.

Kingsley, R. G. and Shapiro, J. (1977) A comparison of three behavioral programs for the control of obesity in children, *Behavior Therapy*, **8**, 30–36.

Kirby, F. D. and Toler, H. C., Jr. (1970) Modification of preschool isolate behavior: A case study, *Journal of Applied Behavior Analysis*, **3**, 309–314.

Kirscht, J. P. and Rosenstock, I. M. (1979) Patients' problems in following recommendations of health experts, in G. C. Stone, F. Cohen and N. E. Adler (Eds.), *Health Psychology*, Jossey-Bass, San Francisco.

Knapp, T. J. (1977) Behavior management procedures for diabetic persons, Paper presented at the meeting of the Midwestern Association of Behavior Analysis, Chicago, May, 1977.

Koski, M. L. (1969) The coping processes in childhood diabetes, *Acta Paediatrica Scandinavica*, Supplement, **198**, 7–56.

Kotses, H., Glaus, K. D., Bricel, S. K., Edwards, J. E. and Crawford, P. L. (1978) Operant muscular relaxation and peak expiratory flow rate in asthmatic children, *Journal of Psychosomatic Research*, **22**, 17–23.

Kotses, H., Glaus, K. D., Crawford, P. L., Edwards, J. E. and Scherr, M. S. (1976) Operant reduction of frontalis EMG activity in the treatment of asthma in children, *Journal of Psychosomatic Research*, **20**, 453–459.

Lambert, N. M., Sandoval, J. and Sassone, D. (1978) Prevalence of hyperactivity in elementary school children as a function of social system definers, *American Journal of Orthopsychiatry*, **48**, 446–463.

Lewis, M. and Rosenblum, L. (Eds.) (1974) *The effect of the infant on its caregiver*, John Wiley, New York.

Lipton, E. L., Sternschneider, A. and Richmond, J. B. (1966) Psychophysiological disorders in children, in L. W. Hoffman and M. L. Hoffman (Eds.), *Review of child development research*, Vol. 2, Russel Sage, New York.

Loughlin, W. and Mosenthal, H. (1944) Study of the personalities of children with diabetes, *American Journal of Diseases of Children*, **68**, 13–15.

Lovibond, S. H. and Coote, M. A. (1970) Enuresis, in C. G. Costello (Ed.), *Symptoms of Psychopathology*, Wiley, New York.

Lowe, K. and Lutzker, J. R. (1979) Increasing compliance to a medical regimen with a juvenile diabetic, *Behavior Therapy*, **10**, 57–64.

Lubar, J. F. and Bahler, W. W. (1976) Behavioral management of epileptic seizures following biofeedback training of the sensorimotor rhythm, *Biofeedback and Self-Regulation*, **1**, 77–104.

Lukeman, D. (1975) Conditioning methods of treating childhood asthma, *Journal of Child Psychology and Psychiatry*, **16**, 165–168.

Lutzker, J. and Drake, J. (1976) A comparison of toilet training techniques to produce rapid toilet training in children, Paper presented at the 1976 meeting of the American Psychological Association, Washington, D.C.

Malament, I. B., Dunn, M. E. and Davis, R. (1975) Pressure sores: An operant conditioning approach to prevention, *Archives of Physical Medicine and Rehabilitation*, **56**, 161–165.

Marks, I. M. (1969) *Fears and phobias*, Academic Press, New York.

Marston, M. V. (1970) Compliance with medical regimens: A review of the literature, *Nursing Research*, **19**, 312–323.

Mattson, A. (1972) Long-term physical illness in childhood: A challenge to psycho–social adaptation. *Pediatrics*, **50**, 801–811.

Meichenbaum, D. W. and Goodman, J. (1971) Training impulsive children to talk to themselves: A means of developing self-control, *Journal of Abnormal Psychology*, **77**, 115–126.

Melamed, B. G. (1977) Psychological preparation for hospitalization, in S. Rachman (Ed.), *Contributions to medical psychology*, Vol. 1, Pergamon Press, Oxford.

Melamed, B. G., Hawes, R., Heiby, E. and Glick, J. (1975) Use of filmed modeling to reduce uncooperative behavior of children during dental treatment, *Journal of Dental Research*, **54**, 797–801.

Melamed, B. G. and Johnson, S. B. (1980) Assessment of chonic illness: Asthma and diabetes, in E. Mash and L. Terdal (Eds.), *Behavioral assessment of childhood disorders*, Guilford, N. J. In press.

Melamed, B. G., Meyer, R., Gee, C. and Soule, L. (1976) The influence of time and type of preparation on children's adjustment to hospitalization, *Journal of Pediatric Psychology*, **1**, 31–37.

Melamed, B. G. and Siegel, L. J. (1975) Reduction of anxiety in children facing hospitalization and surgery by use of filmed modeling, *Journal of Consulting and Clinical Psychology*, **43**, 511–521.

Melamed, B. G. and Siegel, L. J. (1980) *Behavioral medicine: Practical applications in health care*, Springer Publishing, New York.

Melamed, B. G., Weinstein, D., Hawes, R. and Katin-Borland, M. (1975) Reduction of fear-related dental management problems with use of filmed modeling, *Journal of the American Dental Association*, **90**, 822–826.

Melamed, B. G., Yurcheson, R., Fleece, E. L., Hutcheson, S. and Hawes, R. (1978) Effects of film modeling on the reduction of anxiety-related behaviors in individuals varying in level of previous experience in the stress situation, *Journal of Consulting and Clinical Psychology*, **46**, 1357–1367.

Meunier, P., Mollard, P. and Marechal, J. M. (1976) Physiopathology of megarectum: The association of megarectum with encopresis, *Gut*, **17**, 224–227.

Miklich, D. R. (1973) Operant conditioning procedures with systematic desensitization in a hyperkinetic asthmatic boy, *Journal of Behavior Therapy and Experimental Psychiatry*, **4**, 177–182.

Miklich, D. R., Renne, C. M., Creer, T. L., Alexander, A. B., Chai, M., Davis, M. H., Hoffman, A. and Danker-Brown, P. (1977) The clinical utility of behavior therapy as an adjunctive treatment for asthma, *Journal of Allergy and Clinical Immunology*, **60**, 285–294.

Miller, N. (1969) Learning of visceral and glandular responses, *Science*, **163**, 434–445.

Miller, P. M. (1973) An experimental analysis of retention control training in the treatment of nocturnal enuresis in two institutionalized adolescents, *Behavior Therapy*, **4**, 288–294.

Millichap, J. G. (1968) Drugs in management of hyperkinetic and perceptually-handicapped children, *Journal of the American Medical Association*, **206**, 1527–1530.

Minskoff, J. G. (1973) Differential approaches to prevalence estimates of learning disabilities, *Annals of New York Academy of Sciences*, **205**, 139–145.

Minuchin, S., Baker, L., Rosman, B., Liebman, R., Milman, L. and Todd, T. (1975) A conceptual model of psychosomatic illness in children, *Archives of General Psychiatry*, **32**, 1031–1038.

Minuchin, S., Rosman and Baker, L. (1978) *Psychosomatic families*, Harvard University Press, Cambridge, Mass.

Moore, N. (1965) Behavior therapy in bronchial asthma: A controlled study, *Journal of Psychosomatic Research*, **9**, 257–276.

Mostofsky, D. I. and Balaschak, B. A. (1977) Psychobiological control of seizures, *Psychological Bulletin*, **84**, 723–750.

Mowrer, O. H. and Mowrer, W. M. (1938) Enuresis: A method for its study and treatment, *American Journal of Orthopsychiatry*, **8**, 436–459.

Muellner, S. R. (1960) The development of urinary control in children: A new concept in cause, prevention, and treatment of primary enuresis, *Journal of Urology*, **84**, 714–716.

Mussen, P. (1970) Preface, *Carmichael's manual of child psychology*, John Wiley, New York.

Neisworth, J. T. and Moore, F. (1972) Operant treatment of asthmatic responding with the parent as therapist, *Behavior Therapy*, **3**, 95–99.

Nimmer, W. H. and Kapp, R. A. (1974) A multiple impact program for the treatment of an injection phobia, *Journal of Behavior Therapy and Experimental Psychiatry*, **5**, 257–258.

O'Conner, R. D. (1969) Modification of social withdrawal through symbolic modeling, *Journal of Applied Behavior Analysis*, **2**, 15–22.

O'Conner, R. D. (1972) Relative efficacy of modeling, shaping, and the combined procedures for modification of social withdrawal, *Journal of Abnormal Psychology*, **79**, 327–334.

O'Leary, K. D. and Wilson, G. T. (1975) *Behavior therapy: Application and outcome*, Prentice-Hall, Englewood Cliffs, N.J.

O'Leary, K. D., Pelham, W. F., Rosenbaum, A. and Price, G. H. (1976) Behavioral treatment of hyperkinetic children: An experimental evaluation and its usefulness, *Clinical Pediatrics*, **15**, 510–515.

Parrino, J. J. (1971) Reduction of seizures by desensitization, *Journal of Behavior Therapy and Experimental Psychiatry*, **2**, 215–218.

Paschalis, A., Kimmel, H. and Kimmel, E. (1972) Further study of diurnal instrumental conditioning in the treatment of enuresis nocturna, *Journal of Behavior Therapy and Experimental Psychiatry*, **3**, 253–256.

Patterson, G. R. (1976) The aggressive child: Victim and architect of a coercive system, in E. J. Mash, L. A. Hamerlynck and L. C. Handy (Eds.), *Behavior modification and families*, Brunner/Mazel, New York.

Patterson, G. R., Cobb, J. and Ray, R. (1970) A social engineering technology for retraining aggressive boys, in H. Adams and J. Unikel (Eds.), *Georgia symposium in experimental clinical psychology*, Vol. 2, Pergamon, New York.

Patterson, G. R. and Gullion, M. E. (1968) *Living with children*, Research Press, Champaign, Ill.

Patterson, G. R. and Reid, J. B. (1970) Reciprocity and coercion: Two facets of social systems, in C. Neuringer and J. Michael (Eds.), *Behavior modification in clinical psychology*, Appleton-Century-Crofts, New York.

Patterson, G. R., Reid, J. B., Jones, R. R. and Conger, R. E. (1975) *A social learning approach to family intervention: Families with aggressive children*, Vol. 1, Castalia Publishing, Eugene, Ore.

Patterson, R. (1972) Time-out and assertive training for a dependent child, *Behavior Therapy*, **3**, 466–468.

Peterson, L and Ridley Johnson, R. (1980) Pediatric hospital response to prehospital preparation for children. *Journal of Pediatric Psychology*, in press.

Purcell, K., Brady, K., Chai, H., Muser, J., Molk, L., Gordon, N. and Means, J. (1969) The effect on asthma in children of experimental separation from the family, *Psychosomatic Medicine*, **31**, 144–164.

Reid, J. B. (1967) Reciprocity and family interaction, Unpublished doctoral dissertation, University of Oregon.

Renne, C. M., Nau, E., Dretiker, K. E. and Lyon, R. (1976) Latency in seeking asthma treatment as a function of achieving successively higher flow rate criteria, Paper presented at the Tenth Annual Convention of the Association for the Advancement of Behavior Therapy, New York, December, 1976.

Ross, A. O. (1976) *Psychological aspects of learning disabilities and reading disorders*, McGraw–Hill, New York.

Sackett, D. L., Haynes, R. B., Gibson, E. S., Hackett, B. C., Taylor, D. W., Roberts, R. S. and Johnson, A. L. (1975) Randomized clinical trial of strategies for improving medication compliance in primary hypertension, *Lancet*, **1**, 1205–1207.

Safer, D. J. and Allen, R. P. (1976) *Hyperactive children: Diagnosis and management*, University Park Press, Baltimore.

Satterfield, J. H., Cantwell, D. P. and Satterfield, B. T. (1974) Pathophysiology of the hyperactive child syndrome, *Archives of General Psychiatry*, **31**, 839–844.

Schaefer, C. E., Millman, H. L. and Levine, G. F. (1979) *Therapies for psychosomatic disorders in children*, Jossey-Bass, San Francisco.

Schuster, M. M. (1974) Operant conditioning in gastrointestinal dysfunction, *Hospital Practice*, **9**, 135–143.

Schwabb, J. J., McGinnis, N. H., Morris, L. B. and Schwab, R. B. (1970) Psychosomatic medicine and the contemporary social scene, *American Journal of Psychiatry*, **126**, 1632–1642.

Sherman, H. and Farina, A. (1974) Social inadequacy of parents and children, *Journal of Abnormal Psychology*, **83**, 327–330.

Siegel, L. J. and Richards, C. S. (1977) Behavioral intervention with somatic disorders in children, in D. Marholin II (Ed.), *Child behavior therapy*, Gardner Press, New York.

Simonds, J. J. (1977) Psychiatric status of diabetic youth matched with a control group, *Diabetes*, **26**(10), 921–925.

Sirota, A. D. and Mahoney, M. J. (1974) Relaxing on cue: The self-regulation of asthma, *Journal of Behavior Therapy and Experimental Psychiatry*, **5**, 65–66.

Sroufe, L. A. (1975) Drug treatment of children with behavior problems, in F. Horowitz (Ed.), *Review of child development research*, Vol. 4, University of Chicago Press, Chicago.

Sroufe, L. A. and Stewart, M. A. (1973) Treating problem children with stimulant drugs, *New England Journal of Medicine*, **289**, 407–413.

Stableford, W., Butz, R., Hasazi, J., Leitenberg, H. and Peyser, J. (1976) Sequential withdrawal of stimulant drugs and use of behavior therapy with two hyperkinetic boys, *American Journal of Orthopsychiatry*, **46**, 302–312.

Stedman, D. (1970) The applications of learning principles in pediatric practice, *Pediatric Clinics of North America*, **17**, 427–436.

Steinhauser, H., Borner, S. and Koepp, P. (1977) The personality of juvenile diabetics, in Z. Laron (Ed.), *Pediatric and adolescent endocrinology*, Vol. 3.

Sterman, M. B. (1973) Neurophysiological and clinical studies of sensorimotor EEG biofeedback training: Some effects of epilepsy, *Seminars in Psychiatry*, **5**, 507–525.

Sterman, M. B. and Macdonald, L. R. (1978) Effects of central cortical EEG feedback training on incidence of poorly controlled seizures, *Epilepsia*, **19**, 207–222.

Sterman, M. B., Macdonald, L. R. and Stone, R. K. (1974) Biofeedback training of the sensorimotor electroencephalogram rhythm in man: Effects on epilepsy, *Epilepsia*, **15**, 395–416.

Stersky, G. (1963) Family background and state of mental health in a group of diabetic school children, *Acta Paediatrica*, **52**, 377–390.

Straker, N. and Tamerin, J. (1974) Aggression and childhood asthma: A study in a natural setting, *Journal of Psychosomatic Research*, **18**, 131–135.

Tahmasian, J., and McReynolds, W. (1971) Use of parents as behavioral engineers in the treatment of a school phobic girl. *Journal of Counseling Psychology*, **18**, 225–228.

Tal, A. and Miklich, D. R. (1976) Emotionally induced decreases in pulmonary flow rates in asthmatic children, *Psychosomatic Medicine*, **38**, 190–199.

Taylor, C. B., Ferguson, J. M. and Wermuth, B. M. (1977) Simple techniques to treat medical phobias, *Postgraduate Medical Journal*, **53**, 28–32.

Turnage, J. R. and Logan, D. L. (1974) Treatment of a hypodermic needle phobia by *in vivo* systematic desensitization, *Journal of Behavior Therapy and Experimental Psychiatry*, **5**, 67–69.

Vernon, D. and Bailey, W. C. (1974) The use of motion pictures in the psychological preparation of children for induction of anesthesia, *Anesthesiology*, **40**, 68–72.

Wahler, R. G., Leske, G. and Rogers, E. S. (1977) The insular family: A deviance support system for oppositional children (Unpublished manuscript), Presented in part to the Banff International Conference on Behavior Modification, Ganff, Alberta, Canada, March.

Walker, H. M. and Hops, H. (1973) Group and individual reinforcement contingencies in modification of social withdrawal, in L. A. Hamerlynck, L. C. Hardy and E. J. Mash (Eds.), *Behavior change: Methodology, concept and practice*, Research Press, Champaign, Ill.

Wender, P. H. (1971) *Minimal brain dysfunction in children*, Wiley, New York.

Wender, P. H. (1973) *The hyperactive child: A handbook for parents*, Crown, New York.

Werry, J. (1967) Enuresis nocturna, *Medical Times*, **95**, 985–991.

Werry, J. and Cohressen, J. (1965) Enuresis—An etiologic and therapeutic study, *Journal of Pediatrics*, **67**, 423–431.

Werry, J. S. and Sprague, R. L. (1970) Hyperactivity, in C. Costello (Ed.), *Symptoms of Psychopathology*, John Wiley, New York.

Whalen, C. and Henker, B. (1976) Psychostimulants and children: A review and analysis, *Psychological Bulletin*, **83**, 1113–1130.

Wheeler, M. E. and Hess, K. W. (1976) Treatment of juvenile obesity by successive approximation control of eating, *Journal of Behavior Therapy and Experimental Psychiatry*, **7**, 235–241.

Williams, C. (1959) The elimination of tantrum behavior by extinction procedures, *Journal of Abnormal Social Psychology*, **59**, 269.

Wright, L. (1973a) Aversive conditioning of self-induced seizures, *Behavior Therapy*, **4**, 712–713.

Wright, L. (1973b) Handling the encopretic child, *Professional Psychology*, **4**, 137–144.

Wright, L. (1977) Conceptualizing and defining psychosomatic disorders, *American Psychologist*, 625–628.

Wright, L. and Walker, E. (1977) Treatment of the child with psychogenic encopresis, *Clinical Pediatrics*, **16**, 1042–1045.

Wright, L., Nunnery, A., Eichel, B. and Scott, R. P. (1968) Application of operant conditioning principles to problems of tracheostomy addiction in children, *Journal of Consulting and Clinical Psychology*, **32**, 603–606.

Wyler, A. R., Robbins, C. A. and Dodrill, C. B. (1979) EEG operant conditioning for control of epilepsy, *Epilepsia*, **20**, 279–286.

Yates, A. J. (1970) *Behavior therapy*, John Wiley, New York.

Young, G. V. and Turner, R. (1965) CNS stimulant drugs and conditioning of nocturnal enuresis, *Behavior Research and Therapy*, **3**, 93–101.

Zeisat, H. A. (1978) Behavior modification in the treatment of hypertension, *International Journal of Psychiatry in Medicine*, **8**, 257–265.

Zimbardo, P., Pilkonis, P. and Norwood, R. (1974) The silent prison of shyness (Unpublished manuscript), Department of Psychology, Stanford University, Stanford, California.

Zimbardo, P., Pilkonis, P. and Norwood, R. (1975) The social disease called shyness, *Psychology Today*, **8**, 69–72.

Zlutnick, S., Mayville, W. J. and Moffat, S. (1975) Modification of seizure disorders: The interruption of behavioral chains, *Journal of Applied Behavior Analysis*, **8**, 1–12.

11

PROCESS EVALUATION: APPLICATION OF A BEHAVIOURAL APPROACH WITHIN A GENERAL HOSPITAL PSYCHIATRIC UNIT

ROBERT W. SANSON-FISHER and A. DESMOND POOLE

The University of Western Australia

"Speaking for myself, I too believe that humanity will win in the long run; I am only afraid that at the same time the world will have turned into one huge hospital where everyone is everyone else's human nurse."

Goethe, Italienische Reise
27 May, 1787

CONTENTS

1. INTRODUCTION

The purpose of this chapter is to illustrate one way in which we believe medical psychologists, as they broaden the scope of their interests beyond the traditional association with assessment and treatment of individual patients, particularly psychiatric, may contribute to the evaluation of health care delivery systems. In particular we will seek to demonstrate how the use of direct observation techniques may be employed to quantify aspects of the functioning of hospital-based treatment services, and provide information which is necessary for the adequate assessment of therapeutic effectiveness. This we propose to do by describing a series of studies we have undertaken to examine the behaviour of staff and patients within a general hospital psychiatric unit. However, we believe that *these procedures are readily applicable and easily adaptable to the process evaluation of many areas of hospital treatment* and other forms of institutional care.

2. THE NEED FOR EVALUATION

With rapidly expanding demands for health care services, but severely limited resources, the need for evaluation and accountability assumes ever increasing importance. Lack of adequate research into the effectiveness of treatment may result in inappropriate and unnecessary expenditure on services which are without demonstrated value for the patient group. That this may, indeed, occur is suggested by developments in the treatment of ischaemic heart disease.

The relationship between heart disease and "life style" is too well known to require repeating. Despite this, the greatest medical expenditure for the treatment of heart disease has been in the provision of coronary care units. The introduction of such units was heralded as a major advance in medical technology (Powles, 1973). It has been estimated that some 3,000 specialized coronary units had been established in the U.S.A. prior to the end of 1971 and that they employed the services of 10 per cent of all trained nursing staff (Holland, 1971). In Britain, the Office of Health Economics (1971) estimated that £21.9 million was spent in 1969 on the provision of hospital services for the treatment of ischaemic heart disease. However, all this expenditure preceded the reporting of the first randomized controlled trial undertaken to examine the effects of coronary care units, compared with management of patients in their own homes by general practitioners (Mather *et al.*, 1971). That study, in fact, failed to demonstrate any significant benefits, in terms of morbidity or mortality, deriving from the specialized and costly hospital-based treatment.

This example clearly points to the need for outcome research, which is generally regarded as the most fundamental and significant type of evaluation data (McLean, 1974). Within medicine, outcome evaluation is generally associated with group-comparison experimental techniques, of which the classical double-blind drug trial is a typical example. However, while such procedures may succeed in demonstrating whether or not one procedure is superior to another, on a group basis, the extent to which the findings apply to an individual patient is often difficult, if not impossible, to determine. Consequently, as Yule and Hemsley (1977) have argued, the application of single-case methodology offers an economical and potentially powerful means to evaluate the relationship between intervention and outcome.

Since the outcome of any treatment should be capable of being shown to be related to the intervention employed, a fundamental concern of applied behaviour analysis, from which single-case methodology developed, has been to demonstrate that therapeutic process and outcome are lawfully related (Yates, 1970; Yule and Hemsley, 1977). As a result there has been an emphasis on the precise description and quantification of the treatment procedures employed. Less concern appears to have been devoted to this issue in the case of group-comparison outcome studies of the type common in medicine. Yet without adequate specification of the process of treatment the findings of any outcome studies, using either single-case or group-comparison techniques, may be difficult, if not impossible, to interpret. This is particularly true in areas such as the evaluation of a health care delivery system where outcome measures themselves may be difficult to specify.

For example, Kahn and Zarit (1974) point out, in relation to the evaluation of psychiatric treatment, that frequently employed dependent measures, such as duration of stay, discharge rates, time in the community and readmission rates, should not be used as outcome variables. Rather, they suggest, these measures should be viewed as treatment variables since they may be manipulated by treatment personnel, for example by altering admission criteria, thereby distorting apparent outcome findings. It is, therefore, important to seek to discover what actually occurs in existing health care services.

Loeber and Weisman (1975) have argued that there is a need to extend our knowledge of naturally occurring events in so-called therapeutic settings in order to be able to specify the important dimensions of inpatient treatment. Indeed, they suggest that this is a necessary and critical first step in the evaluation and ultimate improvement of the current psychiatric delivery system. However, an inherent problem of process research is the effect which the evaluative procedures themselves may have upon the system under scrutiny. Obviously to find out what actually occurs it is essential to undertake studies of a type which produce minimal distortion, or change, in the system. Furthermore, since there is ample evidence to indicate that there may be marked discrepancies between what people say they do and how they actually behave (Ajzen and Fishbein, 1977), the use of indirect measures of behaviour, such as those obtained by interviews or questionnaires, may be inappropriate. It can be argued that, if what one is seeking to examine is people's behaviour, direct observation of that behaviour is the most appropriate strategy.

Since the objective of the research reported upon in this chapter was to seek to quantify the behaviour of staff and patients within a general hospital psychiatric unit, the methodology employed was that of naturalistic behavioural observation (Jones, Reid and Patterson, 1975). As such, the focus of the research was observable behaviour rather than inferred constructs. According to Jones, Reid and Patterson (1975) the defining characteristics of naturalistic observation techniques are: "the recording of behavioural events in their natural settings at the time they occur, not retrospectively; the use of trained impartial observer-coders; and descriptions of behaviour which require little if any inference by observers to code the events" (p. 46). Although not without methodological problems (Johnson and Bolstad, 1973; Wildman and Erickson, 1977) such procedures provide a means of quantifying complex behaviour interactions in field settings in an objective fashion and in a manner which causes few, if any effects on the system being observed. However, prior to illustrating the way in which these procedures may be employed in process evaluation, it is appropriate to describe briefly the development of psychiatric units within general hospitals, both to set the research in context and to clarify the theoretical framework within which the observations were carried out.

3. DEVELOPMENT OF GENERAL HOSPITAL PSYCHIATRIC UNITS

Perhaps more than any other branch of medicine, psychiatry has been subject to frequent and sometimes violent shifts in approaches to management. These have often taken place as a consequence of ideological pressures within society rather than on the basis of well-documented research evidence (Mechanic, 1976). For example, despite difficulties in evaluating the therapeutic effectiveness of psychiatric hospitalization (Erickson, 1975), during the 1950s and early 1960s there was mounting professional and public criticism of the then traditional mental hospital. Studies undertaken from a sociological perspective frequently concluded that such institutions may have detrimental effects on the patient group (Caudill, 1958; Dunham and Weinberg, 1960; Stanton and Schwartz, 1954; Wessen, 1964). However, this research was primarily concerned with the examination of the process of psychiatric hospitalization and not with its outcome effectiveness. Whatever the validity of criticism of the large psychiatric institutions, a variety of forces within society and the mental health professions gave rise to a renewed emphasis on environmental factors in psychiatric treatment.

The role of environmental factors in psychiatric management had, of course, previously been recognized, particularly during the "moral treatment" era of the early 19th Century (Bockoven, 1963). Although moral treatment was never clearly defined and consisted of a variety of techniques, the approach may be considered as essentially behavioural (Ullmann and Krasner, 1975). Carlson and Dain (1960), for example, argue that a major therapeutic tool for the elimination of symptoms was the use of reward and punishment. However, perhaps the most important component of the moral approach was the positive expectation that patients could, and would, get better if they accepted responsibility for their condition and an appropriate environment was provided.

During that period treatment institutions were small and the superintendent lived, with his family, as part of the hospital community. They, along with other members of the staff, provided models of appropriate behaviour (Alexander and Selesnick, 1967). Patients were expected, by both treatment personnel and other patients, to emulate the example set by staff and appropriate social behaviour was emphasized, encouraged and actively taught. If appropriate skills were demonstrated by patients the result was discharge and the pronouncement of cure. As a result the entire life of patients and staff within the hospital was organized in an effort to approximate the larger society and to re-establish desirable social behaviour (Magaro, 1976).

Although reports of the time suggest that the approach was successful, to the extent that a high discharge rate was achieved, it was criticized for its failure to remove the "cause of the illness" (Ullmann and Krasner, 1975). Rapid developments in medical knowledge and the discovery of physical causes for a variety of diseases resulted in a growing belief that there were physical and internal causes of disordered behaviour. As a result, centres were built in which patients could be contained until an organic solution was found for their problems. With the rise of the organic, or medical, model of psychiatric illness, the importance of environmental factors was largely ignored.

Following the decline of moral treatment in the mid-19th Century, hospitals became larger and the ratio of staff to patients decreased. Interaction between a patient and the environment was no longer seen as of critical importance and psychiatric hospitals became largely custodial. Within such a system staff had little option but to encourage patient behaviour which facilitated control of the increasing patient numbers. Unfortunately, such passive and dependent patient behavioural patterns were incompatible with successful adjustment in the external world (Ullmann and Krasner, 1975).

The early part of the 20th Century saw the introduction of psychosurgery, insulin and electro-convulsive therapy, and the extensive use of psychotropic drugs which continues today. The development of these new physical treatments resulted in optimism once more becoming associated with mental hospitals (Clark, 1964). This optimism not only had an impact on physical treatment but observers also commented on resulting changes in the hospital milieu. For example, Clark (1964) noted that the relationship between patients and staff in an insulin-therapy ward was generally more relaxed and informal, with an apparently greater number of interactions between the two groups, than occurred in other hospital wards. Such observations lend some support to arguments that some of the positive effects of physical treatment may be, in part, attributable to the non-specific effects of the milieu (Baruch and Treacher, 1978).

Certainly, the claims of those who advocated a milieu therapy approach to treatment (e.g. Abroms, 1969; Jones, 1953) and the research of behavioural psychologists who demonstrated the effects of environmental contingencies on abnormal behaviour (e.g. Ayllon and Azrin, 1968; Franks, 1969; Krasner and Ullmann, 1965) contributed, during the 1950s and 1960s, to a reappraisal of approaches to psychiatric treatment. The widespread disenchantment with the large psychiatric hospitals, as appropriate centres for treatment, was reflected within society. In Britain, for example, the Royal Commission on the Law Relating to Mental Illness and Mental Deficiency (1957) recommended a change in emphasis from hospital- to community-based treatment. In the U.S.A., the introduction of the Community Mental Health Centers Act of 1963 was heralded as the start of "the third revolution" in psychiatric practice and paved the way for the proliferation of community mental health programmes (Liberman, King and De Risi, 1976).

It has, however, been argued that one of the major consequences of the community mental health movement has simply been the reallocation of traditional services to new settings (Chu and Trotter, 1974) and specifically the development of psychiatric units within general hospitals. Certainly there has been a dramatic increase in such units both in Britain (Baruch and Treacher, 1978) and in the U.S.A. (Levenson, 1972), where, according to Agras (1976), they now admit more new patients each year than state mental hospitals. Thus, despite widespread recognition of the need for an ecological approach to the major contemporary problems of physical and mental health, consistent with developments in other branches of medicine, current psychiatric practice appears to have adopted an engineering response to management, through the provision of specialized inpatient treatment facilities within general hospitals (Powles, 1973).

Bloom (1977) has argued that, contrary to the basic philosophy of the community mental health movement, the linking of physical and psychiatric services within general hospitals has tended to reinforce the theoretical stance that psychiatric symptoms are primarily organic in nature. Despite this, there are obvious dangers in generalizing the findings of studies of behaviour in large, poorly staffed custodial psychiatric hospitals to the small, well-staffed general hospital units. For example, while Glasscote and Kanno's (1965) survey of general hospital psychiatric units in the U.S.A. indicated that 91 per cent used chemotherapy on a regular basis and 67 per cent employed E.C.T. frequently, they also found that 75 per cent utilized occupational therapy, 60 per cent various forms of recreational therapy and 72 per cent responded that individual psychotherapy was an important part of their offered treatment.

The greater emphasis placed upon interaction and the overall therapeutic milieu is reflected in the employment of professionals whose area of expertise is in altering or modifying the environment surrounding a patient. For example, Glasscote and Kanno (1965) report that 64 per cent of the surveyed units employed social workers and occupational therapists. Typically, such units also have more nurses per patient than state mental hospitals and nursing educators have increasingly argued that the psychiatric nurses' main contribution to treatment is made through interaction with the patient (Altschul, 1972). It appears reasonable, therefore, to assume that an interactional approach (Paul, 1969), i.e. milieu and social learning therapy, is given support in such settings. Consequently, although general hospital psychiatric units may operate within a medical administrative structure and diagnostic system, and although physical treatments are employed, they have features in common with approaches adopted during the moral treatment era.

Given the rapid development of psychiatric units in general hospitals, their high cost and the large number of patients being admitted to them, there is an urgent need to evaluate their functioning. One such unit was, therefore, the setting for our research. In view of the renewed interest and apparently increased emphasis being placed on the interactional aspects of psychiatric management it was this aspect of care which was the prime focus of the present research. In the following sections we describe the observational findings and discuss some possible implications of the obtained results.

4. NATURALISTIC OBSERVATIONS ON THE FUNCTIONING OF A GENERAL HOSPITAL PSYCHIATRIC UNIT

Naturalistic observations within a behavioural framework have tended to emphasize the functional relationships between defined target behaviour and environmental events, which are either the immediate antecedents or consequences of the specified behaviour (Buehler, Patterson and Furness, 1966; Gelfand, Gelfand and Dobson, 1967; Patterson and Cobb, 1971). Such a methodology provides a basis for the fine grain analysis of the content of interactional exchange. However, group care environments include numerous and important variables which may not be temporally related to the occurrence of specific behaviour, although they may be related to therapeutic outcome (Erickson, 1975).

Among those factors which have been demonstrated to influence the behaviour of psychiatric patients in hospital settings are: arrangement of the physical environment (Barker, 1968; Holahan, 1972); number of people in a room (Fairbanks, *et al.*, 1977); size of room (Ittelson, Proshansky and Rivlin, 1970a); and the type of activity (Doke and Risley, 1972; Zarlock, 1966). As a result, various behaviourally based measurement techniques, often termed "behavioural maps" (Ittelson, Rivlin and Proshansky, 1970), have been developed and used to analyse aspects of an institution's social environment (Fairbanks, *et al.*, 1977; Hunter, Schooler and Spohn, 1962; Ittelson, Proshansky and Rivlin, 1970b; McGuire, *et al.*, 1977). It was such a behavioural mapping procedure which was employed in the initial study by Sanson-Fisher, Poole and Thompson (1979) to examine the naturally occurring patterns of interaction in a typical general hospital psychiatric unit.

Description of Unit

All of the studies reported upon in this chapter were conducted in a 40-bed psychiatric unit attached to a 450-bed general teaching hospital. In common with the general hospital psychiatric units surveyed by Glasscote and Kanno (1965) in the U.S.A., this unit is physically well equipped. Apart from patient bedrooms, dining-hall and other basic ward facilities, there are extensive patient activity areas. These include: a day-room, several group rooms, art therapy room, well-equipped workshop, T.V. area, laundry and kitchen facilities for use by patients. There are also readily accessible outdoor recreation areas.

The unit is essentially short-stay, with the average period of hospitalization being approximately four weeks. It has a reputation for providing a high quality of patient care and while it operates within a medically organized framework its orientation is said to be eclectic. Treatment tends to involve chemotherapy, E.C.T., supportive short-term individual and group psychotherapy, behavioural, occupational and general milieu therapy. Glasscote and Kanno's (1965) survey findings indicate that 82 per cent of general hospital psychiatric units state that they share these components of offered treatment.

The total full-time medical staff consists of three consultant psychiatrists, one senior psychiatric registrar, three psychiatric registrars and three resident medical officers. In addition there are three social workers, three occupational therapists and three therapy assistants, one of whom is a trade instructor responsible for the workshop. Nursing staff consist of three senior (charge) nurses and 24 registered nurses/nursing aides. One clinical psychologist provides services to both the in-patient unit and the adjacent 30-patient psychiatric day hospital. The overall ratio of full-time therapeutic staff to patients is, therefore, 1.2 to 1, which is somewhat higher than the majority of similar units in the U.S.A. (Glasscote and Kanno, 1965).

Patterns of Interaction

To obtain data on where, when and with whom patients interacted within the unit all staff and patients were the subjects of the initial study. Observations were undertaken, using the behavioural mapping technique, during two six-day periods separated by a six-week interval. This allowed some assessment of the stability of interaction patterns across time.

Data were reliably collected by observers who moved throughout the unit, at random times twice per hour, between 9.00 a.m. and 9.00 p.m. from Monday to Saturday, during both observation periods. They visited each location in the unit and noted patient and staff deployment and their behavioural patterns. Persons in the unit were categorized according to group membership and their behaviour, at the time of each observation, was coded according to a seven-category rating scale, described in detail by Sanson-Fisher, Poole and Thompson (1979).

Patients' behavioural profiles and interaction rates

There was an almost total change in patient population between the two observation periods, with only five of the original patients still being resident in the unit during the second period. However, since the findings obtained during the two periods were highly stable, only the combined results will be discussed. Table 1 summarizes the percentage of occasions during which patients were observed to engage in each of the seven defined categories of behaviour.

Consistent with findings in other psychiatric settings (Dinitz, et al., 1958; Fairbanks, et al., 1977) it is apparent that patients spend approximately half of their time in solitary activities. Of such solitary behaviour by far the greatest proportion was classified as egocentric. In fact, egocentric behaviour was found to be the most frequently observed patient behaviour. Tudor (1952) has argued that egocentricity is symptomatic of the psychiatric patient group, and that this behaviour may contribute to their initial admission. If this is accepted, the observed high rate of non-interactive behaviour would appear to be a cause for concern. Not only does the frequency of solitary, especially egocentric, behaviour represent a loss of potential therapeutic opportunities for the teaching of new adaptive social skills (Sanson-Fisher and Jenkins, 1978), but it may also contribute to patients becoming bored and "institutionalized" if hospitalization is protracted (Goldman, Bohr and Steinberg, 1970).

Those who adhere to an interaction view of psychiatric therapy suggest that it is at the point of communication between a patient and another person that therapy occurs (Jones, 1953; Paul, 1969). If this is the case, then, a high rate of interaction within a therapeutic environment would be considered desirable. Some support for the view that increased interaction may increase the efficiency of offered treatment comes from findings on the effectiveness of the "total push" approach to psychiatric management (Erickson, 1975). Furthermore, staff of the unit indicated that they believed interaction to be an important part of the therapeutic process since they stated that patients should spend 79.9 per cent (S.D. = 10.5) of their waking time in hospital engaged in interactive behaviour (Sanson-Fisher, Poole and Thompson, 1979). The finding, then, that patients spent approximately 50 per cent of their time in solitary, primarily egocentric, behaviour suggests that the therapeutic potential of the unit may be underutilized.

Of the time that patients were observed in interaction the greatest percentage (21.1 per cent) was on a one-to-one basis, i.e. individual interaction. To examine

TABLE 1.
Percentage of Total Observations During which Patients were Engaged in each Category of Behaviour

Category	%
Individual task	12.4
Egocentric	29.9
T.V. watching	6.8
Total solitary behaviour	(49.1)
Individual interaction	21.1
Group task formal	12.7
Group task informal	5.3
Group interaction	11.8
Total interactive behaviour	(50.9)

TABLE 2.
Percentage of Observed Individual
Interaction Between Patients and
other Groups Within the Unit

Patients in individual interaction with	%
Patients	78.4
Professionals (doctors, social workers, psychologists)	5.1
Nurses	12.0
Occupational therapists	4.5

more closely the pattern of such interaction the percentage of time that patients were engaged in individual interaction, with members of the various groups, was analyzed and is summarized in Table 2.

These findings highlight the potential therapeutic importance of the patients' peer group, since they were observed to spend the majority (78.4 per cent) of observed individual interaction communicating with other patients. Observational research by Gelfand, Gelfand and Dobson (1967), on chronic psychiatric patients, has, in fact, suggested that patients' peers may be more effective behavioural engineers than are staff members. However, the therapeutic potency of the patient peer group may be limited, since research also suggests that patients place less value on interaction with other patients than they do on that with staff members (Ballinger, 1971; Gould and Glick, 1973). Despite this, the observed frequency of peer contacts supports Jones' (1953) contention that patients must be involved as therapeutic agents in the inpatient psychiatric treatment process.

Of all observed individual interactions, those between patients and staff accounted for only 21.6 per cent of the total, of which more than half were with nursing personnel. This not only reinforces findings regarding the extremely low rate of patient/staff interaction but also emphasizes the importance of "aide groups" in the therapeutic endeavours of psychiatric units (Belknap, 1956; Dunham and Weinberg, 1960). Given the observed levels of patients' interaction with staff a number of variables, which may have contributed to these findings, were examined.

Staff's behavioural profiles and interaction rates

Since patients were found to spend little time in interaction with staff it appeared necessary to examine how staff deployed their time. The percentage of occasions on which staff were observed to engage in each defined category of behaviour is summarized in Table 3.

As can be seen, this indicates that the most frequently observed category of staff behaviour was individual task activity, which accounted for nearly one-third of all staff behaviour. Such a finding may indicate that, as suggested by Brown (1973), psychiatric staff have considerable bureaucratic demands placed upon their time. Alternatively, it may be that the completion of such activities is deemed important, because of its association with professional advancement (Ullmann and Krasner, 1975). Whatever the reason such tasks must diminish staff time available for inter-

TABLE 3.
Percentage of Total Observa-
tions During which Staff were
Observed in each Category of
Behaviour

Category	%
Individual task	31.3
Egocentric	0.3
T.V. watching	0.2
Total solitary behaviour	(31.8)
Individual interaction	24.6
Group task formal	29.1
Group task informal	4.6
Group interaction	9.9
Total interactive behaviour	(68.2)

action with patients. It should also be noted that the proportion of time that staff were observed to devote to bureaucratic tasks was at variance with their attitudes about how much of their time should be allocated to such activities. Responding to a questionnaire they indicated that only 16.5 per cent of their time should be devoted to individual tasks (Sanson-Fisher, Poole and Thompson, 1979).

Staff were observed to spend 68.2 per cent of their time in interactive behaviour, while patients had been found to be in interaction for 50.9 per cent of the time. However, the data in Table 3 do not allow examination of with whom staff interacted. Therefore, Table 4 presents the percentage of time the various staff groups were involved in interaction with other staff and with patients.

These data show that staff spend almost twice as much time interacting with other staff (41.1 per cent) as they do with patients (23.5 per cent). These findings are in striking contrast to the staff's questionnaire responses in which they indicate that 62.0 per cent of the time should be in direct contact with patients and only 21.5 per cent in interaction with other staff (Sanson-Fisher, Poole and Thompson, 1979). This discrepancy, between questionnaire responses regarding what should happen and what was observed to occur, illustrates the value of a direct observation approach in process research. Several interpretations of why there is a divergence between the attitudinal and behavioural data are possible.

If, for example, as Premack (1965) has pointed out, the relative frequency with which persons engage in various types of behaviour, when free to choose between alternatives, indicates the reinforcing quality of different activities for them, then,

TABLE 4.
Patterns of Observed Staff Interaction by Occupational Group

Staff group	% of time in interaction with:			% in solitary activity
	Patients	Staff	Others	
Professionals	19.7	44.3	3.4	32.6
Nurses	21.5	42.9	3.9	31.7
Occupational therapists	33.9	33.5	2.2	30.4

while staff attitudes may suggest what they consider therapeutically desirable their behaviour may reflect that interaction with their peers and task activities are more reinforcing than patient contact. However, such an interpretation presupposes that staff have complete freedom in their choice of activities which is not necessarily the case for all staff groups.

Occupational therapy staff, for example, are routinely assigned responsibility for organizing the majority of the patients' daily programmes. Consequently, between 9.00 a.m. and 5.00 p.m. they are obliged to organize and attend various patient activities. As a result they lack the comparative flexibility of the other staff groups, in terms of choosing when and with whom they will interact. The effects of such constraints are, perhaps, reflected in the fact that it is the occupational therapists who spend the greatest proportion of their time in interaction with patients, while the group with potentially greatest freedom of choice, the professional staff, spend least of their time with patients (see Table 4).

If the importance of interaction between staff and patients is considered therapeutically desirable, a view which is held by the unit's staff, it would seem beneficial that the greatest proportion of staff time be devoted to interacting with patients. However, if the frequency with which staff were observed to engage in task activities, in interaction with their peers and with patients reflects the differential reinforcing quality of these activities, such a change may be difficult to effect without altering the contingencies operating on the staff. One possible means of increasing staff/patient interaction rates might be to allocate staff to activities which force them into direct contact with patients. The fact that the occupational therapists, who have specific patient-oriented responsibilities, had the highest rate of interaction with patients suggests the merit of such a strategy.

The foregoing discussion does not, however, provide a causal explanation for the observed profiles of patient and staff behaviour but the low rate of interaction between the two groups suggests that there may be a pattern of avoidance between staff and patients.

Utilization of space by patients and staff

One factor which may contribute to the observed low rate of interaction between patients and staff might be the manner in which the two groups utilize space in the unit. For example, research by Fairbanks *et al.* (1977) suggests that within psychiatric hospitals there is a territorial segregation of staff and patients which contributes to, and maintains low rates of, interaction between the two groups. In order to assess whether staff and patients isolate themselves from one another, in the studied unit, the rates at which they were observed to occupy various functional locations were examined. The results are summarized in Table 5, together with the percentage of time spent by the two groups in three broad territories defined on an *a priori* basis as patient, staff and general areas.

Staff were observed most frequently in the areas designated the nurses' station (22.0 per cent of the time), an observation commonly made in other studies examining the use of space in hospital settings (McLaughlin, 1976; Plutchik, Shulman and Conte, 1972). In contrast the patient group was observed in that area only 1.0 per cent of their time, indicating a decreased opportunity for interaction with staff. The impor-

TABLE 5.
Percentage of Total Observations During which
Staff and Patients were Observed in each Location

Location	Patients %	Rank	Staff %	Rank
Group room	11.2	4	9.9	5
Activity room	6.1	7	5.7	7
Day room	16.0	2	7.4	6
Dining room	11.1	5	1.2	11.5
T.V. area	12.2	3	1.2	11.5
Bedrooms	28.3	1	3.1	8
Total patient areas	(84.9)	—	(28.5)	—
Passages/stairs	6.8	6	12.0	4
Outpatient reception area	2.4	8	1.6	9.5
Courtyard	2.3	9	1.6	9.5
Total general areas	(11.5)	—	(15.2)	—
Nurses station	1.0	11	22.0	1
Offices/conference area	0.9	12	21.5	2
Coffee room	1.7	10	12.8	3
Total staff areas	(3.6)	—	(56.3)	—

tance of design in influencing interaction has been demonstrated by Holahan (1972) and Holahan and Saegert (1973). However, since the nursing station area in the unit was deliberately designed, and located, to encourage communication between the two groups, the present findings suggest that architectural design alone is not sufficient to prevent territorial segregation. The relative frequency with which staff and patients were observed in the nursing station suggests that explicit or implicit modes of communication are utilized by staff to discourage patients entering the area, e.g. by ignoring the patients' presence, or through the use of technical language (Lyman and Scott, 1967).

Other areas used frequently by staff, in descending order, were: their offices, the conference room and the coffee room; all of which are designated staff areas. Clearly patients respect the designation of these as staff areas since they were observed in those settings during only 2.6 per cent of the total observations. This finding also indicates that these areas are used by staff for individual tasks or staff–staff interaction rather than for interaction with patients.

The area in which patients were most frequently observed was their bedrooms, followed by the dayroom, T.V. area and group rooms. The frequent use of bedrooms, despite the fact that few patients were restricted to, or required, bed rest is consistent with the findings of Plutchik, Shulman and Conte (1972) and Willer *et al.* (1974). Spending such a large proportion (28.3 per cent) of their time in their bedrooms suggests that patients avoid a significant part of the offered therapeutic programme, which is something frequently commented upon by the occupational therapy staff. Such a finding may also reflect the patients' perception of the reinforcement value of the offered programme and may suggest the need to institute a token or similar contingency system to ensure greater patient participation.

However, it may also be the case that by remaining in their bedrooms patients can gain some degree of privacy and control over their environment, i.e. choice of with whom they interact (Proshansky, Ittelson and Rivlin, 1976). Such control is less likely if one joins the offered programme. However, whether it is therapeutically or, in view of the cost of hospitalization, ethically acceptable that patients should be able to control their environment in this manner is open to debate. Whatever conclusions are reached the results of these observations clearly indicate that there is a spatial segregation of the unit into staff and patient areas.

This territorial separation is further indicated by the fact that a significant negative correlation was obtained between the ranking of the locations according to frequency of usage by the two groups ($R_s = -0.52$; $P < 0.05$). While patients were found to spend 84.9 per cent of their time in defined patient areas, staff were observed in these locations only 28.5 per cent of the time. Even more striking was the finding that staff spent 56.3 per cent of their time in defined staff areas but patients were observed in these during only 3.6 per cent of the total observation. Obviously given such spatial segregation the opportunity for interaction is decreased since it is impossible to interact with those who do not occupy the same areas as oneself.

In general the pattern of territorial usage suggests that a non-reciprocity system is in operation. Staff appear to behave on the basis of their right to invade patients' areas, where they spend 28.5 per cent of their time. However, they effectively keep patients out of staff areas where patients were observed for only 3.6 per cent of the total observation period. If Proshansky, Ittelson and Rivlin's (1976) argument, that territoriality confers freedom of choice and the maintenance of privacy, is accepted, then it appears that this is generally better preserved by staff than by patients. This staff control of the unit's space, while understandable, is likely to be a factor contributing to the low rate of interaction between the two groups. As such it may suggest the desirability of decreasing the number of locations, and the opportunities for certain areas to be labelled, explicitly or implicitly, as staff territories. However, the findings regarding usage of the nurses station indicate that this will involve more than administrative directive, or architectural design, and may require a change on the part of staff in terms of their willingness to interact with the patient group.

Time and interaction rate

It has been suggested that inpatient psychiatric services frequently function as therapeutic environments for only a limited part of the patients' total waking time each day (Dinitz, *et al.*, 1958). Since most staff members work predominantly between 9.00 a.m. and 5.00 p.m. from Monday to Friday this is likely to be the period of maximum interaction and, hence, potential therapy. Such a suggestion has led to the argument that a therapeutic day operates in inpatient treatment centres, with little of value, other than custodial care, occurring outside that period (Dinitz, *et al.*, 1958). Since the foregoing analyses assume that the rate at which interactions occur is evenly distributed over the period of observation, the relationship between time and interaction was examined. Table 6 presents the rates at which patients were observed in interaction with staff and with their peers as a function of time.

These data do indicate that a therapeutic day phenomenon is in operation in the

TABLE 6.
Percentage of Total Observations of Interaction
Between Patients and Staff and Patients and
other Patients as a Function of Time

Time of day	Type of interaction	
	Patient–staff	Patient–patient
Therapeutic day		
9.00 a.m.–12.00 noon	52.0	23.6
2.00 p.m.–5.00 p.m.	31.0	28.0
Total	(83.0)	(51.6)
Meal periods		
12.00 noon–2.00 p.m.	10.0	18.2
5.00 p.m.–6.00 p.m.	1.6	9.2
Total	(11.6)	(27.4)
Evening		
6.00 p.m.–9.00 p.m.	4.4	16.9
Saturday		
9.00 a.m.–9.00 p.m.	1.0	4.1

studied unit with by far the greatest proportion of patient–staff interaction (83.0 per cent) occurring during designated therapeutic periods. Relatively little interaction between patients and staff occurred during meal times (11.6 per cent) and only 4.4 per cent of such interactions were observed in the evenings after 6.00 p.m. In view of the reduced staff numbers on duty at weekends it was not surprising that few patient–staff interactions were observed on Saturdays. However, the fact that only 1.0 per cent of all such interactions occurred between 9.00 a.m. and 9.00 p.m. on Saturdays suggests that very little therapeutic interaction takes place at weekends.

The pattern of patient–patient communication indicates a greater spread of inter-action over the period of observation, than is the case for patient–staff interaction. More communication between patients and their peers takes place during meal times (27.4 per cent), in the evenings (16.9 per cent) and on Saturdays (4.1 per cent). As such these findings point to the potential therapeutic importance of the peer group, as agents for establishing and maintaining desirable patterns of patient behaviour, particularly outside the period of the therapeutic day.

In general these findings lend further support to the view that the therapeutic potential of the unit may be underutilized. There is, for example, no systematic attempt to enrol the patient group as therapeutic agents and little patient–staff interaction occurs outside the defined therapeutic day. The latter finding may suggest that the unit serves an essentially custodial function during the evening and weekend periods. If this is the case then it can be suggested that, for all but the most disturbed patients, partial hospitalization, on a day basis, might be an equally effective, but more economical, use of limited health care resources.

Even if patients could not be maintained in their home environments the use of hostels and/or group homes could well be employed as alternative evening and weekend accommodation. Not only would such facilities be less expensive than a hospital bed but, appropriately organized, they are more likely to encourage and maintain appropriate patient skills than is total hospitalization. Such an alteration in management style might also permit the transfer of psychiatric staff to work with individuals in their natural environments thus decreasing problems in the generalization of therapeutic effects. However, if total hospitalization is deemed necessary the obtained findings suggest that more staff should be employed on a shift-work basis. If this was done it should provide increased opportunities for patients to interact with the staff group.

The results of the initial observational study, employing a behavioural mapping technique, suggest that, viewed from an interactional approach to psychiatric management, the therapeutic potential of the studied unit is being underutilized. Patients were found to spend approximately half of their waking time engaged in solitary activities, which was considerably greater than the unit staff considered desirable. On the basis of the observational data factors which were hypothesized to contribute to the low rate of patient-staff interaction were: the amount of time staff were observed to spend in interaction with each other, the time staff allocated to solitary task activities, the observed spatial segregation of the staff and patient groups, and the fact that a majority of the staff are present in the unit during only a limited part of the patients' waking day. However, while some suggestions have been advanced as to how the rate of interaction between staff and patients might be increased, it would be naive to assume that merely increasing the rate of interaction will necessarily be linearly related to enhanced therapeutic outcome. Consideration must also be given to the nature of that interaction.

Content of Interaction

From a social learning perspective, of equal importance to the frequency of interaction is the nature of such interaction and the manner in which behaviour is responded to by others. Support for this view is provided by research on "token economies" (Ayllon and Azrin, 1968; Kazdin, 1977; Kazdin and Bootzin, 1972). Such research has indicated that environmental contingencies can modify psychiatric patients' behaviour. Furthermore, research on the contingent application and withdrawal of social attention has also been demonstrated to alter a wide range of abnormal behaviour (Milby, 1970; Meichenbaum, 1966), suggesting that the "behavioural engineering" concept espoused by Ayllon and Michael (1959) should be employed by staff in psychiatric settings. Ayllon and Michael (1959) argue that defined appropriate patient behaviour should be consistently responded to with positive attention, while inappropriate behaviour should be ignored or punished. The experimental literature suggests that the application of these procedures results in the reduction of psychiatric symptomatology (e.g. Ayllon and Haughton, 1964; Little, 1966; Rickard and Dinoff, 1962).

Despite the importance of environmental contingencies for the rehabilitation of psychiatric patients there have been few well-controlled behavioural studies which have examined the type of naturally occurring interactions between patients and others in treatment settings, especially well-staffed acute units. Findings of studies which have been reported tend to support the assertion that, within a social learning context, treatment institutions may be centres in which negative, rather than positive, behaviour is encouraged (Buehler, Patterson and Furness, 1966; Gelfand, Gelfand and Dobson, 1967; Sanson-Fisher and Jenkins, 1978; Trudel et al., 1974;

Warren and Mondy, 1971). Consequently, before concluding that it would be beneficial to increase the rate of interaction, observed within the studied unit, Sanson-Fisher and Poole (1980) undertook a study to examine the content of those interactions which do occur.

Twenty newly admitted patients (ten neurotic and ten psychotic patients matched with respect to age and sex) were the subjects of this study. Each subject was observed on eight separate randomly selected occasions, each of five-minute duration. Observations occurred twice per day, on consecutive week days, between 9.00 a.m. and 5.00 p.m. These limits were selected since the previous research had indicated that maximum interaction occurred between these times.

The content of patient behaviour was coded by trained observers using the Data Acquisition in Real Time (DART 1) recording system, a more detailed description of which is provided by Sanson-Fisher, Poole, Small and Fleming (1979). Subjects' behaviour was coded according to seven mutually exclusive categories, viz: Positive self concept; Independent altruism; Talk; On task; Negative self concept; Egocentric and Bizarre. Staff ratings of the desirability of patient behaviours indicated that the Positive self concept, Independent altruism and Talk categories represented an Appropriate behaviour cluster, while the Negative self concept, Egocentric and Bizarre categories constituted an Inappropriate behaviour cluster. The On task category was viewed by staff as a Neutral behaviour (Sanson-Fisher and Poole, 1980). The responses of those who interacted with the subjects were recorded as being Positive attention, Negative attention and Ignore. A full description of the rating scale is provided by Sanson-Fisher and Poole (1980), with data suggesting that the scale had both content and concurrent validity.

A total of 13 hr 12 min of reliable observations on the behaviour of the target subjects was obtained. Table 7 summarizes the circumstances under which the subjects' behaviour was observed.

From this it can be seen that over half (56.7 per cent) of the observed behaviour occurred in the absence of a potential responder. Such a finding is consistent with that in the previously described study in which patients were observed to spend 49.1 per cent of their time in solitary activity. Of the behaviour observed in the absence of a potential responder 51.4 per cent was coded as Egocentric, 41.0 per cent as On task and 7.6 per cent was Bizarre. In fact Bizarre behaviour emitted in the absence of a potential responder accounted for 98.1 per cent of the total behaviour within that category. Such a finding may suggest that there is a tendency to

TABLE 7.
Percentage of Subjects' Total Behaviour Observed in Isolation and in Interaction with the Different Response Groups

Response group	%
No potential responder	56.7
Visitors/non-clinical staff	1.8
Mixed response, i.e. staff and patients	10.2
Staff	15.9
Patients	15.4

avoid patients when they are behaving in a bizarre fashion in which case it might be argued that this is evidence of "good" behavioural engineering. However, as will be shown later, this does not appear to be the case.

During only 1.8 per cent of the time that the subjects were observed was their behaviour responded to by either visitors or non-clinical members of staff, indicating the relative social isolation of the patient group. During 10.2 per cent of the time subjects were coded as being responded to by a mixed group, i.e. in situations in which the responses were so confused that the observers could not reliably distinguish the input source. Subject behaviour was responded to by staff during 15.9 per cent of the total observation time, again pointing to the low rate of patient–staff interaction. Patients' peers were found to respond to the target subjects during 15.4 per cent of the total observation time.

The content of staff responses to subjects' behaviour is summarized in Table 8. From these data it can be seen that most patient behaviour receives a high rate of positive attention from staff, independent of the desirability of that behaviour.

This finding is consistent with the results reported by Gelfand, Gelfand and Dobson (1967) which also indicated that staff do not discriminate in the way in which they respond to defined appropriate and inappropriate patient behaviour. However, that research was undertaken using a limited, chronic psychotic patient group and in an era when the impact of the social learning approach was not likely to have been extensive in psychiatric management. Consequently, that essentially similar findings should be obtained in a well-staffed acute unit is surprising. The target subjects in the Sanson-Fisher and Poole (1980) study consisted of both diagnosed neurotic and psychotic patients, but no chronic patients were represented, so that staff might be expected to adopt a more active approach towards treatment. That they were indiscriminate in their application of contingencies is all the more surprising since, in response to a questionnaire, they indicated that

TABLE 8.
Subjects' Behaviour Responded to by Staff and Type of Staff Response

Behaviour category	% duration to which staff responded to each category of subjects' behaviour	% duration to which subjects' behaviour was responded to by staff with:		
		Positive attention	Negative attention	Ignore
Appropriate				
Positive self concept	3.7	100.0	—	—
Independent altruism	0.6	100.0	—	—
Talk	3.1	100.0	—	—
Total	(7.4)	(100.0)	(—)	(—)
Neutral				
On task	76.5	70.5	1.5	28.0
Inappropriate				
Negative self concept	5.6	100.0	—	—
Egocentric	10.0	95.6	—	4.4
Bizarre	0.5	100.0	—	—
Total	(16.1)	(97.3)	(—)	(2.7)
Total all behaviour	(100.0)	(77.0)	(1.1)	(21.9)

defined undesirable patient behaviour should not be responded to with positive attention.

Within a social learning framework the obtained results, then, suggest that to increase the interaction rate between staff and patients in the studied unit, without also modifying the style of such communication, might not be therapeutic. It would appear that prior to, or at the same time as, attempting to increase the rate of staff-patient interaction, there should also be training undertaken to make staff more therapeutic in their application of social contingencies.

The nature of peer group responses to target subject behaviour is summarized in Table 9, and indicates that patients are also indiscriminate in their use of social contingencies. This finding is contrary to that of Gelfand, Gelfand and Dobson (1967) whose data suggest that patients are better behavioural engineers, i.e. apply contingencies more appropriately, than staff. The present findings suggest that intervention with the patient group would also be required if an optimum social learning environment is to be achieved.

Sanson-Fisher and Poole (1980) also found that, when target subjects were rank-ordered according to the total time they were observed to exhibit defined inappropriate behaviour, a significant correlation was obtained between that ranking and amount of time each subject was observed in solitary behaviour ($R_s = 0.62$, $P < 0.01$). It therefore appears that the more inappropriate behaviour patients exhibit, the greater is the likelihood that they will be left in isolation. That is, the more behaviourally disturbed a patient the less time he is likely to receive from staff. Such a finding might superficially appear to be good behavioural engineering. However, since the ignoring of behaviour is not confined to the inappropriate actions, such is not the case, i.e. once again it is evidence of indiscriminate use of contingencies. This finding, while consistent with that reported by Tudor (1952), is of concern, since Fairbanks, *et al.* (1977) report that disturbed behaviour is more

TABLE 9.
Subjects' Behaviour Responded to by Patients and Type of Patient Response

Behaviour category	% duration to which patients responded to each category of subjects' behaviour	% duration to which subjects' behaviour was responded to by patients with:		
		Positive attention	Negative attention	Ignore
Appropriate				
Positive self concept	4.2	99.0	—	1.0
Independent altruism	0.4	100.0	—	—
Talk	8.3	99.0	—	1.0
Total	(12.9)	(99.1)	(—)	(0.9)
Neutral				
On task	58.3	86.9	7.7	5.4
Inappropriate				
Negative self concept	9.8	100.0	—	—
Egocentric	18.0	97.2	—	2.8
Bizarre	0.0	—	—	—
Total	(27.8)	(98.1)	(—)	(1.9)
Total all behaviour	100.0	91.7	4.5	3.8

likely to occur when patients are not in interaction. Their observation is, in fact, supported by the present findings in that 98.1 per cent of all observed Bizarre behaviour occurred in the absence of a potential responder.

The findings of the two observational studies reported this far have been discussed within a theoretical framework which leads to the suggestion that there is a need both to increase the rate and to alter the content of interactions, which occur naturally within the unit, if an optimum social learning therapeutic environment is to be created. This interpretation, of course, presupposes that a social learning, or interactional, approach to psychiatric care is deemed to be most appropriate.

Glasscote and Kanno's (1965) survey suggested that, in the U.S.A., general hospital psychiatric units espouse a treatment orientation which combines both medical and environmental approaches to the management of psychiatric patients. However, Benson (1976) has argued that the most appropriate model to employ in such settings is the organic, or medical, model. While the relative effectiveness of different approaches to psychiatric management can only be evaluated by appropriately controlled outcome research it is important, within the context of process evaluation, to attempt to determine the actual treatment orientation, since this in itself may influence the treatment process.

Therapeutic Ideology

Over recent decades there has been a proliferation of theories put forward to conceptualize psychiatric care (Magaro, 1976). These have included the "imprisonment" model (Goffman, 1961), the "hedonistic" model (Braginsky, Braginsky and Ring, 1969), the "medico-social" model (Caplan, 1961) and the "self-help" approach (Illich, 1975). However, there appear to be three orientations, or ideologies, which currently predominate in the day-to-day work of mental health professionals.

The first, and perhaps best known, is the "medical" orientation according to which abnormal behaviour is viewed in terms of psychiatric, or mental, illness (Bates, 1977). Those who adopt this model believe that patients can be reliably and validly diagnosed and that explanations of aetiology conform to those which apply in physical medicine. As a consequence the emphasis of treatment is on somatic methods, such as chemotherapy and E.C.T. (Armor and Klerman, 1968).

The second major psychiatric ideology is the "psychotherapeutic" orientation. Within this model emphasis is placed on the individual's intrapsychic systems and causal explanations are sought within the individual, in terms of the psychodynamics which contribute to the development of personality and of abnormal behaviour (Reiss et al., 1977; Armor and Klerman, 1968). This model emphasizes the efficacy of individual psychotherapy and consequently treatment is usually attempted by means of such techniques.

The third major orientation has been termed the "sociotherapeutic" or "interactional" ideology (Paul, 1969). This approach stresses the importance of social or environmental factors which are hypothesized to contribute to abnormal behaviour (Ullmann and Krasner, 1975). Sociotherapists consequently emphasize the utilization and manipulation of the patient's environment for therapeutic purposes (Armor and Klerman, 1968). The objective of therapy is either towards modifying the patient's ability to cope with the environment, or towards altering the environ-

ment directly, and includes various forms of behavioural intervention (Paul and
Lentz, 1977).

The importance of therapeutic ideology has been stressed by writers who have
described the impact of staff attitudes and values on the treatment process (Hanley,
1966; London, 1969; Sullivan, 1971; Ullmann, 1967; Wilder, 1969). Among those
factors which may be influenced by therapeutic ideology are: the extent to which
individual patients are held responsible for their actions; whether physical or other
forms of treatment are employed; the perceived desirability of staff-patient interaction; the nature and rate of such interaction; length of hospitalization; discharge
rates, and whether after-care is provided following discharge and the form which it
may take (Atthowe and Krasner, 1968; Blaney, 1975; Cumming and Cumming,
1962; Ellsworth and Stokes, 1963; Paul and Lentz, 1977; Ullmann and Krasner,
1975).

As ideology may have a profound impact on the care and management of
patients it is of critical importance, in any studies seeking to assess the functioning
of psychiatric institutions, to attempt to examine the treatment orientation of staff.
Without such data it may be invalid to generalize observational findings across
institutions. Therefore, in order to determine what ideological approach was
employed by staff within the studied unit, Sanson-Fisher, Poole and Harker (1979)
carried out a further naturalistic observation study to determine the ideological
models employed by staff when making decisions concerning patient care.

As the ward round, or team meeting, is the traditional setting for discussing
patients' problems and management (Shamsie and Clark, 1971; Hirschowitz, 1971)
it provides a logical setting for observing the orientations utilized by staff to conceptualize the care of psychiatric patients. However, although medical teaching
rounds have been studied (Payson and Barchas, 1965) there is little empirical
research examining the content, or functioning, of psychiatric ward rounds. This
setting was, therefore, selected to attempt to examine the basis on which decisions
were made regarding the management of patients. The choice of the ward round
for the observation of decisions relating to patient care appeared justified since
staff, responding to a questionnaire, indicated that they also considered it to be the
prime setting for such decision-making (Sanson-Fisher, Poole and Harker, 1979).

Ideology employed during ward rounds

The study was conducted in the regular ward round setting in the unit. A recording of verbal behaviour during ward rounds was obtained by means of a microphone installed in the ceiling of the room. The microphone was installed three
months prior to the commencement of the study in order to reduce reactivity. In
addition, all recording equipment was located outside the room so that staff were
unaware when rating was actually taking place.

The subject group consisted of all staff members in the two therapeutic teams
which were selected for observation. The total sample, therefore, consisted of two
consultant psychiatrists, two registrars, two resident medical officers, four fifth-year
medical students, two social workers, two occupational therapists, twelve psychiatric nurses and four nursing aides. While not all members of the teams attended
every ward round, at least one member of each professional group was present on

every occasion a ward round was observed. Staff verbal discussion on twenty inpatients, during the ward rounds, constituted the behavioural data to be rated.

Patients were selected on the basis of their being newly admitted as inpatients and being diagnosed as either "psychotic" or "neurotic" throughout the entire period of their inpatient stay. Within each team five psychotic and five neurotic patients were randomly chosen, from those who met the selection criteria, and staff discussion of their treatment was observed in each ward round. In order to obtain the total ward round discussion on each of the twenty patients 23 ward rounds were observed, and 9 hr 17 min of data were collected over a four-month period.

Each time a selected patient was discussed within a ward round, interaction was coded using the DART 1 equipment. This permitted information to be obtained regarding each staff member who spoke during the discussion, and the content of what was said (according to the employed observation scale), together with the duration of each statement. The observational scale employed allowed the examination of which professional group made statements and whether they did so within a Medical, Sociotherapeutic or Psychotherapeutic orientation. In addition, it permitted the calculation of the number of defined Authority Statements, made by each staff member, within each of the three orientations. Details of the observational scale, together with reliability estimates, indicating that two observers independently coding the same sequence of interaction achieved satisfactory levels of agreement, are provided by Sanson-Fisher, Poole and Harker (1979).

It was found that only 10.6 per cent of all observed discussion was not categorized according to one of the three specified treatment orientations (see Table 10). Such a finding suggests that the three defined ideologies are, indeed, predominant when decisions are made about inpatient care within the unit.

That there is a strong commitment to the medical orientation is apparent since 55.1 per cent of the total duration of discussion took place within this framework. In contrast, only 2.9 per cent of the time the target patients were discussed was reference made to the psychotherapeutic orientation. However, consideration was given to the sociotherapeutic orientation since it was utilized for 31.4 per cent of the total discussion time. Consequently the data suggests that to some extent an eclectic approach is employed when discussing inpatient management.

However, the unequal representation of the three models supports the contention that the creation of psychiatric units in general hospitals has tended to perpetuate the long-term dominance of a medical orientation in conceptualizing of psychiatric

TABLE 10.
Percentage of Ward Round Discussion Time for the Total Patient Sample within the Three Treatment Orientation and other Verbal Behaviour Categories

Category	% total discussion time
Medical orientation	55.1
Sociotherapeutic orientation	31.4
Psychotherapeutic orientation	2.9
Other verbal behaviour	10.6

patients' problems (Bloom, 1977; Brown, 1973), and that traditional ideology is being reapplied within new settings (Chu and Trotter, 1974).

The foregoing analysis considered the ward round discussions on the total 20 patients without considering their diagnoses. Staff attitudes indicated that they believe the three models should be applied differentially to patients diagnosed as neurotic or psychotic, as can be seen in Table 11. These data indicate that, while staff believe the medical model is most appropriate for the management of psychotic patients, the sociotherapeutic and psychotherapeutic approaches are considered more appropriate to the conceptualization of neurotic patients.

TABLE 11.
Staff Attitudes Regarding Percentage of Ward Round Discussion Time which should be Devoted to each of the Three Ideological Orientations for Patients Diagnosed as Psychotic or Neurotic

Orientation		% discussion time		
		Psychotic	Neurotic	
Medical	$\overline{X}$	49.0	22.7	$t(21) = 4.87$†
	SD	20.4	11.2	
Sociotherapeutic	$\overline{X}$	26.3	40.4	$t(21) = 3.58$*
	SD	12.5	12.2	
Psychotherapeutic	$\overline{X}$	22.0	35.9	$t(21) = 3.57$*
	SD	12.5	11.8	

* $P < 0.01$.
† $P < 0.001$.

When one examines what actually occurs in practice within the ward rounds it is apparent that both neurotic and psychotic patients are discussed within a predominantly medical model (see Table 12). There is, in fact, no behavioural discrimination in the way in which staff apply the models to psychotic and neurotic patients ($\chi^2 = 2.63$, d.f. = 2, N.S.). It is also apparent that, within the ward rounds, staff generally employ the medical model with greater, and the psychotherapeutic model with considerably less, frequency than their questionnaire responses would lead one to expect.

Such a discrepancy between staff attitudes and behaviour again indicates the desirability of obtaining behavioural data wherever possible. Furthermore, these findings suggest that previous research, on the ideology of psychiatric staff groups,

TABLE 12.
Percentage Duration of Discussion, by Ideological Orientation, per Patient Per Ward Round, for Patients Diagnosed as Psychotic or Neurotic

Orientation	% duration of discussion	
	Psychotic	Neurotic
Medical	62.5	60.0
Sociotherapeutic	35.6	34.0
Psychotherapeutic	1.9	6.0

which has employed attitude data (Hollingshead and Redlich, 1958; Kreitman, 1962; Strauss, *et al.*, 1964; Caine and Smail, 1969) should be interpreted with caution, and no assumption made that such responses will predict the way in which psychiatric workers may discuss, or actually make decisions about, patient care.

Table 13 presents the percentage of discussion engaged in by the members of the various professional groups during the ward rounds. When the differing numbers of persons in each professional group are accounted for, the consultant psychiatrist was found to talk twice as much as other members of the medical profession, approximately ten times as much as the occupational therapy and nursing staff and twenty times as much as the social worker.

TABLE 13.
Percentage Duration of Discussion, Per Patient Per Ward Round, by each Staff Group. (Data Standardized to Account for Unequal Numbers within each Group.)

Staff group	% duration of discussion
Consultant psychiatrist	46.1
Registrar/resident	21.3
Medical student	21.2
Total medical staff	(88.6)
Occupational therapist	4.6
Social worker	2.0
Nurse	4.8
Total non-medical staff	(11.4)

These findings suggest that, within the examined unit, there is an adherence to an hierarchical model of organization in which the communication process is dominated by the medical profession, with the consultant psychiatrist being at the top of the organizational pyramid. That this type of organizational model is employed within the unit may not be surprising in view of the dominance of medical ideology found throughout the study. However, the data presented earlier, on interaction rates within the unit, indicate that medical staff have fewer contacts with patients than any other professional group. In contrast, occupational therapists were found to allocate approximately one-third of their working time to patient contact, yet they only speak for an average of 4.6 per cent of each ward round. Nurses, while they were found to have the greatest rate of individual patient contact within the unit, talked for only 2.0 per cent of each ward round.

This discrepancy, between rate of interaction by different staff groups with patients outside the ward rounds and their relative contribution to discussions in the ward rounds, may suggest that decisions regarding patient management are not determined on the basis of knowledge of an individual patient acquired through interaction in the ward. Rather it appears that the information-giving process in the ward rounds operates on the basis that greater knowledge is acquired by medical personnel in their limited and formalized contacts with patients (e.g. mental state examinations). That the consultant psychiatrists dominate the discussion time during ward rounds may suggest that they believe that knowledge of a "patient type", or psychiatric classification, represents a valid data base for discussion and decision-making. If this interpretation is correct it may indicate that treatment occurs on the basis of patient classification, rather than on the unique characteristics and behavioural functioning of a particular individual.

In order to examine the decision-making process more closely, an analysis of the defined Authority Statements made by each professional group was undertaken. Table 14 summarizes the number of authority statements, within each ideological orientation, made by the various professional groups.

TABLE 14.
Percentage of Authority Statements Per Ward Round made by each Staff Group. (Data Standardized to Account for Unequal Numbers within each Group.)

| Staff group | % Authority statements within: | | | % total authority statements |
	Medical orientation	Sociotherapeutic orientation	Psychotherapeutic orientation	
Consultant psychiatrist	86.9	74.6	77.6	84.0
Registrar/resident	10.6	2.3	19.5	9.6
Medical student	2.5	—	—	1.9
Total medical staff	(100.0)	(77.1)	(97.1)	(95.5)
Occupational therapist	—	20.4	—	3.8
Social worker	—	2.5	—	0.5
Nurse	—	—	2.9	0.2
Total non-medical staff	(—)	(22.9)	(2.9)	(4.5)
Total staff	74.8	18.8	6.4	100.0

Examination of this table indicates that, on average, the consultant psychiatrist makes 86.9 per cent of all medically oriented authority statements. When combined with the registrar/resident and medical student data, 100 per cent of medically oriented authority statements were made by medically qualified staff members. This finding is consistent with previous research in which it was found that psychiatrists perceived themselves, and were perceived by other occupational groups, to have "exclusive competence" in determining medical diagnosis and treatment (Miles, 1977). However, the present findings suggest that medical personnel also act as if they have "exclusive competence" in both the sociotherapeutic and psychotherapeutic orientations, since they made 77.1 and 97.1 per cent respectively of all authority statements within these orientations. Overall, in fact, the medical personnel make 95.5 per cent of all authority statements, as against 4.5 per cent of such statements made by non-medical team members. In combination with the finding that 88.6 per cent of total discussion time during ward rounds is accounted for by medical personnel, these data suggest that this group feels it has the necessary knowledge to make decisions about all activities concerning the treatment and care of psychiatric patients.

The data also suggest that the idealized concept of the therapeutic multidisciplinary team (Holzberg, 1960), in which each professional makes an equal contribution, is not adhered to. Rather ward rounds appear to be settings for decision-making, and information-giving, by the medical profession, with little contribution from the other professional groups. The value of ward rounds as currently structured may, therefore, be questioned given their high economic cost and the diversion of staff time away from patient contact that such meetings represent. In addition, the finding regarding the predominance of the medical orientation suggests a further factor which may be contributing to the observed rate of interaction between staff and patients, and the style of that interaction which takes place.

5. CONCLUDING REMARKS

In this brief overview of some of our recent research we have attempted to describe aspects of the functioning of a general hospital psychiatric unit, in order to illustrate the use of naturalistic behavioural observation procedures in the area of process evaluation. In doing so we have not only summarized the quantitative results but have also suggested some possible implications of the findings, viewed from a social learning perspective on psychiatric management. Obviously the conclusions we have drawn are limited by the fact that only one unit was observed and naturalistic observations, of the type employed, do not permit causal relationships to be specified. However, given these constraints, we believe that the results suggest that there is an underutilization of the therapeutic potential of the studied unit.

Certainly the data indicate that the observed rate of interaction, between patients and staff, is both objectively low and less than that considered desirable by the staff. In addition, the content of such interaction as does occur fails to conform to the requirements of an optimum social learning environment. A number of factors which may contribute to the observed rate and style of interaction are also suggested by the data. These include the ways in which staff spend their time, the manner in which staff and patients utilize space within the unit, the working hours of the majority of staff groups, and the predominance of a medical orientation in the conceptualization of patients' problems.

Obviously there is a need to determine whether similar results are obtained in other general hospital psychiatric units. Even if they are replicated it is more important to determine the relationship between process variables, of the type we have quantified, and therapeutic effectiveness. The value of this research, then, is not so much in interpretation of the obtained data as in the methods whereby they were collected. As such we see the main contribution of these studies to be to demonstrate how direct behavioural observation may be employed in the evaluation of health care services.

In view of the reported discrepancies between staff attitudes, as assessed by questionnaire techniques, and their behaviour, as directly observed, the advantages of naturalistic observations appear self-evident. Not only do such procedures enable one to assess whether or not treatment services are being provided in the manner stated to be desirable, they also facilitate the interpretation of outcome research. By obtaining quantitative data on the actual functioning of different treatment facilities it is possible to determine more reasonably those factors contributing to therapeutic effectiveness. Consequently, we believe that the use of behavioural observation techniques, which are easily adaptable and readily applicable to many areas of the health care delivery system, represent a potentially significant contribution of psychology to evaluative research in medicine.

REFERENCES

Abroms, G. M. (1969) Defining milieu therapy, *Archives of General Psychiatry*, **21**, 553–560.

Agras, W. S. (1976) Behavior modification in the general hospital psychiatric unit, in H. Leitenberg (Ed.) *Handbook of Behavior Modification and Behavior Therapy*, Prentice-Hall, Englewood Cliffs, New Jersey.

Ajzen, I. and Fishbein, M. (1977) Attitude-behavior relations: A theoretical analysis and review of the literature, *Psychological Bulletin*, **84**, 888–918.

Alexander, F. C. and Selesnick, S. T. (1967) *The History of Psychiatry*, Allen & Unwin, London.

Altschul, A. (1972) *Patient–Nurse Interaction: A Study of Interaction Patterns in Acute Psychiatric Wards*, Churchill Livingstone, London.

Armor, D. J. and Klerman, G. L. (1968) Psychiatric treatment orientations and professional ideology, *Journal of Health and Social Behavior*, **9**, 243–255.

Atthowe, J. M. and Krasner, L. (1968) A preliminary report on the application of contingent reinforcement procedures (token economy) in a chronic psychiatric ward, *Journal of Abnormal Psychology*, **73**, 37–43.

Ayllon, T. and Azrin, N. H. (1968) *The Token Economy: A Motivational System for Therapy and Rehabilitation*, Appleton-Century-Crofts, New York.

Ayllon, T. and Haughton, E. (1964) Modification of symptomatic verbal behaviour of mental patients, *Behaviour Research and Therapy*, **3**, 87–97.

Ayllon, T. and Michael, J. (1959) The psychiatric nurse as a behavioral engineer, *Journal of the Experimental Analysis of Behavior*, **2**, 323–334.

Ballinger, E. R. (1971) The patient's view of psychiatric treatment, *Health Bulletin*, **29**, 192–195.

Barker, R. E. (1968) *Ecological Psychology*, Stanford University Press, Stanford, California.

Baruch, G. and Treacher, A. (1978) *Psychiatry Observed*, Routledge & Kegan Paul, London.

Bates, E. (1977) *Models of Madness*, University of Queensland Press, St. Lucia, Queensland.

Belknap, I. (1956) *Human Problems of a State Mental Hospital*, McGraw-Hill, New York.

Benson, R. (1976) The function of a psychiatric unit in a general hospital—a five-year experience, *Diseases of the Nervous System*, **37**, 573–577.

Blaney, P. H. (1975) Implications of the medical model and its alternatives, *American Journal of Psychiatry*, **132**, 911–914.

Bloom, B. L. (1977) *Community Mental Health: A General Introduction*, Brooks Cole, Monterey, California.

Bockoven, J. S. (1963) *Moral Treatment in American Psychiatry*, Springer, New York.

Braginsky, B. M., Braginsky, D. D. and Ring, K. (1969) *Methods of Madness: The Mental Hospital as a Last Resort*, Holt, Rinehart & Winston, New York.

Brown, G. W. (1973) The mental hospital as an institution, *Social Science and Medicine*, **7**, 407–424.

Buehler, R., Patterson, G. R. and Furness, J. (1966) The reinforcement of behaviour in institutional settings, *Behaviour Research and Therapy*, **4**, 157–167.

Caine, T. M. and Smail, D. J. (1969) *The Treatment of Mental Illness*, University of London Press, London.

Caplan, G. (1961) *An Approach to Community Mental Health*, Tavistock Publications, London.

Carlson, E. T. and Dain, N. (1960) The psychotherapy that was moral treatment, *American Journal of Psychiatry*, **115**, 519–524.

Caudill, W. (1958) *The Psychiatric Hospital as a Small Society*, Harvard University Press, Cambridge, Massachusetts.

Chu, F. D. and Trotter, S. (1974) *The Madness Establishment*, Grossman, New York.

Clark, D. H. (1964) *Administrative Therapy*, Tavistock Publications, London.

Cumming, E. and Cumming, J. (1962) *Ego and Milieu*, Atherton, New York.

Dinitz, S., Lefton, M., Simpson, J. E., Pasamanick, B. and Patterson, R. M. (1958) The ward behavior of psychiatric patients, *Social Problems*, **6**, 107–115.

Doke, L. A. and Risley, T. R. (1972) The organization of day-care environments: required versus optional activities, *Journal of Applied Behavior Analysis*, **5**, 405–420.

Dunham, H. W. and Weinberg, S. K. (1960) *The Culture of the State Mental Hospital*, Wayne State University Press, Detroit.

Ellsworth, R. B. and Stokes, H. A. (1963) Staff attitudes and patient release, *Psychiatric Studies and Projects*, **7**, 1–6.

Erickson, R. C. (1975) Outcome studies in mental hospitals: a review, *Psychological Bulletin*, **82**, 519–540.

Fairbanks, L., McGuire, M., Cole, B., Sbordone, R., Silvers, F., Richards, M. and Akers, J. (1977) The ethological study of four psychiatric wards: patient, staff and system behaviours, *Journal of Psychiatric Research*, **13**, 193–209.

Franks, C. M. (1969) *Behavior Therapy: Appraisal and Status*, McGraw-Hill, New York.

Gelfand, D. M., Gelfand, S. and Dobson, W. R. (1967) Unprogrammed reinforcement of patients' behaviour in a mental hospital, *Behaviour Research and Therapy*, **5**, 201–207.

Glasscote, R. M. and Kanno, C. K. (1965) *A National Survey: General Hospital Psychiatric Units*, Joint Information Services of the American Psychiatric Association and the National Association of Mental Health, Washington D.C.

Goffman, E. (1961) *Asylums: Essays on the Social Situation of Mental Patients and Other Inmates*, Anchor Books, New York.

Goldman, A. R., Bohr, R. H. and Steinberg, T. A. (1970) On posing as mental patients: reminiscences and recommendations, *Professional Psychology*, **1**, 427–434.

Gould, E. and Glick, I. D. (1973) Patient-staff judgement of treatment programme helpfulness on a psychiatric ward, *British Journal of Medical Psychology*, **49**, 23–33.

Hanley, F. W. (1966) Some social attitudes to personality with implications for psychotherapy, *Canadian Psychiatric Association Journal*, **11**, 492–496.

Hirschowitz, R. G. (1971) Promotion of change in the state mental hospital: the "organic consultation" strategy, *Psychiatric Quarterly*, **45**, 317–332.

Holahan, C. (1972) Seating patterns and patient behavior in an experimental dayroom, *Journal of Abnormal Psychology*, **80**, 115–124.

Holahan, C. and Saegert, S. (1973) Behavioral and attitudinal effects of large-scale variation in the physical environment of psychiatric wards, *Journal of Abnormal Psychology*, **82**, 454–462.

Holland, W. W. (1971) Clinicians and the use of medical resources, *The Hospital* (*London*), **67**, 236–239.

Hollingshead, A. and Redlich, F. (1958) *Social Class and Mental Illness*, Chapman & Hall, London.

Holzberg, J. D. (1960) Problems in the team treatment of adults in state mental hospitals, *American Journal of Orthopsychiatry*, **30**, 87–94.

Hunter, M., Schooler, C. and Spohn, H. E. (1962) The measurement of characteristic patterns of ward behavior in chronic schizophrenics, *Journal of Consulting Psychology*, **26**, 69–73.

Ittelson, W. H., Proshansky, H. M. and Rivlin, L. G. (1970a) Bedroom size and social interaction of the psychiatric ward, *Environment and Behaviour*, **2**, 255–270.

Ittelson, W. H., Proshansky, H. M. and Rivlin, L. G. (1970b) The environmental psychology of the psychiatric ward, in H. M. Proshansky, W. H. Ittelson and L. G. Rivlin (Eds.), *Environmental Psychology: Man and His Physical Setting*, Holt, Rinehart & Winston, New York.

Ittelson, W. H., Rivlin, L. G. and Proshansky, H. M. (1970) The use of behavioral maps in environmental psychology, in H. M. Proshansky, W. H. Ittelson and L. G. Rivlin (Eds.), *Environmental Psychology: Man and His Physical Setting*, Holt, Rinehart & Winston, New York.

Illich, I. (1975) *Medical Nemesis*, Trinity Press, London.

Johnson, S. M. and Bolstad, O. D. (1973) Methodological issues in naturalistic observation: some problems and solutions for field research, in L. A. Hamerlynck, L. C. Handy and E. J. Mash (Eds.), *Behavior Change: Methodology, Concepts and Practice*, Research Press, Champaign, Illinois.

Jones, R. R., Reid, J. B. and Patterson, G. R. (1975) Naturalistic observation in clinical assessment, in P. McReynolds (Ed.), *Advances in Psychological Assessment*, Vol. 3, Jossey-Bass, San Francisco.

Jones, M. (1953) *The Therapeutic Community*, Basic Books, New York.

Kahn, R. S. and Zarit, S. H. (1974) Evaluation of mental health programs for the aged, in P. O. Davidson, F. W. Clark and L. A. Hamerlynck (Eds.), *Evaluating Behavioral Programs in Community, Residential and School Settings*, Research Press, Champaign, Illinois.

Kazdin, A. E. (1977) *The Token Economy: A Review and Evaluation*, Plenum, New York.

Kazdin, A. E. and Bootzin, R. R. (1972) The token economy: an evaluative review, *Journal of Applied Behavior Analysis*, **5**, 343–372.

Krasner, L. and Ullmann, L. P. (1965) *Research in Behavior Modification*, Holt, Rinehart & Winston, New York.

Kreitman, N. (1962) Psychiatric orientation: a study of attitudes among psychiatrists, *Journal of Mental Science*, **108**, 317–328.

Levenson, A. I. (1972) The community mental health centers program, in S. E. Golann and C. Eisdorfer (Eds.), *Handbook of Community Mental Health*, Appleton-Century-Crofts, New York.

Liberman, R. P., King, L. W. and De Risi, W. J. (1976) Behavior analysis and therapy in community mental health, in H. Leitenberg (Ed.), *Handbook of Behavior Modification and Behavior Therapy*, Prentice-Hall, Englewood Cliffs, New Jersey.

Little, L. K. (1966) Effects of interpersonal interaction on abstract thinking performance in schizophrenia, *Journal of Consulting Psychology*, **30**, 158–164.

Loeber, R. and Weisman, R. G. (1975) Contingencies of therapist and trainer performance: a review, *Psychological Bulletin*, **82**, 660–688.

London, P. (1969) Morals and mental health, in S. C. Plog and R. B. Edgerton (Eds.), *Changing Perspectives in Mental Illness*, Holt, Rinehart & Winston, New York.

Lyman, S. M. and Scott, M. B. (1967) Territoriality: a neglected sociological dimension, *Social Problems*, **15**, 236–249.

McGuire, M. T., Fairbanks, S. R., Cole, R., Sbordone, F. M., Silvers, M., Richards, M. and Akers, J. (1977) The ethological study of four psychiatric wards: behavior changes associated with new staff and new patients, *Journal of Psychiatric Research*, **13**, 211–224.

McLaughlin, H. (1976) Evaluating the effectiveness of innovative design for a community mental health center, *Hospital and Community Psychiatry*, **27**, 566–571.

McLean, P. D. (1974) Evaluating community based psychiatric services, in P. O. Davidson, F. W. Clark and L. A. Hamerlynck (Eds.), *Evaluation Behavioral Programs in Community, Residential and School Settings*, Research Press, Champaign, Illinois.

Magaro, P. A. (1976) The cultural context of madness and its treatment, in P. A. Magaro (Ed.), *The Construction of Madness*, Pergamon, Oxford.

Mather, H. G., Pearson, N. G., Read, K. L. Q., Shaw, D. B., Steed, G. R., Thorne, M. G., Jones, S., Guerrier, C. J., Eraut, C. D., McHugh, P. M., Chowdhury, N. R., Jafary, M. H. and Wallace, T. J. (1971) Acute myocardial infarction: home and hospital treatment, *British Medical Journal*, **3**, 334–338.

Mechanic, D. (1976) Judicial action and social change, in S. Golann and W. F. Fremouw, *The Right to Treatment for Mental Patients*, Irvington, New York.

Meichenbaum, D. H. (1966) Effects of social reinforcement on the level of abstraction in schizophrenics, *Journal of Abnormal and Social Psychology*, **71**, 354–362.

Milby, J. B. (1970) Modification of extreme social isolation by contingent social reinforcement, *Journal of Applied Behavior Analysis*, **3**, 149–152.

Miles, A. (1977) Staff relations in psychiatric hospitals, *British Journal of Psychiatry*, **130**, 84–88.

Office of Health Economics (1971) *Hypertension. A Suitable Case for Treatment*, Office of Health Economics, London.

Patterson, G. R. and Cobb, J. A. (1971) A dyadic analysis of "aggressive" behaviors, in J. P. Hill (Ed.), *Minnesota Symposia on Child Psychology*, Vol. 5, University of Minnesota Press, Minneapolis, Minnesota.

Paul, G. L. (1969) Chronic mental patient: current status, future directions, *Psychological Bulletin*, **71**, 81–94.

Paul, G. L. and Lentz, R. J. (1977) *Psychosocial Treatment of Chronic Mental Patients: Milieu versus Social-Learning Programs*, Harvard University Press, Cambridge, Massachusetts.

Payson, H. E. and Barchas, J. D. (1965) A time study of medical teaching rounds, *The New England Journal of Medicine*, **273**, 1468–1471.

Plutchik, R., Shulman, R. and Conte, H. (1972) Territorial and communication patterns of patients and staff members in a mental hospital, *Mental Hygiene*, **56**, 102–104.

Powles, J. (1973) On the limitations of modern medicine, *Science, Medicine and Man*, **1**, 1–30.

Premack, D. (1965) Reinforcement theory, in D. Levine (Ed.), *Nebraska Symposium on Motivation*, University of Nebraska Press, Lincoln, Nebraska.

Proshansky, H. M., Itteleson, W. H. and Rivlin, L. G. (1976) Freedom of choice and behavior in a physical setting, in H. M. Proshansky, W. H. Ittelson and L. G. Rivlin (Eds.), *Environmental Psychology: People and Their Physical Settings*, Holt, Rinehart & Winston, New York.

Reiss, D., Peterson, R. A., Eron, L. D. and Reiss, M. M. (1977) *Abnormality: Experimental and Clinical Approaches*, Macmillan, New York.

Rickard, H. C. and Dinoff, M. (1962) A follow-up note on "verbal manipulation" in a psychotherapeutic relationship, *Psychological Reports*, **11**, 506.

Royal Commission on the Law Relating to Mental Illness and Mental Deficiency (1957) Command 169, HMSO, London.

Sanson-Fisher, R. W. and Jenkins, H. (1978) Interaction patterns between inmates and staff in a maximum security institution for delinquents, *Behavior Therapy*, **9**, 703–716.

Sanson-Fisher, R. W. and Poole, A. D. (1980) The content of interactions: naturally occurring contingencies within a short-stay psychiatric unit, *Advances in Behaviour Research and Therapy*, **2**, 145–157.

Sanson-Fisher, R. W., Poole, A. D. and Harker, J. (1979) Behavioural analysis of ward rounds within a general hospital psychiatric unit, *Behaviour Research and Therapy*, **17**, 333–348.

Sanson-Fisher, R. W., Poole, A. D., Small, G. A. and Fleming, I. R. (1979) Data acquisition in real time—an improved system for naturalistic observations, *Behavior Therapy*, **10**, 543–554.

Sanson-Fisher, R. W., Poole, A. D. and Thompson, V. (1979) Behaviour patterns within a general hospital psychiatric unit: an observational study, *Behaviour Research and Therapy*, **17**, 317–332.

Shamsie, S. J. and Clark, J. E. (1971) Effectiveness of ward meetings, *Canadian Psychiatric Association Journal*, **16**, 217–222.

Stanton, A. H. and Schwartz, M. S. (1954) *The Mental Hospital*, Basic Books, New York.

Strauss, A., Schatzman, L., Bucher, R., Ehrlich, D. and Sabshin, M. (1964) *Psychiatric Ideologies and Institutions*, Free Press, Glencoe, Illinois.

Sullivan, P. R. (1971) Influence of personal values on psychiatric judgement: a military example, *Journal of Nervous and Mental Diseases*, **152**, 193–198.

Trudel, G., Boisvert, J., Maruca, F. and Le Roux, P. (1974) Unprogrammed reinforcement of patients' behaviors in wards with and without token economy, *Journal of Behavior Therapy and Experimental Psychiatry*, **5**, 147–149.

Tudor, G. (1952) A sociopsychiatric nursing approach to intervention in a problem of mutual withdrawal on a mental hospital ward, *Psychiatry*, **15**, 193–217.

Ullmann, L. P. (1967) *Institution and Outcome: A Comparative Study of Psychiatric Hospitals*, Pergamon, New York.

Ullmann, L. P. and Krasner, L. (1975) *A Psychological Approach to Abnormal Behavior*, 2nd Edition, Prentice-Hall, Englewood Cliffs, New Jersey.

Warren, S. A. and Mondy, L. W. (1971) To what behaviors do attending adults respond? *American Journal of Mental Deficiency*, **75**, 449–455.

Wildman, B. G. and Erickson, M. T. (1977) Methodological problems in behavioral observation, in J. D. Cone and R. P. Hawkins (Eds.), *Behavioral Assessment: New Directions in Clinical Psychology*, Brunner/Mazel, New York.

Wessen, A. F. (1964) *The Psychiatric Hospital as a Social System*, Charles C. Thomas, Springfield, Illinois.

Wilder, J. (1969) Values and psychotherapy, *American Journal of Psychotherapy*, **23**, 405–414.

Willer, B., Stasiak, E., Pinfold, P. and Rogers, M. (1974) Activity patterns and the use of space by patients and staff on the psychiatric ward, *Canadian Psychiatric Association Journal*, **19**, 457–462.

Yates, A. J. (1970) *Behavior Therapy*, Wiley, New York.

Yule, W. and Hemsley, D. (1977) Single-case method in medical psychology, in S. Rachman (Ed.), *Contributions to Medical Psychology*, Vol. 1, Pergamon, Oxford.

Zarlock, S. P. (1966) Social expectations, language and schizophrenia, *Journal of Humanistic Psychology*, **6**, 68–74.

AUTHOR INDEX

319

SUBJECT INDEX